Mediation as a Mandatory Pre-condition to Arbitration

Nijhoff International Investment Law Series

Series Editors

Prof. Eric De Brabandere (*Leiden University*)
Prof. Tarcisio Gazzini (*University of East Anglia*)
Prof. Stephan W. Schill (*University of Amsterdam*)
Prof. Attila Tanzi (*University of Bologna*)

VOLUME 21

The titles published in this series are listed at *brill.com/iils*

Mediation as a Mandatory Pre-condition to Arbitration

Alternative Dispute Resolution in Investor-State Dispute Settlement

By

Ana Ubilava

BRILL
NIJHOFF

LEIDEN | BOSTON

The Library of Congress Cataloging-in-Publication Data is available online at https://catalog.loc.gov
LC record available at https://lccn.loc.gov/2022044606

Typeface for the Latin, Greek, and Cyrillic scripts: "Brill". See and download: brill.com/brill-typeface.

ISSN 2351-9542
ISBN 978-90-04-53253-3 (hardback)
ISBN 978-90-04-53254-0 (e-book)

To my husband David and my daughters Ellie and Lily

Contents

Foreword

In recent days, mediation is getting renewed attention in the global community as a means of settling disputes while maintaining a long-term relationship between disputing parties. The advent of the Singapore Convention on Mediation, which entered force in September 2020, is the driving force behind this development. On the other hand, another issue that is drawing global attention at the moment is a reform of the existing investor-state dispute settlement proceedings. For the past several years robust discussions and active debates are being undertaken at various fora such as the United Nations Commission on International Trade Law, Organisation for Economic Co-operation and Development, and International Centre for Settlement of Investment Disputes.

Dr. Ana Ubilava's book, *Mediation as a Mandatory Pre-condition to Arbitration*, is an important academic achievement that combines the two novel trends in the fields of international law and international dispute settlement. It then examines whether and how mediation would work in the context of settling international investment disputes. This book presents a strong argument for the unique benefits of mediation in settling international disputes and its critical contribution to the improvement of ISDS proceedings.

By all accounts, this book could not be more timely and relevant. Few in-depth academic researches have been taken on this topic, and many relevant issues are still on the drawing board. In that regard, Dr. Ubilava's book will be able to guide the current global discussion on this very topic (mediation in ISDS proceedings), and also on two respective topics (mediation, and ISDS reform) in the right direction.

In the book, Dr. Ubilava presents both academic analyses and empirical evidence to support the conclusion that the introduction of a mandatory mediation mechanism will improve ISDS proceedings. In the process, she presents a coherent, persuasive and succinct argument. If the scheme she proposes in the book works, it will probably be able to handle much of the concerns being raised against the current ISDS proceedings. It will help foreign investors and host state governments find common ground and settle their disputes in a cost-efficient and time-efficient manner. Most importantly, the disputing parties will be able to maintain their existing relationship and explore future growth together. I believe Dr. Ubilava hits the nail on the head and I fully agree to her assessment.

The difficulty so far in addressing this particular issue has been the lack or absence of details: it is not clear how mediation can be introduced to and coordinated with the existing ISDS mechanism. It is one thing to say "mediation would help", it is quite another to present a specific scheme to achieve the goal. This book achieves exactly that objective. And for that, many in academia and governments would appreciate Dr. Ubilava's effort in this book very much.

I am confident that this book will offer a significant contribution to the continuing academic and policy debates on this issue, and also to the development of international investment law generally.

Jaemin Lee
Professor of Law, School of Law, Seoul National University

Figures and Tables

Figures

Tables

Annexes

Abbreviations

AAA	American Arbitration Association
ACDC	Australian Commercial Disputes Centre Limited
ACICA	Australian Centre for International Commercial Arbitration
ADR	Alternative Dispute Resolution
ASEAN	Association of Southeast Asian Nations
BIT	Bilateral Investment Treaty
CEDR	Centre for Effective Dispute Resolution
CETA	EU-Canada Comprehensive Economic and Trade Agreement
CIETAC	China International Economic and Trade Centre
CIFA	Cooperation and Investment Facilitation Agreements
CPTPP	Comprehensive and Progressive Agreement for Trans-Pacific Partnership
ECT	Energy Charter Treaty
FDI	Foreign Direct Investment
FET	Fair and Equitable Treatment
FNC	Friendship, Commerce and Navigation Treaty
FTA	Free Trade Agreement
HKIAC	Hong Kong International Arbitration Centre
IA-CEPA	Indonesia-Australia Comprehensive Economic Partnership Agreement
IAMA	Institute of Arbitrators and Mediators Australia
IBA	International Bar Association
ICC	International Chamber of Commerce
ICDR	International Centre for Dispute Resolution
ICSID	International Centre for Settlement of Investment Disputes
IIA	International Investment Agreement
IMI	International Mediation Institute
ISA	Investor-State Arbitration
ISDS	Investor-State Dispute Settlement
ISM	Investor-State Mediation
JSCOT	Joint Standing Committee on Treaties
LCIA	London Court for International Arbitration
MAI	Multilateral Agreement on Investment
MFN	Most-Favoured-Nation
NADRAC	National Alternative Dispute Resolution Advisory Council
NAFTA	North Atlantic Free Trade Agreement
NGO	Non-government organisation
OECD	Organisation for Economic Co-operation and Development
PCA	Permanent Court of Arbitration

QMUL	Queen Mary University London
RCEP	Regional Comprehensive Economic Partnership
SCC	Stockholm Chamber of Commerce
SIAC	Singapore International Arbitration Centre
SIMC	Singapore International Mediation Centre
SIMI	Singapore International Mediation Institute
TPP	Trans-Pacific Partnership agreement
TTIP	EU-US Transatlantic Trade and Investment Partnership
UNCITRAL	United Nations Commission on International Trade Law
UNCTAD	United Nations Conference on Trade and Development
WTO	World Trade Organization

CHAPTER 1

Introduction

Mediation as an alternative dispute resolution (ADR) mechanism is relatively new to investor-state dispute settlement (ISDS). Investor-state mediation (ISM) has been actively promoted as an additional step in the ISDS process over the last few years.[1] The need for ISM in an already established ISDS regime can be explained by increasingly formalised, time- and cost-consuming arbitration procedures, albeit with unpredictable and inconsistent outcomes.[2] There is no universal definition of mediation. Overall, however, it can be described as a process through which a neutral third-party is actively engaged in the resolution of a dispute between parties by facilitating a mutually favourable outcome. Conciliation, a process similar to mediation, offers a more formal and structured dispute resolution procedure with relevant procedural rules in place.[3] Historically, the term conciliation applied to investor-state disputes, whereas the term mediation was more common for international commercial

1 Frauke Nitschke, 'The ICSID Conciliation Rules in Practice' in Catharine Titi and Katia Fach Gómez (eds), *Mediation in International Commercial and Investment Disputes*, (Oxford University Press, 2019) 121; Susan Franck, 'Using Investor–State Mediation Rules to Promote Conflict Management: An Introductory Guide' (2014) 29(1) ICSID Review 66; Susan Franck and Anna Joubin-Bret, 'Investor–State Mediation: A Simulation' (2014) 29(1) ICSID Review 90; Wolf von Kumberg, Jeremy Lack, and Michael Leathes, 'Enabling Early Settlement in Investor–State Arbitration: The Time to Introduce Mediation Has Come' (2014) 29(1) ICSID Review 133; Nancy Welsh and Andrea Schneider, 'Becoming Investor-State Mediation' (2012) 1(1) Penn State Journal of Law and International Affairs 86.

2 By the end of 2020, there were 1061 known treaty-based investor-state arbitration cases, comprising 707 concluded cases, 347 pending cases, and seven status-unknown cases. The number of new cases also appears to be rising. This information was collected from UNCTAD's Investment Policy Hub, available at <https://investmentpolicy.unctad.org/> and the ICSID Case Database in December 2020 'ICSID Caseload Database', available at <https://icsid.worldbank.org/en/Pages/cases/AdvancedSearch.aspx>. Susan Franck, 'The Legitimacy Crisis in Investment Treaty Arbitration: Privatizing Public International Law through Inconsistent Decisions' (2004) 73(4) Fordham Law Review 1521; Anthea Roberts and Zeineb Bouraoui, 'UNCITRAL and ISDS Reforms: Concerns about Costs, Transparency, Third Party Funding and Counterclaims' (6 June 2018) EJIL:TALK! Blog of the European Journal of International Law, available at <https://www.ejiltalk.org/uncitral-and-isds-reforms-concerns-about-costs-transparency-third-party-funding-and-counterclaims/>.

3 For the purposes of this book, ADR includes conciliation, mediation, negotiation, and consultations. Jaemin Lee, 'Settling Investment Disputes Through Mediation' in Mahdev Mohan and Chester Brown (eds), *The Asian Turn in Foreign Investment* (Cambridge University Press 2021).

 | DOI:10.1163/9789004532540_002

dispute settlement. Today the difference between these two terms has largely disappeared.[4]

Various reforms have been explored for rebalancing the current ISDS regime, including eschewing or restructuring international investment agreements (IIAs).[5] Some countries changed their treaty practices by denouncing the Convention on the Settlement of Investment Disputes between States and Nationals of Other States (the ICSID Convention),[6] and others rejected ISDS provisions altogether[7] or incorporated dispute prevention policies in their national legislation.[8] The EU now advocates for a Permanent Investment Court.[9] The United Nations Conference on Trade and Development (UNCTAD)

---

4 The terms conciliation and mediation are set in this broader definition and used interchangeably. More on the definition of mediation can be found in Chapter 3.3 of this book. See also on the interchangeable use of the terms mediation and conciliation Chester Brown and Phoebe Winch, 'The Confidentiality and Transparency Debate in Commercial and Investment Mediation' in Catharine Titi and Katia Fach Gómez (eds), *Mediation in International Commercial and Investment Disputes* (Oxford University Press 2019) 321.

5 Stephan Schill, 'Reforming Investor–State Dispute Settlement: A (Comparative and International) Constitutional Law Framework' (2017) 20(3) Journal of International Economic Law 649; Jarrod Hepburn and Luke Nottage, 'A Procedural Win for Public Health Measures' (2017) 18(2) Journal of World Investment & Trade 307; Luke Nottage, 'Rebalancing Investment Treaties and Investor-State Arbitration: Two Approaches' (2016) Journal of World Investment & Trade 1015.

6 Discussed in detail in Chapter 3. Convention on the Settlement of Investment Disputes between States and Nationals of Other States, opened for signature 18 March 1965, 575 UNTS 159, entered into force 14 October 1966 (The ICSID Convention); Marco Tulio Montanes, 'Bolivia's Denunciation of the Convention on the Settlement of Investment Disputes between States and Nationals of Other States' (2007) 46(5) International Legal Materials 969; Rodrigo Polanco Lazo, 'Is there a life for Latin American countries after denouncing the ICSID convention?' (2014) 11(1) Transnational Dispute Management, available at <https://www.transnational-dispute-management.com/article.asp?key=2037>.

7 Ana Ubilava and Luke Nottage, 'Novel and Noteworthy Aspects of Australia's Recent Investment Agreements and ISDS Policy: The CPTPP, Hong Kong, Indonesia and Mauritius Transparency Treaties' in Luke Nottage et al (eds), *New Frontiers in Asia-Pacific International Arbitration and Dispute Resolution* (Wolters Kluwer 2021) 115.

8 Catharine Titi, 'Mediation and the Settlement of Investment Disputes: Between Utopia and Realism' in Catharine Titi and Katia Fach Gómez (eds), *Mediation in International Commercial and Investment Disputes* (Oxford University Press 2019) 21.

9 Ruggiero Cafari Panico and Fabrizio Di Benedetto, 'Recent Developments in the Most Controversial Aspects of EU International Investment Agreements: Portfolio Investments and Investor-State Dispute Settlement', (2016) 13(1) Transnational Dispute Management, available at <https://www.transnational-dispute-management.com/article.asp?key=2317>; Trade Agreement and an Investment Protection Agreement, signed 30 June 2019, trade agreement entered into force 1 August 2020, investment protection agreement not yet in force (EU-Vietnam FTA); Nguyen Manh Dzung and Nguyen Thi Thu Trang, 'International Investment Dispute Resolution in Vietnam: Opportunities and Challenges' in Julien Chaisse and Luke Nottage (eds), *International Investment Treaties and Arbitration Across*

has been working on prevention and alternatives to arbitration since 2010,[10] and the United Nations Commission on International Trade Law (UNCITRAL) Working Group III has been tasked with ISDS reform since 2017.[11] Among these reforms is the proposal to promote more ISM.[12] Mediation can serve as a time- and cost-saving dispute resolution mechanism, and is also more likely to preserve investment relationships between investors and states. It can prevent disputes from escalating to investor-state arbitration (ISA) or resolve an already commenced case before the tribunal renders the final award.[13]

Steps, therefore, have been made towards promoting more ISM, notably by ensuring the enforceability of settlement agreements and supporting the earlier procedural phase of conducting ISM. In June 2018, after four years of discussions, UNCITRAL Working Group II finalised the United Nations Convention on International Settlement Agreements Resulting from Mediation (the Singapore Convention on Mediation) and the UNCITRAL Model Law on International

Asia (Brill-Nijhoff 2018) 280; Comprehensive Economic and Trade Agreement (CETA), signed 20 October 2016, entered into force provisionally 21 September 2017; Barton Legum, 'Appellate Mechanisms for Investment Arbitration: Worth a Second Look for the Trans-Pacific Partnership and the Proposed EU-US FTA?' (2014) 11(1) Transnational Dispute Management, available at <https://www.transnational-dispute-management.com/article.asp?key=2073>.

10 UNCTAD, Investor–State Disputes: Prevention and Alternatives to Arbitration, UN Doc UNCTAD/DIAE/IA/2009/11, 1 August 2010.

11 UNCIRAL Working Group III, available at <https://uncitral.un.org/en/working_groups/3/investor-state>.

12 Jeswald Salacuse, 'Is There a Better Way? Alternative Methods of Treaty-Based, Investor-State Dispute Resolution' (2007) 31(1) Fordham International Law Journal 138; Investor–State Disputes: Prevention and Alternatives to Arbitration (n 10); Submission from the Government of Indonesia (A/CN.9/WG.III/WP.156) para. 19; Submission from the European Union and its member States (A/CN.9/WG.III/WP.159/Add.1) para. 12; Submission from the Government of Morocco (A/CN.9/WG.III/WP.161) para. 14; Submission from the Government of Thailand (A/CN.9/WG.III/WP.162) para. 24; Submission from the Governments of Chile, Israel, and Japan (A/CN.9/WG.III/WP.163) p. 6- 7, annex I; Submission from the Government of South Africa (A/CN.9/WG.III/WP.176) paras. 40 and 41; Submission from the Government of China (A/CN.9/WG.III/WP.177) p. 5; Submission from the Government of Mali (A/CN.9/WG.III/WP.181) s F.

13 For the purposes of this paper, ADR includes conciliation, mediation, negotiation, and consultations. The terms conciliation and mediation are used interchangeably. Nitschke (n 1); Franck, 'Using Investor-State Mediation Rules to Promote Conflict Management: An Introductory Guide' (n 1); Franck and Joubin-Bret (n 1); von Kumberg, Lack and Leathes (n 1); Welsh and Schneider (n 1); Anthea Roberts and Taylor St. John, 'UNCITRAL and ISDS Reforms: The Divided West and the Battle by and for the Rest' (30 April 2019) EJIL:TALK! Blog of the European Journal of International Law, available at <https://www.ejiltalk.org/uncitral-and-isds-reforms-the-divided-west-and-the-battle-by-and-for-the-rest/>.

Commercial Mediation and International Settlement Agreements Resulting from Mediation, 2018.[14] The Convention was signed by 46 nations on the same day that it was open for signature on 7 August 2019, which marks the highest number of signatories on the first day in the history of United Nations (UN) trade conventions.[15] It came into effect on 12 September 2020.[16] The Singapore Convention on Mediation is the instrument that will ensure the universal enforceability of settlement agreements reached during both international commercial and ISDS proceedings. Some level of controversy remains among scholars and practitioners whether the Singapore Convention, apart from international commercial disputes, will also apply to investor-state disputes. This question has arisen mainly because the term 'commercial' was left undefined in the Convention.[17] However, it is quite widely agreed that at least a significant proportion of investor-state mediated settlement agreements will fall under the scope of the Singapore Convention on Mediation. On 2 August 2018, ICSID announced the fourth and most extensive changes to its rules, which

14 United Nations Convention on International Settlement Agreements Resulting from Mediation, opened for signature 7 August 2019, entered into force 12 September 2020 (Singapore Convention on Mediation); Model Law on International Commercial Mediation and International Settlement Agreements Resulting from Mediation, GA Res 73/199, UN Doc A/RES/73/199, 3 January 2019, adopted 20 December 2018 (Model Law on International Commercial Mediation and International Settlement Agreements Resulting from Mediation); Nadja Alexander, 'It's DONE: The Singapore Convention on Mediation' (9 August 2019) Kluwer Mediation Blog, available at <http://mediationblog.kluwerarbitration.com/2019/08/09/its-done-the-singapore-convention-on-mediation/>.

15 United Nations Treaty Collection, 'United Nations Convention on International Settlement Agreements Resulting from Mediation', available at <https://treaties.un.org/pages/ViewDetails.aspx?src=TREATY&mtdsg_no=XXII-4&chapter=22&clang=_en>.

16 Hal Abramson, 'New Singapore Convention on Cross-Border Mediated Settlements: Key Choices' in Catharine Titi and Katia Fach Gómez (eds), *Mediation in International Commercial and Investment Disputes* (Oxford University Press 2019) 360.

17 More in-depth discussion on this point and the Singapore Convention on Mediation is provided in Chapter 3. See generally Esme Shirlow, 'The Promises and Pitfalls of Investor-State Mediation' in Lisa E Sachs, Lise Johnson and Jesse Coleman (eds), *Yearbook on International Investment Law and Policy 2019* (Oxford University Press 2021), 461; Surya Kapoor, 'Singapore Convention Series: How Does The Singapore Mediation Convention Affect International Dispute Resolution? ISDS Perspective' (15 November 2019) Kluwer Mediation Blog, available at <http://mediationblog.kluwerarbitration.com/2019/11/15/singapore-convention-series-how-does-the-singapore-mediation-convention-affect-international-dispute-resolution-isds-perspective/>; Timothy Schnabel, 'The Singapore Convention on Mediation: A Framework for the Cross-Border Recognition and Enforcement of Mediated Settlements'(2019) 19(1) Pepperdine Dispute Resolution Law Journal 1.

include the new ICSID Mediation Rules.[18] Since then, ICSID has published four working papers, with the latest (Working Paper Number 4) released in February 2020.[19] The new ICSID Mediation Rules as well as proposed amendments to the ICSID Conciliation Rules (originally adopted in 1967) rely on the Singapore Convention on Mediation for providing an enforcement mechanism to settlement agreements reached through these rules.[20] Increased express reference to ISM can also be observed in a new generation of IIAs, which is quite atypical for older generation treaties such as bilateral investment treaties (BITs).[21] This is because in most BITs, the ISDS clauses usually only provide negotiation/consultations in the early stages of a dispute, whereas third-party procedures (with reference usually to conciliation as an option alongside arbitration) are

18 Ana Ubilava and Luke Nottage, 'ICSID's New Mediation Rules: A Small but Positive Step Forward' (17 October 2018) ICSID, available at <https://icsid.worldbank.org/sites/default/files/amendments/public-input/Ubilava_Notage_10.17.2018.pdf>; ICSID, Proposals for Amendment of the ICSID Rules, Working Paper No 1, Synopsis, 3 August 2018, (ICSID WP1 – Synopsis).

19 ICSID, Proposals for Amendment of the ICSID Rules, Working Paper No 1, Consolidated Rules, 3 August 2018, (ICSID WP1 – Consolidated Rules); ICSID, Proposals for Amendment of the ICSID Rules, Working Paper No 2, Consolidated Rules, 15 March 2019, (ICSID WP2 – Consolidated Rules); ICSID, Proposals for Amendment of the ICSID Rules, Working Paper No 3, 16 August 2019, (ICSID WP3); ICSID, Proposals for Amendment of the ICSID Rules, Working Paper No 4, 28 February 2020, (ICSID WP4).

20 Ubilava and Nottage (n 18); ICSID, Rules of Procedure for Conciliation Proceedings (Conciliation Rules) (2006); (ICSID WP1 – Synopsis) (n 18). A more detailed discussion of the ICSID Conciliation Rules and the new amendments is provided in Chapter 3.

21 For example, Comprehensive Economic and Trade Agreement (CETA) (n 9) art 8.20; Investment Protection Agreement, signed 19 October 2018, not yet in force, annex 6 (EU-Singapore IPA); Comprehensive and Progressive Agreement for Trans-Pacific Partnership (CPTPP), opened for signature 8 March 2018, entered into force 30 December 2018, art 9.18 (Comprehensive and Progressive Agreement for Trans-Pacific Partnership (CPTPP)); Agreement for the Reciprocal Promotion and Protection of Investments Between the Argentine Republic and the United Arab Emirates, signed 16 April 2018, not yet in force, art 20 (Argentina-UAE BIT); Peru-Australia Free Trade Agreement, signed and entered into force 11 February 2020, art 8.19 (Peru-Australia Free Trade Agreement); Free Trade Agreement between the Republic of Korea and the Republics of Central America, signed 21 February 2018, entered into force 1 November 2019, art 9.16 (Free Trade Agreement between the Republic of Korea and the Republics of Central America); Agreement between the Government of the Republic of Kazakhstan and the Government of the United Arab Emirates on Promotion and Reciprocal Protection of Investments, signed 24 March 2018, not yet in force, art 10 (Kazakhstan – United Arab Emirates BIT); Agreement between the United States of America, the United Mexican States, and Canada, signed and entered into force 1 July 2020, art 14.D.2 (USMCA); Titi (n 8); Malcolm Langford, Daniel Behn and Laura Létourneau-Tremblay, 'Empirical Perspectives on Investment Arbitration: What Do We Know? Does It Matter?' (2020) 21(2–3) Journal of World Investment & Trade 188.

typically offered for the later stages of an investor-state dispute.[22] These cooperative efforts promise an unprecedented 'treatification' of ISM.

Notwithstanding these recent incentives, mediation has almost always been regarded as a voluntary step in the ISDS process, until recently. In a 2020 Queen Mary University of London (QMUL) survey, which was designed to determine the position of investors, 63% of the respondents expressed their support for mandatory mediation as a pre-condition to arbitration in ISDS.[23] More specifically, 30% said they 'strongly favour' mandatory ISM, 34% – 'somewhat favour', 22% – 'strongly oppose', 11% – 'somewhat oppose', and 3% did not have a view on the subject. However, unlike the investors, who seem to be more receptive to mandatory ISM in ISDS, academics and commentators are largely sceptical, and indeed deem it unnecessary.[24] The opponents of mandatory ISM argue that greater enforceability of settlement agreements through the Singapore Convention on Mediation will suffice to increase recourse to optional and purely voluntary ISM, diminishing the need to make ISM a mandatory step.[25] Sceptics also argue that mediation is not a universally and automatically applicable dispute resolution mechanism for all investor-state disputes.[26] Therefore, it is suggested that ISM should not be incorporated as a compulsory, automatic step as a pre-condition to arbitration, which would then apply to all investor-state disputes under the relevant treaty.

However, it is questionable whether the (pre-Singapore Convention) non-enforceability of settlement agreements was, indeed, a primary cause for the underutilisation of ADR (mediation/conciliation) in ISDS in the first place.

22 Gabriel Bottini and Veronica Lavista, 'Conciliation And BITs' in Arthur W Rovine (ed), *Contemporary Issues in International Arbitration and Mediation: The Fordham Papers (2009)* (Brill Nijhoff 2010) 358.

23 Queen Mary University London (QMUL) and Corporate Counsel International Arbitration Group (CCIAG), QMUL-CCIAG Survey: Investors' Perceptions of ISDS (2020) 24–25.

24 Nancy Welsh and Andrea Kupfer Schneider, 'The Thoughtful Integration of Mediation into Bilateral Investment Treaty Arbitration' (2013) 18(1) Harvard Negotiation Law Review 71; Wolf von Kumberg, 'Making Mediation Mainstream: An Application for Investment Treaty Disputes' in Susan Franck and Anna Joubin-Bret (eds), *Investor-State Disputes: Prevention and Alternatives to Arbitration II* (UNCTAD 2011) 71; Lou Wells, 'Investor State Conciliation – A Comment', (2005) 2(5) Transnational Dispute Management, available at <https://www.transnational-dispute-management.com/article.asp?key=678>; UNCITRAL Working Group III, Draft Summary Possible Reform of Investor-State Dispute Settlement (Addendum), UN Doc A/CN.9/WG.III/XXXIX/CRP.1/Add.1 [18].

25 Asian Academy of International Law, 'UNCITRAL Working Group III Virtual Pre-Intersessional Meeting (Afternoon Session)' (15 November 2020) virtual conference, Youtube, available at <https://www.youtube.com/watch?v=AEjp_ASQfj8>.

26 Kun Fan, 'Mediation of Investor-State Disputes: A Treaty Survey', (2020) 2 Journal of Dispute Resolution 327.

A doctrinal analysis, presented under Chapter 4, identifies a significant conflict in the interpretation of the advance consent to conciliation and arbitration provided by host states in ISDS clauses of various IIAs, which could be contributing to the underuse of ADR in ISDS. A commonly found interpretation suggests that the choice of one method (such as conciliation) is to the exclusion of the other (usually arbitration). If this is correct, meaning the usual treaty wording creates a sort of 'fork in the road', it is not surprising that investors and their legal advisors almost always choose the arbitration route over conciliation or mediation. Relatedly, we should question the assumption that improving the enforceability of settlement agreements will result in significantly increased use of voluntary ADR, including ISM, because there exist other significant impediments to such use.

Nevertheless, while providing relevant ISM procedural rules and implementing a better enforcement mechanism are promising developments, and may facilitate increased recourse to ISM, there remain other obstacles, such as common misconceptions attributed to ISM by legal practitioners and academics that make this dispute resolution mechanism unattractive for ISDS disputants.[27] Some of the common misconceptions about ADR, or, in particular, settlement agreements reached during ADR proceedings (for example through ISM), include:

- States would 'look weak' or admit the blame if they agreed on settling an investor-state dispute rather than going forward with arbitration. Therefore, sceptics argue that forcing governments to engage in mandatory ISM may not be suitable for some investor-state disputes;
- Depending on the type of investor-state dispute, determining an authority to settle disputes on behalf of a sovereign state may prove to be challenging for a respondent state. Therefore, opponents of mandatory ISM argue that having an arbitrator make the decision is a more suitable option for certain cases rather than having to go through mandatory ISM without a representative authorised to conclude settlements;
- It is easier for state representatives to shift the blame for the final decision to arbitrators rather than be accountable to the public for the terms of a settlement agreement;

27 Michael Reisman, 'International Investment Arbitration and ADR: Married but Best Living Apart' (2009) 24(1) ICSID Review 185; Lucy Reed, 'Synopsis of Closing Remarks' in Susan Franck and Anna Joubin-Bret (eds), *Investor-State Disputes: Prevention and Alternatives to Arbitration II* (UNCTAD 2011) 30; Jacqueline Nolan-Haley, 'Mediation: the new arbitration' (2012) 17(1)Harvard Negotiation Law Review 61.

- Not all investor-state disputes may be suitable for mediation. For example, some scholars argue that disputes with non-monetary claimed relief, where the state is required to take policy or legislative action, may be beyond the scope of any settlement agreement capacities;[28]
- Another common misconception is that claimants are paid less through settlements compared to what they receive through arbitral awards. Therefore, opponents believe that if ISM were to be a mandatory pre-condition to arbitration, claimant investors would have no intention of genuinely trying to settle the dispute, and participate in ISM only for the sake of progressing to arbitration;
- One of the most common concerns regarding settlements through ADR mechanisms such as ISM, especially if it were a mandatory step of ISDS, is that mediation could be used with the intention to bypass crucial transparency requirements otherwise in place for ISA. This concern builds on the long-existing belief that settlements are used to maintain the secrecy of outcomes.[29]

However, it can be argued that, despite the critiques, unless ISM is made a mandatory pre-condition to ISA, mediation in a purely voluntary or optional format will remain underutilised. Therefore, unless sceptics' arguments are challenged, the prospect of mandatory ISM will remain unattractive to ISDS stakeholders.

The critiques of mandatory ISM seem to be largely speculative or hypothetical, with arguments against mandatory ISM historically not subject to robust, critical, and empirical investigation. The primary cause of this dearth of research is a lack of information on ISM cases. Without sufficient data, it is nearly impossible to empirically examine the validity of these arguments and to determine whether certain characteristics of ADR (for which a successful outcome is a settlement agreement) do indeed make ADR mechanisms incompatible with ISDS.

An original alternative approach, presented in Chapter 5 of this book, empirically investigates the validity of key arguments (and indeed misconceptions) against mandatory mediation in ISDS.[30] The chapter examines the legitimacy

28 Seraphina Chew, Lucy Reed and J Christopher Thomas, 'Report: Survey on Obstacles to Settlement of Investor-State Disputes' (2018) National University of Singapore Working Paper, available at <https://papers.ssrn.com/sol3/papers.cfm?abstract_id=3247492>.

29 Luke Nottage, 'Confidentiality and Transparency in International Arbitration: Asia-Pacific Tensions and Expectations' (2020) 16(1) Asian International Arbitration Journal 1.

30 These critiques will be discussed individually in Chapters 4 and 5. All the presented figures and tables here are based on calculations and analysis of a database developed and coded by this author, consisting of a total of 656 investor-state treaty-based arbitration

of the common critiques questioning the compatibility of ADR with investment disputes, for example through mandatory ISM, by quantitatively analysing known ISA cases (as of the end of 2019). It is important to note that the main arguments against mandatory ISM build on critiques that are not exclusive to mediation. In fact, they could be extended to any ADR mechanism (including mandatory negotiation between disputing parties, already commonly required by IIAs) that concludes with a settlement agreement. Therefore, regardless of which ADR mechanism was used to reach such settlements – mediation or conciliation, or negotiations and consultations – by empirically examining the concluded ISA cases, it is possible to determine whether the critiques have adequate empirical foundations. If insufficient evidence is found in previously concluded cases to support the validity of these critiques, then an argument can be made that mandatory ISM before arbitration should be applied to any investor-state dispute. After all, if settlements are often reached in many types of investment disputes through negotiations, adding a neutral third-party skilled in mediation should further increase prospects for an early and amicable resolution of the dispute, with very little extra cost and delay.

The book, therefore, makes the following original and significant contributions to an important and evolving area of international investment law and dispute resolution practice. Chapter 2 highlights an existing trend that seems to be characteristic of new incentives in an already established dispute resolution platform. Generally, whenever a new dispute resolution procedure is introduced, it is initially met with scepticism. (We see this, for example, in relation to remote hearings in international arbitration, which were possible technologically for many years but not much used in practice due to various objections, until the COVID-19 pandemic and its consequences forced participants to use them pervasively – and largely without the feared negative consequences). In fact, Chapter 2 shows that when arbitration and then consequently mediation were first actively promoted in *domestic* judicial systems, the arguments that sceptics had back then were very similar to the concerns that were later voiced against mediation pre-commitments through a multi-tiered dispute

cases that were concluded by 2020. The database does not contain cases that have been concluded since 2020 for several reasons: First, the author had to stop collecting data at some point and start the data analysis on the existing database. Secondly, the main platform for data collection (UNCTAD) updates its database of concluded cases every July–August. When data analysis commenced, the newly concluded cases of 2020 were not yet published. Third, due to the unforeseen global events from early 2020, adding subsequent data could skew the results and suggest misleading findings. Future statistical research, including several more years of data for cases completed during and preferably also after the Covid-19 pandemic, can examine new trends.

resolution clause in *international* commercial dispute resolution platforms. Similar arguments are now advanced against the role of mandatory mediation in ISDS (empirically examined in Chapter 5). Chapter 3 explores the factors that contribute to the necessity of an additional dispute resolution step in ISDS in the form of mediation. It first investigates the problems associated with ISA that contributed to the incentive of incorporating and promoting more ISM in ISDS. The chapter then investigates the current role of mediation in ISDS, including its anticipated benefits and possible shortcomings.

Moving from these general critical observations to more specific arguments, the doctrinal study presented under Chapter 4, which makes significant and original contributions to the field, identifies the issue of conflicting interpretations of advance consent to ISDS in IIAs. It challenges the view that there is no need to promote mandatory mediation for ISDS because once the procedural rules (such as the proposed ICSID Mediation Rules) and a better enforcement mechanism (the Singapore Convention) are widely in place, recourse to voluntary opt-in ISM will increase. The unique counter-argument in Chapter 4 builds on the fact that conciliation in ISDS has been seldom used throughout the years. While there exist relevant procedural rules such as the ICSID Conciliation Rules, blame for conciliation's underuse often falls on the fact of the non-binding and non-enforceable outcome (the "report" proposed by mediators, which the disputant need not accept in settlement). There exists significant conflict regarding interpretation of the advance consent provided by host states through ISDS clauses in IIAs that allows investors to choose between conciliation and arbitration. A commonly found interpretation, mostly by the stakeholders of ISDS, is that choice of one method (such as conciliation) results in excluding access to the other (usually arbitration). Chapter 4 draws on principles of treaty interpretation to argue for the alternative view, that an investor choosing conciliation is not usually precluded from going to arbitration if no settlement is achieved in conciliation. Nonetheless, this view is not shared by all commentators. Therefore, the 'fork in the road' interpretation will most likely lead to investors overwhelmingly choosing arbitration (with its guaranteed binding outcome) over conciliation (which may not resolve the dispute if no settlement is reached). If the latter interpretation is and remains pervasive, commentators' assumption that the non-enforceability of settlement agreements is a principal reason for the underutilisation of ADR mechanisms is rather questionable. Relatedly, we should question the assumption that improving the enforceability of settlement agreements (notably through the recent Singapore Convention on Mediation) will, even if that Convention is widely ratified, result in significantly increased use of ADR – and, in particular, voluntary ISM.

Chapter 5 details how arguments, parallel to those discussed in Chapter 2, are now being advanced against the concept of mandatory ISM as a pre-condition to ISA, meaning a multi-tiered dispute resolution clause for IIAs. Most importantly, through descriptive statistical analysis, as well as regression-based results, the chapter debunks major common arguments against the compatibility of mandatory ISM with ISDS by empirically analysing patterns in existing ISA cases that terminate based on party settlement before the arbitration award is rendered.[31] It investigates whether, and to what extent, common misconceptions attributed to amicable settlements generally – that similarly underpin arguments against mandatory ISM – are evident in practice. Chapter 5 begins with extensive descriptive statistics for 656 known ISA cases resolved by the end of 2019. One interesting feature is that a significant proportion of settled cases do not turn the outcome into a consent award, which would enhance legal enforceability under the 1958 New York Convention or the 1965 ICSID Convention. This finding further undermines the view that enforceability for mediation agreements under the new Singapore Convention on Mediation will be enough to promote voluntary ISM. Chapter 5 then poses four specific research questions that correspond with the major critiques of ISM, but which can be applied to any ADR mechanism that results in settlement agreements in ISDS:

(1) Would mandatory ISM be futile because certain types of investor-state disputes cannot be resolved through settlement agreements?
(2) Would mandatory ISM through settlement agreements contribute to the secrecy of outcomes and impede transparency?
(3) Would mandatory ISM be a waste of time (and hence unattractive for disputants) because settlements pay less compared to when investors win?
(4) Has the non-enforceability of settlement agreements been a problem in practice?

The findings from this pioneering econometric analysis suggest that not all these purported problematic aspects of ADR, including mandatory ISM, are as evident in practice as is commonly believed.

Based on these findings, Chapter 6 sets forth recommendations for policymakers on possible ways forward to integrate mandatory ISM, as a precondition to arbitration, into the current ISDS regime. It concludes that for the full utilisation of the benefits of ISM – as a timely and cost-effective method to

31 Ana Ubilava, 'Amicable Settlements in Investor-State Disputes: Empirical Analysis of Patterns and Perceived Problems' (2020) 21(4) Journal of World Investment and Trade 528.

resolve investment disputes on mutually agreeable terms and preserve investment relationships – mediation is best provided as a mandatory pre-condition to arbitration during the 'cooling-off' or negotiation periods usually provided anyway in IIAs. This can be done when drafting new treaties, as well as through amendments to some Rules applicable to future IIAs. In addition, for the many pre-existing IIAs worldwide, a mandatory mediation step should be introduced through a multilateral instrument similar to the 2014 United Nations Convention on Transparency in Treaty-based Investor-State Arbitration (the Mauritius Convention on Transparency), which retrofits transparency obligations to prior treaties.[32]

32 United Nations Convention on Transparency in Treaty-based Investor-State Arbitration, opened for signature 10 December 2014, entered into force 18 October 2017 (Mauritius Convention on Transparency).

CHAPTER 2

Mediation to Address Drawbacks of Domestic and International Commercial Arbitration

2.1 Introduction

Over time, with the formation of complex socio-economic relations, the nature of conflicts metamorphosed from primitive to more sophisticated and complex forms. The court system is believed to be the oldest and most practised dispute resolution procedure in the world. However, from the early days, courts seemed to fail to manage excessive numbers of cases. In fact, it is known that ancient societies, such as the Greeks, actively practised out-of-court dispute settlement mechanisms such as arbitration and mediation.[1] At present, apart from court adjudication, arbitration and mediation are the two most practised dispute settlement mechanisms. Moreover, both have been incorporated into court systems of various countries to help unclog overloaded court dockets.

The beginning of the twentieth century witnessed the rise of court-annexed (civil) commercial and international arbitrations. In the second half of the twentieth century, mediation and conciliation were put under the spotlight due to the pitfalls of arbitration.[2] Today, in the twenty-first century, mediation is once again advanced as a possible solution to the shortcomings of ISDS and a prevention mechanism for disputes escalating to arbitration.[3]

The first part of this Chapter describes the origins of arbitration, its historical development, its role in domestic and international dispute resolution systems, and problems associated with it. The second part examines mediation and its role in domestic, commercial and international commercial dispute resolution platforms as a supplementary or alternative procedure to arbitration.

This Chapter serves as a reminder of the significant role mediation has long played in tackling the shortcomings of domestic and international commercial

1 Jerome Barrett and Joseph Barrett, *A History of Alternative Dispute Resolution: The Story of a Political, Social, and Cultural Movement* (John Wiley & Sons 2004); Derek Roebuck, *Ancient Greek Arbitration* (Holo Books 2001) 348.

2 Thomas Stipanowich and Ryan Lamare, 'Living with ADR: Evolving Perceptions and Use of Mediation, Arbitration, and Conflict Management in Fortune 1000 Corporations' (2014) 19(1) Harvard Negotiation Law Review 1.

3 Discussed separately in Chapter 3. Titi (n 8 in ch 1).

 | DOI:10.1163/9789004532540_003

arbitration. Initially, when mediation was first added to these modes of dispute resolution, the arguments that its opponents had were remarkably similar to those advanced against mandatory ISM today. Despite the resistance, over time, mediation proved to be an appropriate and applicable dispute resolution mechanism for both domestic and international commercial disputes. This resonates with what mediation is going through now in the new context of ISDS, where mediation will hopefully prove to be similarly successful.

2.2 Popularisation of Arbitration

2.2.1 *Early Days of Arbitration*

Arbitration as a form of international dispute resolution is a product of the 20th century and is widely accepted to have emerged in the West.[4] However, according to Derek Roebuck, an arbitration historian, ancient civilisations across the world had practised dispute resolution mechanisms resembling arbitration for centuries.[5] Ancient Romans, for example, used arbitration for commercial disputes based on a so-called *compromissum* – an agreement for referring a dispute to a private arbitrator.[6]

In the Middle Ages, merchants conducting cross-border trade across European markets were entitled to a specific form of dispute resolution built on trade customs, the *lex mercatoria,* that was different from courts.[7] These customs were later incorporated into domestic legislation, forming the foundation of arbitration laws, and spreading from Europe to the rest of the world, partly through colonialism.[8] The first legislative regulation of commercial arbitration took place in England since commercial arbitration had already

4 Muthucumaraswamy Sornarajah, 'The Climate of International Arbitration', (1991) 8(2) Journal of International Arbitration 47; Amr A Shalakany, 'Arbitration and the Third World: A Plea for Reassessing Bias Under the Specter of Neoliberalism' (2000) 41(2) Harvard International Law Journal 419; Julian DM Lew, Loukas A Mistelis and Stefan Kröll, *Comparative International Commercial Arbitration* (Kluwer Law International 2003) 18. But see James Crawford, 'Continuity and Discontinuity in International Dispute Settlement: An Inaugural Lecture' (2009) 1(1) Journal of International Dispute Settlement 801.

5 Derek Roebuck, 'Sources for the History of Arbitration: A Bibliographical Introduction' (1998) 14(3) Arbitration international 237.

6 Derek Roebuck and Bruno de Loynes de Fumichon, *Roman arbitration* (Holo Books 2004) 94.

7 Frank Emerson, 'History of Arbitration Practice and Law' (1970) 19(1) Cleveland State Law Review 1585.

8 Rene David, *Arbitration in International Trade* (Kluwer Law and Taxation Publishers 1985) 85–86; Kate Miles, *The Origins of International Investment Law: Empire, Environment, and the Safeguarding of Capital,* vol 99 (Cambridge University Press 2013) 22.

become a common practice through *lex mercatoria*.[9] England enacted the Arbitration Act in 1698, which later spread to the majority of Commonwealth countries.[10] Australia inherited the English Arbitration Act from the time of settlement in 1788. About two centuries later, in 1979, England significantly reformed the arbitration law, which further contributed to the number of commercial arbitration Acts adopted by individual Australian states.[11]

The origins of international commercial arbitration in France were similar to the origins in England. Extensive trade relationships established commercial arbitration practices throughout the country, as well as throughout the region. This led to the incorporation of arbitration in the 1793 and 1795 Constitutions of France, amid the French Revolution.[12] Across the Atlantic, the US took a very similar path to England in incorporating arbitration for the resolution of commercial disputes, which was further encouraged by courts.[13]

Over time, international arbitration was increasingly seen as a preferred method of resolving international disputes. In 1899 and 1907, the Hague Conventions were adopted under the auspices of the First and Second International Peace Conference.[14] These Conventions addressed peaceful settlement of inter-state disputes, with states multilaterally agreeing that international arbitration was the preferred method of dispute resolution for inter-state disputes that diplomacy had failed to settle.[15] The Permanent Court of Arbitration (PCA) was established by the 1899 Hague Convention.[16] After

9 David (n 8).

10 Jan Schaefer, 'Leaving the Colonial Arbitration Laws Behind: Southeast Asia's Move into the International Arbitration Arena' (2000) 16(3) Arbitration International 297; Rashda Rana and Michelle Sanson, 'International Commercial Arbitration' (2011) 6(4) Construction Law International 39.

11 The Australian states were not uniform in legislative incentives and thus enacted individual commercial arbitration acts eventuating in disconnected and non-uniform arbitration laws around the country; NSW and Victoria in 1984, WA and the Northern Territory in 1985, and Queensland in 1990. See Hilary Astor and Christine Chinkin, *Dispute resolution in Australia* (LexisNexis Butterworths 2002) 300.

12 David (n 8) 90.

13 Paul Carrington, 'ADR and the Future of Adjudication: A Primer on Dispute Resolution' (1996) 15(1) Review of Litigation 485; Bruce Benson, 'An exploration of the impact of modern arbitration statutes on the development of arbitration in the United States' (1995) 11(2) Journal of Law, Economics, & Organization 479.

14 Convention for the Pacific Settlement of International Disputes (Hague Convention I), signed 29 July 1899, entered into force 4 September 1900; Convention for the Pacific Settlement of International Disputes (Hague Convention II), signed 18 October 1907, entered into force 26 January 1910.

15 Hague Convention I (n 14) art 16.

16 Lew, Mistelis and Kröll (n 4) 19.

World War I, the international community seemed even more determined to create a peaceful, international dispute resolution mechanism that would further facilitate international trade.[17]

2.2.2 *International Commercial Arbitration*

International commercial arbitration has become the primary dispute resolution mechanism for international commercial disputes. This is due to its unique combination of characteristics such as widespread adoption of treaties facilitating now near-universal enforceability of foreign arbitration agreements and awards, party autonomy and flexibility throughout arbitral proceedings, the impartiality of arbitrators, and neutrality and confidentiality of proceedings.[18]

The process of the 'treatification' of international commercial arbitration began with the founding of the International Chamber of Commerce (ICC) in 1919. Since World War I, due to the increasing role of arbitration in settling international disputes, the ICC not only established a Court of International Arbitration, but also facilitated the creation of the 1923 Geneva Protocol on Arbitration Clauses.[19] The Protocol made the agreement to arbitrate valid for ongoing and future disputes. The Geneva Protocol was soon followed by the adoption of the 1927 Geneva Convention of the Execution of Foreign Arbitral Awards, which regulated the international enforcement of arbitral awards that were made under the 1923 Protocol.[20] However, while the 1927 Geneva Convention facilitated the international recognition of arbitration agreements and awards, it faced a 'double exequatur' problem:[21] the party seeking enforcement had to provide proof that the award was final in the place of the seat of

17 Rana and Sanson (n 10).

18 Margaret Moses, *The Principles and Practice of International Commercial Arbitration* (Cambridge University Press 2017) 1; Rémy Gerbay, 'Is the End Nigh Again? An Empirical Assessment of the 'Judicialization' of International Arbitration' (2014) 24(2) American Journal of International Arbitration 223; Lew, Mistelis and Kröll (n 4) 1–9; Filip De Ly, Mark Friedman and Luca Radicati Di Brozolo, 'International Law Association International Commercial Arbitration Committee's Report and Recommendations on 'Confidentiality in International Commercial Arbitration'' (2012) 28(3) Arbitration International 355.

19 Geneva Protocol on Arbitration Clauses, opened for signature 24 September 1923, 27 LNTS 157, entered into force 28 July 1924 (Geneva Protocol on Arbitration Clauses).

20 Albert Jan Van den Berg and TMC Den Haag, *The New York Arbitration Convention of 1958: Towards a Uniform Judicial Interpretation* (Kluwer law and taxation Deventer 1981) 6–7; Geneva Convention on the Execution of Foreign Arbitral Awards, opened for signature 26 September 1927, 92 LNTS 301, entered into force 25 July 1929 (Geneva Convention on the Execution of Foreign Arbitral Awards).

21 Lew, Mistelis and Kröll (n 4) 20.

arbitration (that proof, for most countries, had to be obtained through national courts) before seeking enforcement abroad.

In 1958, a new treaty, the Convention on the Recognition and Enforcement of Foreign Arbitral Awards (the New York Convention), was adopted by the United Nations to promote the universal enforceability of foreign arbitration agreements and awards.[22] It has been considered a major milestone and catalyst for the development of modern-day international commercial arbitration.[23] It established a universal regime for the enforcement of arbitration agreements, as well as the recognition and enforcement of arbitral awards by the signatory states of the New York Convention.[24] The near-universal enforceability of arbitral awards is an advantage that neither settlement agreements through mediation and other ADR mechanisms, nor court decisions, have.[25] However, the Convention did not provide procedural provisions for conducting arbitrations. In 1966, UNCITRAL was created to develop uniform commercial law, including a procedural regime for international commercial arbitration. In 1976, the UNCITRAL Arbitration Rules were adopted, followed by the UNCITRAL Conciliation Rules in 1980, and the former then heavily influenced the drafting of the Model Law in 1985.[26] The UNCITRAL Rules were created initially for ad hoc arbitrations and were not associated with any arbitral institution, but their success led to them being widely used by such institutions.[27]

Unlike Europe and the West in general, the Asia-Oceania region was relatively slow to embrace modern-day international arbitration. This was arguably for two reasons. One was political tension and the region's sometimes strained relationship with the West. The other, at least according to some commentators, was Asia's non-confrontational approach towards disputes, allegedly favouring settlements through negotiations and mediation over adjudication

22 Convention on the Recognition and Enforcement of Foreign Arbitral Awards, opened for signature 10 June 1958, 330 UNTS 3, entered into force 7 June 1959 (The New York Convention).

23 Pieter Sanders, 'The History of the New York Convention' in Albert Jan van den Berg (ed), *Improving the Efficiency of Arbitration Agreements and Awards: 40 Years of Application of the New York Convention* (Kluwer Law International 1999) 11; Herbert Kronke, *Recognition and Enforcement of Foreign Arbitral Awards: A Global Commentary on the New York Convention* (Kluwer Law International 2010).

24 Van den Berg and Den Haag (n 20) 383.

25 Michael Reisman and Brian Richardson, 'Tribunals and Courts: An Interpretation of the Architecture of International Commercial Arbitration' in Albert Jan van den Berg (ed), *Arbitration-The Next Fifty Years* (Kluwer Law International 2012) 21.

26 Pieter Sanders, 'Procedures and Practices under the UNCITRAL Rules' (1979) 27(2–3) American Journal of Comparative Law 453.

27 Lew, Mistelis and Kröll (n 4) 26.

or arbitration.[28] The latter reasoning, however, is debatable. This is because the international commercial disputes tend to be international by nature and therefore, less constrained by culturally conditioned mentality. As expected, the reluctance to embrace global international commercial arbitration practices continued in Asia up until the end of the 20th century, when parties from the region started to use cross-border arbitration and states began adopting relevant legislation for international commercial arbitration, mostly based on the Model Law.[29]

Australia ratified the New York Convention on 26 March 1975, which entered into force on 24 June 1975 without any reservations. Australia was also one of the first countries to adopt the UNCITRAL Model Law on International Commercial Arbitrations, and to amend its national legislation (the *International Arbitration Act 1974* (Cth)) accordingly.[30] That Act now comprises the 1958 New York Convention, the UNCITRAL Model Law (including almost all 2006 amendments), and the 1966 (Washington) Convention on the Settlement of Investment Disputes between States and Nationals of Other States. In 1985, the Institute of Arbitrators in Australia helped establish the Australian Centre for International Commercial Arbitration (ACICA).[31] Similar trends were observed in other countries of Asia-Oceania. In 1956, the Chinese government established the Foreign Trade Arbitration Commission, renamed in 1988 and currently known as the China International Economic and Trade Arbitration Commission (CIETAC). CIETAC has held a dominant position in Chinese international arbitrations ever since.[32] The Hong Kong International Arbitration Centre (HKIAC) was established in 1985. HKIAC has become another leading institution for arbitration in Asia, although it only developed its own rules for administering arbitrations in 2008 as, initially, it administered arbitrations under the UNCITRAL Arbitration Rules.[33] Also leading is the

---

28 Simon Chesterman, 'Asia's Ambivalence about International Law and Institutions: Past, Present and Futures' (2016) 27(4) European Journal of International Law 945.

29 See generally, Gary Born, *International Commercial Arbitration*, vol. 1 (Kluwer Law International 2009); Chesterman (n 28).

30 See generally, Malcolm Holmes and Chester Brown, *The International Arbitration Act 1974: A Commentary* (3rd ed, LexisNexis Butterworths Australia 2018); See generally, Luke Nottage and Richard Garnett (eds), *International Arbitration in Australia* (The Federation Press 2010).

31 Nottage and Garnett (n 30) 79; Luke Nottage and Richard Garnett, 'The Australian Centre for International Commercial Arbitration' in Helene Ruiz Fabri (ed), *Max Planck Encyclopedia of International Procedural Law* (Oxford University Press 2019) 1–18.

32 Michael Moser, 'CIETAC Arbitration: A Success Story', (1998) 15(1) Journal of International Arbitration 27.

33 Michael Pryles, *Dispute Resolution in Asia* (Kluwer Law International 2006) 109.

Singapore International Arbitration Centre (SIAC), established in 1991, which applies either the UNCITRAL Arbitration Rules or the SIAC Rules (in various editions since 1997).[34]

Unlike Europe, where the recognition and enforcement of judicial decisions of member states are regulated under European Union law, Asia-Oceania jurisdictions do not have such a uniform instrument.[35] Thus, the adoption of the New York Convention was especially beneficial for the region, facilitating the uniform recognition and enforcement of foreign arbitral agreements and awards. Soon, international commercial arbitration became the preferred method of international commercial dispute resolution in the Asia-Oceania region.[36] For example, in 2019, the ICC reported 869 new filed cases.[37] For the same year, CIETAC reported 3333 arbitration cases (617 international arbitration cases and 2716 domestic).[38] HKIAC had 308 arbitration cases in 2019, with about 81% being international, with similar numbers also in SIAC.[39]

Initially, arbitration was deemed to be a time-efficient and hence cheaper alternative to litigation. A 2017 study by the American Arbitration Association found that, on average, court cases took more than 12 months longer to reach the trial compared to arbitrated cases (24.2 months vs 11.6 months for domestic arbitrations). When cases went through appeal, the court cases (US district and circuit courts) took 21 months longer to resolve compared to arbitration (33.6 months vs 11.6 months). The study also found that compared to arbitrated cases, the costs associated with delays were significantly higher for court cases.[40] However, from the 1990s onwards, international commercial

34 SIAC has adopted revised SIAC rules almost every three or four years since 1997. Christopher Drahozal, 'Empirical Findings on International Arbitration: An Overview' in Thomas Schultz and Federico Ortino (eds), *The Oxford Handbook on International Arbitration* (Oxford University Press 2020) 643.

35 Schaefer (n 10).

36 Michael Hwang and Shaun Lee, 'Survey of South East Asian Nations on the Application of the New York Convention' (2008) 25(6) Journal of International Arbitration 873; Diana Hu and Luke Nottage, 'The International Arbitration Act Matters in Australia: Where to Litigate and Why (Not)' (2016) 35(1) The Arbitrator and Mediator 91; Drahozal (n 34).

37 'ICC Celebrates Case Milestone, Announces Record Figures for 2019', International Chamber of Commence, available at <https://iccwbo.org/media-wall/news-speeches/icc-celebrates-25000th-case-milestone-and-announces-record-figures-for-2019/>.

38 'Statistics', China International Economic and Trade Arbitration Commission, available at <http://www.cietac.org/index.php?m=Page&a=index&id=40&l=en>.

39 'Statistics', Hong Kong International Arbitration Centre, available at <https://www.hkiac.org/about-us/statistics>.

40 'Measuring the Costs of Delays in Dispute Resolution: Arbitration is Faster to Resolution than Court – and the Difference Can be Assessed Monetarily' American Arbitration Association, available at <https://go.adr.org/impactsofdelay.html>.

arbitration was increasingly criticised for starting to resemble litigation.[41] The proceedings became very costly, including skyrocketing arbitrator's fees and party (legal and witness) expenses.[42] Relatedly, the disputes became unreasonably time-consuming.[43]

More and more experts in the field began exploring ADR mechanisms to tackle such issues afflicting the international commercial arbitration regime.[44] Accordingly, in the past decade, the interest in international commercial mediation has been increasing in proportion to the rising pitfalls of international commercial arbitration. Consequently, mediation was incorporated in international commercial contracts through multi-tier/multi-step dispute resolution clauses. By then, mediation had already been widely practised in courts as both a civil and commercial dispute settlement mechanism.[45]

2.2.3 *Court-Annexed Arbitration*

Traditionally, arbitration was extensively used in trade and construction disputes, as well as shipping and commodities trade. In domestic legislation, arbitration was initiated either through a court mandate or mutual party agreement.[46] The process of formation of court-annexed arbitration – also known as mandatory arbitration – was facilitated by similar factors in the 20th century, as it was back in the times of Plato and Cicero.[47] The major purpose was to

41 Thomas Stipanowich, 'Arbitration: The New Litigation' (2010) 1 University of Illinois Law Review 1; Luke Nottage, *International Commercial and Investor-State Arbitration: Australia and Japan in Regional and Global Contexts* (Edward Elgar Publishing 2021); Luke Nottage, 'A Weather Map for International Arbitration: Mainly Sunny, Some Clouds, Possible Thunderstorms' (2015) 26(4) American Review of International Arbitration 495.

42 Micha Bühler, 'Awarding Costs in International Commercial Arbitration: An Overview (1/2)' (2004) 22(2) ASA Bulletin 249; Lisa Baertlein, 'Starbucks to Pay $2.76 Billion in Kraft Grocery Rift' (13 November 2013) Reuters, available at <https://www.reuters.com/article/us-starbucks-kraft-idUSBRE9AB17920131112>.

43 Born (n 29) 21. The case of *Tessera Inc. v Amkor Technology, Inc* was pending in front of an arbitration tribunal for 8 years in total; see *Amkor Technology v Tessera* 5:14-cv-03604, ND Cal, 2014.

44 Thomas Stipanowich, 'The International Evolution of Mediation: A Call for Dialogue and Deliberation' (2015) 46(4) Victoria University of Wellington Law Review 1191.

45 Robert A Baruch Bush, 'Substituting Mediation for Arbitration: The Growing Market for Evaluative Mediation, and What it Means for the ADR Field' (2002) 3(1) Pepperdine Dispute Resolution Law Journal 111; Michael Schneider, 'Combining Arbitration with Conciliation' (2004) 1(1) Transnational Dispute Management, available at <https://www.transnational-dispute-management.com/article.asp?key=35>.

46 Astor and Chinkin (n 11) 297.

47 Barrett and Barrett (n 1).

address court congestion.[48] Litigation was also time-consuming and therefore costly for litigants.

Half a century ago, a movement began in the US towards the multi-door courthouse system, which entailed making justice accessible for everyone. This was achieved by referring many court cases to arbitration or instead mediation, for fast, efficient and inexpensive resolution.[49] The first steps toward court-annexed arbitration were made in Philadelphia in 1952, followed by legislative amendments by other states and finally by its implementation in federal courts from 1978 to 1985.[50] Hensler observed the following differences between court-annexed arbitration and commercial arbitration, litigation, and mediation: (a) unlike private commercial arbitration, court-annexed arbitration was neither voluntary nor binding;[51] (b) unlike a traditional mediator, the arbitrator was not trying to help the disputants reach a mutually agreeable compromise; and (c) unlike most judicial settlement conferences, there was a true hearing of the case and an opportunity for litigants to participate.[52]

During the same period, similar developments took place on the other side of the world – Australia. Court-annexed arbitration (or 'referee' procedures) came to be quite widely used and implemented by the courts of various Australian states.[53] Australia began practising court-annexed arbitrations for the same reasons as the US: to give relief to courts by shifting less complicated cases to arbitration and providing litigants with an opportunity to resolve their disputes quickly and cheaply.[54]

Over time, it became apparent that court-annexed arbitration, predominantly in the US, was unable to maintain the advantages it had over litigation. Robert A Baruch Bush observes several reasons why arbitration fell short of its high expectations.[55] One of the possible causes was the extensive

48 Deborah R Hensler, 'Our Courts, Ourselves: How the Alternative Dispute Resolution Movement Is Re-Shaping Our Legal System' (2017) 122(1) Dickinson Law Review 349.

49 Ettie Ward, 'Mandatory Court-Annexed Alternative Dispute Resolution in the United States Federal Courts: Panacea or Pandemic' (2007) 81(1) St. John's Law Review 77.

50 Hensler (n 48).

51 Deborah R Hensler, 'What We Know and Don't Know About Court-Administered Arbitration' (1985) 69(5) Judicature 270.

52 Ibid 271.

53 Federal Court of Australia Act 1976 (Cth) s 53A.

54 Tania Sourdin, *Alternative Dispute Resolution* (5th ed, Thomson Reuters Professional Australia Pty Limited 2016) 23–26; Erik Ficks, 'Models of General Court-Connected Conciliation and Mediation for Commercial Disputes in Sweden, Australia and Japan' (2008) 13(25) Journal of Japanese Law 131.

55 Bush (n 45).

institutionalization of arbitration.[56] The formation of court-like, judicial arbitration was the result of constant court referrals of various types of disputes, such as commercial, antitrust, employment, and especially consumer disputes.[57] Arbitrators were often expected to act in a more judicial way, which contributed to arbitration's 'judicialization', which was most evident in the US.[58] This in turn resulted in court-annexed arbitration losing its cost-effectiveness and time efficiency.[59]

2.3 Spread of Mediation

2.3.1 *History of Mediation*

Mediation has been a part of the dispute resolution system since the impetus of primitive society and existed alongside arbitration for centuries, but the development paths of arbitration and mediation, throughout history, differ tremendously.[60] Mediation practices are encountered in many ancient civilisations of the world.[61] However, the origins of mediation are unknown. It could have been the Emperor Shun of China who first introduced mediation to his people around 4000 years ago, or the earlier cases of mediation in Babylonian

---

56 Ibid.

57 Deborah R Hensler, 'Suppose It's Not True: Challenging Mediation Ideology' (2002) 1 Journal of Dispute Resolution 81. The US is one of the few countries allowing consumer disputes to be arbitrated with little to no limitations. See Michael Barr, 'Mandatory arbitration in consumer finance and investor contracts' (2015) 11(4) New York University Journal of Law and Business 793.

58 Some authors believe that arbitrated consumer disputes can be beneficial and facilitate settlements if regulated properly. However, as in the US, the risk of judicializing arbitration may have been overlooked. See Therese Wilson, 'Setting Boundaries Rather than Imposing Bans: Is it Possible to Regulate Consumer Arbitration Clauses to Achieve Fairness for Consumers?' (2016) 39(3) Journal of Consumer Policy 349.

59 Bush (n 45); Stipanowich (n 41).

60 See generally, David Spencer and Michael Brogan, *Mediation Law and Practice* (Cambridge University Press 2006).

61 Confucianism in China, panchayats in India, and community elders in ancient Egypt. Stanley Lubman, 'Mao and Mediation: Politics and Dispute Resolution in Communist China' (1967) 55(5) California Law Review 1284; Ellen Reinstein, 'Finding a Happy Ending for Foreign Investors: The Enforcement of Arbitration Awards in the People's Republic of China' (2005) 16(1) Indiana International & Comparative Law Review 37; Vikram Raghavan, 'New Horizons for Alternative Dispute Resolution in India-The New Arbitration Law of 1996' (1996) 13(4) Journal of International Arbitration 5; Derek Roebuck, 'Cleopatra Compromised: Arbitration in Egypt in the First Century BC' (2008) 74(3) Arbitration: the Journal of the Chartered Institute of Arbitrators 263.

culture 2300 BC and Phoenician commerce,[62] between Assyrian tradesmen 40 centuries ago, or in an *Anno Domini* reference to mediation in St Paul's letter to the people of Corinth.[63]

While there is no universal definition of mediation, it is generally agreed that mediation is an amicable dispute resolution mechanism that requires the parties to try to reach an agreement on mutually beneficial terms with the help of a neutral third-party.[64] The term international mediation was first formally mentioned at the First Hague Peace Conference in 1899, where mediation was considered as the method for settlement of international disputes alongside arbitration. In 1999, during another Hague conference, mediation once again stood out as the primary method for the peaceful settlement of international disputes.[65] During these 100 years, mediation as a concept for both domestic and international dispute resolution platforms experienced drastic changes.

The spread of mediation began with its initial incorporation into domestic court systems, as court-annexed mediation.[66] It then progressed to commercial disputes, and from there mediation was gradually introduced to the international commercial dispute resolution platform. The proponents of mediation argued that mediation would bring more benefits compared to other, adversarial dispute resolution mechanisms: it was less formal and more flexible, tailored by the disputants and in response to party and dispute needs.[67] In addition, mediation was believed to be a more suitable method for preserving long-term business relations.

2.3.2 *Court-Annexed Mediation*

Court-annexed mediation originated from the common law system and spread throughout the world, including into countries with different legal backgrounds and jurisdictions.[68] The journey of modern mediation towards its successful implementation into the judicial system, similarly to court-annexed arbitration, starts in the US. As early as 1947, the Federal Mediation

62 Cyril Chern, *The Commercial Mediator's Handbook* (CRC Press 2014) 15.

63 Derek Roebuck, 'Cultural Differences and Mediation: An Introduction' (2002) 4(2) Asian Dispute Review 135.

64 More on the existing definitions of mediation can be found in Chapter 3.

65 Jacob Bercovitch, *Studies in International Mediation* (Macmillan 2002) 1.

66 The term court-annexed mediation includes all other terms used to describe a similar process in different jurisdictions, eg court-connected mediation and court-ordered mediation.

67 Stipanowich (n 41).

68 Dimitri Vanoverbeke, *Community and State in the Japanese Farm Village: Farm Tenancy Conciliation (1924–1938)*, vol 29 (Leuven University Press 2004) 171.

and Conciliation Service was formed, which managed labour disputes.[69] From the mid-1960s to the 1970s, mediation proponents began marketing its benefits to unclog overloaded courts from family and neighbourhood disputes.[70] In the 1960s, community justice centres began gaining support in the US. These centres preferred amicable dispute resolution methods over adjudication.[71] The ideology behind the community justice movement was that legal institutions were allegedly serving the interests of privileged groups of society, while 'ordinary people' lost control over their own fates.[72] Therefore, the community centres embraced the conciliatory means of dispute resolution because the participating individuals had full control over the outcomes of their disputes.[73]

Gradually, mediation expanded to more complex civil matters between 1970 and 1980.[74] The major milestone for the institutionalisation of ADR mechanisms was the introduction of a multi-door courthouse system in the US.[75] This was the proposal of Professor Frank Sander at a prominent Pound Conference in 1976.[76] Since then, courts began referring the majority of commercial, family, community and personal injury disputes to mediation, as the first step to dealing with disputes.[77] These mediated cases returned to the courts only if they were not successfully resolved.[78]

In the beginning, participation in mediation was voluntary for disputants. However, because of its non-mandatory character and the unfamiliarity of the parties and their representatives with this new process, mediation was seldom requested voluntarily, and therefore, was rarely used. In those rare occasions when mediation was initiated, the rates of the settlement were significantly high.[79] Consequently, proponents of mediation offered to make court-annexed mediation mandatory for parties. Some judges and legislators supported the introduction of compulsory mediation. They argued that parties to disputes

69 Chris Poole, 'The Future of Mediation' (2015) Mediate.com, available at <https://www.mediate.com/articles/PooleFutures.cfm>.
70 Spencer and Brogan (n 60) 79.
71 Hensler (n 48).
72 Ibid.
73 Ibid.
74 Spencer and Brogan (n 60) 81.
75 Discussed earlier in Chapter 2.2.3.
76 Louise Phipps Senft and Cynthia A Savage, 'ADR in the Courts: Progress, Problems, and Possibilities' (2003) 108(1) Penn State Law Review 327.
77 Bush (n 45).
78 Hensler (n 48).
79 Nancy Welsh, 'The Thinning Vision of Self-Determination in Court-Connected Mediation: The Inevitable Price of Institutionalization' (2001) 6(1) Harvard Negotiation Law Review 1.

generally favoured non-adversarial approaches over litigation and that the popularity of mediation was not defined by its mandatory character but by overall preference.[80] However, Hensler contended that the rates of settlement went up not because a non-adversarial approach was more appealing to an individual's psychology, as some claimed, but because disputants rarely chose voluntary mediation and the rates of use increased once it had become mandatory through courts.[81]

This journey of mediation from voluntary to a court-annexed, mandatory ADR mechanism is a very good analogy to the current voluntary ISM and the proposition of this book to attribute mediation with mandatory characteristics and make it a pre-condition to arbitration. Experience suggests that unless mediation is made mandatory in ISDS, in its current voluntary opt-in format, chances are it will remain significantly underutilised, as it happened with court-annexed mediation.[82] It is less likely for the disputants to choose an additional step voluntarily when their main focus is the outcome of an arbitration award, or in the case of court-annexed mediation, the court's decision.

The gradual popularisation of mediation in domestic dispute resolution can be attributed to the need to remedy costly and time-consuming litigation.[83] Court-annexed mediation was welcomed by the US courts for the same reasons arbitration was once welcomed: to relieve pressure from overloaded courts.[84] This time, it was mediation promising time- and cost-efficiency.[85] Court-annexed mediation gained popularity over court-annexed arbitration, which had been accused of being 'overjudicialized'.[86] Donald Dugdale discussed the oppressive nature of arbitration in cases of insurance claims and argued that arbitration was unsuitable for these types of commercial claims.[87] Baruch Bush argued that court-annexed arbitration lacked the characteristic of finality, unlike private arbitration, and therefore constituted a mechanism for predicting outcomes of a case once it had returned back to the courts.[88]

80 Hensler (n 57).
81 Ibid.
82 More on the reasons why investor-state mediation may remain underutilised unless made mandatory are discussed in Chapters 4 and 5.
83 Welsh (n 79).
84 Ibid.
85 Ibid.
86 Bush (n 45).
87 Cited in Astor and Chinkin (n 11).
88 Bush (n 45).

By contrast, mediation seemed more promising with its evaluative method, which pressured parties to settle.[89]

Similar factors contributed to the popularisation of court-annexed mediations in Australia, whose path was similar to that of its US counterpart. Australian courts also struggled with caseload and lengthy and costly dispute resolution procedures. Domestic mediation in Australia emerged in the 1960s and was triggered by several events: (a) the introduction of the ombudsman's institution; (b) the establishment of an administrative tribunal in 1970; and (c) the creation of the Family Court, which mediated child custody and property matters for divorcing partners, in 1975.[90] In the 1980s, mediation was also strongly encouraged via community justice centres.[91] Moreover, the Australian Federal Court had been practising court-annexed mediation since 1987.[92] Court-annexed mediation referrals were originally voluntary, but over time, a compulsory court-annexed procedure was adopted.[93] For example, Part 4 of the *Civil Procedure Act 2005* (NSW) refers to the procedure of conducting mediation and arbitration for civil cases without requiring the disputants' consent.[94] In Australia, it was judges who were the major supporters of implementing court-annexed mediation in Federal courts.[95] They encouraged disputants to start ADR mechanisms as early as possible during the pre-hearing stages of court proceedings.[96]

Today, court-annexed ADR extends from federal to state legislative systems.[97] For example, the then Chief Justice of the Victorian Supreme Court, Hon Marilyn Warren, emphasised the twenty-year practice of mediation by the Victorian Supreme Court and noted that before going to trial, the majority of civil cases first went through mediation.[98] In fact, just as the decline of trials

89 Craig McEwen and Roselle Wissler, 'Finding Out if It Is True: Comparing Mediation and Negotiation Through Research' (2002) 1 Journal of Dispute Resolution 131.

90 Luke Nottage, 'Comparing ADR in Australia and New Zealand: Introduction and Update', Working Paper No 22, Sydney Centre for International Law, Faculty of Law, the University of Sydney, 22 May 2009, available at <http://web.archive.org/web/20130920012624/http://sydney.edu.au/law/scil/documents/2009/SCILWP22_Nottage.pdf>.

91 Ibid.

92 Rhain Buth, 'Limits to the Quantitative Data on Court-Connected Mediation in the Federal Courts of Australia' (2009) 20(4) Australasian Dispute Resolution Journal 229.

93 Laurence Boulle, *Mediation: Principles, Process, Practice* (3rd ed, LexisNexis Butterworths 2011) 562.

94 Sourdin (n 54); Civil Procedure Act 2005 (NSW) No 28, s 26(1).

95 Justice TF Bathurst, 'The Role of the Courts in the Changing Dispute Resolution Landscape' (2012) 35(3) University of New South Wales Law Journal 870.

96 Boulle (n 93) 559–566.

97 Ibid.

98 Sourdin (n 54) 309.

in US courts during the 1962–2002 year period was referred to as the 'vanishing trial phenomenon' by the American Bar Association, similar trends were also identified in the Australian civil court system (based on a NSW District Court case study from 1990–2009).[99] The increased use of ADR mechanisms, such as mediation, by the courts, was discussed among other factors that could have influenced the decrease of trials in Australia. In 2010, the then NSW Chief Justice James Spigelman characterised mediation as an undoubtedly cost-effective and more settlement-oriented practice.[100] According to the NSW Supreme Court Review of 2014, *'mediation is the most popular form of alternative dispute resolution for Supreme Court proceedings'.*[101] According to the review, out of 486 court-annexed mediation cases, 54% were successfully and amicably settled by the parties.[102]

While mediation has been widely practised through the court systems of Australia, the US, and other countries worldwide, such as the UK, Canada, and New Zealand, over time, its shortcomings became increasingly apparent.[103] At the same time, mediation started becoming more institutionalised and formalised. According to Nolan-Haley, mediation has become more like arbitration.[104] Coben noted that instead of resolving existing disputes, mediation was creating grounds for new claims and disputes, when, for example, settlement agreements were not complied with.[105] Welsh argues that over-institutionalisation could pose a threat to 'self-determination', the fundamental principle of mediation, as there have been instances in which disputants claimed they were pushed into settlement by mediators.[106]

2.3.3 *Commercial Mediation*

Mediation then made its way from domestic courts to the commercial dispute resolution platform.[107] However, the degree of incorporation of mediation

---

99 David L Spencer, 'The Decline of the Trial in Australia' (2011) The Arbitrator and Mediator 1.

100 Chris Merritt, 'Mediation in NSW Supreme Court works: Spigelman' (1 October 2010) The Australian, available at <www.theaustralian.com.au>.

101 2014 Annual Review, Supreme Court of New South Wales, 34 (2014 Annual Review).

102 Ibid.

103 Stipanowich (n 44).

104 Nolan-Haley (n 27 in ch 1).

105 James Cohen, 'Barnacles, Aristocracy and Truth Denial: Three Not So Beautiful Aspects of Contemporary Mediation' (2014) 16(3) Cardozo Journal of Conflict Resolution 779.

106 Welsh (n 79).

107 David Lipsky and Ronald Seeber, 'The Appropriate Resolution of Corporate Disputes: A Report on the Growing Use of ADR by US Corporations' (1998) 4 Martin and Laurie Scheinman Institute on Conflict Resolution; Amanda Leigh Torres and Hernando Otero, 'Commercial Mediation in the Americas' (2016) 13(1) Transnational Dispute

into the commercial platform was not the same as in domestic court systems. Whilst 64% of countries have laws regulating court-annexed mediations, only 46% have consolidated laws for commercial mediation, with 54% having no regulation for commercial mediation.[108]

In the early 1990s, construction contracts were amongst the first to include mediation in their dispute resolution clauses. This field has favoured mediation over arbitration for over two decades, believing that mediation provides better results. This is because, apart from being time and cost-effective, unlike arbitration, mediation preserved business relationships.[109] From construction contracts, mediation then spread to the commercial and business sector, where it was incorporated in the dispute resolution process through Arb-Med-Arb or the hybrid procedures through which arbitration and mediation are used in combination.[110]

One of the common practices of incorporating mediation in a contract as a dispute resolution procedure is through multi-step/tier dispute resolution clauses.[111] This is because such clauses are drafted with a negotiation – mediation – adjudication sequence.[112] However, these clauses do not always mean mediation is followed by arbitration or the other way around. They may also involve litigation instead of arbitration. According to Stipanowich, parties will consider litigation as the final binding step if arbitration does not offer benefits that would outweigh the drawbacks related to costs.[113]

A problem with multi-step clauses occurs when mediation is a mandatory pre-condition to arbitration or litigation. While some clauses may be

Management, available at <https://www.transnational-dispute-management.com/article.asp?key=2334>.

108 Sophie Pouget, 'Arbitrating and Mediating Disputes: Benchmarking Arbitration and Mediation Regimes for Commercial Disputes Related to Foreign Direct Investment' (1 October 2013) The World Bank, available at <https://openknowledge.worldbank.org/handle/10986/16849>.

109 Kent Scott and Cody Wilson, 'Questions Clients Have About Whether (and How) to Mediate and How Counsel Should Answer Them' (2008) 63(2) Dispute Resolution Journal 26; Thomas Stipanowich, 'Beyond Arbitration: Innovation and Evolution in the United States Construction Industry' (1996) 31(1) Wake Forest Law Review 65.

110 Dilyara Nigmatullina, 'The Combined Use of Mediation and Arbitration in Commercial Dispute Resolution: Results from an International Study' (2016) 33(1) Journal of International Arbitration 37, Table 2; Stipanowich (n 109).

111 Alexander Jolles, 'Consequences of Multi-tier Arbitration Clauses: Issues of Enforcement' (2006) 72(4) Arbitration: The International Journal of Arbitration, Mediation and Dispute Management 329.

112 American Arbitration Association, 'Drafting Dispute Resolution Clauses A Practical Guide' (2013) 16.

113 Stipanowich (n 41).

quite straightforward, clearly informing parties about the pre-condition requirements, others may be more ambiguous. For example, in the case of *International Research Corp PLC v Lufthansa Systems Asia Pacific Pte Ltd*, the invoked dispute resolution clause was drafted in such a vague manner that the respondent had to make jurisdictional challenges at various stages of the dispute.[114] The respondent argued that mandatory mediation was a pre-condition to arbitration, and thus non-compliance with the requirement was indeed a valid challenge to the jurisdiction of the arbitral tribunal.

The risks associated with mandatory mediation as a pre-condition to arbitration can be eliminated if the dispute resolution clause has a time limit and an opt-out provision. Such provision would ensure that the respondent does not use the mediation step as the means to deliberately delay the process without any real intent of settlement. Once an allocated time frame is over and no settlement is reached, the claimant should have the right to proceed with arbitration. Otherwise, it would be hard for a party to prove its compliance with the pre-condition in cases where the respondent avoids taking part in the proceedings, or intentionally delays the proceedings. The same opt-out provision can apply to mandatory mediation in ISDS.

In March 2013, the World Intellectual Property Organisation conducted a survey on dispute resolution in technology transactions.[115] According to the survey:

> Respondents indicated that mediation took on average 8 months, and 91% of Respondents stated that costs of mediation typically did not exceed USD 100,000. Respondents indicated that arbitration took on average slightly more than 1 year and cost on average slightly over USD 400,000.[116]

The findings of the survey suggest that when mediation yields a successful outcome (disputants reach an agreement), it is four times cheaper and offers outcomes in a significantly shorter time compared to arbitration.

114 *International Research Corp PLC v Lufthansa Systems Asia Pacific Pte Ltd and another* [2013] SGCA 55, 130.

115 The World Intellectual Property Organization's (WIPO) Arbitration and Mediation Center (WIPO Center), 'Results of the WIPO Arbitration and Mediation Center International Survey on Dispute Resolution in Technology Transactions' (2013), available at <https://www.wipo.int/amc/en/center/survey/results.html>.

116 Ibid.

Despite extensive institutionalisation and other concerns of some commentators as discussed earlier, mediation was incorporated into private commercial contracts as an additional step in the dispute resolution process. With the growing awareness of mediation in the commercial sphere, a new wave of professionals started to emerge, specialising in mediations. Higher education providers and ADR institutions also began offering various training degrees in dispute resolution, with a special focus on mediation. All these steps were orchestrated by the increased market demand for mediation, which has been gradually increasing in many countries (especially those with common law systems).[117]

In a 2011 survey with respondents predominantly from the US, mediation was mentioned as a 'natural response to the cost, length, perceived risks and loss of control associated with litigation'.[118] The survey interviewed 1000 corporate representatives regarding their preferred method of dispute resolution.[119] The study was conducted as a comparison between the findings of the previous 1997 study and the current one of 2011. The research analysis showed that the use of mediation in 2011 was significantly higher compared to 1997. According to the findings, mediation was not limited to construction and employment disputes anymore but had spread to other areas such as commercial/contract, consumer, intellectual property and product liability.[120] Unsurprisingly, while the popularity of mediation increased, the use of arbitration was reducing quite drastically not only in commercial disputes, but also in employment disputes.[121] These changes were most probably caused by the shortcomings of arbitration, which started resembling litigation with increased formality, costs and delays. Thus, dissatisfaction with litigation and arbitration led to the promotion of ADR mechanisms predominantly in the form of mediation.[122]

On a regional scale, while many European countries have long had their national legal frameworks in place for domestic mediations, there was no uniform regulation for cross-border mediations in Europe until 2008.[123] In that

117 Randall Kiser, *How Leading Lawyers Think: Expert Insights Into Judgment and Advocacy* (Springer Science & Business Media 2011) 217.

118 Stipanowich and Lamare (n 2).

119 Ibid.

120 Ibid.

121 Ibid.

122 Ibid.

123 William A Herbert et al, 'International Commercial Mediation' (2011) 45(1) The International Lawyer 111; Irina Paliashvili, Ethan Burger and Michael Lewis, 'Resolution of Commercial Disputes in Russia and Ukraine: is Mediation a Viable Option?' (2004) 1(3) Transnational Dispute Management, available at <https://www.transnational-dispute-management.com/article.asp?key=249>.

year, the European Union (EU) adopted an EU Directive on Certain Aspects of Mediation in Civil and Commercial Matters to facilitate the formation of minimum requirements and basic principles applicable to all EU countries.[124]

Despite this unification attempt, findings from studies on commercial mediation in the EU have not been coherent. A study conducted by the European Parliament in 2014 illustrated that despite the widespread implementation of the Directive into national legislation by EU member states, the number of mediated cases concluded within the EU was less than 1% of all litigated cases.[125] Only Germany, Italy, the Netherlands and the UK showed more than 10,000 mediated cases per year.[126] Focusing on Germany, it is widely accepted that its judicial system works relatively more efficiently compared to the judicial systems of other EU countries, which can explain the relatively insignificant impact of the EU Directive on rates of mediated cases.[127] Moreover, German courts provide financial aid for legal representation, and according to civil procedure, judges are required to facilitate settlement during the proceedings. This practice is common across the EU, which may very well be one of the reasons why commercial mediation is not utilised throughout the Union more often.[128]

As in Europe and the West, mediation expanded from courts to commercial contracts in the Asia-Oceania region as well.[129] In Australia, apart from the

---

124 Council of the European Union, 'Parliamentary Debates, on certain aspects of mediation in civil and commercial matters' European Parliament, Directive 2008/52/EC (which does not apply to Denmark). Interesting issues will arise for Great Britain due to Brexit. Nadja Alexander, 'Brexit and EU mediation' (18 July 2016) Kluwer Mediation Blog, available at <http://mediationblog.kluwerarbitration.com/2016/07/18/brexit-and-london-as-a-mediation-venue/>.

125 Giuseppe De Palo, Leonardo D'Urso, Mary Trevor, Bryan Branon, Romina Canessa, Beverly Cawyer and L. Reagan Florence, 'Rebooting the Mediation Directive: Assessing the Limited Impact of its Implementation and Proposing Measures to Increase the Number of Mediations in the EU' (2014) Directorate General for Intenrational Policies, Policy Department C: Citizens' Rights and Constitutional Affairs 162, available at <https://www.europarl.europa.eu/thinktank/en/document/IPOL-JURI_ET(2014)493042>.

126 Ibid; Centre for Effective Dispute Resolution, 'The Seventh Mediation Audit A survey of commercial mediator attitudes and experience' (2016) CEDR, available at <https://www.cedr.com/wp-content/uploads/2020/01/The_Seventh_Mediation_Audit_2016-1.pdf>.

127 Greg Bond, 'Who Should Be Promoting Mediation and Why? Mediation in Germany: The Poor Cousin to the Courts?' (24 November 2016) Kluwer Mediation Blog, available at <http://mediationblog.kluwerarbitration.com/2016/11/24/who-should-be-promoting-mediation-and-why-mediation-in-germany-the-poor-cousin-to-the-courts/>.

128 Ibid.

129 Throughout this book, the term 'Asia-Pacific' only includes East Asia, South Asia, Southeast Asia, and Oceania.

development of court-annexed mediation in the 1980s, several factors further contributed to the expansion of mediation into commercial contracts.[130] These factors were the legislative incentives and local institutional developments such as the foundation of the Institute of Arbitrators and Mediators Australia (IAMA) in 1975,[131] the establishment of the Australian Commercial Disputes Centre Limited (ACDC) in 1986,[132] and the National Alternative Dispute Resolution Advisory Council (NADRAC) in 1995.[133] These institutions and their successors[134] played a significant role in developing commercial mediation practices through their practice guidelines, training lawyers, and increasing the necessity for university programmes specialising in mediation.[135] Today, due to the diversification of out-of-court dispute resolution mechanisms in Australia, the exact numbers of ADR cases are unlikely to be determined. In 2014, the Australian Government Productivity Commission issued a Report on 'Access to Justice Arrangements',[136] which illustrated that during the years 2011–2012, a total of 542,000 cases were administered by 'Ombudsman and complaint bodies'. This is only a limited number of reported cases because there are numerous contractual and banking matters that are referred to as being ADR but are under no obligation to be reported.[137]

Japan also had a positive move towards the promotion of mediation/conciliation, with an emphasis recently on promoting privately supplied services.[138] Court-annexed conciliation has been known in Japan for some time. Judicial conciliation procedures have been included in the Code of Civil Procedure since 1890.[139] Similarly, court-annexed conciliation has been regulated by the

130 Boulle (n 93).

131 The Institute of Arbitrators & Mediators Australia, available at <https://www.iama.org.au/about-us>.

132 Australian Disputes Centre, available at <https://www.disputescentre.com.au/history>.

133 Australian Government Attorney General's Department, available at <https://www.ag.gov.au/LegalSystem/AlternateDisputeResolution/Pages/default.aspx>.

134 ACDC folded into the Australian Disputes Centre and IAMA was transformed into the Resolution Institute.

135 Spencer and Brogan (n 60).

136 Australian Government Productivity Commission, 'Access to Justice Arrangements: Overview' (2014) Inquiry Report No. 72.

137 Sourdin (n 54) 17.

138 Luke Nottage, 'Will Privately-Supplied ADR Keep Growing in Japan?' (17 March 2010) Japanese Law And The Asia-Pacific, available at <https://japaneselaw.sydney.edu.au/2010/03/will-privately-supplied-adr-keep-growing-in-japan/>; Nottage, *International Commercial and Investor-State Arbitration: Australia and Japan in Regional and Global Contexts* (n 41).

139 Nottage, 'Will Privately-Supplied ADR Keep Growing in Japan?' (n 138).

Civil Conciliation Act since 1951.[140] However, despite the existence of privately supplied forms of ADR mechanisms, such mechanisms have rarely been used. In order to promote ADR in Japan, based on the recommendations of the Justice System Reform Council and as part of justice system reform, a new act was enacted in 2004 and entered into force in 2007 – The Act for Promotion of Use of Alternative Dispute Resolution.[141] Despite these attempts and the official government certifications issued to mediation centres, the number of privately supplied mediations in the commercial field remains low.[142] Various dispute resolution centres have periodically been reporting the statistics of cases. Overall, most cases are referred to mediation rather than arbitration.[143] But the Japan Commercial Arbitration Association reported 26 arbitrations and only 5 mediations for the year 2013.[144]

Out-of-court mediation has long been practised in China.[145] However, reflecting socio-economic developments, People's Mediation (for neighbourhood disputes) lost its popularity since the 1990s despite government efforts to promote it by enacting the People's Mediation Law in 2010.[146] Unlike People's Mediation, commercial mediation provided by mediation institutions such as the mediation centre of CIETAC and the conciliation centre of the China Council for the Promotion of International Trade (CCPIT) is enjoying higher degrees of trust and popularity.[147]

A survey was conducted in 2013 by the International Institute for Conflict Prevention & Resolution, which focused on the Asia-Pacific region's attitude towards ADR, and in particular mediation.[148] It found that 82% of respondents

---

140 Ibid.

141 Shusuke Kakiuchi, 'Regulating Mediation in Japan: Latest Development and Its Background' in Carlos Esplugues and Louis Marquis (eds), *New Developments in Civil and Commercial Mediation* (Springer 2015) 367.

142 Hideaki Irie, 'An Overview on the Current Status of Japanese Private Dispute Resolution – Small Impact of the ADR Act and it's still at the Early Stage' (2010) The Japan Commercial Arbitration Association.

143 Kakiuchi (n 141).

144 Ibid; Nottage, 'Will Privately-Supplied ADR Keep Growing in Japan?' (n 138).

145 Yuanshi Bu and Xuyang Huo, 'The Revival of ADR in China: The Path to Rule of Law or the Turn Against Law?' in Carlos Esplugues and Louis Marquis (eds), *New Developments in Civil and Commercial Mediation* (Springer 2015) 191.

146 Ibid.

147 Jun Wu, 'Annual Review on Commercial Mediation' in *Beijing Arbitration Commission Commercial Dispute Resolution in China: An Annual Review and Preview* (2014) Beijing Arbitration Commission 44.

148 CPR International Institute for Conflict Preservation & Resolution, 'Attitudes Toward ADR In the Asia-Pacific Region: A CPR Survey' (2013) (including results from the Cornell/CPR/Pepperdine 2010–11 Survey of the Fortune 1000 ADR Study for comparison).

from 15 countries of the region welcomed ADR mechanisms. Mediation received 72% in terms of positive responses whereas arbitration received 69%. The study reported that 82% of respondents gave mediation a positive evaluation due to its cost-efficiency whereas 77% stated that mediation provided results much faster compared to litigation and arbitration, which made it the most preferred method for dispute resolution among survey participants.[149]

The situation may be different now, for example, for commercial mediation in New Zealand.[150] The mediation market increased in New Zealand from the 1990s to the 2000s, but, since then, there has been no evidence showing maintenance of this trend in the past 21 years. In fact, while there has been an increase in the number of qualified mediators, supply is more than market demand.[151]

Despite the differences and shifts at an individual state level, it appears that in the past 30 years, mediation in both the Asia-Oceania region and across much of the world has become more established in dispute resolution systems than ever before.

2.3.4 *International Commercial Mediation*

Gradually, with the growth of international commerce, commercial mediation acquired an international character as well.[152] At the beginning of the twentieth century, mediation was actively utilised by disputants and benefited from institutional support alongside arbitration.[153] Since 1923, international commercial conciliation and mediation have been regulated by the relevant ICC rules, which were most recently replaced by the Mediation Rules, adopted on 1 January 2014.[154] In 1929, the ICC Court of Arbitration reported 337 requests out of which 120 were concluded cases.[155] Out of these 120 concluded disputes,

149 Ibid.

150 Grant Hamilton Morris, 'From Anecdote to Evidence: The New Zealand Commercial Mediation Market' (2016) 22(1) New Zealand Business Law Quarterly 10.

151 Ibid.

152 Thomas Wälde, 'Efficient Management of Transnational Disputes: Mutual Gain by Mediation or Joint Loss in Litigation' (2006) 22(2) Arbitration International 205; Stacie Strong, 'Beyond International Commercial Arbitration-The Promise of International Commercial Mediation' (2014) 45(1) Washington University Journal of Law and Policy 10.

153 Linda Reif, 'The Use of Conciliation or Mediation for the Resolution of International Commercial Disputes' (2007) 45(1) Canadian Business Law Journal 20.

154 Strong (n 152).

155 Michel Gaudet, 'Overcoming regional differences' (1988) 5(4) Journal of International Arbitration 67.

80 were settled amicably, 21 were concluded through conciliation and only 19 disputes were concluded with an arbitral award.[156]

Recourse to mediation decreased after World War II as the global business community shifted to arbitration as the preferred means for dispute resolution.[157] The period of 1983–1987 already shows this trend, with only 42 requests for conciliation and 1545 requests for arbitration. In 2019, out of 869 new registered cases, 851 cases were administered under Arbitration Rules while the ICC acted as an appointing authority only in the remaining 18.[158]

The first significant step towards the promotion of more ADR mechanisms in international dispute resolution was the adoption of the UNCITRAL Conciliation Rules in July 1980. Yet they have hardly been used. Arguably, it was not the result of badly tailored rules, but rather a general preference of arbitration over conciliation.[159] There was a theory that the West was culturally more adjudicatory than the East and that this was reflected in the number of arbitrated versus conciliated disputes. However, it is very unlikely, considering the transcultural nature of contemporary international economic relations, making it impossible to limit the origins of the commercial dispute participants to a particular are of the world.[160] Overall, it has been agreed that the adoption of the New York Convention, which provides universal enforceability for arbitral agreements and awards, was the major contributing factor for arbitration taking over the international dispute resolution platform.[161]

In the 1990s, mediation was again gaining popularity globally, for both domestic and international commercial disputes.[162] The increased use of

---

156 Ibid.

157 Stacie Strong, 'Realizing Rationality: An Empirical Assessment of International Commercial Mediation' (2016) 73(4) Washington and Lee Law Review 1973.

158 Gaudet (n 155); Linda Reif, 'Conciliation As A Mechanism For The Resolution Of International Economic And Business Disputes' (1990) 14(3) Fordham International Law Journal 578; 'ICC releases 2019 Dispute Resolution statistics' (15 July 2020) ICC News, available at <https://iccwbo.org/media-wall/news-speeches/icc-releases-2019-dispute-resolution-statistics/>.

159 Gavan Griffith and Andrew Mitchell, 'Contractual Dispute Resolution in International Trade: The UNCITRAL Arbitration Rules (1976) and the UNCITRAL Conciliation Rules (1980)' (2002) 3(1) Melbourne Journal of International Law 184.

160 Tai-Heng Cheng, 'Reflections on Culture in Med-Arb' in Arthur W Rovine (ed), *Contemporary Issues in International Arbitration and Mediation: The Fordham Papers (2009)* (Brill Nijhoff 2010) 419.

161 See earlier Chapter 2.2.2; The New York Convention (n 22).

162 Stephen Huber and E Wendy Trachte-Huber, 'Top Ten Developments in Arbitration in the 1990s' (2000) 55(4) Dispute Resolution Journal 24; Julie Barker, 'International Mediation-A Better Alternative for the Resolution of Commercial Disputes: Guidelines for a US

mediation facilitated the creation of various regulatory frameworks in different jurisdictions around the world, but these legislations were not uniform.[163] On the fortieth anniversary of the New York Convention in 1998, it was suggested to unite the individual regulations into one uniform instrument.[164] In 2002, UNCITRAL adopted a Model Law on International Commercial Conciliation to facilitate the creation of a uniform legal framework.[165] Yet this Model Law has hardly been ratified by states (it was adopted by 33 states, in total 45 jurisdictions).[166] This is partly because it does not provide any guidance on the enforceability of settlement agreements and leaves it to the discretion of individual states adopting the Model Law.

International arbitration institutions also started adopting rules for ADR mechanisms, such as mediation and providing relevant dispute resolution services.[167] Over the last few decades, new institutions with a special mediation profile have been established. For example, the Mediation Institute of the Stockholm Chamber of Commerce was established in 1999, the International Mediation Institute (IMI) came into being in the Hague in 2007, the Singapore International Mediation Centre (SIMC), which administers mediations, and the Singapore International Mediation Institute (SIMI), which promotes mediation education, were both incorporated in 2014, and, more recently, the

---

Negotiator Involved in an International Commercial Mediation with Mexicans' (1996) 19(1) Loyola of Los Angeles International and Comparative Law Journal 1.

163 Stipanowich (n 44); Carlos Esplugues, *New Developments in Civil and Commercial Mediation: Global Comparative Perspectives*, vol 6 (Springer International Publishing 2015) 1199.

164 Eric van Ginkel, 'The UNCITRAL Model Law on International Commercial Conciliation' (2004) 21(1) Journal of International Arbitration 1.

165 Model Law on International Commercial Conciliation, GA Res 57/18, UN Doc A/RES/57/18, 24 January 2003 (Model Law on International Commercial Conciliation); Stipanowich (n 44).

166 'Status: UNCITRAL Model Law on International Commercial Conciliation (2002)', UNCITRAL, available at <https://uncitral.un.org/en/texts/arbitration/modellaw/commercial_conciliation/status>.

167 The institutions include the American Arbitration Association (AAA), which also adopted the International Mediation Rules, the International Chamber of Commerce (ICC) with its ADR rules, the London Court of International Arbitration with its Mediation Rules, the Vienna International Arbitration Center (VIAC) with its 2016 Mediation Rules, and The World Intellectual Property Organisation (WIPO) with its Mediation Rules. Anthony Connerty, 'Alternative Dispute Resolution' (2007) 4(5) Transnational Dispute Management, available at <https://www.transnational-dispute-management.com/about-author-a-z-profile.asp?key=1088>.

Japan International Mediation Centre in Kyoto (JIMC-Kyoto) was launched in 2018.[168]

Despite best efforts, international commercial mediation has still not reached its anticipated level of use. According to Stipanowich, civil law countries are sceptical of common-law-style mediation, which continental Europe sees as the result of the common law's faulty judicial system.[169] Curiously, when quoting the 2013 global international arbitration survey on 'Corporate Choices in International Arbitration, Industry perspectives' by QMUL, commentators usually emphasise the findings that mediation was the least preferred dispute resolution mechanism, with the arbitration, court litigation and adjudication/ expert determination taking the first, second and third places respectively.[170] However, the survey also reported that:

> On average, respondents said that they managed to settle 57% of their disputes through direct negotiation or mediation. Interestingly, of those disputes that do not settle, only a minority (32%) are referred to litigation or arbitration.[171]

The respondents did not differentiate between mediation and negotiation; and indeed, this wording does not necessarily mean that mediation was used in every dispute. However, it does not exclude the possibility that mediation was used in the preliminary stages of these disputes as often as any other dispute resolution mechanism. Accordingly, the findings of the survey do not marginalise the role and success of mediation. On the contrary, the findings emphasise the important and positive role that ADR mechanisms play (settling 57% of respondents' disputes) in otherwise hostile dispute resolution processes.

Amidst the increased demand for mediation on the international commercial stage, this dispute resolution mechanism also faces criticism. Opponents of mediation question its capabilities and argue that it is not an appropriate

168 Victoria Pernt and Sebastian Lukic, 'Mediation on the Heels of Arbitration – Competition or Peaceful Coexistence?' (6 October 2016) Kluwer Arbitration Blog, available at <http://arbitrationblog.kluwerarbitration.com/2016/10/06/mediation-on-the-heels-of-arbitration-competition-or-peaceful-coexistence/>; James Claxton, Luke Nottage, and Nobumichi Teramura, 'Disruption as a Catalyst for International Dispute Services in Japan: No Longer Business as Usual?' in Luke Nottage et al (eds), *New Frontiers in Asia-Pacific International Arbitration and Dispute Resolution* (Wolters Kluwer 2021) 237.

169 Stipanowich (n 44).

170 QMUL, 'Corporate choices in International Arbitration: Industry perspectives' (2013) 6–7; Esplugues (n 163).

171 QMUL (n 170) 5.

dispute resolution mechanism for intricate international commercial disputes.[172] Yet, against such critiques, both in theory and in practice, mediation has proven to be suitable for complex cases due to its key characteristics, such as providing parties with a variety of options and widening horizons that they never knew existed.[173] For example, in the *AMD v Intel* case in the US, the dispute was resolved after only two days of mediation proceedings between the manufacturers of computer chips. Notably, parties had been litigating the same dispute from 2004 until 2009, in multiple cross-border jurisdictions.[174] The parties agreed that Intel would pay USD1.25 billion to AMD and withdraw from litigation.[175] Another complex yet successful mediation settlement took place in the UK regarding toxic waste. The Corby case was disputed for 10 years until it was settled by mediation on 16 April 2010.[176]

Mediation has also become used for disputes involving government-linked entities. New Zealand experienced a mega mediation case settlement in 2013 known as the 'Canterbury earthquake claims': insurers agreed to pay Lyttelton Port more than USD400 million and Christchurch City Council more than USD600 million.[177] Since the 2011 disaster in Japan, which caused the leakage of radioactive material from the Fukushima Dai-ichi Nuclear Power Plant, a special Dispute Resolution Centre for Nuclear Damage Compensation was established to conduct mediation proceedings. The necessity of creating a special profile centre was due to the complexity and extremely high volume of cases.[178] By 2013, out of 7313 lodged mediation cases to the centre, 4239 were

---

172 John Lande and Rachel Wohl, 'Listening to Experienced Users: Improving Quality and Use of Commercial Mediation' (2007) 13(3) Dispute Resolution Magazine 18.

173 Peter Kamminga, 'Overcoming Barriers to Using Mediation in Multi-Party Disputes' (27 July 2013) SSRN, available at <https://papers.ssrn.com/sol3/papers.cfm?abstract_id=2298874>; Mark Kelly, 'No Case Too Big to Mediate' (2016) 892(1) LawTalk 28; Jeff Kichaven, 'A Tool for Multi-Party Insurance Litigation Mediation with "Additional Insureds"'(2008) Mediate.com, available at <https://www.mediate.com/articles/kichavenJ15.cfm>.

174 Arik Hesseldahl, 'The Intel-AMD Settlement: A Play-by-Play' (16 November 2009) Bloomberg, available at <https://www.bloomberg.com/news/articles/2009-11-15/the-intel-amd-settlement-a-play-by-play>.

175 'AMD and Intel Announce Settlement of All Antitrust and IP Disputes' (12 November 2009) Intel Newsroom, available at <https://www.intel.com/pressroom/archive/releases/2009/20091112corp_a.htm>.

176 Press Association, 'Corby Council Agrees Compensation for Birth Defects in Toxic Waste Case' (17 April 2010) The Guardian, available at <https://www.theguardian.com/environment/2010/apr/16/corby-compensation-birth-defects-toxic-steel>.

177 Kelly (n 173).

178 Naoki Idei, 'The Nuclear Damage Claim Dispute Resolution Center' (2012) Japan Commercial Arbitration Association Newsletter 1.

successfully settled.[179] Recently, the Dominican state-owned power holdings company CDEEE settled a USD one billion dispute with an Odebrecht-led consortium for just under USD400 million, using mediation.[180] According to the Dominican government, the mediator 'guided the parties through "extensive discussions", analysing their positions and "the advantages and disadvantages of reaching an agreement"'.[181] Similar arguments that were posed against mediation in an international commercial dispute resolution setting, as discussed earlier, are now advanced against the prospect of mandatory ISM. It is often argued that mediation, due to its non-binding and less confrontational nature, is not universally applicable or relevant to all investor-state disputes. This misconception then adds to the argument against making such futile dispute resolution mechanisms mandatory, which is queried in detail in Chapters 3 to 5.

Another argument against mediation is that it may not serve its purpose, and will instead be an additional, time-consuming step in an already prolonged dispute resolution process. The concern is that some disputants may participate in mediation with the sole intention to get information that they may later use in adjudication against their opponents. These tactics in commercial disputes may give significant financial relief to one party while causing considerable damage to the other.[182] Mediation is not only accused of being a possible timewaster, but also of not being cost-effective. Strong, for example, observes that the presumption that international commercial mediation is more time- and cost-efficient is not supported by facts.[183] Strong relies on the empirical study conducted in 2002 by Roselle Wissler, which studied court-annexed mediation in civil cases in Ohio. According to that study, mediation reduced client costs in only half of the mediated disputes.[184]

179 Joel Rheuben and Luke Nottage, 'Resolving Claims from the Fukushima Nuclear Disaster' (26 Janaury 2015) Japanese Law And The Asia-Pacific (Japanese Law in Asia-Pacific Socio-Economic Context), available at <https://japaneselaw.sydney.edu.au/2015/01/resolving-claims-from-the-fukushima-nuclear-disaster/>.

180 *The Odebrecht-Tecnimont-Estrella consortium v Corporación Dominicana de Empresas Eléctricas Estatales* (CDEEE) (March 2020) Mediated Settlement Agreement, International ADR Center of the International Chamber of Commerce (ICC); Cosmo Sanderson, 'Billion-dollar Odebrecht dispute settled through mediation' (2020) Global Arbitration Review, available at <https://globalarbitrationreview.com/settlements/billion-dollar-odebrecht-dispute-settled-through-mediation>.

181 Sanderson (n 180).

182 Cyril Chern, *International Commercial Mediation* (Informa Law from Routledge 2008) 1–30. The same concern is also raised when discussing the role of mediation in ISDS, as discussed in Chapters 3 and 4.

183 Strong (n 152).

184 Ibid.

However, if we are comparing international commercial mediation to court-annexed mediation from a costs perspective, it would only be fair to also compare them from a time perspective, particularly because the same study by Wissler addressed the effects of mediation on both cost and time.[185] It found that although a very small number of cases were referred to mediation by courts back in 2002 in the US, courts still reported that mediation referrals significantly reduced their caseload.[186] Moreover, apart from settled disputes, the attempted but unsuccessful mediation cases which were reverted back to the courts overall still took less time to be resolved than cases that went straight to litigation without first being mediated.[187] Finally, Wissler makes a reference to an empirical research study conducted by Schildt, which found that the majority of the respondent insurance companies believed mediation to be more time- and cost-effective than litigation.[188]

A detailed comparison of costs was made by Timothy Martin.[189] He compared the amounts an identical dispute would incur under international commercial arbitration and international commercial mediation. According to the study, for the same dispute, the total cost of international commercial mediation would be 5% of the total cost of international commercial arbitration.[190] Moreover, the study found that based on the accumulative statistical data on international mediations conducted by the ICC, international disputes mediated by the International Centre for Dispute Resolution (ICDR) and the London Court of International Arbitration (LCIA) had increased by 45% over a five-year period, from 2005 to 2009.[191]

An interesting trend can also be observed in the QMUL 2013 survey.[192] Most of the respondents reported that due to the 2008 financial crisis, the budgets for litigation were limited and, therefore, they utilised mediation more. This

185 Roselle Wissler, 'Court-Connected Mediation in General Civil Cases: What We Know from Empirical Research' (2002) 17(3) Ohio State Journal on Dispute Resolution 641.

186 Ibid.

187 Ibid.

188 Ibid discussing K Schildt, JJ Alfini and P Johnson, 'Major Civil Case Mediation Pilot Program: 17th Judicial Circuit of Illinois', Preliminary Report, 1994.

189 Timothy Martin, 'International Mediation: An Evolving Market' in Arthur W Rovine (ed), *Contemporary Issues in International Arbitration and Mediation: the Fordham Papers 2010* (Brill Nijhoff 2010) 404.

190 Ibid.

191 Ibid.

192 QMUL (n 170).

is also supported by the Director General's Reports for the LCIA.[193] In 2008, there were 6 mediation cases, whereas in 2009 the figure more than doubled to 13 cases. The rise continued in 2010, reaching 21 mediated cases, but then plummeting to 13 cases in 2011, and gradually falling to 6 cases in 2015.[194] These practices illustrate that mediation is indeed considered to be a cheaper mechanism for dispute resolution than litigation and arbitration.[195] Now, due to the recent COVID-19 pandemic, it is anticipated that there will be an abundance of disputes in all areas of both commercial and investment regimes concerning virtually every state and nation around the world.[196] While settlements through mediation are encouraged, some commentators believe that in the post-pandemic social mentality, there will be no place for amicable settlements.[197] However, such a prediction builds on the subjective and, in fact, arguable statement that settlements are equivalent to losses:

> What is required now for successful settlement negotiations is the ability and willingness to decide under uncertainty. However which manager will now be inclined to accept the responsibility for far-reaching and certainly "lossmaking" settlement decision?[198]

If we replace the statement 'settlements equal a loss' with 'settlements lead to a win-win outcome', then the abovementioned prediction is false.

Notwithstanding the significant steps forward made by international commercial mediation in the past two decades, the biggest limitation of this dispute resolution mechanism remained unresolved until 2019. Before the Singapore Convention, mediation could not promise a binding and enforceable cross-border settlement agreement, which meant it was unable to guarantee the final resolution of disputes. The stakeholders in international disputes believed that mediation would become more popular and heavily utilised if

193 LCIA, 'Director General's Report 2008', available at <https://www.lcia.org/LCIA/reports.aspx; LCIA, 'Director General's Report 2009', available at <https://www.lcia.org/LCIA/reports.aspx.

194 LCIA, 'Director General's Report 2010', available at <https://www.lcia.org/LCIA/reports.aspx>; LCIA, 'Registrar's Report 2015', available at <https://www.lcia.org/LCIA/reports.aspx>.

195 QMUL (n 170).

196 Investment Policy Responses to the Covid-19 Pandemic, UN Doc Special Issue No. 2, UNCTAD, 4 May 2020.

197 Jörg Risse, 'Thinking Ahead: Dispute Resolution after the Corona Crisis' (2020) 18(4) German Arbitration Journal (SchiedsVZ) 165.

198 Ibid.

mediation settlement agreements were made universally enforceable as international arbitration awards.[199]

However, survey responses regarding the possible impact of the enforceability of mediated settlement agreements are not uniform.[200] A 2007 survey conducted by the International Bar Association (IBA) illustrated that the enforceability of mediated settlement agreements was extremely important and that it would have a positive effect on the increased recourse to mediation at an international level.[201] A 2014 survey by IMI also showed that 90% of respondents believed that non-enforceability of international mediated settlement agreements would have a negative effect on the facilitation of international commercial mediation.[202] By contrast, in a 2015 study concluded by QMUL, only 54% of respondents gave a positive answer to the question of whether the creation of a convention on the enforcement of mediated settlement agreements would encourage them to engage in mediation more frequently.[203] Nonetheless, respondents could have been less enthusiastic about the idea of a convention for enforcement of mediated settlement agreements due to enforcement problems associated with arbitral awards under the New York Convention, and not because of their dislike of mediation per se.

There are no comprehensive data that could illustrate the rates of compliance with international commercial mediated settlement agreements. And even when an international mediation is concluded successfully, the reasons for later non-compliance may vary.[204] For example, the parties may regret the compromises made during the mediation or rethink the outcome and thus not

---

199 Ellen Deason, 'Enforcement of Settlement Agreements in International Commercial Mediation: A New Legal Framework' (2015) 22(1) Dispute Resolution Magazine 32.

200 Dorcas Quek Anderson, Nadja Alexander and Anna Howard, 'UNCITRAL and the Enforceability of iMSAs: the Debate Heats Up – Part 3' (22 September 2016) Kluwer Mediation Blog, available at <http://mediationblog.kluwerarbitration.com/2016/09/22/uncitral-and-the-enforceability-of-imsas-the-debate-heats-up-part-3/>.

201 Ibid; 'IBA Mediation Committee Reports on UNCITRAL Model Law Regarding Conciliation', International Bar Association, available at <https://www.ibanet.org/ENews_Archive/IBA_November_2007_ENews_MediationSummary.aspx>.

202 Anderson, Alexander and Howard (n 200); 'How Users View the Proposal for a UN Convention on the Enforcement of Mediated Settlements', International Mediation Institute, available at <https://www.imimediation.org/wp-content/uploads/2018/06/IMI-UN-Convention-on-Enforcement-Survey-Summary-final-27.11.14.pdf>.

203 QMUL, 'International Arbitration Survey: Improvements and Innovations in International Arbitration', 2015; Anderson, Alexander, and Howard (n 200).

204 Chang-Fa Lo, 'Desirability of a New International Legal Framework for Cross-Border Enforcement of Certain Mediated Settlement Agreements' (2014) 7(1) Contemporary Asia Arbitration Journal 119.

comply with the terms of the settlement agreement;[205] or, the bargain received from the intentionally delayed enforcement may be directly relevant to economic benefits.[206]

The legal framework for enforceability, and generally, the status of mediated settlement agreements, have not been uniform – neither on national nor international platforms. As noted above, in 2002, UNCITRAL promulgated the Model Law on International Commercial Conciliation.[207] This was the perfect opportunity for the proposal of legislative provisions which would make settlement agreements binding and enforceable. Yet the opportunity was squandered.[208] The enforcement of settlement agreements was left to the discretion of individual states.[209] According to Article 14 of the UNCITRAL *Model Law*:

> If the parties conclude an agreement settling a dispute, that settlement agreement is binding and enforceable ... [*the enacting State may insert a description of the method of enforcing settlement agreements or refer to provisions governing such enforcement*].[210]

Thus, it is not surprising that this incentive did not do much to promote more international commercial mediation. The EU directive also attempted to create a more unified legal system among EU member states regarding cross-border commercial mediations, but it was unable to reach the desired goal. This incentive did influence various jurisdictions to enact relatively similar, mediation-friendly, domestic legislation.[211] Yet, the Directive was ambiguous about many aspects of the mediation procedure, leaving the regulation of major topics (such as enforcement measures) to the discretion of member states.[212]

205 Deason (n 199).

206 Ibid.

207 Model Law on International Commercial Conciliation (n 165); William Slate, 'UNCITRAL (United Nations Commission on International Trade Law) Its Workings in International Arbitration and a New Model Conciliation Law' (2004) 6(1) Cardozo Journal of Conflict Resolution 73.

208 Jernej Sekolec and Michael B Getty, 'The UMA and the UNCITRAL Model Rule: An Emerging Consensus on Mediation and Conciliation', (2003) 1 Journal of Dispute Resolution 175.

209 Pieter Sanders, 'UNCITRAL's Model Law on International Commercial Conciliation' (2007) 23(1) Arbitration International 105; Deason (n 199).

210 Model Law on International Commercial Conciliation (n 165).

211 Bond (n 127).

212 Stipanowich (n 44).

In June 2018, UNCITRAL approved the final draft of the Singapore Convention on Mediation.[213] UNCITRAL also adopted amendments to the 2002 Model Law on Conciliation and replaced it with the title 'Model Law on International Commercial Mediation and International Settlement Agreements Resulting from Mediation'.[214] Neither the Singapore Convention on Mediation nor the Model Law provides a specific procedure for enforcing settlement agreements. Article 3(1) of the *Convention* instead states:

> Each Party to the Convention shall enforce a settlement agreement in accordance with its rules of procedure and under the conditions laid down in this Convention.

This is similar to the 1958 New York Convention. The members of UNCITRAL Working Group II acknowledged the diverse enforcement mechanism provided in the legislation of different economies. Accordingly, a more flexible method was chosen which could accommodate diverging legislative conditions for enforcement. The main achievement here is that the enforcement of settlement agreements is now backed by a binding instrument such as a convention, instead of soft law. There is also a clear enforcement mechanism, qualified by grounds for refusing enforcement, largely inspired by those provided in the New York Convention for arbitral awards.[215] Despite 53 signatures in 2019, as of February 2022, only 9 states have ratified it and other than Singapore, none of them are major players in international dispute resolution.[216]

Before the creation of the Singapore Convention on Mediation (and before it enters into force for each country), there existed several methods for enforcing mediated settlement agreements both nationally and internationally.[217]

---

213 Singapore Convention on Mediation (n 14 in ch 1).

214 Model Law on International Commercial Mediation and International Settlement Agreements Resulting from Mediation (n 14 in ch 1).

215 Schnabel (n 17 in ch 1); Alexander (n 14 in ch 1); Shouyu Chong and Felix Steffek, 'Enforcement of International Settlement Agreements Resulting from Mediation under the Singapore Convention: Private International Law Issues in Perspective' (2019) 31(1) Singapore Academy of Law Journal 448. Chapter 3 goes into more detail on the Singapore Convention on Mediation in the investor-state dispute settlement framework.

216 States that ratified the Singapore Convention, as of February 2022, are Belarus, Ecuador, Fiji, Georgia, Honduras, Qatar, Saudi Arabia, Singapore, and Turkey. See United Nations, 'Status: United Nations Convention on International Settlement Agreements Resulting from Mediation, available at <https://uncitral.un.org/en/texts/mediation/conventions/international_settlement_agreements/status>.

217 Bobette Wolski, 'Enforcing Mediated Settlement Agreements (MSAs): Critical Questions and Directions for Future Research' (2014) 7(1) Contemporary Asia Arbitration Journal 87.

These methods are the enforcement as contracts, enforcement as court orders or via notaries, and enforcement as consent awards. It is worth mentioning that the Singapore Convention on Mediation will not apply to settlement agreements that have been concluded during court proceedings or approved by a court, settlements that are enforceable as judgements of a court, or settlement agreements that have been embodied in arbitral awards or are enforceable as such.[218]

2.3.4.1 Enforcement as Contracts

International mediation settlement agreements represent ordinary contracts in most jurisdictions.[219] The problem with settlement agreements being enforced as contracts is that if one of the parties later breaches the terms of such settlement agreements, the aggrieved party would have to again seek damages through litigation or arbitration.[220] Thus, the parties to the dispute would be confined to the circle of contractual breach and restitution. Yet international mediation settlement agreements and ordinary agreements/contracts are two very different things.[221]

The procedure used to conclude settlement agreements is different from that of concluding simple contracts. Settlement agreements are the result of the mediation process, are designed to settle an existing dispute amicably by the parties, are concluded during a specifically tailored procedure that ensures the fairness of the agreement and use the assistance of a neutral third-party chosen and appointed by the parties.[222] Most jurisdictions around the world do not have regulations for the enforcement of national or international mediated settlement agreements. For example, there is no statutory regulation for the enforcement of mediated settlement agreements in Australia, a common law country.[223] There is also no such regulation in Georgia, a civil law tradition country located on the other side of the globe. Unless international mediated settlement agreements are approved by arbitral tribunals and embedded into arbitral awards, they fall under the category of contracts in both

218 Singapore Convention on Mediation (n 14 in ch 1) art 1(3).

219 Wolski (n 217).

220 Ibid.

221 Lo (n 204).

222 Ibid.

223 Settlement of Commercial Disputes – Enforcement of Settlement Agreements Resulting from International Commercial Conciliation/Mediation – Compilation of Comments by Governments, 48th sess, UN Doc A/CN.9/846/Add.2, 22 April 2015.

countries. This practice is identical to many other jurisdictions that adopted the UNCITRAL Model Law on International Commercial Arbitration.[224]

2.3.4.2 Enforcement as Court Orders or through Notaries

In some jurisdictions, mediated settlement agreements (both domestic and international) can acquire enforceability powers once registered as court orders or judgements. For example, in Canada, settlement agreements obtained using international commercial mediation are enforced as court judgements. International settlement agreements are enforced in a similar manner.[225]

Some countries are part of multilateral or bilateral treaties on reciprocal recognition of court judgements, including, for example, the Hague Convention on Choice of Court Agreements[226] and the Brussels I Regulation. Therefore, court judgements issued by the judicial organs of one country can be readily enforceable in another.[227] In Europe, mediated settlement agreements fall under the category of contracts and are either confirmed by the notary or by judges.[228] The enforcement of such settlements, which are considered as contracts, is easier inside the borders of the EU under the Brussels I Regulation. The same enforceability problems occur when one of the parties to the mediation is from outside EU borders, bringing in the international element.[229] This is because foreign court judgements do not have the same recognition and enforceability potential as arbitral awards supported by the New York Convention, with there being no worldwide, unifying multilateral convention for the recognition of foreign court judgements.[230] A mediated settlement agreement via court order can be enforced in the country where it was concluded, but international

---

224 Ibid.

225 Jeffrey Talpis, 'Recent Developments Relating to the Use of Mediation to Resolve International Disputes in Canada' (28 August 2015) Advisory Committee on Private Commercial Disputes (Article 2022, NAFTA) Conference Paper.

226 Richard Garnett, 'The Hague Choice of Court Convention: Magnum Opus or Much Ado About Nothing?' (2009) 5(1) Journal of Private International Law 161.

227 Convention on Jurisdiction and the Enforcement of Judgements in Civil and Commercial Matters, opened for signature 27 September 1968, entered into force 1 February 1973 (Brussels Convention). Extended by the Lugano Convention of September 16, 1988.

228 Piet Taelman and Stefaan Voet, 'Mediation in Belgium: A Long and Winding Road' in Carlos Esplugues and Louis Marquis (eds), *New Developments in Civil and Commercial Mediation* (Springer 2015) 89.

229 Burkhard Hess and Nils Pelzer, 'Mediation in Germany: Finding the Right Balance between Regulation and Self-Regulation' in Carlos Esplugues and Louis Marquis (eds), *New Developments in Civil and Commercial Mediation*, (Springer 2015) 291.

230 Stacie Strong, 'Recognition and Enforcement of Foreign Judgements in US Courts: Problems and Possibilities' (2014) 33(1) The Review of Litigation 45.

enforceability would be unpredictable.[231] The notary certification represents a part of a domestic legal system of individual jurisdiction and therefore faces similar issues as enforcement as court judgements.[232]

In Japan, mediated settlement agreements represent contracts, as in European countries.[233] They are therefore not enforceable and simply fall under contractual obligations via relevant provisions of the civil code. Another way is for mediation settlements to be issued as court judgements, or for a notary to certify the monetary claims.

Singapore is making further steps towards asserting its position as the centre for international dispute resolution. On 10 January 2017, the Parliament of Singapore passed the Mediation Act according to which mediated settlement agreements are recorded as court orders.[234] What is special about this incentive is that under the new Act, mediated settlement agreements, subject to public policy requirements, can be directly recorded and enforced as court orders without further application to courts for consent orders or seeking enforcement through contractual claims.[235] By contrast, with the new Singapore Convention on Mediation, mediated settlement agreements can be universally enforceable unless they are court orders. Therefore, parties would have to choose which enforcement instrument to use, the Singapore Mediation Act or the Singapore Convention on Mediation.

2.3.4.3 Enforcement as Consent Arbitral Awards

This method is also called a hybrid dispute resolution system, or hybrid proceedings.[236] The hybrid of mediation and arbitration is not a novelty and has been around for some time now.[237] In China, mediated settlement agreements

231 Brette Steele, 'Enforcing International Commercial Mediation Agreements as Arbitral Awards Under the New York Convention' (2006) 54(5) UCLA Law Review 1385.

232 In Germany, out-of-court mediation settlement agreements can be certified by a notary or by a court. Hess and Pelzer (n 229); Carlos Esplugues and Louis Marquis, *New Developments in Civil and Commercial Mediation* (Springer 2015) 145.

233 Kakiuchi (n 141).

234 Alfred Chua, 'Law Passed to Boost Framework for Commercial Mediation in S'pore' (11 January 2017) Today, available at <https://www.todayonline.com/singapore/law-passed-boost-framework-commerical-mediation-spore>.

235 Dylan Loh, 'Two Bills Passed to Boost Singapore's Position as Dispute Resolution Hub' (11 January 2017) Channel News Asia, available at <https://www.channelnewsasia.com/news/singapore/two-bills-passed-to-boost-singapore-s-position-as-dispute/3428178.html>.

236 Wolski (n 217).

237 Barry C Bartel, 'Med-Arb as a Distinct Method of Dispute Resolution: History, Analysis, and Potential' (1991) 27(3) Willamette Law Review 661; Schneider (n 45).

are considered to be contracts similar to People's Mediation settlement agreements.[238] They can be enforced via judicial ratification (in limited circumstances) or as arbitral awards in case of arbitration-mediation-arbitration procedures.

Hybrid procedures are believed to be beneficial in comparison to multi-tier dispute resolution clauses where mediation and arbitration proceedings are separate and the neutral third-parties are different individuals.[239] Hybrids give financial relief to the parties when the same person wears two hats without the need to hire another individual for the job.[240] Due to the flexibility of this role transformation, a significant amount of time is saved in contrast to establishing a new panel.[241] Moreover, the neutral third-party who wears two hats already knows the dispute and can easily proceed with the award instead of taking additional time to understand the details of the dispute.[242]

The two most common forms of arbitration-mediation hybrids discussed here are Mediation-Arbitration (Med-Arb) and Arbitration-Mediation (Arb-Med) or Arbitration-Mediation-Arbitration (Arb-Med-Arb). Med-Arb is a procedure during which mediation is followed by arbitration.[243] Arb-Med or Arb-Med-Arb is a procedure during which arbitration is initiated before mediation.[244] Once the arbitration begins and the arbitrator is chosen, the process pauses and transforms into mediation which is usually allocated a specific timeframe.[245] If the mediation is unsuccessful, then the mediator switches back to arbitration and continues as an arbitrator.

238 Bu and Huo (n 145).

239 Lucy Greenwood, 'A Window of Opportunity? Building a Short Period of Time into Arbitral Rules in Order for Parties to Explore Settlement' (2011) 27(2) Arbitration International 199.

240 Jacob Rosoff, 'Hybrid Efficiency in Arbitration: Waiving Potential Conflicts for Dual Role Arbitrators in Med–Arb and Arb–Med Proceedings' (2009) 26(1) Journal of International Arbitration 89; Edna Sussman, 'Developing an Effective Med-arb/Arb-med Process' (2010) 7(1) Transnational Dispute Management, available at <https://www.transnational-dispute-management.com/article.asp?key=1592>.

241 Gerald Phillips, 'Same-Neutral Med-Arb: What does the Future Hold?' (2005) 60(2) Dispute Resolution Journal 24.

242 Gabrielle Kaufmann-Kohler, 'When Arbitrators Facilitate Settlement: Towards a Transnational Standard: Clayton Utz/University of Sydney International Arbitration Lecture' (2009) 25(2) Arbitration International 187.

243 Edna Sussman, 'Combinations and Permutations of Arbitration and Mediation: Issues and Solutions' in Arnold Ingen-Housz (ed), *ADR in Business Practice and Issues across Countries and Cultures* (Kluwer Law International 2011) 381.

244 Nottage and Garnett (n 31) 179.

245 Greenwood (n 239).

There are some concerns about hybrid dispute resolution procedures.[246] The issues arise once a successful mediation procedure, being the first step of the dispute resolution, proceeds to arbitration.[247] This is because, after a successful mediation, a Med-Arb hybrid attempts to enforce settlement agreements under the New York Convention.[248] According to Article 1 of the *New York Convention*:

> This Convention shall apply to the recognition and enforcement of arbitral awards … arising out of differences between persons …[249]

Once the dispute has been resolved by mediation, there seems to be no legal ground for initiating arbitration, because there is no dispute which can be arbitrated.[250] Therefore, Med-Arb, when there is a successful mediation, is a fiction, a tool to gain enforceability through consent awards.

The issue of Med-Arb becomes further complicated when arbitration rules of one country allow mediated settlement agreements to be transformed into arbitral awards, but then such consent awards may not be enforceable under the rules of another country.[251] The question arises whether a consent award rendered under the Med-Arb in one country will be refused enforcement under Article V of the New York Convention in another country based on the invalid agreement of the parties to arbitrate (because there was no dispute to arbitrate in the first place).[252]

According to Article 30 of the UNCITRAL Model Law on International Commercial Arbitration 1985 and the arbitration rules of various state jurisdictions implementing the Model Law, consent awards issued during arbitral proceedings are recognised as arbitral awards:

246 Bartel (n 237).

247 Christopher Newmark and Richard Hill, 'Can a Mediated Settlement Become an Enforceable Arbitration Award?' (2014) 16(1) Arbitration International 81.

248 Edna Sussman, 'The New York Convention Through a Mediation Prism' (2009) 15(4) Dispute Resolution Magazine 10; Wolski (n 217).

249 The New York Convention (n 22) art I.

250 Newmark and Hill (n 247).

251 Sussman (n 248); Donna Ross, 'Med-Arb/Arb-Med: A More Efficient ADR Process or an Invitation to a Potential Ethical Disaster?' in Arthur W Rovine (ed), *Contemporary Issues in International Arbitration and Mediation: The Fordham Papers (2012)* (Brill Nijhoff 2013) 352.

252 Newmark and Hill (n 247).

> (1) If, during arbitral proceedings, the parties settle the dispute, the arbitral tribunal shall terminate the proceedings and, if requested by the parties and not objected to by the arbitral tribunal, record the settlement in the form of an arbitral award on agreed terms.[253]

This means that mediated settlement agreements are recognised as agreed/ consent awards only if the parties are given the opportunity to mediate during the arbitration proceedings. This approach is also shared by the ICC Mediation Guidance Notes.[254] Therefore, the problem of enforceability can be eliminated by initiating arbitration first, and only after that using the mediation window, as in the Arb-Med-Arb hybrid.[255]

There is another problem often associated with such hybrid proceedings regardless of the successful or unsuccessful outcome of mediation. It is the issue of the same neutral third-party in both mediation and arbitration procedures.[256] There is a reasonable risk that the same neutral third-party may raise confidentiality, impartiality, natural justice and public policy concerns.[257] Although the same neutral third-party is allowed by UNCITRAL Model Law on International Commercial Conciliation 2002 Article 12,[258] this practice could potentially invoke enforcement refusal under Article V(2) of the New York Convention, although this would be quite rare.[259]

One of the major beneficial traits of mediation is the process of ex parte communications between the parties and the mediator, also known as

---

253 Model Law on International Commercial Arbitration, GA Res 40/72, UN Doc A/40/17, Annex I, 21 June 1985, art 30 (1).

254 'ICC 2014 Mediation Guidance Notes', International Chamber of Commerce (ICC), para 34.

255 Newmark and Hill (n 247); Wolski (n 217); Sussman (n 248).

256 Sussman (n 243); Wolski (n 217); Jeremy Lack, 'Appropriate Dispute Resolution (ADR): the Spectrum of Hybrid Techniques Available to the Parties' in Arnold Ingen-Housz (ed), *ADR in Business Practice and Issues across Countries and Cultures* (Kluwer Law International 2011) 339.

257 Nottage and Garnett (n 31).

258 'Unless otherwise agreed by the parties, the conciliator shall not act as an arbitrator in respect of a dispute that was or is the subject of the conciliation proceedings or in respect of another dispute that has arisen from the same contract or legal relationship or any related contract or legal relationship': Model Law on International Commercial Conciliation (n 165).

259 Brian Pappas, 'Med-Arb and the Legalization of Alternative Dispute Resolution' (2015) 20(1) Harvard Negotiation Law Review 157; Sussman (n 243); Gabrielle Kaufmann-Kohler and Kun Fan, 'Integrating Mediation into Arbitration: Why It Works in China' (2008) 25(4) Journal of International Arbitration 479.

'caucusing'.[260] This is a process during which a mediator conducts one-to-one conversations with the parties to the dispute.[261] These ex parte meetings help the parties open up to the mediator, tell their version of facts, and express their intentions and hopes in relation to the outcome of the dispute, without reservation.[262] Communications between the mediator and the parties are allowed by the UNCITRAL Model Law on International Commercial Mediation 2018. According to Article 8, '[t]he mediator may meet or communicate with the parties together or with each of them separately'.[263]

By contrast, private ex parte communications are not allowed during arbitral proceedings and can qualify as grounds for refusal of enforcement under the New York Convention.[264] Legislators in some jurisdictions (for example, Australia, Hong Kong and Singapore) have attempted to address the grounds for refusal and make it easier to enforce consent awards following Arb-Med.[265] Once the mediation proceedings are concluded, parties are allowed to opt-out of the further continuance of arbitration with the same neutral.[266] In Hong Kong and Singapore, the consent of one of the disputants is enough for the proceedings to continue with the same individual as the arbitrator. In NSW, the old Commercial Arbitration Act (which was based on English law and could be used for either domestic or international arbitrations) was amended to allow one-consent Arb-Med.[267] However, according to the current *Commercial Arbitration Act 2010* (which is based on the Model Law and applies to domestic arbitrations only), double consent is required for a dispute resolution to

260 Edna Sussman, 'Med-Arb: An Argument for Favoring Ex Parte Communications in the Mediation Phase' (2013) 7(2) World Arbitration and Mediation Review 421.

261 Michael Hollingdale, 'Mediation in the Resources Sector: 'Alternative' Dispute Resolution or Now the Norm?' in Gabriël A Moens and Philip Evans (eds), *Arbitration and Dispute Resolution in the Resources Sector* (Springer 2015) 101.

262 Sussman (n 260); Ross (n 251).

263 Model Law on International Commercial Mediation and International Settlement Agreements Resulting from Mediation (n 14 in ch 1).

264 Pappas (n 259); Carlos De Vera, 'Arbitrating Harmony: Med-Arb and the Confluence of Culture and Rule of Law in the Resolution of International Commercial Disputes in China' (2004) 18(1) Columbia Journal of Asian Law 149; Kaufmann–Kohler and Fan (n 259).

265 Commercial Arbitration Act 2010 (NSW) s 27D; New Hong Kong Arbitration Ordinance 2010 (Hong Kong) s 33; International Arbitration Act (Chapter 143A) 1994 (Singapore) s 17.

266 Stephen Mau, 'Arbitration to Mediation to Arbitration With the Same Parties in the Same International Commercial Dispute Before the Same Neutral: Innovative Evolution or Recipe for Disaster?' (2015) 31(8) Construction Law Journal 429.

267 Luke Nottage and Richard Garnett, 'Top 20 Things to Change in or Around Australia's International Arbitration Act' (2010) 6(1) Asian International Arbitration Journal 1; Luke Nottage, 'International Commercial Arbitration in Australia: What's New and What's Next?' (2013) 30(5) Journal of International Arbitration 465.

continue from mediation to arbitration with the same person as arbitrator.[268] Moreover, mediators are required to disclose all the information made known to them during failed mediation proceedings that they deem important for the parties to know.[269]

Similarly, according to the Centre for Effective Dispute Resolution (CEDR) guidelines, if the arbitrator is acting as a mediator, they will not conduct caucuses with the parties unless the information that was shared with the mediator is disclosed to both parties.[270] While the whole purpose of disclosure is to eliminate the risks of arbitrator bias, some commentators believe it has jeopardized the whole purpose of caucusing, which is to encourage the honesty and freedom of expression of the parties. It has been argued that parties to the dispute will not disclose true intentions and a caucus will not be fruitful if the parties know that everything they say may be disclosed to the other party.[271] In fact, disputants may even use this opportunity to gain the sympathy of the now-mediator-future-arbitrator, to win them over.[272] The neutral third-party could be influenced by the information received in confidence during the mediation proceedings, impacting the neutrality of the arbitral award.[273]

The issue surrounding full disclosure has somewhat been remedied by the UNCITRAL Model Law on International Commercial Mediation 2018. Article 9 gives a conditional obligation to disclose information:

> When the mediator receives information concerning the dispute from a party, the mediator may disclose the substance of that information to any other party to the mediation. However, when a party gives any information to the mediator, subject to a specific condition that it be kept

268 Pappas (n 259). Similarly, informed consent is required by US courts for a consent award to be deemed successful. See Sussman (n 240); Nottage and Garnett, 'Top 20 Things to Change in or Around Australia's International Arbitration Act' (n 267).

269 Commercial Arbitration Act 2010 (n 265); New Hong Kong Arbitration Ordinance (n 265); International Arbitration Act (Chapter 143A) (n 265).

270 Centre for Effective Dispute Resolution, 'CEDR Commission on Settlement in International Arbitration' (2009), para 4.2.6.

271 Mau (n 266); Alan Limbury, 'Getting the Best of Both Worlds with Med-Arb' (2010) 48(8) Law Society Journal 62.

272 Sussman (n 243).

273 Pappas (n 259); Sussman (n 243); Kun Fan, 'The Risks of Apparent Bias When an Arbitrator Act as a Mediator-Remarks on Hong Kong Court's Decision in Gao Haiyan' in Andrea Bonomi and Gian Paolo Romano (eds), *Yearbook of Private International Law Volume XIII* (Sellier European Law Publishers 2011) 535.

confidential, that information shall not be disclosed to any other party to the mediation.[274]

In 2011, the Hong Kong Court of First Instance rendered a judgement refusing the enforcement of a Chinese arbitral award based on the grounds of public policy violation.[275] Despite the ruling being later overturned by the Court of Appeal of Hong Kong, one cannot deny the possibility of future refusals for enforcement on similar public policy grounds. Arbitration and mediation proceedings are so different by nature – one generally requires a caucus and the other generally prohibits it – that it is not safe to allow the same individual to conduct both mediation and arbitration.[276] There should be an express provision mandating the mediator and arbitrator to be different individuals, to ensure a legitimate dispute resolution process.[277] SIAC and SIMC developed an Arb-Med-Arb Protocol according to which, unless the parties agree otherwise, the arbitrator(s) and the mediator(s) will generally be different persons. Another proposed approach is for the parties to agree that information received during caucusing will not be disclosed by the mediator/arbitrator to the parties if Arb-Med reverts to issuing an award. However, this practice could put into question whether the information received during caucusing affected the impartiality of the arbitrator issuing an award.[278] Moreover, the information received during caucusing is required to be disclosed to the parties under Article 24(3) of the Model Law.[279]

There is another way to have the same person as a mediator and later as an arbitrator without triggering the refusal grounds of the New York Convention; through a 'Sealed award'.[280] Arbitrators conduct arbitral proceedings. Then,

274 Model Law on International Commercial Mediation and International Settlement Agreements Resulting from Mediation (n 14 in ch 1).

275 *Gao Haiyan and Xie Heping v Keeneye Holdings Limited and New Purple Golden Resources Development Limited*, Hong Kong, Court of First Instance, Decision No HCCT 41/2010, 12 April 2011; Mark Goodrich, 'Arb-Med: Ideal Solution or Dangerous Heresy' (2012) 15(1) International Arbitration Law Review 12.

276 Philip Evans and Gabriel Moens, 'Reflections on the Role of Mediators and Arbitrators Can a Good Mediator Also Be a Good Arbitrator' (2009) 6(1) Macquarie Journal of Business Law 265.

277 Ibid.

278 Goodrich (n 275).

279 Nottage, 'International Commercial Arbitration in Australia: What's New and What's Next?' (n 267).

280 Michael McIlwrath and John Savage, *International Arbitration and Mediation: A Practical Guide* (Kluwer Law International BV 2010) 186; Haig Oghigian, 'The Mediation/Arbitration Hybrid' (2003) 20(1) Journal of International Arbitration 75.

once an award is made, it is sealed without being disclosed to the parties.[281] After this, the parties are given time to try and reach an agreement through an amicable dispute resolution procedure.[282] If mediation is not successful, the parties then open the sealed award, which becomes binding.[283] If they manage to agree and conclude a mediated settlement agreement, the sealed arbitral award is destroyed without its contents ever being known to the disputants.[284] During the arbitral proceedings, parties are more or less able to see where the dispute is going and acknowledge the strength of each party's position in the dispute. This way, the arbitral award would not be subject to public policy grounds of refusal. The only criticism around this type of practice is that anything the mediator later says or does to facilitate the mediation settlement may be interpreted by the parties as a hint regarding what might be in the envelope, the parties thus feeling coerced into an agreement that they did not want.[285]

The hybrids are believed to be a product of flawed arbitration, offering a timely and cost-effective alternative.[286] But this is from the perspective of arbitration. The picture is different when we evaluate the consequences of hybrids from the perspective of mediation. Hybrids are not really a cost-effective alternative to (costly) arbitrations as they do not offer financial relief to the parties.[287] Unlike freestanding mediation, in hybrids, parties are usually required to have lawyers during the proceedings, thus acquiring further expenses during mediation. Moreover, the right neutral with both arbitrator and mediator skills will most probably charge more, as experts with skills in both fields would be rare.[288]

Notwithstanding the regulatory attempts to create a symbiosis of two totally different types of dispute resolution mechanisms, they do not seem to fit together. That is why neither Med-Arb nor its better version – Arb-(Med-Arb) – has had a wide application in Australia as well as other non-Asian countries.[289] A study conducted by Nigmatullina in 2014 revealed that only 34.6% of participants reported having participated in the combined use of mediation

281 Laurence Boulle, 'International Enforceability of Mediated Settlement Agreements: Developing the Conceptual Framework' (2014) 7(1) Contemporary Asia Arbitration Journal 35.
282 Lack (n 256).
283 Boulle (n 281).
284 Lack (n 256).
285 Spencer and Brogan (n 60).
286 Phillips (n 241).
287 Pappas (n 259).
288 Sussman (n 243).
289 Hollingdale (n 261).

and arbitration procedures.[290] Of those participants, 84.6% had taken part in combined mediation and arbitration proceedings where the mediator and the arbitrator were two different individuals.[291] Moreover, the Arb-Med hybrid has become less common even in some Asian countries.[292] A research survey conducted by Mau illustrated that 52% of respondents would not recommend their clients to engage in Arb-(Med-Arb) proceedings and this was mostly due to the enforceability issue and public policy concerns.[293] According to the survey conducted by QMUL on Improvements and Innovations in International Arbitration, 78% of respondents said they would prefer to stay arbitration proceedings whilst mediation was attempted.[294] Thus, the survey found '[w]hen arbitration and mediation are used in conjunction, it appears that a minimal overlap between the two processes is preferred'.[295]

Now, if more states ratify the Singapore Convention on Mediation and the Model Law on International Commercial Mediation, mediation settlement agreements may start to enjoy universal enforceability. Therefore, the need for embedding settlement agreements into arbitral awards would be expected to decrease. Hopefully, with these new changes, mediation practice will increase through multi-tier dispute resolution clauses. Staying arbitration proceedings and recourse to separate mediation should also be more encouraged.

2.4 Conclusion

The historical review illustrates how each new procedure introduced into the well-established dispute resolution processes was initially met with scepticism and varying levels of resistance. Moreover, each of the incentives to upgrade the existing dispute resolution processes was triggered by the drawbacks of the mechanism that were already in place. For example, arbitration was injected into domestic court systems due to overloaded court dockets, which made adjudication lengthy and costly. While this change was met with resistance, with time, it served its purpose, and relieved the pressure on the courts. Yet,

290 Nigmatullina (n 110).

291 Ibid.

292 Nottage, 'A Weather Map for International Arbitration: Mainly Sunny, Some Clouds, Possible Thunderstorms' (n 41).

293 Mau (n 266); Limbury (n 271).

294 QMUL (n 203) 30. But see Kun Fan, 'An Empirical Study of Arbitrators Acting as Mediators in China' (2014) 15(3) Cardozo Journal of Conflict Resolution 777, which finds that arbitrators acting as mediators is common practice in China.

295 QMUL (n 203); Lack (n 256).

over time, arbitration too started resembling litigation and, therefore, court-annexed mediation was introduced. While this incentive was also met with distrust, through practice, mediation proved to be a beneficial addition to domestic litigation.

This trend continued with the promotion of mediation in international commercial dispute resolution. Once international commercial arbitration became problematic, mediation was inserted into the international commercial dispute settlement process through multi-tier dispute resolution clauses. Commentators expressed doubt about the suitability of mediation for international commercial disputes and were sceptical about mediation's ability to handle international cases. Yet mediation has been successfully utilised in international commercial dispute resolution for some time now, particularly in multi-tier dispute resolution clauses involving separate mediators and (if necessary) arbitrators.

Presently, arbitration in investor-state dispute resolution is facing similar drawbacks to those it experienced in domestic and international commercial dispute resolution. Once again, mediation as an ADR mechanism is being put forward as a remedy to the costly and time-consuming investor-state dispute resolution process. Yet opinions about what it can bring to the table are divided when ISM is discussed as a mandatory pre-condition to arbitration, instead of a voluntary opt-in step of ISDS, as explored generally next in Chapter 3.

CHAPTER 3

Mediation to Address Drawbacks of Arbitration in the Investor-State Dispute Settlement Regime

3.1 Introduction

Growing dissatisfaction with ISDS, centred on ISA, paved the way for the promotion and integration of ISM into the current ISDS regime. More stakeholders of ISDS have started to believe that mediation can serve as a time- and cost-saving dispute resolution mechanism, which is also more likely to preserve investment relationships between investors and states. On 12 September 2020 the Singapore Convention on Mediation entered into force.[1] The number of the new-generation IIAs with express reference to mediation is also on the rise, which is atypical for older generation BITs.[2] These cooperative efforts reflect an unprecedented 'treatification' of ISM.[3]

This chapter examines the need for ISM by first analysing the current factors impacting ISA. It outlines the progression of ISA from its conception to the present day. It then examines three major drawbacks of ISA: high costs, prolonged arbitral process, and the so-called 'legitimacy crisis'. It concludes by discussing current steps taken by ISDS stakeholders to tackle these issues and, in particular, the incentive of integrating mediation into ISDS.

1 It was signed by 46 nations on the first day. This marks the highest number of signatories on the first day in the history of UN trade conventions. However, it has only been ratified by 6 States so far. Singapore Convention on Mediation (n 14 in ch 1).

2 Titi (n 8 in ch 1). For example, art 8.20 of the Comprehensive Economic and Trade Agreement (CETA) (n 9 in ch 1) is dedicated to mediation. The EU-Singapore IPA (n 21 in ch 1) provides a whole annex for mediation between investors and states (Annex 6 in ch 1). Article 9.18(1) of the Comprehensive and Progressive Agreement for Trans-Pacific Partnership (CPTPP) (n 21 in ch 1) provides a voluntary conciliation and mediation step before arbitration. See also Fan, 'Mediation of Investor-State Disputes: A Treaty Survey' (n 26 in ch 1); James Claxton, 'Faithful Friend and Flattering Foe: How Investment Treaties Both Facilitate and Discourage Investor-State Mediation' (2 November 2020) SSRN, available at <https://papers.ssrn.com/sol3/papers.cfm?abstract_id=3690682>.

3 Stacie Strong, 'The Role of Empirical Research and Dispute System Design in Proposing and Developing International Treaties: A Case Study of the Singapore Convention on Mediation' (2018) 20(4) Cardozo Journal of Conflict Resolution 1103.

 DOI:10.1163/9789004532540_004

The chapter then investigates the current role of ISM in ISDS. It starts by defining mediation.[4] It then proceeds with examining the benefits of mediation, especially over arbitration in ISDS. This is followed by an analysis of the current steps and incentives that have been taken towards the promotion of ISM in ISDS. The Chapter concludes that the current ISDS regime will benefit most if mediation is incorporated as a mandatory prerequisite of ISA rather than made a voluntary step in the dispute resolution process.

3.2 Investor-State Arbitration

In the second half of the twentieth century, ISA as a new form of international arbitration was becoming increasingly popular alongside international commercial arbitration. The ISDS regime had been designed and developed under the strong influence of burgeoning international commercial arbitration, with procedural regulation, particularly through ICSID.[5] Since the late 1960s, most IIAs have provided investor-state dispute resolution clauses in addition to state-to-state dispute resolution provisions. These ISDS clauses carried the advance consent of a sovereign state to settle disputes with foreign investors under specific arbitration or conciliation procedures. The increased number of BITs (and later free trade agreement (FTA) investment chapters) that contained ISDS clauses opened the doors for foreign investors to bring claims against host states.

After a slow start, the number of new ISA cases has increased annually, especially from the beginning of the 21st century. The size and complexity of claims grew considerably with the progression of socio-economic relations and investments over time. Especially over the last decade or so, arbitration of investor-state disputes has become a time- and cost-consuming dispute resolution process. Factors contributing to prolonged ISA procedures are, for example (a) sparsity of procedural rules limiting the volume of materials submitted to tribunals by the parties and the experts; and (b) common practice of billable hours of lawyers and (some) arbitrators who consequently become invested in delayed proceedings.[6] Calls have been made for rebalancing the existing

4 As mentioned in Chapter 1, the terms mediation and conciliation are used interchangeably throughout this book.

5 Mark Clodfelter, 'The Future Direction of Investment Agreements in the European Union' (2013) 12(1) Santa Clara Journal of International Law 159.

6 Nick Papadimos and Sebastian King, 'Australian Arbitration Week Recap: Re-assessing Australia's Bilateral Investment Treaty Practices' (29 October 2020) Kluwer Arbitration

ISDS regime, especially through dispute prevention and ADR mechanisms.[7] In 2017, UNCITRAL Working Group III was tasked with identifying concerns regarding ISDS and developing reform solutions. Among these proposals is to increase dispute prevention and mitigation through ADR mechanisms such as mediation.[8]

3.2.1 *Promotion of Investor-State Arbitration*

The growth of trade and commerce among nations led to the spread of foreign investments initially from Europe to non-European countries. It expanded through various channels and instruments such as European imperialism (colonialism) and the conclusion of treaties and investment agreements, namely bilateral friendship, commerce and navigation (FCN) treaties, and then standalone BITS, FTAs and multilateral regional treaties.[9]

The peaceful 18th and 19th centuries in Europe, which are associated with the post-Napoleonic Wars, the industrial revolution, and newly emerged liberal economic theory facilitated the metamorphosis of the international economy.[10] That economy required regulation though, so states began concluding FCN treaties.[11] However, these treaties mostly focused on the protection of property rights rather than investments.[12]

The principles of foreign investment protection were developed with the primary goal of protecting the investment rights of capital-exporting states and the investors who were nationals of these states.[13] The first case that very

Blog, available at http://arbitrationblog.kluwerarbitration.com/2020/10/29/australian-arbitration-week-recap-re-assessing-australias-bilateral-investment-treaty-practices/; Luke Nottage, 'In/formalisation and Glocalisation of International Commercial Arbitration and Investment Treaty Arbitration in Asia' in Joachim Zekoll, Moritz Bälz, and Iwo Amelung (eds), *Formalisation and Flexibilisation in Dispute Resolution* (Brill 2014) 211.

7 Official Records of the General Assembly, Seventy -second Session, Supplement No. 17 (A/72/17) paras. 263 and 264; UNCITRAL Working Group III, Possible reform of investor-State dispute settlement (ISDS) – Dispute prevention and mitigation – Means of alternative dispute resolution A/CN.9/WG.III/WP.190; Franck, 'The Legitimacy Crisis in Investment Treaty Arbitration: Privatizing Public International Law through Inconsistent Decisions' (n 2 in ch 1) ch 1.

8 Schill (n 5 in ch 1).

9 Miles (n 8 in ch 2) 19–31.

10 Chester Brown, 'The Evolution of the Regime of International Investment Agreements: History, Economics and Politics' in Marc Bungenberg et al (eds), *International Investment Law* (1st ed, Nomos Verlagsgesellschaft mbH & Co KG 2015) 153.

11 Ibid.

12 Kenneth J. Vandevelde, *The First Bilateral Investment Treaties: U.S. Postwar Friendship, Commerce, and Navigation Treaties* (Oxford University Press 2017).

13 Muthucumaraswamy Sornarajah, *The International Law on Foreign Investment* (Cambridge University Press 2010) 6.

much resembles modern-day ISA took place as early as the 19th century: *Suez Canal Co. v Egypt*.[14] The arbitral proceeding was initiated on the basis of a concession agreement between the company and Egypt in 1864. The arbitrators for the case were appointed by the Emperor of France, Napoleon III.[15]

The peaceful period did not last long. The catastrophic consequences of two World Wars were reflected both on the domestic economies of directly affected countries as well as the international economy in general. In the first half of the 20th century, the uncertainties of customary international law on investment protection principles became impossible to ignore. Developed and developing states struggled to agree on standards of treatment, compensation for expropriation, and rights of investors to sue states.[16] On the one hand, capital-exporting states believed that the standard of treatment of foreign investors should have been the international minimum standard provided by customary international law. On the other hand, capital importing states tended to give foreign investors the standard of treatment as defined under national laws.[17] Some states supported the 'Hull formula' for compensation for expropriation, according to which compensation should be 'prompt, adequate and effective'. Others believed that fitting one formula to all cases would not be fair and instead favoured the idea of considering further factors, for example, a state's financial situation.[18]

Another issue for debate was the lack of legal personality for investors under international law.[19] In the early days, investors were not attributed with the right to bring claims against host states directly.[20] The later versions of FCN treaties at most provided for inter-state arbitration.[21] Therefore, investors had two options: try their luck before the national courts or turn to their home state for diplomatic protection. None of these measures was reliable for investors. Firstly, the national courts of host states often favoured their own states.[22]

14 Jason Yackee, 'The First Investor-State Arbitration: The Suez Canal Company v Egypt (1864)' (2016) 17(3) Journal of World Investment & Trade 401.

15 Ibid.

16 Jeswald Salacuse, *The Law of Investment Treaties* (OUP Oxford 2015) 46.

17 Brown (n 10).

18 Ibid.

19 Ibid.

20 Daniel Meyers, 'In Defense of the International Treaty Arbitration System' (2008) 31(1) Houston Journal of International Law 47.

21 American Society of International Law, 'Thailand and United States: Treaty of Amity and Economic Relations' (1966) 5(5) International Legal Materials 876.

22 See generally Doak Bishop, Michael Reisman and James Crawford, *Foreign Investment Disputes: Cases, Materials and Commentary* (Kluwer International 2005).

Secondly, home states seldom reacted to their investors' appeals, to avoid escalation of diplomatic sanctions into an armed conflict between two states. Moreover, even when countries engaged in diplomatic negotiations regarding the matter in dispute, investors had little to no say in those dispute resolution procedures.[23]

As a result, investors avoided investing in foreign states due to unreliable and unfavourable means for safeguarding their investment rights.[24] This created a strong belief within the international community that without a proper and functioning system of international investment dispute resolution, there would be no proliferation of international investment relations.[25] For this purpose, lawyers and legal scholars came to an understanding that the creation of a unified convention regulating investment disputes between states would facilitate world peace and encourage more foreign direct investments.[26] There have been multiple unsuccessful attempts of concluding multilateral investment treaties throughout modern history.

The 20th century was an active period for draft proposals of investment conventions such as the Abs-Shawcross Draft Convention of 1959, the Harvard Draft Convention of 1961[27] and the OECD Draft Convention on the Protection of the Foreign Property of 1962.[28] These incentives did not eventuate into a successful multilateral investment treaty. However, the attempted drafts did contribute towards the development of modern-day standards of treatment in international investment law and were reflected in the texts of future BITs.[29]

On 18 March 1965, with the efforts of Mr Aron Broches, the General Counsel of the World Bank, the ICSID Convention opened for signature.[30] The ICSID Convention entered into force in 1966, thereby establishing ICSID.[31] The first

---

23 Ibid.

24 Meyers (n 20).

25 See generally Lauge Poulsen, *Bounded Rationality and Economic Diplomacy: The Politics of Investment Treaties in Developing Countries* (Cambridge University Press 2015).

26 Jonathan Bonnitcha, Lauge N Skovgaard Poulsen and Michael Waibel, *The Political Economy of the Investment Treaty Regime* (Oxford University Press 2017) 9.

27 Brown (n 10).

28 Andrew Paul Newcombe and Lluís Paradell, *Law and Practice of Investment Treaties: Standards of Treatment* (Wolters Kluwer Law & Business 2009) 30.

29 Joachim Karl, 'The Negotiations on the OECD Multilateral Agreement on Investment' in Marc Bungenberg et al (eds), *International Investment Law* (1st ed, Nomos Verlagsgesellschaft mbH & Co KG 2015) 342; John Gaffney and Zeynep Akçay, 'European Bilateral Approaches' in Marc Bungenberg et al (eds), *International Investment Law* (1st ed, Nomos Verlagsgesellschaft mbH & Co KG 2015) 186.

30 Brown (n 10); The ICSID Convention (n 6 in ch 1).

31 Brown (n 10); The ICSID Convention (n 6 in ch 1).

versions of the ICSID Arbitration Rules and the ICSID Conciliation Rules were adopted in 1967. They were later amended in 2006. The first country to sign the ICSID Convention was Tunisia and the first to ratify it was Nigeria (in 1965).[32] As of December 2020, there are 163 signatory and contracting states to the Convention.

The unique feature that distinguishes dispute resolution under the ICSID Convention from such resolution under any other instrument is that arbitration under ICSID is 'delocalised'. This means that awards are not subject to the laws and courts of any seat. Domestic courts do not have the authority to set aside, or review awards rendered under the ICSID Convention. The awards may only be annulled according to self-contained annulment procedures provided by the Convention itself. Awards are also treated like final judgments of courts in the member state, where enforcement may be sought by the award creditor. This explains why foreign investors generally prefer to invoke this Convention regime, and the related ICSID Arbitration Rules, if advance consent to those Rules is provided by the host state and both it and the foreign investor's home state have ratified the ICSID Convention.

By contrast, the ICSID Additional Facility Rules only apply when either the host state or the home state of the investor is a party to the ICSID Convention. The arbitral awards rendered under these rules are not subject to ICSID annulment procedures. Instead, they are subject to domestic court review at the seat of arbitration. In addition, arbitral awards rendered under the ICSID Additional Facility Rules are typically enforced via the New York Convention on the Recognition and Enforcement of Foreign Arbitral Awards.

ICSID is not a judicial body and does not itself perform arbitration procedures, but instead administers the registration and rules of arbitration.[33] The consensus on the text of the Convention was reached only because, unlike previous efforts, the ICSID Convention is a framework convention, addressing only procedural aspects for the resolution of investment disputes, and indeed requiring separate advance consent to arbitration administered by ICSID to be provided by the host state (typically nowadays through a BIT or FTA with the foreign investor's home state). This way, the fiercely disagreed issues of substantive characters, such as applicable standards of treatment, were bypassed, and significant steps were made towards the goal of establishing a unified system of international investment dispute resolution.

---

32 Meg Kinnear and Geraldine R Fischer, *Building International Investment Law: The First 50 Years of ICSID* (Kluwer Law International BV 2015) 11.

33 The ICSID Convention (n 6 in ch 1) art 1(2).

Standards of treatment are still separately provided in national laws on foreign investment, investor-state contracts and especially nowadays IIAs.[34] These IIAs provide the consent of a state under which the latter waives its sovereign immunity against enforcement (but not necessarily execution), and often subjects itself to investor-state dispute resolution under the ICSID Convention.[35] According to Article 25(1) of the ICSID Convention:

> The jurisdiction of the Centre shall extend to any legal dispute arising directly out of an investment, between a Contracting State (or any constituent subdivision or agency of a Contracting State designated to the Centre by that State) and a national of another Contracting State, which the parties to the dispute consent in writing to submit to the Centre. When the parties have given their consent, no party may withdraw its consent unilaterally.[36]

The first modern BIT was signed by Germany and Pakistan in 1959, which was followed by other countries concluding BITs in subsequent years.[37] BITs initially only provided state-to-state dispute resolution opportunities.[38] In

34 See, for example, the ASEAN Comprehensive Investment Agreement, signed 26 February 2009, entered into force 24 February 2012, and ASEAN+ agreements, such as the ASEAN-Australia-New Zealand Free Trade Agreement, signed 27 February 2009, entered into force 1 January 2010 (AANZFTA).

35 Carolyn Lamm, Hansel Pham and Alexandra Meise Bay, 'Consent and Due Process in Multiparty Investor-State Arbitrations' in Christina Binder et al (eds), *International Investment Law for the 21st Century: Essays in Honour of Christoph Schreuer* (Oxford University Press 2009) 54; Luke Nottage, 'Do Many of Australia's Bilateral Treaties Really Not Provide Full Advance Consent to Investor-State Arbitration? Analysis of Planet Mining v Indonesia and Regional Implications' (2015) 12(1) Transnational Dispute Management available at <https://www.transnational-dispute-management.com/article.asp?key=2177>; Antonio Parra, 'Advancing Reform at ICSID' (2014) 11(1) Transnational Dispute Management, available at <https://www.transnational-dispute-management.com/article.asp?key=2031>; Andreas F Lowenfeld, 'The ICSID Convention: Origins and Transformation' (2009) 38(1) Georgia Journal of International and Comparative Law 47.

36 The ICSID Convention (n 6 in ch 1).

37 France and Switzerland in 1960, the Netherlands in 1963, Italy and the Belgium–Luxembourg Economic Union in 1964, Sweden and Denmark in 1965, Norway in 1966, the United Kingdom in 1975, Austria in 1976, and Japan and the US in 1977. See Brown (n 10).

38 Gaffney and Akçay (n 29).

1968, the first BIT with an ISDS clause was concluded between Indonesia and Netherlands.[39] Article 11 of the BIT stated:[40]

> The Contracting Party in the territory of which a national of the other Contracting Party makes or intends to make an investment, shall assent to any demand on the part of such national and any such national shall comply with any request of the former Contracting Party, to submit, for conciliation or arbitration, to the Centre established by the Convention of Washington of March 18, 1965, 1 any dispute that may arise in connection with the investment.[41]

However, the first BIT to have included an unqualified consent, unlike the Indonesia-Netherlands 1968 BIT, was the Chad-Italy BIT, concluded in 1969.[42] Ironically, 50 years later, Indonesia was the first to announce that it would allow its BITs to lapse in order to possibly renegotiate them and omit or reformulate any ISDS provisions. The first BIT Indonesia terminated was the one it had with the Netherlands.[43] It also terminated its 1992 BIT with Australia, which was replaced by a new FTA in 2020; the Indonesia-Australia Comprehensive Economic Partnership Agreement (IA-CEPA).[44] The IA-CEPA will coexist with the ASEAN-Australia-New Zealand FTA, both of which have an ISDS provision. However, the IA-CEPA multi-tier ISDS clause has an element that is not normally found in other treaties (a similar exceptional provision is found in the

39 Chester Brown, 'Introduction: The Development and Importance of the Model Bilateral Investment Treaty' in Chester Brown (ed), *Commentaries on Selected Model Investment Treaties* (Oxford University Press 2013) 8.

40 Gaffney and Akçay (n 29).

41 Netherlands and Indonesia Agreement on Economic Cooperation, signed 7 July 1968, entered into force 7 July 1971, art 11 (Indonesia-Netherlands BIT).

42 Agreement Between the Republic of Chad and the Republic of Italy to Protect and Promote Investment Capital, signed 11 June 1969, entered into force 11 June 1969, art 7 (Chad-Italy BIT); Anthea Roberts, 'State-to-State Investment Treaty Arbitration: A Hybrid Theory of Interdependent Rights and Shared Interpretive Authority' (2014) 55(1) Harvard International Law Journal 1, fn 4 and 44.

43 Michael Ewing-Chow and James Losari, 'Indonesia is Letting its Bilateral Treaties Lapse so as to Renegotiate Better Ones' (15 April 2014) Centre for International Law-National University of Singapore, available at <https://cil.nus.edu.sg/wp-content/uploads/2010/12/Ewing-Chow+Losari-FT-Article-Indonesia-is-letting-its-bilateral-treaties-lapse-15Apr2014.pdf>; Alvin Yeo and Smitha Menon, 'Indonesia-Arbitrating with Foreign Parties: A Closer Look at Indonesia's Approach to Investor-State Dispute Settlement' (2016) 18(3) Asian Dispute Review 124.

44 Indonesia-Australia Comprehensive Economic Partnership Agreement, signed 4 March 2019, entered into force 5 July 2020 (IA-CEPA).

Hong Kong-United Arab Emirates BIT, Armenia-United Arab Emirates BIT, Serbia-United Arab Emirates BIT, Estonia-United Arab Emirates BIT and the Jordan-United Arab Emirates BIT).[45] According to the ISDS provisons of these treaties, apart from the Jordan-UAE BIT, once mediation (conciliaton) is initiated by a disputing party, it becomes mandatory for the claimant investor – a unilaterally mandatory mediation provision as a pre-condition to arbitration.[46] A more detailed analysis of these ISDS provisions is provided in Chapter 4.

Since the dissolution of the Soviet Union and Eastern communist bloc in 1991, newly formed, developing countries emerged on the international arena eager to attract foreign direct investments (FDI) and engage in the global investment economy.[47] They began concluding numerous BITs, signing and ratifying as many treaties as they could.[48] Poulsen and Aisbett argue:

> For most Western States, the treaties were designed and negotiated primarily to protect their investors abroad, whereas for most States in Africa, Latin America, Asia and Eastern Europe the treaties were entered into primarily in the expectation that it would help them attract foreign investment.[49]

---

45 Agreement Between the Government of the Hong Kong Special Administrative Region of the People's Republic of China and the Government of The United Arab Emirates for the Promotion and Reciprocal Protection of Investments, signed and entered into force 6 March 2020 (Hong Kong-UAE BIT); Agreement Between the Government of the Republic of Armenia and the Government of The United Arab Emirates for the Promotion and Reciprocal Protection of Investments, signed 22 July 2016, entered into force 21 November 2017 (Armenia-UAE BIT); Agreement Between the Government of the Republic of Serbia and the Government of The United Arab Emirates for the Promotion and Reciprocal Protection of Investments, signed 17 February 2013, entered into force 25 December 2014 (Serbia-UAE BIT); Agreement Between the Government of the Republic of Estonia and the Government of The United Arab Emirates for the Promotion and Reciprocal Protection of Investments, signed 20 April 2011, entered into force 21 March 2012 (Estonia-UAE BIT); Agreement Between the Hashemite Kingdom of Jordan and the United Arab Emirates for the Promotion and Reciprocal Protection of Investments, signed 15 April 2009, entered into force 12 February 2010 (Jordan-UAE BIT).

46 Ubilava and Nottage (n 18 in ch 1); The Jordan-UAE BIT is only available in Arabic, however, an English translation was provided to the tribunal in *Itisaluna Iraq LLC and others v Republic of Iraq (Award)*, (ICSID Arbitral Tribunal, Case No. ARB/17/10, 3 April 2020, 60.

47 Brown (n 39).

48 Kenneth Vandevelde, 'Of Politics and Markets: The Shifting Ideology of the BITs' (1993) 11(2) International Tax & Business Lawyer 159; Kenneth Vandevelde, 'A Brief History of International Investment Agreements' (2005) 12(1) UC Davis Journal of International Law & Policy 157.

49 Lauge Poulsen and Emma Aisbett, 'Diplomats Want Treaties: Diplomatic Agendas and Perks in the Investment Regime' (2016) 7(1) Journal of International Dispute Settlement 72.

Developing countries believed that by creating a welcoming and safe environment for foreign investors, FDI flows would increase to their benefit.[50] Hence they undertook to treat foreign investments in compliance with the requirements of BITs, granting investors substantive rights and increasingly adding an ISDS provision to the treaties.[51]

In 1992, the North Atlantic Free Trade Agreement (NAFTA) was concluded between the United States, Mexico and Canada. Chapter Eleven of NAFTA, which regulated the investment part of the FTA, also included an ISDS clause for investment protection purposes, with the Unites States believing such a clause was necessary given Mexico's unstable political situation.[52] Ironically, a few years later it was the US and Canada who also became regular respondents of ISA under NAFTA, not just Mexico. Throughout the years, NAFTA generated 63 ISA cases which also contributed to the interpretation of national treatment,[53] the minimum standard of treatment (fair and equitable treatment (FET))[54] and unlawful expropriations.[55] Due to being quite frequent respondents to ISA, the US and Canada adapted their investment agreement templates or Model BITs, developing unusually detailed provisions and voluminous subsequent investment agreements.[56] Such 'NAFTA +' provisions in turn heavily influenced the BITs and then FTAs signed by other Asia-Pacific states.[57] In 2020 NAFTA was replaced by the United States-Mexico-Canada Agreement (USMCA) that entered into force on July 1, 2020. According to the new USMCA, Canada is no longer part of the ISDS regime and overall, investor access to ISDS has been reduced considerably compared to its predecessor, NAFTA.[58]

---

50 Ibid.

51 Franck (n 2 in ch 1).

52 Andrew Newcombe, 'The Americas' in Marc Bungenberg et al (eds), *International Investment Law* (1st ed, Nomos Verlagsgesellschaft mbH & Co KG 2015) 202.

53 *Pope & Talbot Inc. v The Government of Canada (Award on the Merits of Phase II)*, 10 April 2001, [79]; *Methanex Corporation v United States of America (Final Award)*, 7 August 2005, Part IV Ch B [18] and [22].

54 Christopher Thomas, 'Reflections on article 1105 of NAFTA: History, State Practice and the Influence of Commentators' (2002) 17(1) ICSID Review 21.

55 Newcombe (n 52); Andrea K. Bjorklund, 'NAFTA's Contributions to Investor-State Dispute Settlement' in Marc Bungenberg et al (eds), *International Investment Law* (1st ed, Nomos Verlagsgesellschaft mbH & Co KG 2015) 261.

56 Newcombe (n 52); Bjorklund (n 55).

57 Wolfgang Alschner and Dmitriy Skougarevskiy, 'The New Gold Standard? Empirically Situating the Trans-Pacific Partnership in the Investment Treaty Universe' (2016) 17(3) Journal of World Investment & Trade 339. However, NAFTA was renegotiated under the Trump Administration and the ISDS provisions were heavily curtailed.

58 NAFTA, Agreement Between the United States of America, the United Mexican States, and Canada 7/1/20.

In 1998, the Energy Charter Treaty (ECT) entered into force, which built on the principles of the 1994 European Energy Charter.[59] Under the ECT, only transit disputes are referred to conciliation procedures. All other types of investor-state disputes are settled under ISA.[60] ECT has over fifty states and the EU as signatories. As of the latest report of December 2020, ECT has contributed 135 ISA cases to the total number of the known treaty-based ISDS cases of the UNCTAD database.[61]

Treaty-based disputes have not been the only investor-state disputes known to history. The origins of contract-based investor-state disputes can be traced back to the 19th century.[62] This is when a contract concluded between a foreign investor and a sovereign state, regardless of the existence of an international investment agreement, refers the dispute to arbitration instead of to the national courts of the host state.[63] In such cases, the substantive provisions of the dispute are not the standards of treatment under an investment treaty but instead consist of the substantive obligations that are contained in those individual investor-state contracts. Modern-day investor-state contracts may contain *ad hoc* instead of institutional arbitration clauses. This means that apart from the UNCITRAL Arbitration Rules, the contracts may also provide prior consent to the ICC, the LCIA, the American Arbitration Association (AAA), the Arbitration Institute of the Stockholm Chamber of Commerce (SCC), and most importantly the ICSID Arbitration or Additional Facility Rules.[64] According to the ICSID database, the oldest known investor-state contract arbitration case

59 The Energy Charter Treaty (ECT), opened for signature December 1994, entered into force April 1998; Richard Happ, 'The Energy Charter Treaty' in Marc Bungenberg et al (eds), *International Investment Law* (1st ed, Nomos Verlagsgesellschaft mbH & Co KG 2015) 240.

60 Energy Charter Secretariat, 'The International Energy Charter Consolidated Energy Charter Treaty', 2016; Energy Charter Secretariat, 'Decision of the Energy Charter Conference', 2016.

61 International Energy Charter, 'List of Cases', available at <https://www.energychartertreaty.org/cases/list-of-cases/>; UNCTAD, 'Investment Policy Hub' (n 2 in ch 1).

62 André von Walter, 'Investor-State Contracts in the Context of International Investment Law' in Marc Bungenberg et al (eds), *International Investment Law* (1st ed, Nomos Verlagsgesellschaft mbH & Co KG 2015) 80.

63 Ibid. Arthur Nussbaum, 'Arbitration Between the Lena Goldfields Ltd. and the Soviet Government' (1950) 36(1) Cornell Law Quarterly 31.

64 Morris Besch, 'Typical Questions Arising within Negotiations' in Marc Bungenberg et al (eds), *International Investment Law* (1st ed, Nomos Verlagsgesellschaft mbH & Co KG 2015) 93. Moreover, ICSID also offers model ICSID arbitration clauses, which are publicly available on its website. See ICSID, 'Model ICSID Arbitration Clauses', available at <http://icsidfiles.worldbank.org/icsid/icsid/staticfiles/model-clauses-en/main-eng.htm>.

is *Holiday Inns S.A. and others v Morocco*, which was discontinued in 1978 due to party settlement after an award on jurisdiction.[65]

The final attempt for multilateralization took place between 1995 and 1998 under the auspices of the Organisation for Economic Co-operation and Development (OECD). Despite the apparent readiness of international society for such a step, the Multilateral Agreement on Investment (MAI) failed, for several reasons.[66] The MAI was based on three main pillars: investment liberalisation, protection, and dispute settlement. While participants in the negotiations agreed on these major points, there was much disagreement on the content of the individual provisions.[67]

The first problem was encountered at the very beginning, when the negotiators failed to define the term "investment".[68] Secondly, each negotiator party presented its own list of industries that were excluded from the investment liberalisation provisions, causing asymmetry in commitments that became impossible to harmonise. Thirdly, some countries were against allowing pre-establishment disputes to be covered by MAI, whereas others fully opposed the inclusion even of post-establishment disputes.[69] Moreover, non-governmental organisations (NGOS) were strongly against the whole concept of ISDS and started protests against MAI, thereby pressuring the delegates. Many of these NGOs had earlier mobilised unsuccessfully against trade and (services) investment liberalisation under the World Trade Organisation (WTO) (established in 1994 and officially commenced in 1995).[70] Additionally, the already agreed parts of the negotiations were constantly renegotiated and more topics further overloaded the negotiation agenda. There was also a lack of political support

---

65 *Holiday Inns S.A. and others v Morocco (Discontinued)* (ICSID Arbitral Tribunal, Case No ARB/72/1, 17 October 1978).

66 The Multilateral Agreement on Investment: Draft Consolidated Text, DAFFE/MAI(98)7/REV1; The Multilateral Agreement on Investment: Commentary to the Consolidated Text, DAFFE/MAI(98)8/REV1. See also the database containing documents from the negotiations OECD Database, available at <http://www1.oecd.org.ezproxy.library.sydney.edu.au/daf/mai/index.htm>; Karl (n 29); Newcombe and Paradell (n 28) 55.

67 See generally, David Henderson, *The MAI affair: A Story and its Lessons* (Royal Institute of International Affairs 1999).

68 Pierre Sauve, 'Multilateral Rules on Investment: Is Forward Movement Possible?' (2006) 9(2) Journal of International Economic Law 325.

69 Jurgen Kurtz, 'A General Investment Agreement in the WTO? Lessons from Chapter 11 of NAFTA and the OECD Multilateral Agreement on Investment' (2002) 23(4) University of Pennsylvania Journal of International Economic Law 713.

70 Jeswald W Salacuse, 'Towards a Global Treaty on Foreign Investment: the Search for a Grand Bargain' in Norbert Horn and Stefan Kroll (eds), *Arbitrating Foreign Investment Disputes* (Kluwer Law International 2004) 51.

from the higher echelons of participating countries. For example, MAI, unlike NAFTA, was not publicly promoted by the then US president (Bill Clinton) and many politicians of European countries started criticising and distancing themselves from MAI.[71] Negotiations were conducted by experts in the field who lacked political authority. Due to pressure particularly from civil society, France announced that it would no longer take part in the OECD MAI negotiations. The EU followed France as it could not stay in the project without the latter, and hence the whole negotiations came to an end.[72]

Despite the failed attempts to adopt a multilateral convention, efforts to create regional multilateral treaties have been more successful.[73] In 2009, the Association of Southeast Asian Nations (ASEAN) member states signed the ASEAN Comprehensive Investment Agreement (ACIA), which entered into force in 2012. The original aim of ASEAN was the promotion of security, then trade. Gradually, its major objective shifted to include the facilitation of mutual investment within the region through ACIA. During the time of its signature and entry into force, ASEAN also entered into FTAs with Korea, Japan, China, Australia-New Zealand, and India (ASEAN Plus Agreements). Meanwhile, from 2012, ASEAN began working on a unified FTA, a Regional Comprehensive Economic Partnership (RCEP) to include ten ASEAN states and the six ASEAN Plus Agreement countries.[74] RCEP was signed on 15 November 2020, and while India declared it would not sign the treaty, it still represents the world's largest FTA.[75] The initial leaked draft of RCEP in 2015 included ISDS provisions.[76] However, according to the announcement in late 2019 and the final signed text, RCEP does not have ISDS provisions. However, within two years of coming into force, there will be further negotiations to consider adding ISDS. Regardless,

71 Ibid.

72 Karl (n 29).

73 August Reinisch, 'The Future of Investment Arbitration' in Christina Binder et al (eds), *International Investment Law for the 21st Century: Essays in Honour of Christoph Schreuer* (Oxford University Press 2009) 894.

74 Vivienne Bath and Luke Nottage, 'The ASEAN Comprehensive Investment Agreement and 'ASEAN Plus'–The Australia-New Zealand Free Trade Area (AANZFTA) and the PRC-ASEAN Investment Agreement' in M. Bungenberg et al (eds), *International Investment Law: A Handbook* (Nomos Verlagsgellschaft 2015) 283.

75 Amokura Kawharu and Luke Nottage, 'Models for Investment Treaties in the Asian Region: An Underview' (2017) 34(3) Arizona Journal of International and Comparative Law 461.

76 The leaked RCEP draft can be found at <https://www.keionline.org/23065>.

almost all pairs of 15 RCEP states already have at least one ISDS-backed IIA in force between them.[77]

It was not until the mid-2000s that investor-state treaty-based arbitration cases started to increase, with foreign investors invoking various investment agreements and treaties as well as investor-state contracts. While the explosion of BITS, FTAS and multilateral investment treaties made investor-state claims possible, other events also facilitated the growth of ISA cases. A notable example is Argentina's financial crisis, which alone has generated 59 known ISA cases since 1997.[78] As of December 2020 (the latest report), there have been 1104 registered treaty-based ISA cases, with 797 already concluded.[79] According to the UNCTAD database, of these 797 cases, 298 were decided in favour of the state, 227 were decided in favour of the investor, 155 were settled before the final award was rendered, 98 were discontinued, and in 19 cases liability was found but no damages were awarded.[80]

With extensive practice and growing experience in conducting ISA proceedings, arbitration started to show the same weaknesses in the new field of international investment dispute settlement as it had on the international commercial dispute resolution platform. Notwithstanding the structural differences between international commercial arbitration and ISA – one is based on the contracts governed by national law between private parties, and the other (between investors and states) is based mainly on treaties as public international law instruments – they are still part of the same family: arbitration.[81] This extensive common ground is why these two forms have some similar positive and negative traits.

77 Luke Nottage and Bruno Jetin, 'New Frontiers in Asia-Pacific Trade, Investment and International Business Dispute Resolution' in Luke Nottage et al (eds), *New Frontiers in Asia-Pacific International Arbitration and Dispute Resolution* (Wolters Kluwer 2021) 1.

78 Christoph Schreuer, 'The Future of International Investment Law' in Marc Bungenberg et al (eds), *International Investment Law* (1st ed, Nomos Verlagsgesellschaft mbH & Co KG 2015) 1904; UNCTAD, 'Investor-State Dispute Settlement: Review of Developments in 2015', 2016 (IIA Issue Note, No. 2, 2016); Cédric Dupont, Thomas Schultz and Merih Angin, 'Political Risk and Investment Arbitration: An Empirical Study' (2016) 7(1) Journal of International Dispute Settlement 136.

79 UNCTAD, 'Investment Policy Hub' (n 2 in ch 1).

80 My database, which is analysed empirically in Chapter 5, consists of 656 concluded ISA cases as of December 2019.

81 Gus Van Harten and Martin Loughlin, 'Investment Treaty Arbitration as a Species of Global Administrative Law' (2006) 17(1) European Journal of International Law 121.

3.2.2 *Investor-State Arbitration Drawbacks*

The 2013 QMUL focusing on Energy, Financial Services and Construction industries found that 22% of respondents believed cost was the major drawback of arbitration, while 17% considered arbitration extremely time-consuming.[82] In a more recent (2018) QMUL survey, the costs and delays of ISA continued to be arbitration's worst features among other issues, such as 'the lack of effective sanctions during the arbitral process' and the 'lack of power in relation to third parties'.[83] Issues with delays and costs (party costs, tribunal costs and damages awarded) are not only evident in investor-state dispute settlement but also in international commercial dispute settlement.[84] However, these drawbacks are particularly important in ISA rather than in international commercial arbitration. As much as corporate interests may be infringed by time-consuming and costly arbitration proceedings, both the public interest and legitimate concerns caused by the alleged 'regulatory chill' of state legislators are of greater importance.[85]

3.2.2.1 Arbitration Costs

There is rising dissatisfaction with the magnitude of costs associated with international arbitration.[86] Arbitration costs include party costs (for example, expert and especially legal counsel fees, travel expenses), tribunal costs

---

82 QMUL (n 170 in ch 2).

83 QMUL, 'International Arbitration Survey: The Evolution of International Arbitration', 2018; Nottage (n 6).

84 WIPO Arbitration and Mediation Center, 'Results of the WIPO Arbitration and Mediation Center International Survey on Dispute Resolution in Technology Transactions' (2013); International Chamber of Commerce Commission Report, 'Controlling Time and Costs in Arbitration' (2018) ICC Publication 861–2 ENG; Matthew Hodgson, 'Costs in Investment Treaty Arbitration: The Case for Reform' (2014) 11(1) Transnational Dispute Management, available at <https://www.transnational-dispute-management.com/article.asp?key=2088>; Susan Franck, 'Rationalising Costs in Investment Treaty Arbitration' (2011) 88(4) Washington University Law Review 769.

85 UNCITRAL Working Group III, 'Possible Reform of Investor-State Dispute Settlement (ISDS) – Cost and Duration' UN Doc A/CN.9/WG.III/WP.153; Nottage, 'A Weather Map for International Arbitration: Mainly Sunny, Some Clouds, Possible Thunderstorms' (n 41 in ch 2).

86 Robert Smit and Tyler Robinson, 'Cost Awards in International Commercial Arbitration: Proposed Guidelines for Promoting Time and Cost Efficiency' (2010) 20(3) The American Review of International Arbitration (ARIA) 267; Jean-Claude Najar, 'Inside Out: A User's Perspective on Challenges in International Arbitration' (2009) 25(4) Arbitration International 515; Loukas Mistelis and Crina Baltag, 'Trends and Challenges in International Arbitration: Two Surveys of In-House Counsel of Major Corporations' (2008) 2(5) World Arbitration and Mediation Review 83.

(administrative fees and arbitrator remuneration), and the size of damages (claimed and awarded). Some commentators argue that international arbitration is often more expensive than litigation or any other dispute resolution procedure.[87]

An exceptional case, which resulted in the largest award so far of all publicly available cases, is *Yukos v Russia*. That award was rendered by a tribunal sitting in the Hague under the auspices of the PCA.[88] The claimants were three former shareholders of Yukos, a company whose assets Russia had unlawfully expropriated. In the final three awards rendered on 18 July 2014, the Russian Federation was ordered to pay damages in excess of USD50 billion to the claimants, plus USD60 million in legal fees (75% of the incurred costs of the proceedings) and USD9,165,047 for arbitration costs.[89] Another ISA with a significantly large amount awarded was *Tethyan v Pakistan*, where the tribunal ordered Pakistan to pay to the claimant over USD5.9 billion in compensation (including interest and USD62 million for the legal costs of both parties).[90] In *Crystallex v Venezuela*,[91] the ICSID tribunal awarded damages of USD1.2 billion plus pre- and post-award interest. Crystallex sought an award in the amount of USD30.4 million in its party expenses, whereas Venezuela sought

87 Franck (n 84); Hugues Arthur, 'Where do We Stand? Where Should We Go? An Assessment of Recent Costs Allocation Trends in International Commercial and Investment Arbitration' (2015) 12(6) Transnational Dispute Management, available at <https://www.transnational-dispute-management.com/article.asp?key=2279>; David D Caron and Lee M Caplan, *The UNCITRAL Arbitration Rules: a Commentary* (Oxford University Press 2013) 840; Lucy Reed, 'Allocation of Costs in International Arbitration' (2011) 26(1) ICSID Review 76.

88 The award was appealed by Russia and set aside by the District Court of the Hague on April 20, 2016. Yukos filed an appeal and on 18 February 2020, the Court of Appeal in The Hague overturned the previous annulment decision of 2016, reviving the awards rendered in July 2014. See *Veteran Petroleum Limited (Cyprus) v The Russian Federation (Final Award)* (PCA, Case No 2005-05/AA228, 18 July 2014); *Yukos Universal Limited (Isle of Man) v The Russian Federation (Final Award)* (PCA, Case No 2005-04/AA227, 18 July 2014); *Hulley Enterprises Limited (Cyprus) v The Russian Federation (Final Award)* (PCA, Case No 2005-03/AA226, 18 July 2014).

89 Applying the average 2014 EUR to USD exchange rate as the original award amount was in Euros. See Chester Brown, 'The End of the Affair? Hulley Enterprises Ltd (Cyprus) v Russian Federation; Yukos Universal Ltd (Isle of Man) v Russian Federation; Veteran Petroleum Ltd (Cyprus) v Russian Federation, UNCITRAL, PCA Nos AA 226, 227, 228, Final Awards, 18 July 2014 (Yves Fortier, Charles Poncet, Stephen Schwebel)' (2016) 17(1) *Journal of World Investment & Trade* 126.

90 *Tethyan Copper Company Pty Limited v Islamic Republic of Pakistan (Award)* (ICSID Arbitral Tribunal, Case No ARB/12/1, 12 July 2019).

91 *Crystallex International Corporation v Bolivarian Republic of Venezuela (Award)* (ICSID Arbitral Tribunal, Case No ARB(AF)/11/2, 2 April 2016).

USD14.3 million. Each party paid their own party costs.[92] In *Palma Consortium v Bulgaria*, and *Pey Casado v Chile*, legal costs were over USD15 million.[93]

The above are extreme cases with exceptionally high costs and do not reflect the real costs of ISA. Some commentators even argue that the empirical research in this field is limited and that costs of arbitration are more reasonable than those of litigation. They therefore state that the benefits offered by ISA outweigh the costs.[94]

Nevertheless, in UNCITRAL Working Group III, deliberations on multilateral ISDS reform, which have been underway since late 2017, it was widely felt that costs and length of ISA were grounds for concern. This was especially true for both developing states with limited financial capacity and small to medium-sized enterprises (claimants).[95] Recent studies show that party costs represent 90% of the total cost of arbitration, averaging USD six million for the claimant and USD five million for the respondent.[96] The average tribunal costs amount to USD one million, usually split between the disputants.

The cause for increasing arbitration costs (as well as delays) can be found in the way legal counsel usually charge their clients.[97] It is common practice to charge clients by billable hours for the services of legal counsel. It may well be in the interests of such counsel to prolong the dispute resolution process and thereby charge more billable hours. The fees of legal counsel do not have a cap in ISA. That could be introduced through the relevant arbitration rules or IIAs, but this is very unlikely, especially for the IIAs to cover the details of legal counsel costs, since the topic is beyond the treaty regulation scope.[98]

The costs conundrum continues with the inconsistency in how they are distributed between the parties.[99] This makes awards on costs very unpredictable

92 Luke Peterson, 'In-Depth: Arbitrators in Crystallex Case Sidestep Debate Over Lawful vs Unlawful Expropriation, and Accept Validity of Two of Four Damages Valuation Methods' (9 April 2016) IAReporter, available at <https://www-iareporter-com.ezproxy1.library.usyd.edu.au/articles/24957/>.

93 *Victor Pey Casado and President Allende Foundation v Republic of Chile (Award)* (ICSID Arbitral Tribunal, Case No ARB/98/2, 2 May 2008).

94 Chiara Giogetti, 'Is the Truth in the Eyes of the Beholder-The Perils and Benefits of Empirical Research in International Investment Arbitration' (2013) 12(1) Santa Clara Journal of International Law 263; Susan Franck, 'Empirically Evaluating Claims About Investment Treaty Arbitration' (2007) 86(1) North Carolina Law Review 1.

95 UNCITRAL Working Group III, 'Possible Reform of Investor-State Sispute Settlement (ISDS) – Cost and Duration' (n 85).

96 Langford, Behn and Létourneau-Tremblay (n 21 in ch 1).

97 Nottage (n 6).

98 Ubilava and Nottage (n 18 in ch 1).

99 Franck (n 84).

TABLE 1 Average arbitration costs from recent empirical studies

Empirical study	Study period	Arbitral rules	Sample	Average claimant costs	Sample	Average respondent costs	Sample	Average tribunal costs
Behn and Daza, (2019)[a]	1987–2019	ICSID & UNCITRAL	169	6,067,184	177	5,223,974	193	947,622
Franck, (2019)[b]	1987–2012	ICSID & UNCITRAL	161	5,000,000	161	4,100,000	160	800,000
Hodgson and Campbell, (2017)[c]	2013–2017	ICSID & UNCITRAL	96	7,414,000	96	5,188,000	89	1,118,000
Commission and	2011–2017	ICSID	90	6,043,915	88	5,217,247	68	922,087
Moloo, (2018)[d]	2010–2017	UNCITRAL	36	6,077,585	41	4,596,807	48	960,641

a Daniel Behn and Ana Maria Daza, 'The Defense Burden in Investment Arbitration' (2019) PluriCourts Working Paper.

b Susan Franck, *Arbitration Costs: Myths and Realities in Investment Treaty Arbitration* (Oxford University Press 2019) 135.

c Matthew Hodgson and Alistair Campbell, 'Damages and Costs in Investment Treaty Arbitration Revisited' (14 December 2017) Global Arbitration Review, available at <https://globalarbitrationreview.com/damages-and-costs-in-investment-treaty-arbitration-revisited>.

d Jeffery Commission and Rahim Moloo, *Procedural Issues in International Investment Arbitration* (Oxford University Press 2018) 187.

SOURCE: ANA UBILAVA AND LUKE NOTTAGE, 'NOVEL AND NOTEWORTHY ASPECTS OF AUSTRALIA'S RECENT INVESTMENT AGREEMENTS AND ISDS POLICY: THE CPTPP, HONG KONG, INDONESIA AND MAURITIUS TRANSPARENCY TREATIES' IN LUKE NOTTAGE ET AL (EDS), *NEW FRONTIERS IN ASIA-PACIFIC INTERNATIONAL ARBITRATION AND DISPUTE RESOLUTION* (WOLTERS KLUWER 2021) 115

for the parties, which could increase the settlement prospects of a dispute.[100] However, unpredictability may work either way. Disputants may prefer to settle their dispute on their own terms rather than wait for an unknown outcome. Alternatively, they may push their luck with arbitration, hoping the other party pays its fees.

There are two major cost distribution systems in the world.[101] One is the English system according to which the 'costs follow the event', otherwise known as the 'loser pays' principle. Traditionally, at common law, parties to judicial proceedings paid their own expenses.[102] Over time, as common law traditions evolved, England amended its rules and shifted to a new system where the losing party bears all (reasonable) costs of the winning party, including legal expenses.[103] This system, although originally an element of judicial proceedings, has largely been adopted by both civil and common law countries.[104] The other is the American system, according to which each party pays its own party costs whilst the procedural costs are divided equally.[105] In practice, tribunals use their own discretion to allocate costs by applying either of the cost allocation systems, largely depending on individual case circumstances.[106]

The non-existence of a uniform cost allocation system is also affected by how the two most commonly applied rules to an ISA, the ICSID and UNCITRAL Rules, define the cost allocation principles for arbitration costs. According to Rule 28 of the ICSID Arbitration Rules:

> Without prejudice to the final decision on the payment of the cost of the proceeding, the Tribunal may, unless otherwise agreed by the parties, decide: with respect to any part of the proceeding, that the related costs (as determined by the Secretary-General) shall be borne entirely or in a particular share by one of the parties.[107]

By contrast, Article 42 of the UNCITRAL Arbitration Rules, states that:

100 Franck (Table 1, n b 98); Arthur (n 87).

101 John Gotanda, 'Consistently Inconsistent: The Need for Predictability in Awarding Costs and Fees in Investment Treaty Arbitrations' (2013) 28(2) ICSID Review 420.

102 Christopher Koch, 'Is There a Default Principle of Cost Allocation in International Arbitration?' (2014) 31(4) Journal of International Arbitration 485.

103 *Arbitration Act 1996* (UK) s 61.

104 Arthur (n 87).

105 Ibid.

106 Hodgson and Campbell (Table 1, n c).

107 ICSID, Rules of Procedure for Arbitration Proceedings (Arbitration Rules) (2006) (ICSID Arbitration Rules).

> The costs of the arbitration shall in principle be borne by the unsuccessful party or parties. However, the arbitral tribunal may apportion each of such costs between the parties if it determines that apportionment is reasonable, considering the circumstances of the case.[108]

Both sets of Rules provide discretion for arbitrators in awarding and allocating costs, but the formulation of the UNCITRAL Rules (used in one third of ISA cases) by default sets the principle for shifting the costs to the losing party.

While historically, ISA tribunals more often applied the American cost allocation system (where parties bear their own costs), a more recent practice shows increased application of the English system (where costs follow the event).[109] Several studies have shown that in practice, ISA case law is shifting towards the 'loser pays' principle or the English cost allocation system.[110] A study by Hodgson found that 56% of arbitral tribunals ruled in favour of the American system while 44% ordered only one party to fully or partially bear both party costs as well as the tribunal costs: the English system.[111] The American system however has remained the most widely practised cost allocation system for international law disputes used by the WTO.[112] Nonetheless, sometimes, even if a party wins, it still 'loses' financially when not awarded full legal costs. For example, in *Philip Morris v Australia*, despite winning, Australia ended up paying millions in arbitration costs.[113]

---

108 UNCITRAL Arbitration Rules, GA Res 31/98, UN GAOR, 31st sess, 99th plen mtg, Supp No 39, adopted 15 December 1976 (UNCITRAL Arbitration Rules).

109 Hodgson and Campbell (Table 1, n c).

110 Thomas Webster, 'Efficiency in Investment Arbitration: Recent Decisions on Preliminary and Costs Issues' (2009) 25(4)Arbitration International 469, n 15; Koch (n 102); Reed (n 87); Hodgson (n 84); Inna Uchkunova and Oleg Temnikov, 'Allocation of Costs in ICSID Arbitration' (3 December 2014) Kluwer Arbitration Blog, available at <http://arbitrationblog.kluwerarbitration.com/2014/12/03/allocation-of-costs-in-icsid-arbitration/>; *ADC Affiliate Limited and ADC & ADMC Management Limited v The Republic of Hungary (Final Award)* (ICSID Arbitral Tribunal, Case No ARB/03/16, 27 September 2006) [531]-[533]; *Gemplus, S.A., SLP, S.A., and Gemplus Industrial S.A. de C.V. v United Mexican States (Award)* (ICSID Arbitral Tribunal, Case No ARB(AF)/04/3, 16 June 2010).

111 Hodgson (n 84).

112 Noah Rubins, 'The Allocation of Costs and Attorney's Fees in Investor-State Arbitration' (2003) 18(1) ICSID Review 109; Ben Hamida, 'Cost Issue in Investor-State Arbitration Decisions Rendered Against the Investor: a Synthetic Table' (2005) 2(5)Transnational Dispute Management, available at <https://www.transnational-dispute-management.com/article.asp?key=606>.

113 Hepburn and Nottage (n 5 in ch 1); Patricia Ranald, 'When Even Winning is Losing. The Surprising Cost of Defeating Philip Morris Over Plain Packaging' (27 March 2019)The Conversation, available at <https://theconversation.com/when-even-winning-is-losing-the-surprising-cost-of-defeating-philip-morris-over-plain-packaging-114279>.

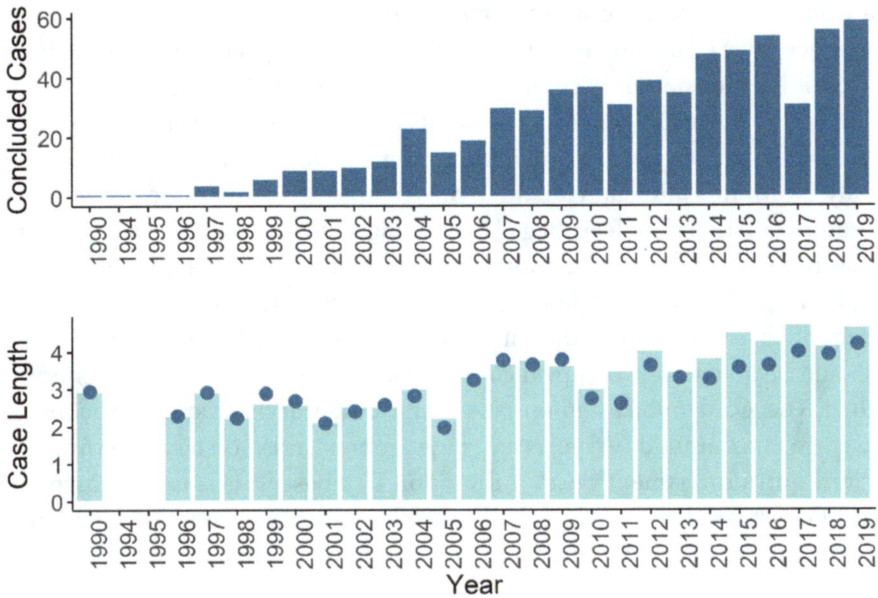

FIGURE 1 Annual number of investor-state arbitration concluded cases and their length
Note: The case length is measured in years. Bars are average and dots are median lengths of concluded cases

3.2.2.2 Delays

Arbitration is not as time efficient as initially anticipated. On average, ISA takes over four years to be concluded from the date of registration and the length of arbitration is growing.[114] If it took a little over three years to conclude an ISA case in 2009, ten years later the average length is four and a half years (Figure 1).

A 2015 QMUL study attempted to determine what the participants of international dispute resolution like and dislike in arbitration.[115] The study found that lengthy proceedings was one of the four main concerns respondents had: 68% of respondents were dissatisfied with costs, 46% were concerned with the lack of effective sanctions during the proceedings, 39% named arbitrators' qualifications (or rather lack thereof) as a disadvantage, and 36% expressed their concerns about delays and lengthy proceedings.[116] The respondents expressed

114 Zachary Douglas, '19th International Arbitration Lecture: A Response to DFAT's Review of Australia's Bilateral Investment Treaties' (14 October 2020,) online lecture, available at <https://youtu.be/bwhUcDyBWlY>.

115 QMUL (n 203 in ch 2).

116 Ibid.

a willingness to work on ways to reduce arbitral timeframes. Nonetheless, in practice, they were reluctant to compromise on any aspects of the proceedings, such as limiting rounds of submissions or even the number of pages of submissions. This is because when losing a case, legal counsel fears being blamed for not exhausting the means available to them.[117] Moreover, due to party autonomy, arbitrators often find it hard to press counsel to adopt more efficient procedures and therefore feel obliged to go along with counsel from each side who may be choosing more conservative or even inefficient procedures.[118]

It is expected for a dispute resolution process to take some time from the date of registration until the final award is rendered. However, the tribunal should be able to rule on jurisdictional matters in relatively shorter periods of time. The Academic Forum on ISDS found that a decision on jurisdiction on average takes around two years and nine months, based on 635 cases from the PluriCourt's Investment Treaty Arbitration Database.[119] It is hard to ascertain what constitutes an excessive amount of time to resolve an ISA dispute unless each case is evaluated individually. For example, it took four and a half years (2011 to 2015) for the *Philip Morris v Australia* case to be announced inadmissible on jurisdictional grounds. Nevertheless, during these four years, Australia attracted tough resistance and anti-ISDS movements from NGOs with multiple Parliamentary discussions and enquiries on the matter.[120] If the arbitral tribunal had taken less time to dismiss the case on jurisdictional grounds, it probably would not have caused the chain of events that followed, with ISDS to the present day remaining a controversial topic in Australia.

Time- and cost-inefficiency are two major drawbacks of both international commercial arbitration and ISA. This indicates that the cause for criticism is rooted in the concept of arbitration itself, rather than the ISDS system involving investors claiming against states. Yet arbitration is not the only dispute resolution mechanism available in the ISDS system. That also includes ADR mechanisms such as conciliation and ISM. Rejecting ISDS due to the shortcomings of arbitration, like anti-ISDS Bills tried to do in Australia and NZ, would

117 Joerg Risse, 'Ten Drastic Proposals for Saving Time and Costs in Arbitral Proceedings' (2013) 29(3) Arbitration International 466.

118 Douglas (n 114).

119 Academic Forum on ISDS – Working Group 2, 'Duration of ISDS Proceedings', Concept Papers Project: Matching Concerns and Reform Options, Geneva Center for International Dispute Settlement, available at <https://www.cids.ch/images/Documents/Academic-Forum/2_Duration_-_WG2.pdf>.

120 Hepburn and Nottage (n 5 in ch 1).

also remove investor-state conciliation and ISM options from the table.[121] Yet arbitration becoming costly and lengthy increases the chances of more ISM. It is in the interests of both parties to (a) reduce costs by quickly settling the dispute and (b) have a say in cost attribution. Therefore, rejecting the whole ISDS regime for one element (arbitration) seems unreasonable and excessive.

3.2.2.3 Legitimacy Crisis

A perceived legitimacy crisis is an issue that predominantly occurs in ISA and is a lesser concern in international commercial arbitration.[122] There has been intensive public debate and calls for fundamental changes to the ISDS system due to its perceived legitimacy crisis.[123] Apart from costs and delays associated with arbitration, as mentioned above, three problematic aspects form part of the legitimacy crisis. These are unpredictable and inconsistent awards, lack of transparency, and constraints to legal sovereignty and allegations of 'regulatory chill'.[124]

3.2.2.3.1 *Unpredictable and Inconsistent Awards*

There can be more than one forum entitled to arbitrate investor-state disputes. This sometimes contributes to fragmented and inconsistent decisions on similar cases. ISA disputes are often resolved by institutional and ad hoc tribunals. Institutional arbitral tribunals are established under the procedural and arbitral rules of particular institutions such as ICSID, ICC, and the SCC. Ad hoc tribunals are usually one-off tribunals based on the UNCITRAL Arbitration rules. They are specifically created for certain disputes and cease to exist once those disputes are resolved. Such independence of tribunals has caused controversial decisions of different tribunals on relatively similar facts or treaty

---

121 Kawharu and Nottage (n 75); Amokura Kawharu and Luke Nottage, 'Foreign Investment Regulation and Treaty Practice in New Zealand and Australia: Getting it Together in the Asia-Pacific?' in Julien Chaisse and Luke Nottage (eds), *International Investment Treaties and Arbitration Across Asia* (Brill Nijhoff 2018) 443.

122 Franck, 'The Legitimacy Crisis in Investment Treaty Arbitration: Privatizing Public International Law through Inconsistent Decisions' (n 2 in ch 1). But see Luke Nottage, 'International Arbitration and Society at Large' in A Bjorklund, F Ferrari and S Kroell (eds), *Cambridge Compendium of International Commercial and Investment Arbitration* (Cambridge University Press 2022) forthcoming.

123 Philip Hainbach, 'The EU's Approach to Investor-State Arbitration in the Comprehensive Economic and Trade Agreement (CETA)' (2016) 13(1)Transnational Dispute Management, available at <https://www.transnational-dispute-management.com/article.asp?key=2315>.

124 Ibid.

provisions.[125] Even within institutional arbitrations there are still possible inconsistencies because arbitrations are independent.[126]

Inconsistent awards can be divided into two types.[127] One type (although rare) is when two or more investment tribunals reach different decisions on the exact same dispute and legal issues. The most prominent inconsistent decisions of this nature were the awards in the Lauder case(s). Two investment arbitrations were initiated, one under the Dutch-Czech Republic BIT (which was seated in Stockholm),[128] and the other under the US-Czech Republic BIT (which was seated in London).[129] The two tribunals (which were differently constituted) reached radically different decisions in a 10-day interval despite the similar investor protection provisions in both BITs and the identical nature of the dispute.[130]

The second type of inconsistent award is when investment tribunals issue opposing awards on different cases even though the cases involve similar legal issues.[131] For example, SGS was the investor and party to investor-state disputes

---

125 Julian Arato, Chester Brown and Federico Ortino, 'Parsing and Managing Inconsistency in Investor-State Dispute Settlement' (2020) 21(2–3) Journal of World Investment & Trade 336.

126 Eun Young Park, 'Appellate Review in Investor-State Arbitration' in Jean E Kalicki and Anna Joubin-Bret (eds), *Reshaping the Investor-State Dispute Settlement System* (Brill Nijhoff 2015) 443; *Republic of Equatorial Guinea v CMS Energy Corporation and others (Report)* (ICSID Arbitral Tribunal, Case No CONC(AF)/12/2, 12 May 2015); *LG&E Energy Corp, LG&E Capital Corp and LG&E International Inc v Argentine Republic (Decision on Liability)* (ICSID Arbitral Tribunal, Case No ARB/02/1, 3 October 2006); *Enron Corporation and Ponderosa Assets, L.P. v Argentine Republic (Award)* (ICSID Arbitral Tribunal, Case No ARB/01/3, 22 May 2007); *Sempra Energy International v The Argentine Republic (Award)* (ICSID Arbitral Tribunal, Case No ARB/02/16, 28 September 2007).

127 Arato, Brown and Ortino (n 125); Lucy Reed, 'Great Expectations: Where Does the Proliferation of International Dispute Resolution Tribunals Leave International Law?' (2002) 96(1) Proceedings of the Annual Meeting (American Society of International Law) 219.

128 Mau (n 266 in ch 2).

129 Additional Protocol Concerning the Reciprocal Encouragement and Protection of Investment, United States of America-The Czech Republic-Czech and Slovak Federal Republic, signed 22 October 1991, entered into force 19 December 1992 (Czech Republic-United States of America BIT).

130 *CME Czech Republic B.V. v The Czech Republic* (UNCITRAL, Partial Award, 13 September 2001); *CME Czech Republic B.V. v The Czech Republic* (UNCITRAL, Dissenting opinion of the Arbitrator JUDr Jaroslav Hándl against the Partial Arbitration Award, 13 September 2001); Agreement Between the Lebanese Republic and the Federal Republic of Germany on the Promotion and Reciprocal Protection of Investments, signed 18 March 1997, entered into force 25 March 1999 (Lebanon-Germany BIT).

131 Franck (n 2 in ch 1).

in two ICSID cases. One was against Pakistan, where the tribunal concluded that the breach of the investment contract did not constitute a breach of the investment treaty (BIT) under the 'umbrella clause'.[132] The other case involved the Philippines. There the tribunal reached a contradictory decision to the previous case against Pakistan and concluded that breaching contractual duties by the host state may constitute a breach of the 'umbrella clause' in the BIT.[133]

Inconsistent interpretations are also evident in a few NAFTA cases on minimum standard of treatment and the condition for exhaustion of local remedies.[134] In particular, tribunals have inconsistent approaches when it comes to the pre-condition of exhausting local remedies before going to arbitration under customary international law. This is not surprising, considering that international investment is an area with multiple investment treaties and forums but without a uniform tool for harmonising these individual elements.[135]

3.2.2.3.2 *Lack of Transparency*

Inconsistency in international investment arbitration awards has been aggravated by an additional deficiency: lack of transparency. In the 1976 UNCITRAL Arbitration Rules, the requirement for transparency was very limited. Article 32(5) stated that an award would be publicly available only if both parties consented.[136] However, these rules did not otherwise include a confidentiality obligation on the parties. Therefore, in theory, parties could disclose information about the arbitration unless precluded by confidentiality required by the law of the seat, or unless the disclosure might impede the integrity of the proceedings.[137] The 2010 UNCITRAL Arbitration Rules offered an upgrade regarding transparency.[138] Article 34(5) stated that a party had an opportunity

---

132 According to the tribunal: 'the State may breach a treaty without breaching a contract, and vice versa, and this is certainly true of these provisions of the BIT'. See *SGS Société Générale de Surveillance S.A. v Islamic Republic of Pakistan (Decision on Jurisdiction)* (ICSID Arbitral Tribunal, Case No ARB/01/13, 6 August 2003).

133 *GS Société Générale de Surveillance S.A. v Republic of the Philippines (Decision on Jurisdiction)* (ICSID Arbitral Tribunal, Case No ARB/02/6, 29 January 2004).

134 Two tribunals reached radically different decisions in a 10-day interval: *Metalclad Corporation v The United Mexican States (Award)* (ICSID Arbitral Tribunal, Case No ARB(AF)/97/1, 30 August 2000); Bjorklund (n 55).

135 Franck (n 2 in ch 1).

136 UNCITRAL Arbitration Rules (n 108).

137 Nottage (n 29 in ch 1).

138 James Harrison, 'Recent Developments to Promote Transparency and Public Participation in Investment Treaty Arbitration' Working Paper No 2011/01, University of Edinburgh School of Law, available at <https://papers.ssrn.com/sol3/papers.cfm?abstract_id=1739181>.

to publicise the arbitral award without the consent of the other party in case the 'disclosure is required of a party by legal duty, to protect or pursue a legal right or in relation to legal proceedings before a court or other competent authority'.[139]

These Rules were still limited in comparison to transparency requirements under the ICSID Arbitration Rules, which provide minimum transparency regardless of party consent.[140] When an ISA case is registered, its existence becomes publicly known.[141] The publication of the award is solely a party discretion and if they choose not to publish, the major contents of the award remain confidential. Yet, regardless of party consent, the ICSID Secretariat will publish the excerpts of the award (but not other decisions, including decisions on jurisdiction).[142] This can put pressure on the parties to the dispute to agree and publicise the whole award instead of just the excerpts.

While it is understandable that sensitive corporate and government information requires confidentiality, minimum transparency is required to allow public scrutiny of matters of public policy, such as environment and health.[143] Some scholars speculate that states may be reluctant to join ICSID because of the relevant transparency requirements.[144] The possibility of non-publication of full awards is also seen as problematic by some scholars. They believe that this practice is detrimental to further case law development, which contributes to inconsistent awards on similar issues.[145] A lack of transparency is also problematic for international commercial law. Because confidentiality is a characteristic strictly protected by stakeholders in international commercial

139 UNCITRAL Arbitration Rules (as revised in 2010), GA Res 65/22, UN Doc A/RES/65/22 (10 January 2011, adopted 6 December 2010) art 34(5) (UNCITRAL Arbitration Rules).

140 Harrison (n 138).

141 ICSID, Administrative and Financial Regulations (2006) reg 22(1) (ICSID Administrative and Financial Regulations).

142 ICSID Arbitration Rules (n 107) r 48(4). See almost identical text in ICSID, Additional Facility Rules (2006) r 53(3) (ICSID Additional Facility Rules).

143 Karl-Heinz Böckstiegel, 'The Future of International Investment Law–Substantive Protection and Dispute Settlement' in Marc Bungenberg et al (eds), *International Investment Law* (Nomos Verlagsgesellschaft mbH & Co KG 2015) 1863.

144 Emilie M Hafner-Burton, Sergio Puig and David G Victor, 'Against Secrecy: The Social Cost of International Dispute Settlement' (2017) 42(2) Yale Journal of International Law 279.

145 Ibid; Harrison (n 138). There are scholars who believe that ISA awards should contribute to case-law, and scholars who do not. The latter claim that international investment law is more of a code-based system rather than a common law system and is therefore not suitable for binding precedents. See Marc Bungenberg and Catharine Titi, 'Precedents in International Investment Law' in Marc Bungenberg et al (eds), *International Investment Law* (Nomos Verlagsgesellschaft mbH & Co. KG 2015) 1505.

arbitration, awards are confidential and therefore do not contribute to the development of substantive international commercial law. However, the need to ensure transparency is especially strong in ISA, where public interests are directly affected by an arbitral award.[146]

In 2014, UNCITRAL adopted the Rules on Transparency in Treaty-based Investor-State Arbitration (Rules on Transparency).[147] Yet these new rules only apply to disputes that are based on treaties which were concluded after 2014.[148] The Rules on Transparency can only be applied to UNCITRAL arbitrations conducted under older treaties if the parties opt in, which is less likely to happen unless these rules are proposed in the form of a convention for states to ratify.[149] With this in mind, the same year, UNCITRAL developed the United Nations Convention on Transparency in Treaty-based Investor-State Arbitration (New York, 2014) (the Mauritius Convention on Transparency).[150] The Mauritius Convention on Transparency is an instrument which allows acceding states to retrofit the Rules on Transparency to disputes arising out of earlier IIAs (if both parties to the relevant IIA have acceded to it).[151] The Mauritius Convention has 23 signatories as of December 2020, and has been ratified by seven states, most recently by Australia on 17 September 2020 and Bolivia a month later. This type of instrument, which allows new provisions to be retrofitted to earlier IIAs, can also be used to incorporate potentially mandatory ISM provisions into already existing IIAs without renegotiating thousands of BITs and FTAs. More on the ways of incorporating ISM into ISDS is discussed in Chapter 6. However, the empirical analysis of concluded ISA cases provided in Chapter 5 of this book shows that overall, ISA awards and awarded amounts are publicly disclosed in over 95% of disputes.[152]

---

146 Nottage (n 29 in ch 1).

147 Nathalie Bernasconi-Osterwalder and Diana Rosert, 'Investment Treaty Arbitration: Opportunities to reform arbitral rules and processes' (12 March 2014) International Institute for Sustainable Development, available at <https://www.iisd.org/publications/investment-treaty-arbitration-opportunities-reform-arbitral-rules-and-processes>; Lise Johnson and Nathalie Bernasconi-Osterwalder, 'New UNCITRAL Arbitration Rules on Transparency: Application, Content and Next Steps' (18 September 2013) Investment Treaty News, available at <https://www.iisd.org/itn/2013/09/18/new-uncitral-arbitration-rules-on-transparency-application-content-and-next-steps-2/>.

148 Bernasconi-Osterwalder and Rosert (n 147); Johnson and Bernasconi-Osterwalder (n 147).

149 Bernasconi-Osterwalder and Rosert (n 147); Johnson and Bernasconi-Osterwalder (n 147).

150 Mauritius Convention on Transparency (n 32 in ch 1).

151 Ubilava and Nottage (n 7 in ch 1).

152 The transparency rates are different for settled outcomes, as discussed in further detail in Chapter 5.

3.2.2.3.3 *Constraints on Sovereignty and Allegations of 'Regulatory Chill'*

International investment treaties are believed to draw a very narrow line between the investment protection obligations of a state and its discretion to issue new laws. For this reason, tribunals are given broad powers to possibly interpret government's non-discriminatory legislative actions as breaches to investment rights.[153] The late 1990s case *Metalclad v Mexico* was the trigger for the first wave of protests against ISA accusing the system of imposing a regulatory chill on government policymaking.[154] This was because Mexico had relied upon environmental concerns when it denied construction of a waste landfill and was consequently found to be in breach of the NAFTA standards of treatment in ISA.[155]

Similarly, the Philip Morris cases against Australia and Uruguay regarding the countries' tobacco regulations triggered strong criticism against the ISDS system, even though claims failed respectively on jurisdictional grounds and on the merits.[156] In Australia, the anti-ISDS movement was enriched by major concerns towards ISA. The movement claimed that ISDS provisions allowed investors to challenge measures issued by a host state and therefore forced a 'regulatory chill' on the government, which would have to either compromise on the necessary public measures or risk facing an investment dispute.[157] The anti-ISDS movement re-emerged once again around the inclusion of ISDS provisions in the Trans-Pacific Partnership agreement (TPP) due to the fear of the litigiousness of US investors. This is because since 1987, US nationals have been the claimants in 183 ISA cases.[158]

On 30 November 2016, Australia's Joint Standing Committee on Treaties (JSCOT) addressed, among other key concerns regarding ISDS, the topic of

153 Caroline Henckels, 'Protecting Regulatory Autonomy Through Greater Precision in Investment Treaties: the TPP, CETA, and TTIP' (2016) 19(1) Journal of International Economic Law 27.

154 Nikos Lavranos, 'The Deafening Silence of the Anti-ISDS Groups After the Philip Morris Decision' (24 February 2016) Kluwer Arbitration Blog, available at <http://arbitrationblog.kluwerarbitration.com/2016/02/24/the-deafening-silence-of-the-anti-isds-groups-after-the-philip-morris-decision/>; Hafner-Burton, Puig and Victor (n 144).

155 *Metalclad Corporation v The United Mexican States* (n 134).

156 Hafner-Burton, Puig and Victor (n 144); Hepburn and Nottage (n 5 in ch 1).

157 Gareth Hutchens, 'Trans-Pacific Partnership Makes Australia Vulnerable to Court Challenges, Report Claims' (25 October 2016,) International Trade News, available at <https://www.theguardian.com/business/2016/oct/25/trans-pacific-partnership-makes-australia-vulnerable-to-court-challenges-report-claims>.

158 The number of claimants from different home states can be found using UNCTAD's search engine. See UNCTAD, 'Investment Policy Hub' (n 2 in ch 1).

'regulatory chill' in its Report 165.[159] According to the Report, investor claims against the laws and regulations passed by a country would be unsuccessful because the TPP has a carve-out for public welfare protection regulations.[160] Moreover, even if the ISDS claim were successful, it would only mean that the regulation was faulty and the investor deserved legitimate compensation. The Report did note the possibility of increased potential for inbound claims from US investors, infamous, as just noted, for their litigiousness. However, the Report also pointed out that litigiousness would not be a problem for a developed country such as Australia. Nottage points out that whilst US investors had filed most of the investment claims made by the end of 2015, when evaluated from a per capita standpoint, they were less litigious than, for example, investors from Canada and Germany.[161]

There have been reports of tobacco companies intimidating developing host countries, mostly in Africa. They threaten those countries with lengthy and costly investment arbitration disputes if the countries pass regulations limiting the companies' brand or marketing freedom or enforce such regulations.[162] Moreover, the economies being threatened are not only poor developing countries but also developed states. For example, Canada gave up on its tobacco regulations twice, approximately 20 years ago. Whereas New Zealand stated that it would wait for the outcome of *Philip Morris v Australia* before issuing tobacco regulations similar to Australia.[163] Therefore, one view is that while big companies seem to influence states with weaker economies into limiting their legislative incentives, developed countries too seem to avoid possible investment disputes, even at the cost of regulatory chill. However, unlike Australia, New Zealand has very few BITs. Therefore, it is arguable that New Zealand waited for the outcome of *Philip Morris v Australia* due to its own ISDS

159 Joint Standing Committee on Treaties (JSCOT), Report 165 Trans-Pacific Partnership Agreement (Report No 165, 2016).

160 Jarrod Hepburn and Mark Huber, 'An Assessment of Australia's Parliamentary Report on ISDS in the TPP' (5 January 2017) Kluwer Arbitration Blog, available at <http://kluwerarbitrationblog.com/2017/01/05/reserved-an-assessment-of-australias-parliamentary-report-on-isds-in-the-tpp/>.

161 Luke Nottage, 'Are US Investors Exceptionally Litigious with ISDS Claims?' (14 November 2016) Kluwer Arbitration Blog, available at <http://kluwerarbitrationblog.com/2016/11/14/are-us-investors-exceptionally-litigious-with-isds-claims/>.

162 Sabrina Tavernise, 'Tobacco Firms' Strategy Limits Poorer Nations' Smoking Laws' (13 December 2013) The New York Times, available at <http://www.nytimes.com/2013/12/13/health/tobacco-industry-tactics-limit-poorer-nations-smoking-laws.html>.

163 Krzysztof Pelc, 'Does the International Investment Regime Induce Frivolous Litigation?' (10 May 2016) SSRN, available at <https://papers.ssrn.com/sol3/papers.cfm?abstract_id=2778056>.

provisions in BITs. But the more likely argument is that it waited for the outcome because the evidence related to the case was connected to pending cases before the WTO. Therefore, any or some regulatory chill came from the WTO rather than ISDS.

In a 2011 study, Allee and Peinhardt researched the impact of states' international investment treaty violations on FDI flows.[164] They found that BITs were beneficial for those states whose actions were in compliance with treaty requirements, but detrimental for those states whose actions led them to ISA because such actions resulted in the decline of their FDI inflows.[165] The authors explained that the negative effect of treaty violations on FDI inflow was caused by a state's stained reputation from being a respondent in an ISA. It was a signal that the state allegedly failed to comply with the standards of treatment of an investor under its IIAs. Therefore, if a state subjects itself to the ISDS provisions under its IIAs and then becomes a respondent to ISA, its reputation declines. Consequently, this adverse effect on a state's reputation results in reduced FDI, which is the opposite of the originally anticipated aim. While such adverse effects of ISDS can be avoided if the state acts in compliance with all of its obligations, states may still face frivolous ISA claims. Therefore, considering the concerns of the "regulatory chill" caused by ISA, it is in the interests of the respondent host state to resolve an investment dispute on its own terms. This can be achieved through dispute resolution processes that allow for the parties to have control over the outcome of their disputes, such as ISM.

3.2.3 *Current ISDS Reform Proposals*

The increasing dissatisfaction with ISA laid grounds for various initiatives towards rebalancing ISDS, and in particular ISA and IIAs.[166] Countries have

164 Todd Allee and Clint Peinhardt, 'Contingent Credibility: The Impact of Investment Treaty Violations on Foreign Direct Investment' (2011) 65(3) International Organization 401.

165 Ibid.

166 Kaj Hobér, 'Does Investment Arbitration have a Future?' in Marc Bungenberg et al (eds), *International Investment Law: A Handbook* (1st ed, Nomos Verlagsgesellschaft mbH & Co KG 2015) 1873; Böckstiegel (n 143); Luke Nottage, 'Investor-State Arbitration Policy and Practice after *Philip Morris Asia v Australia*' in Leon Trakman and Nicola Ranieri (eds), *Regionalism in International Investment Law* (Oxford University Press 2013) 452; Nottage, 'Rebalancing Investment Treaties and Investor-State Arbitration: Two Approaches' (n 5 in ch 1); Kawharu and Nottage (n 75); Leon E Trakman and David Musayelyan, 'The Repudiation of Investor–State Arbitration and Subsequent Treaty Practice: the Resurgence of Qualified Investor–State Arbitration' (2016) 31(1) ICSID Review-Foreign Investment Law Journal 194.

been implementing different measures to deal with the adverse effects of ISDS provisions.

That ISDS has become a problem for some states is reflected in their treaty drafting practices. For example, US international investment agreement policy has been largely influenced by extensive NAFTA claims against the US despite the fact that it has never lost an ISA case.[167] The US and Canadian IIA templates employ very detailed language for clarifying substantive and procedural clauses, which makes them five times more voluminous in comparison to EU IIAs (usually with shorter and more laconic texts).[168]

India took steps to bar easy access to ISA though its new Model BIT, and since June 2016 has terminated many of its existing BITs.[169] The goal is to conclude treaties based on its new Model BIT, which was adopted in December 2015, with its former BIT or future FTA counterparts. The new Model, while still includes ISDS clauses, creates complex pre-conditions before an investor is allowed to proceed to ISA.[170] These pre-conditions are the exhaustion of local remedies for at least five years, and consecutive compulsory consultations/negotiations or (voluntary) mediation with additionally allocated time frame on top of an existing ISDS timeline.[171] The Most-Favoured-Nation (MFN) clause is not included in the new Model BIT.

These steps could be rightly perceived as a response to the famous *White Industries v India* case. An Australian investor tried to enforce a commercial arbitration award in Indian courts for years.[172] Eventually, the investor initiated ISA against India with the facilitation of the MFN clause in the Australia-India BIT, which the tribunal interpreted as permitting it to incorporate a provision requiring states to provide "effective means" for enforcing rights in the India-Kuwait BIT.[173] This ISA case was followed by a number of other investor claims against India, invoking other Indian BITs.[174] Since *White Industries*,

167 Newcombe (n 52).

168 Ibid.

169 Model Text for the Indian Bilateral Investment Treaty 2015 (India) (India Model BIT).

170 For example, the Australia-India BIT 2000 was unilaterally terminated by India on 23 March 2017. See Agreement Between the Government of Australia and the Government of the Republic of India on the Promotion and Protection of Investments, signed 26 February 1999, terminated 23 March 2017, entered into force 4 May 2000 (Australia-India BIT).

171 Kawharu and Nottage (n 75).

172 *White Industries Australia Limited v The Republic of India* (UNCITRAL, Final Award, 30 November 2011) (*White Industries Australia Limited v The Republic of India, UNCITRAL*).

173 Ibid.

174 *Vodafone International Holdings BV v Government of India [I]* (PCA, Case No 2016–35, 17 April 2014); *Deutsche Telekom v India* (PCA, Case No 2014–10, 2 September 2013); Jaivir

Indian BITs have become the centre of an unprecedented debate in the Indian Parliament and other fora.[175]

The IA-CEPA signed in 2019 does have a largely CPTPP-style ISDS clause.[176] Yet it adds an unconventional multi-tier dispute resolution element, including a form of mandatory ISM.[177] After a standard initial consultation phase, a disputing party (being either the respondent or the claimant) may initiate a conciliation step which becomes mandatory only for the investor.

> If the dispute cannot be resolved within 180 days from the date of receipt by the disputing Party of the written request for consultations, the disputing Party may initiate a conciliation process, which shall be mandatory for the disputing investor ...[178]

Arguably, this innovative proposal came from the Indonesian side, which had been raising ISM in UNCITRAL reform deliberations over ISDS. Australia did not include such a provision in its renegotiated BIT with Hong Kong also signed in 2019, along with a wider bilateral FTA, but Hong Kong added a similar provision in its BIT signed in 2019 with the UAE.[179]

Singh, 'Indian Investment Treaty Practice: Qualitatively and Quantitatively Assessing Recent Developments' in Luke Nottage et al (eds), *New Frontiers in Asia-Pacific International Arbitration and Dispute Resolution* (Wolters Kluwer 2021) 287.

175 Prabhash Ranjan, 'India and Bilateral Investment Treaties: From Rejection to Embracement to Hesitance?' in Srinivas Burra and R Rajesh Babu (eds), *Locating India in the Contemporary International Legal Order* (Springer 2018) 101.

176 Antony Crockett, 'Indonesia's Bilateral Investment Treaties: Between Generations?' (2015) 30(2) ICSID Review 437.

177 IA-CEPA (n 44); Ubilava and Nottage (n 7 in ch 1).

178 IA-CEPA (n 44) art 14.24.

179 James Claxton, Luke Nottage and Ana Ubilava, 'Mandatory Investor-State Conciliation Before Arbitration in Asia-Pacific Treaties: New Developments and Implications for India and Australia', (2021) 3 Indian Journal of International Economic 209; James Claxton, Luke Nottage and Ana Ubilava, 'Pioneering Mandatory Investor-State Conciliation Before Arbitration in Asia-Pacific Treaties: IA-CEPA and HK-UAE BIT' (5 September 2020) Kluwer Arbitration Blog, available at <http://arbitrationblog.kluwerarbitration.com/2020/09/05/pioneering-mandatory-investor-state-conciliation-before-arbitration-in-asia-pacific-treaties-ia-cepa-and-hk-uae-bit/>; Adrian Lai and Matthew Suen, 'Background Paper for Session 1 – Overcoming Challenges to the Use of Mediation in ISDS' (9 November 2020) Virtual Pre-Intersessional Meeting on the Use of Mediation in ISDS, available at <https://aail.org/uncitral-wgiii-virtual-pre-intersessional/>; David Ng, 'Background Paper for Session 4 – "The Way Forward for Mediation as a Reform Option for ISDS"' (9 November 2020) Virtual Pre-Intersessional Meeting on the Use of Mediation in ISDS, available at <https://aail.org/wp-content/uploads/2020/11/2020_UNCITRAL_WGIII_Background_Paper_Session_4.pdf>.

Some countries, such as Bolivia, Venezuela, and Ecuador, have decided to withdraw from ICSID while still keeping ISDS provisions under UNCITRAL Rules.[180] On top of critiques such as absence of an appeals mechanism in local courts, high costs, and unrealistic compensation awards, these countries also accused ICSID of being biased against them and favouring multinational corporations.[181] However, denouncing ICSID does not mean the state has recalled its consent for ISA under other treaties. ICSID simply provides an additional procedural framework for investor-state dispute resolution. Denouncing ICSID means only that an investor would not be able to initiate ISA under the auspices of ICSID. Yet these governments are parties to IIAs where they had already given prior consent to ISAs. Therefore, an investor is not precluded from initiating ISA under the UNCITRAL Rules through ad hoc tribunals. This happens to be the case for Bolivia, with 11 UNCITRAL cases and one ICSID AF case,[182] and Ecuador, with six UNCITRAL cases.[183] For these reasons, Bolivia

180 Bolivia notified ICSID of its intention to withdraw on 2 May 2007, and that withdrawal took effect on 3 November 2007. Ecuador notified ICSID on 6 July 2009 and its withdrawal took effect on 7 January 2010. See UNCTAD, 'Denunciation of the ICSID Convention and BITS: Impact on Investor-State Claims' IIA Issues Note, No 2 2010, UN Doc UNCTAD/WEB/DIAE/IA/2010/6); Marco Tulio Montanes, 'Introductory Note to Bolivia's Denunciation of the Convention on the Settlement of Investment Disputes between States and Nationals of Other States' (2007) 46(5) International Legal Materials 969; Keyvan Rastegar, 'Denouncing ICSID' in Christina Binder et al (eds), *International Investment Law for the 21st Century: Essays in Honour of Christoph Schreuer* (Oxford University Press 2009) 278.

181 Polanco Lazo (n 6 in ch 1).

182 *Julio Miguel Orlandini-Ágreda and Compañía Minera Orlandini Ltda. v Plurinational State of Bolivia* (PCA, Case No 2018–39, Pending); *Glencore Finance (Bermuda) Ltd. v Plurinational State of Bolivia* (PCA, Case No 2016–39, Pending); *Paz Holdings Ltd. v Plurinational State of Bolivia* (11 November 2015); *Iberdrola, S.A. and Iberdrola Energía, S.A.U. v Plurinational State of Bolivia* (PCA, Case No 2015–05, 16 February 2016); *Red Eléctrica Internacional S.A.U. v Plurinational State of Bolivia* (13 November 2014); *South American Silver Limited v The Plurinational State of Bolivia (Final Award)* (PCA, Case No 2013–15, 30 August 2018); *Abertis Infraestructuras S.A. v Government of Bolivia* (PCA, Case No 2011–14, 11 May 2017); *Air BP S.A. v Plurinational State of Bolivia* (Pending); *Guaracachi America, Inc. and Rurelec PLC v The Plurinational State of Bolivia (Final Award)* (PCA, Case No 2011–17, 31 January 2014); *Oiltanking GmbH, Graña Montero S.A. and Graña Montero S.A.A. v Bolivia* (PCA, Settled); *E.T.I. Euro Telecom International N.V. v Republic of Bolivia (II)* (PCA, Settled); *Banco Bilbao Vizcaya Argentaria S.A. v Plurinational State of Bolivia* (ICSID Arbitral Tribunal, Case No ARB(AF)/18/5, Pending).

183 *WorleyParsons International, Inc. v Republic of Ecuador* (UNCITRAL, Pending); *Albacora S.A. v Republic of Ecuador (Final Award)* (PCA, Case No 2016–11, 12 July 2017); *Mantenimientos, Ayuda a la Explotación y Servicios S.A. and Sociedad Española de Montajes Industriales S.A. (formerly Consorcio GLP) v Republic of Ecuador (Award on Jurisdiction)* (ICC, 21 December 2018); *Copper Mesa Mining Corporation v Republic of Ecuador (Final Award)* (PCA, Case No 2012–2, 15 March 2016); *Merck Sharpe & Dohme (I.A.) Corporation v*

terminated FTAs with Mexico and its BIT with the US. Ecuador has terminated nine BITs and, consequently, its Constitutional Tribunal in 2010 declared all BITs unconstitutional.[184] In addition, ad hoc arbitrations under UNCITRAL are not the only dispute resolution mechanism that foreign investors can use. They can also have recourse to ISA under the ICSID Convention through the 'survival clauses' of the IIAs that originally included consents to ICSID.[185]

Interestingly, Venezuela has continued concluding new BIT with ISDS clauses, but only under UNCITRAL arbitration.[186] There may be two reasons why states are denouncing the ICSID Convention but at the same time still concluding IIAs with ISDS provisions. One reason may be an attempt to maintain their reputation, signalling that they do not avoid ISA but simply protest ISA under the allegedly biased ICSID Convention. The other reason may be that by shifting their potential ISA cases to ad hoc arbitrations, these states can attempt to maintain confidentiality and avoid publicity of the awards against them.[187]

Some countries have implemented dispute prevention policies in their legislation to prevent disputes from escalating to arbitration.[188] After its first ISA and then subsequent arbitration claims, Peru enacted such a policy via its domestic legislation in the form of law. The local and central bodies of the government coordinate international investment obligations and alert each other about possible investor-state disputes through a Coordinator – a role given to the Ministry of Economy and Finance. Peru has also established a Special Committee responsible for representing Peru in ISA.[189] Countries like Guatemala and Colombia also began appointing responsible government agencies whose actions may affect international investment rights protected under IIAs.[190] Others such as Korea and Morocco have established the office of

The Republic of Ecuador (Partial Final Award) (PCA, Case 2012–10, 25 January 2018); *Murphy Exploration & Production Company – International v The Republic of Ecuador (II) (Final Award)* (PCA, Case No 2012–16, 10 February 2017); Jonathan C Hamilton, Omar E Garcia-Bolivar and Hernando Otero, *Latin American Investment Protections: Comparative Perspectives on Laws, Treaties, and Disputes for Investors, States and Counsel* (Martinus Nijhoff Publishers 2012) 71.

184 Polanco Lazo (n 6 in ch 1).

185 *Pan American Energy LLC v Plurinational State of Bolivia* (ICSID Arbitral Tribunal, Case No ARB/10/8, 24 February 2014); Polanco Lazo (n 6 in ch 1).

186 Polanco Lazo (n 6 in ch 1).

187 Hafner-Burton, Puig and Victor (n 144).

188 Polanco Lazo (n 6 in ch 1).

189 Law No 28933, December 2006, reported in UNCTAD, 'Investor–State Disputes: Prevention and Alternatives to Arbitration' (n 10 in ch 1).

190 Ibid.

the investment ombudsmen and specific institutions responsible for amicable settlement procedures between foreign investors and the government.[191]

Brazil, having recently concluded its Cooperation and Investment Facilitation Agreements (CIFAS), also took measures for risk mitigation,[192] namely the creation of an Ombudsman and Joint Committees. The Ombudsman's responsibility is to 'act directly to prevent disputes and to facilitate their resolution in coordination with the competent government authorities and in collaboration with the appropriate private entities'. Joint Committees 'seek consensus and resolve amicably any questions or conflicts regarding the investments of the Parties'.[193]

Vietnam also took preventative steps by issuing the 2012 Directive No. 01/CT-TTg and a 2014 Regulation on Coordinating International Investment Disputes for coordinating among different Government bodies in the event of an investment dispute.[194] These coordinated steps of ministries, state agencies and relevant organisations include information sharing and a potential investor-state dispute alert system. The central and local governments are required to communicate between each other and to inform the Ministry of Justice of all complaints from foreign investors as a way of preventing escalation to ISA.[195] Vietnam also amended its national law on foreign investment to promote mediation before arbitration, but that can be bypassed if an arbitration claim is filed under a relevant investment treaty.[196]

191 Ibid.

192 Fabio Morosini and Michelle Ratton Sanchez Badin, 'The Brazilian Agreement on Cooperation and Facilitation of Investments (ACFI): A New Formula for International Investment Agreements' (2015) 6(3) Investment Treaty News 3.

193 Cooperation and Investment Facilitation Agreement between the Government of the Federative Republic of Brazil and the Government of the Republic of Mozambique, signed 30 March 2015, not yet in force, art 4 (Brazil-Mozambique CIFA); Cooperation and Investment Facilitation Agreement between the Government of the Federative Republic of Brazil and the Government of the Republic of Angola, signed 1 April 2015, entered into force 28 July 2017, art 5 (Brazil-Angola CIFA); Amokura Kawharu, 'Punctuated Equilibrium: The Potential Role of FTA Trade Commissions in the Evolution of International Investment Law' (2017) 20(1) Journal of International Economic Law 87.

194 TT Nguyen and TCQ Vu, 'Investor-State Dispute Settlement from the Perspective of Vietnam: Looking for a "Post-Honeymoon" Reform' (2014) 11(1) Transnational Dispute Management, available at <https://www.transnational-dispute-management.com/article.asp?key=2041>.

195 Nguyen Manh Dzung and Nguyen Thi Thu Trang, 'International Investment Dispute Resolution in Vietnam: Opportunities and Challenges' in Julien Chaisse and Luke Nottage (eds), *International Investment Treaties and Arbitration Across Asia* (Brill Nijhoff 2018) 280.

196 Ibid.

Australia has taken the option of deciding on ISDS on a case-by-case basis. In 2010, the Productivity Commission reported that it was unable to find evidence that ISDS provisions had an impact on the growth of FDI.[197] Relying on that report, in 2011, the (Labor-Greens) Gillard Government announced that it would no longer include ISDS in its future FTAs.[198] However, since 2013, which saw the Coalition Government return to power, Australia has continued to conclude treaties with ISDS provisions, on a case-by-case basis.[199] ISDS was omitted in the bilateral agreement concluded with Malaysia, but this did not really matter, given Australia's membership of 'ASEAN +', which already carries the consent of its member states to ISDS.[200] In March 2018, Australia signed the Comprehensive and Progressive Agreement for Trans-Pacific Partnership (CPTPP), which also has investor-state dispute resolution provisions included in its text.[201] The anti-ISDS movement did, however, affect CPTPP negotiations, specifically tobacco regulations, which were consequently excluded from the scope of ISDS provisions if adopted by the host state.[202]

The EU's response to the problematic aspects of ISDS has been to introduce a permanent international investment court system with a permanent panel of judges and an appeals mechanism to correct errors of law.[203] In 2015, the European Commission finalised the EU-Vietnam FTA and the EU-Vietnam Investment Protection Agreement (IPA). The EU-Vietnam IPA incorporates

197 Productivity Commission, 'Bilateral and Regional Trade Agreements', Productivity Commission Research Report, Australian Government. Cf Shiro Patrick Armstrong and Luke Nottage, 'The Impact of Investment Treaties and ISDS Provisions on Foreign Direct Investment: A Baseline Econometric Analysis' (2016) Research Paper No 16/74, Sydney Law School, available at <https://papers.ssrn.com/sol3/papers.cfm?abstract_id=2824090>.

198 Jürgen Kurtz and Luke Nottage, 'Investment Treaty Arbitration 'Down Under': Policy and Politics in Australia' (2015) 30(2) ICSID Review-Foreign Investment Law Journal 465.

199 Ubilava and Nottage (n 7 in ch 1).

200 Luke Nottage, 'Investor-State Arbitration Policy and Practice in Australia' in Armand De Mestral (ed), *Second Thoughts: Investor-State Arbitration Between Developed Democracies* (Centre for International Governance Innovation 2017) 377.

201 The CPTPP builds on the failed Trans-Pacific Partnership (TPP) agreement, which the United States under the Trump administration refused to sign. The current signatory states of the CPTPP are Australia, Brunei, Canada, Chile, Japan, Malaysia, Mexico, New Zealand, Peru, Singapore, and Vietnam. See Comprehensive and Progressive Agreement for Trans-Pacific Partnership (CPTPP) (n 21 in ch 1); Kurtz and Nottage (n 198).

202 Thomas Bollyky, 'TPP Tobacco Exception Proves the New Rule in Trade' (4 February 2016) Expert Brief, available at <https://www.cfr.org/expert-brief/tpp-tobacco-exception-proves-new-rule-trade>.

203 Panico and Di Benedetto (n 9 in ch 1).

this alternative to traditional ISDS.[204] Similar treaties (FTA and IPA) were also signed between the EU and Singapore. Unlike the ratification of the EU-Singapore FTA, which only required single-step ratification by the EU, the EU-Singapore IPA requires two-step ratification which means it needs to be ratified by the EU and its member states for it to enter into force.[205] The EU further continued on this new path with the final text of the EU-Canada Comprehensive Economic and Trade Agreement (CETA), which includes fundamentals of the permanent investment court and appellate mechanism, and a commitment to make that court system operational as soon as the agreement enters into force.[206] It provisionally entered into force on 21 September 2017, though is pending ratification by 11 EU member states. The EU-US Transatlantic Trade and Investment Partnership (TTIP) draft also included a two-tier court system that uses the permanent international investment court system with its panel of judges and the appeals mechanism.[207] As the then First Vice-President Frans Timmermans said:

> With our proposals for a new Investment Court System, we are breaking new ground. The new Investment Court System will be composed of fully qualified judges, proceedings will be transparent, and cases will be decided on the basis of clear rules. In addition, the Court will be subject to review by a new Appeal Tribunal. With this new system, we protect the governments' right to regulate and ensure that investment disputes will be adjudicated in full accordance with the rule of law.[208]

204 European Commission, 'The EU and Vietnam finalise landmark trade deal' (2 December 2015) News Archive, available at <http://trade.ec.europa.eu/doclib/press/index.cfm?id=1409>.

205 European Commission, 'EU-Singapore Trade and Investment Agreements' (18 April 2018) News Archive, available at <http://trade.ec.europa.eu/doclib/press/index.cfm?id=961>.

206 Comprehensive Economic and Trade Agreement (CETA) (n 9 in ch 1); Hainbach (n 123).

207 European Commission, 'EU Negotiating Texts in TTIP' (14 July 2016) News Archive, available at <http://trade.ec.europa.eu/doclib/press/index.cfm?id=1230>; Legum (n 9 in ch 1); Louise Woods, 'Fit for purpose? The EU's Investment Court System' (23 March 2016) Kluwer Arbitration Blog, available at <http://arbitrationblog.kluwerarbitration.com/2016/03/23/to-be-decided/>.

208 European Commission, 'Commission Proposes New Investment Court System for TTIP and Other EU Trade and Investment Negotiations' (16 September 2015) News Archive, available at <http://trade.ec.europa.eu/doclib/press/index.cfm?id=1364>.

EU civil society argued against the inclusion of ISDS provisions in the TTIP, deeming it to be problematic and unnecessary.[209] German and French civil society groups are strongly outspoken against ISDS, accusing the system of a lack of transparency and claiming that it sacrifices the public interest for the sake of foreign investors.[210] Some scholars have made proposals that investor-state disputes should only be submitted to local courts in order for treaties such as the TTIP to gain political support.[211] They justify the omission of ISA because both the EU and the US are developed economies with well-formed and trustworthy court systems, where investors of both sides will be able to defend their rights. Eventually, however, TTIP negotiations were suspended by the then US President Donald Trump. Despite opposition, the EU has not yet given up on the rights of foreign investors to bring direct claims against states, but has instead introduced a permanent investment court for such disputes.[212]

Notwithstanding the willingness of the international community to address and eliminate concerns associated with ISDS, limiting these efforts to only a few IIAs would not change much in a broader sense for international investment arbitration. The drawback is that creating separate, individual permanent tribunals and appellate tribunals for each and every international investment agreement would result in a multitude of independent bodies concluding awards on similar matters differently.[213] Moreover, creating a permanent

---

209 Cécile Barbière, 'France and Germany to Form United Front Against ISDS' (15 January 2015) EURACTIV, available at <http://www.euractiv.com/section/trade-society/news/france-and-germany-to-form-united-front-against-isds/>.

210 Benedetta Cappiello, 'ISDS in European International Agreements: Alternative Justice or Alternative to Justice?' (2016) 13(1) Transnational Dispute Management, available at <https://www.transnational-dispute-management.com/article.asp?key=2314>.

211 Jan Kleinheisterkamp and Lauge Poulsen, 'Investment Protection in TTIP: Three Feasible Proposals' in Marc Bungenberg et al (eds), *European Yearbook of International Economic Law* (Springer International Publishing 2016) 527.

212 August Reinisch, 'The European Union and Investor-State Dispute Settlement: from Investor-State Arbitration to a Permanent Investment Court' in Armand De Mestral (ed), *Second Thoughts: Investor-State Arbitration between Developed Democracies* (McGill-Queen's University Press 2017) 333; Steffen Hindelang, 'Study on Investor-State Dispute Settlement (ISDS) and Alternatives to Dispute Resolution in International Investment Law' (2016) 13(1) Transnational Dispute Management, available at <https://www.transnational-dispute-management.com/article.asp?key=2313>.

213 Woods (n 207); Anna Joubin-Bret, 'Why We Need a Global Appellate Mechanism for International Investment Law' (27 April 2015) Columbia FDI Perspectives No 146, Columbia Centre on Sustainable Development; Jaemin Lee, 'Mending the Wound or Pulling It Apart: New Proposals for International Investment Courts and Fragmentation of International Investment Law' (2018) 39(1) Northwestern Journal of International Law & Business 1.

investment court would require further regulation of issues, including the relationship between such a court and the ICSID Convention and the enforcement of awards rendered by that court.[214] However, in doing so the aim of eliminating inconsistent awards will not be achieved. On the contrary, chasing after legitimacy will result in increased costs and delays without a final award that could contribute to the uniformity and harmony of global investment arbitration.[215] As Schill pointed out, if the sole aim of permanent investment courts is to remedy the pitfalls of ISA, then there are plenty of other methods that could make a difference, such as for example, increasing transparency or creating an appeals mechanism.

Another approach towards reducing the effects of the problematic aspects of ISA is to promote ISM. Mediation, with the appropriate procedural rules and enforcement mechanisms in place, offers an opportunity to prevent the escalation of investor-state disputes to ISA, thereby resulting in faster and cheaper dispute settlement. ISM is especially relevant now with the increasing inconsistency and unpredictability of ISA awards and allegations of regulatory chill. The inconsistency and unpredictability of ISA awards may in fact become contributing factors towards increased use of ISM. Both claimant investors and respondent host states may want to regain control over the outcome of their dispute, which they can through a dispute resolution mechanism like mediation. Nonetheless, until very recently, ISM was almost always only discussed in a voluntary format and there is strong opposition from legal scholars to making ISM a mandatory pre-condition to arbitration.[216]

3.2.4 *Summary*

ISA has become the preferred dispute resolution mechanism for international investment disputes. Its popularisation was greatly influenced by the adoption of the ICSID Convention and UNCITRAL Arbitration Rules. Unlike court decisions, arbitral awards benefit from near-universal recognition and

---

214 Stephan Schill, 'The TTIP Negotiations: US versus EU Leadership in Global Investment Governance' (4 March 2016) Kluwer Arbitration Blog, available at <http://arbitrationblog.kluwerarbitration.com/2016/03/05/the-ttip-negotiations-us-versus-eu-leadership-in-global-investment-governance/>; Kawharu and Nottage (n 75); Jaemin Lee, 'Introduction of an Appellate Review Mechanism for International Investment Disputes: Expected Benefits and Remaining Tasks' in Jean E Kalicki and Anna Joubin-Bret (eds), *Reshaping the Investor-State Dispute Settlement System Journeys for the 21st Century* (Brill Nijhoff 2015) 474.

215 Jaemin Lee (n 214).

216 Asian Academy of International Law (n 25 in ch 1); Lai and Suen (n 179); QMUL and CCIAG (n 23 in ch 1).

enforceability, simplifying otherwise complex multi-national processes. Yet over time, major flaws of ISA have started to emerge and caused serious problems for the entire ISDS regime. Countries have been managing ISDS related problems in their own ways: changing and adopting their treaty drafting practices, introducing dispute prevention mechanisms, rejecting automatic ISDS and shifting to a case-by-case assessment of treaties, and introducing permanent investment courts and appellate bodies for each individual IIA. While each of these approaches, to a certain degree, serves the purpose of reducing the overuse of ISDS, they still have some drawbacks. Most importantly, the approaches are not uniform.

Discussions are ongoing about the establishment of a Multilateral Investment Court, which would be a permanent multilateral investment court with an appellate mechanism of its own. The mandate of UNCITRAL Working Group III includes a proposal for creating such a court – an idea which builds on an earlier study conducted by Gabrielle Kaufmann-Kohler and Michele Potestà.[217] While the EU and most of its member states, as well as Canada, South Africa, and some Latin American countries, support the idea of a Multilateral Investment Court, Asia-Pacific countries and the US remain unconvinced.[218] Until there is a more harmonised approach towards the concept of a Multilateral Investment Court, its creation in the near future is extremely unlikely.

All the above-mentioned incentives have been proposed by UNCTAD since 2010, with the aim of slowing down the significantly growing number of ISDS claims annually. Interestingly, however, a 2015 QMUL survey found that, in practice, not everyone agreed with the ideas and solutions discussed regarding ISA.[219] For example, the respondents, of which 49% were private practitioners and only 4% were academics, did not agree with the common claim that international arbitration is overly regulated. 70% of the respondents

217 Nikos Lavranos, 'The First Steps Towards a Multilateral Investment Court (MIC)' (13 July 2017) EFILA BLOG, available at <https://efilablog.org/2017/07/19/the-first-steps-towards-a-multilateral-investment-court-mic/>; Gabrielle Kaufmann-Kohler and Michele Potestà, 'Can the Mauritius Convention Serve as a Model for the Reform of Investor-State Arbitration in Connection with the Introduction of a Permanent Investment Tribunal or an Appeal Mechanism?' (3 June 2016) Research Paper, UNCITRAL, available at <https://www.uncitral.org/pdf/english/CIDS_Research_Paper_Mauritius.pdf>.

218 Lavranos (n 217).

219 QMUL (n 203 in ch 2); Sophie Nappert, Luke Nottage and Christian Campbell, 'Assessing Treaty-based Investor-State Dispute Settlement: Abandon, Retain or Reform?' (2014) 11(1) Transnational Dispute Management, available at <https://www.transnational-dispute-management.com/article.asp?key=2024>.

considered the current level of regulation of international arbitration to be rational. Furthermore, 61% of respondents were against the creation of an appeals mechanism for international investment arbitration. The number of votes against an appeals mechanism was even higher for international commercial arbitration: 77%.[220] On the contrary, however, 60% of respondents believed arbitration counsel could be improved if they encouraged settlement during arbitration, including implementing mediation.[221] The 2014 UNCTAD Series concluded that, while ADR mechanisms and dispute prevention policies would not resolve the problems with ISDS, they could eliminate a great number of investor-state disputes by preventing their escalation to arbitration.[222] In a more recent (2018) QMUL survey, the great majority of respondents (97%) indicated that arbitration was their preferred dispute resolution method, with 48% preferring stand-alone arbitration and 49% preferring arbitration in conjunction with ADR.[223] The following section will discuss ISM (conciliation) as an additional step to ISDS: what it has to offer to the ISDS regime, its present status, and critiques.

3.3 Current Role of Investor-State Mediation

3.3.1 *Definition*

As mentioned briefly in Chapter 1, there is no universal definition of mediation.[224] This is partially due to its multitude of forms in practice, but also because of its constantly evolving nature.[225] Bercovitch provides the following definition of international mediation:

> ... a process of conflict management, related to but distinct from the parties' own negotiations, where those in conflict seek the assistance of, or accept an offer of help from, an outsider (whether an individual, an organisation, a group, or a state) to change their perceptions of behaviour,

---

220 QMUL (n 203 in ch 2).

221 Ibid.

222 UNCTAD, 'Investor-State Dispute Settlement: A Sequel' UNCTAD Series on Issues in International Investment Agreements II, UNCTAD/DIAE/IA/2013/2, May 2014, 197.

223 QMUL (n 83).

224 Sourdin (n 54 in ch 2).

225 Boulle (n 93 in ch 2).

> and to do so without resorting to physical force or invoking the authority of law. [226]

According to Wolski, '[m]ediation is a process of assisted negotiation in which an acceptable third party, the mediator, undertakes a range of activities to assist the parties involved in a dispute to negotiate an agreement'.[227] Another commentator suggests: '[b]y definition, mediation will defy complete codification. Its inherent flexibility and strengths will continue to form, and applications will be discovered in new areas'.[228]

A wider definition of Article 2(3) of the Singapore Convention on Mediation includes conciliation among other third-party assisted mechanisms:

> "Mediation" means a process, *irrespective of the expression used or the basis upon which the process is carried out*, whereby parties attempt to reach an amicable settlement of their dispute with the assistance of a third person or persons ("the mediator") lacking the authority to impose a solution upon the parties to the dispute.[229]

To better understand ISM, one must first look at its place in the global dispute resolution system and then define it. There are three schools of thought regarding the dispute resolution mechanisms of ISDS (litigation, arbitration, and mediation).[230]

According to the first and oldest school of thought, the dispute resolution system is divided into two: (a) litigation and (b) ADR, which includes arbitration, mediation, conciliation and negotiation. According to the second school of thought, arbitration is not an ADR mechanism. Instead, litigation and

226 Jacob Bercovitch, 'Mediation in International Conflict: An Overview of Theory, a Review of Practice' in I William Zartman and J Lewis Rasmussen (eds), *Peacemaking in International Conflict: Methods and Techniques* (United States Institute of Peace Press 1997) 125, cited in Karin Aggestam, 'Quasi-informal Mediation in the Oslo Channel: Larsen and Holst as Individual Mediators' in Jacob Bercovitch (ed), *Studies in International Mediation: Essays in Honor of Jeffrey Z. Rubin* (Palgrave Macmillan 2002) 58.

227 Bobette Wolski, 'ARB-MED-ARB (and MSAs): A Whole Which Is Less than, Not Greater than, the Sum of Its Parts' (2013) 6(2) Contemporary Asia Arbitration Journal 249.

228 Sharon Press, 'International Trends in Dispute Resolution a US Perspective' (2000) 3(2) ADR Bulletin 1.

229 Singapore Convention on Mediation (n 14 in ch 1) art 2(3) (emphasis added).

230 Alan Redfern and Martin Hunter, *Law and Practice of International Commercial Arbitration*, Sweet & Maxwell, 2004, 1.

arbitration are grouped together because of their adjudicatory nature, whereas the ADR group only consists of mediation, conciliation, and negotiation.[231]

The third school of thought, and perhaps the most widely accepted today, takes a three-branch approach. According to this school of thought, litigation and arbitration – whilst both adjudicatory by nature – cannot be put in the same group because, unlike litigation, there is a willful agreement of parties to arbitrate. Yet arbitration cannot be placed next to mediation or conciliation either, because:

(a) parties to ADR are not legally bound by its outcome, whereas arbitral awards are binding without the need for further agreement; and
(b) arbitration benefits from universal enforceability through the New York Convention, or the ICSID Convention in cases of investor-state treaty arbitrations, whereas ADR mechanisms do not.[232]

Therefore, according to the third school of thought, litigation, arbitration, and ADR are standalone groups. From today's perspective, this seems to reflect most accurately the contemporary characteristics of all three (arbitration, litigation, and mediation) and so the third school of thought will be followed throughout this book. However, when examining the possibility of adding a mandatory dispute resolution mechanism to the current ISDS process, it can be done without limiting the process with already set characteristics of a classic form of mediation. In fact, ISM can simply reflect a process where the disputants have full autonomy and control over the dispute resolution process with the participation and guidance of a third-party neutral regardless of what we decide to call this ADR step as long as it serves the intended purpose.

3.3.2 *Benefits of Investor-State Mediation*

Mediation is believed to be a beneficial and useful addition to ISDS due to its very high rate of settlement. Around 80% of domestic and international commercial mediated cases settle during such mediation proceedings.[233] In the

231 Ibid. Luke Nottage, 'Is (International) Commercial Arbitration ADR?' (2002) 4(1) The Arbitrator and Mediator 83.

232 Redfern and Hunter (n 230).

233 Edna Sussman, 'The Advantages of Mediation and the Special Challenges to its Utilization in Investor State Disputes' (2014) 11(1) Transnational Dispute Management, available at <https://www.transnational-dispute-management.com/article.asp?key=2081>; Jack Coe Jr, 'Should Mediation of Investment Disputes Be Encouraged, and, If So, by Whom and How?' in Arthur W Rovine (ed), *Contemporary Issues in International Arbitration and Mediation: The Fordham Papers (2009)* (Brill Nijhoff 2010) 339; Franck (Table 1, n b).

wake of the shortcomings of arbitration in ISDS, mediation seems to offer the countering benefits, including:[234]

(1) Flexibility: in mediation, unlike arbitration, parties retain control over the outcome of the process. Mediation is a less formal and more flexible dispute resolution mechanism where parties are the ones who determine the direction of the process.[235] For example, the flexibility, enjoyed by the parties in a mediation process is especially relevant in an expropriation case where the parties are free to agree on any compensation amount.

(2) Time and cost: mediation is more time-efficient than arbitration. Arbitration proceedings take on average over four years to settle (Figure 1) from the date of registration to the date of conclusion.[236] By contrast, mediation can settle disputes that have the potential for early settlement within a few sessions.[237] Some commentators are concerned that adding mediation to the mix would further increase the ISDS timeline. This argument builds on the assumption that disputants would only participate in the mediation process to gain insight into their opponent's case and thus be better prepared for arbitration. Moreover, if mediation were a compulsory pre-condition to arbitration, the only reason parties would participate would be to guarantee their access to arbitration. Either way, mediation would not serve its purpose and therefore, unnecessarily increase the overall timeline of an investor-state dispute. However, this viewpoint is arguable. Mediation can be added to the ISDS process without altering the timeline, by inserting it into 'cooling off' periods.[238] Cooling-off periods are stipulated periods of time in IIAs, mostly three or six months, to allow parties to attempt amicable settlement before initiating ISA.[239]

Timely settlement of conflicts leads to smaller procedural costs.[240] Hence, if the conflict is resolved during the mediation stage, then the time- and

---

234 Strong (n 157 in ch 2); Munir Maniruzzaman, 'A Rethink of Investor-State Dispute Settlement' (30 May 2013,) Kluwer Arbitration Blog, available at <http://arbitrationblog.kluwerarbitration.com/2013/05/30/a-rethink-of-investor-state-dispute-settlement/>.

235 Jack Coe, 'Toward a Complementary Use of Conciliation in Investor-State Disputes-A Preliminary Sketch' (2005) 12(1) UC Davis Journal of International Law & Policy 7; Titi (n 8 in ch 1).

236 See Figure 1.

237 Sussman (n 233).

238 Coe (n 233); Jack Coe, 'Settlement of Investor-State Disputes through Mediation-Preliminary Remarks on Processes, Problems and Prospects' in R Doak Bishop (ed), *Enforcement of Arbitral Awards Against Sovereigns* (Juris Publishers 2009) 73.

239 Investor-State Disputes: Prevention and Alternatives to Arbitration (n 10).

240 As discussed in Chapter 3.2.2.

cost-consuming ISA process could be avoided. The whole idea of promoting more ISM in ISDS is for mediation to serve as a filtering or preventative mechanism for investor-state disputes before they progress to arbitration. Preventing disputes from escalating to costly arbitration proceedings would save both time and money for disputants.

(3) Relationships: mediation is believed to enable parties to meet and communicate, which does not always happen in the negotiation phase.[241] In international investment relations that involve long-term investment interests, preserving business relationships is especially important. During the early stages of a dispute, parties rarely make an effort to discuss their problems constructively. Instead, they often shut down and prepare for battles in courts or arbitral forums.[242] However, ISA, with its win-lose outcome, seldom leaves room for any further relationship. Once investor-state disputes are concluded via arbitration, and even throughout the arbitral proceedings, the relationship between the parties is often shattered, and bridges are burnt. Moreover, the final outcomes of concluded ISA cases where investors win rarely live up to the claimants' expectations. Not only do they not receive the amount they claimed – statistically the awarded amount is 25% of the originally claimed amount (see Chapter 5) – but they also lose or considerably reduce the benefits of their existing investment.[243] Similarly for the state, even in the case of winning, the procedures prove to be costly, time-consuming, and harmful to the state's reputation. Winning merely confirms that the state was never at fault.[244] Unlike arbitration, mediation offers a win-win outcome, where both parties come out with something that benefits their interests. With mediation, unlike direct negotiations, there is always a neutral third-party managing the process and thus keeping the discussions on track.[245]

An interesting observation was made by Wells based on personal experience in the Indonesian Electric Power Cases.[246] Those that wanted to exit

241 Salacuse (n 12 in ch 1); Sussman, (n 233); Coe (n 233).

242 Cathy A Costantino and Christina Sickles Merchant, *Designing Conflict Management Systems: A Guide to Creating Productive and Healthy Organizations* (Jossey-Bass 1996); Mariana Hernandez Crespo, 'From Paper to People: Building Conflict Resolution Capacity and Frameworks for Sustainable Implementation of IIAs to Increase Investor-State Satisfaction' in Susan Franck and Anna Joubin-Bret (eds), *Investor-State Disputes: Prevention and Alternatives to Arbitration II* (UNCTAD 2011) 55.

243 Wälde (n 152 in ch 2).

244 Tillmann Rudolf Braun, 'Investor-State Mediation: Is There A Future?' in Arthur W Rovine (ed), *Contemporary Issues in International Arbitration and Mediation: The Fordham Papers (2009)* (Brill Nijhoff 2010) 374.

245 Sussman (n 233).

246 Wells (n 24 in ch 1).

from their investment in Indonesia were the ones that went to arbitration, whereas those who avoided arbitral proceedings were the ones who wanted to continue doing business in the country despite operating in the same sectors that were affected.[247] Wells argues that the companies that had other ongoing investment projects in Indonesia preferred not to damage their investment relationships with the state and thus endanger their other investments, and so refrained from ISA.[248] In circumstances such as this, when parties want to preserve their business and investment relationships with the disputants, ISM would be the better option. This way, claimants can seek redress for damages in a process fully controlled by the parties, and with the least damage done to the claimants' investment relations with the respondent.

3.3.3 *Promoting Mediation/Conciliation in ISDS*

Extensive literature has discussed the role of ADR mechanisms in the international dispute resolution system in general, but until recently, little has been said about mediation and conciliation in ISDS. A 2005 article by Coe and a 2007 article by Salacuse laid grounds for the current discussion about the functionally meaningful role of ADR mechanisms in investor-state disputes, and specifically the role of mediation and conciliation.[249] Coe argued that because of the success of mediation in international commercial dispute settlement, it could also be a useful addition to the ISDS regime. For mediation to be successfully incorporated into ISDS, it should be cost-effective (not incurring additional costs in an already expensive process) and fast (not prolonging an already time-consuming process). Coe suggested using the cooling-off periods already present in IIAs. He also predicted that mediation/conciliation processes would remain underutilised if not initiated automatically as part of the mandatory ISDS procedure.

Salacuse discussed that disputants may be exclusively resorting to arbitration, resulting in increased ISA cases worldwide, due to the lack of alternative cost- and time-effective remedies. His 2007 paper argued that while mediation was unlikely to replace arbitration, it could nevertheless settle some of the disputes in a time- and cost-effective manner. Salacuse proposed several ways to enhance ADR in ISDS. Among these suggestions was the renegotiation or revision of treaty language, thereby encouraging ADR practice before resorting to arbitration.

247 Ibid.
248 Ibid. But see Reed (n 27 in ch 1).
249 Coe, (n 233); Salacuse (n 12 in ch 1); Coe (n 235).

In 2010, UNCTAD began working on dispute prevention and alternatives to arbitration. Consequently, discussions and studies on the topic of ISM increased significantly.[250] In an international investment agreement Issues Note of 2013, UNCTAD proposed five areas that could be reformed to tackle ISDS problems. Among these suggestions was the promotion of amicable settlements in ISDS, and specifically ISM.[251] The success of mediation in international commercial dispute resolution motivated a new movement towards the idea that mediation could also complement and improve the existing drawbacks of ISDS.[252]

While the role of mediation and conciliation, used interchangeably, may not be significant in the current ISDS, it is set to grow. In the UNCITRAL Working Group III submissions and discussions, questions have been consistently raised regarding dispute prevention and mitigation through mediation what seems to be a common theme of interest among states.[253] The emphasis is largely made on the prevention of disputes rather than the aftermath regulation, as resolving and eliminating them early is deemed to be the most cost-effective approach.[254] A number of initiatives have been put forward by the states, as well as governmental and non-governmental organisations regarding the implementation and further promotion of preventative measures in ISDS. The focus has been predominantly put on three main areas. On national level suggestions include: raising awareness of government officials regarding treaty obligations and dispute prevention practices such as mediation, ensuring communication channels between investors and governments, ensuring early settlement discussions and thereby preventing the escalation of complaints into disputes.[255] On the investment treaty level, certain submissions highlighted the measures for the parties to agree on dispute prevention and pre-arbitration consultation procedures during the treaty negotiation stage

250 Investor-State Disputes: Prevention and Alternatives to Arbitration (n 10 in ch 1); Susan Franck and Anna Joubin-Bret (eds), *Investor-State Disputes: Prevention and Alternatives to Arbitration II* (UNCTAD 2011); Welsh and Schneider (n 24 in ch 1).

251 UNCTAD, 'Reform of Investor-State Dispute Settlement: In Search of a Roadmap', IIA Issues Note N2, June 2013.

252 Coe (n 233); Anna Spain, 'Integration Matters: Rethinking the Architecture of International Dispute Resolution' (2010) 32(1) University of Pennsylvania Journal of International Law 1.

253 UNCITRAL Working Group III, 'Possible reform of investor-State dispute settlement (ISDS) Dispute prevention and mitigation – Means of alternative dispute resolution' A/CN.9/WG.III/WP.190.

254 Submission from the Government of the Republic of Korea (A/CN.9/WG.III/WP.179) p. 5.

255 Submission from the Government of South Africa (n 12 in ch 1) paras. 38 and 39; Submission from the Government of Morocco (n 12 in ch 1) para. 9; Submission from the Government of Brazil, (A/CN.9/WG.III/WP.171) para. 2; Submission from the Governments of Chile, Israel, Japan, Mexico and Peru (A/CN.9/WG.III/WP.182) fn 20.

such as incorporating dispute prevention steps in ISDS clauses.[256] On the international level, it was suggested to narrow the knowledge gap on dispute prevention procedures that is evident on a national level through state-to-state cooperation such as technical assistance and capacity-building activities which would include sharing knowledge and experience on the use of ADR such as mediation.[257] While nearly all submissions from states that highlight the significant role of the ADR in dispute prevention and mitigation process agree on its benefits, such as the cost- and time-effectiveness, flexibility, autonomy and the means for preserving relationships, only Indonesia proposed mediation in a mandatory format.[258] The future premise for exploring the mandatory ISM as a prerequisite of ISA is something UNCITRAL Working Group III has noted in its 2020 discussion, however, currently, in a wider audience, mediation is only offered in an opt-in format.[259]

However, opt-in mediation may not yield the desired results and the progress that has been made towards popularisation and integration of mediation into ISDS can simply end up being futile. A 2014 study by Echandi and Kher, which examined ICSID cases that terminated due to party settlement, investigated at what stage of ISA these settlements took place.[260] The study found that in total, 22% of registered ICSID cases settled tribunals rendered their awards on merits. In 39% of those cases, settlements were reached even before the constitution of the tribunal. Echandi and Kher concluded that a significant portion of investor-state disputes could have been prevented at earlier stages had there been other available dispute resolution mechanisms in place. Negotiations and consultations have always been a part of ISDS clauses in IIAs as the first step in the investor-state dispute resolution process. However, the above-mentioned study illustrated that parties often needed more than negotiations and consultations – possibly something like conciliation or

256 Submission from the Government of China (n 12 in ch 1) p. 5; Submission from the Government of Brazil (n 255); Submission from the Government of South Africa (n 12 in ch 1) paras. 104 and 109.

257 Submission from the Government of Thailand (n 12 in ch 1) para. 25; Submission from the Government of the Republic of Korea (n 254).

258 Submission from the Government of Indonesia (n 12 in ch 1) paras. 19 and 20.

259 UNCITRAL Working Group III, 'Possible reform of investor-State dispute settlement (ISDS) Dispute prevention and mitigation – Means of alternative dispute resolution' A/CN.9/WG.III/WP.190.

260 Roberto Echandi and Priyanka Kher, 'Can International Investor-State Disputes be Prevented? Empirical Evidence from Settlements in ICSID Arbitration' (2014) 29(1) ICSID Review 41.

mediation – to reach settlements, which was usually achieved by registering their dispute for arbitration and then settling the case before the tribunal was constituted.

A similar analysis to that of Echandi and Kher is presented here, which builds on dividing ISA proceedings into four phases (Figure 2). According to the findings of this empirical analysis, it becomes evident that 16% of ISA cases settle before the arbitral tribunal is constituted (First Phase). Another 30% of disputes settle after the constitution of the tribunal – before the award on jurisdiction is rendered, or if there is no jurisdiction phase until the parties exchange their first memorials and counter memorials (Second Phase). A further 16% of disputes are settled after the award on jurisdiction (or after the exchange of memorials) but before the completion of the hearing on merits (Third Phase). Only 11% of disputes settled after the completion of the hearing on merits (Fourth Phase).

These findings suggest that if there is an appropriate dispute resolution mechanism in place, such as mediation or conciliation – more structured than negotiations/consultations but less adjudicatory than arbitration – investor-state disputes have the potential to be settled before they reach the arbitration phase. But even if mediation is available to the disputants, it is arguable

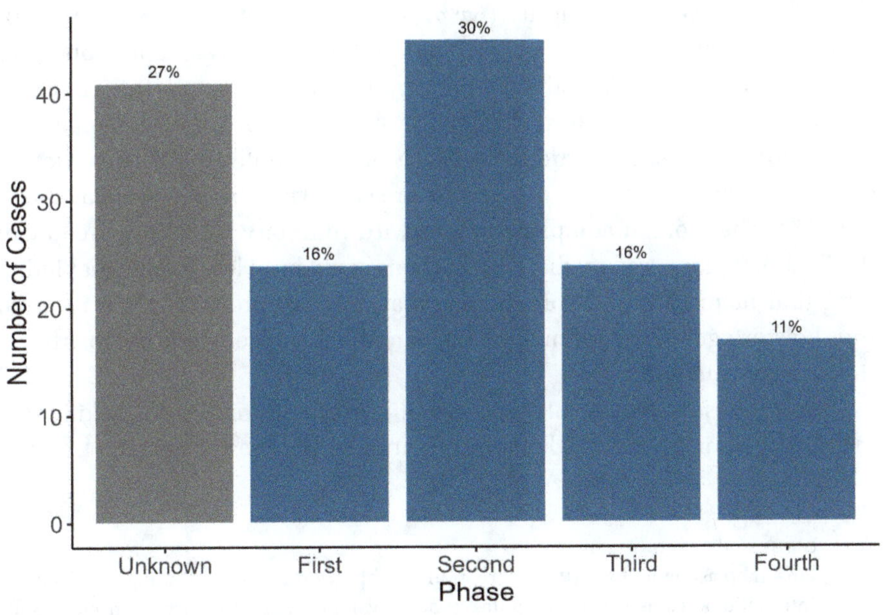

FIGURE 2 Settlements and phases
Note: Author's own calculations

what the rate of recourse and the rate of compliance will be. For example, the recent 2020 Investment Arbitration Survey by QMUL on 'Investors' Views on the Current State of Affairs and Proposed Reforms of Investor-State Dispute Settlement (ISDS)' reported that 64% of respondents were in favour of the idea of introducing mandatory mediation as a pre-condition to arbitration.[261] Specifically, the answers to the question on mandatory mediation were divided as follows: 30% replied with 'strongly favour', 34% replied with 'somewhat favour', 11% had 'no view' on the subject matter, 22% 'somewhat opposed' the idea of mandatory ISM, and 3% were 'strongly opposed'. The extent of support indicated for mandatory ISM as a pre-condition to arbitration is unprecedented, especially with so much being written on the reasons against it in the literature available so far. The findings of this survey suggest that it is not only respondent states that would be open for it, but investors too, as they also see the beneficial prospect of settling disputes without arbitration.

Another example, regarding compliance with decisions of ADR mechanisms, is the relatively recent Pinsent Masons and QMUL Survey 2019 on international arbitration in construction. It reported that, when asked how often they complied with the decisions of voluntary pre-arbitral dispute resolution mechanisms (which includes mediation), only 28% of respondents replied that in their experience compliance was frequent; 41% stated that parties did not comply, and 31% reported that compliance only happened 'half of the time'.[262] Moreover, the majority (67%) of respondents expressed their support for mandatory compliance with pre-arbitral decisions as a pre-condition to arbitration (which includes mandatory mediation). While this survey is about construction dispute settlement, it still serves as a useful comparison to investor-state dispute settlement. This is because, unlike ISDS, construction dispute settlement was one of the first areas to which mediation was introduced.[263] Therefore, if compliance rates with voluntary mediation are low in the field that pioneered mediation, then this could be at least somewhat indicative that mediation in a voluntary format may not progress much in ISDS, thus bolstering the case for making ISM a mandatory pre-condition to arbitration of investment disputes.

Despite these survey results and seemingly overall interest in making ISM mandatory, as indicated by the abovementioned Indonesia-Australia FTA and

---

261 QMUL and CCIAG (n 23 in ch 1).

262 Pinsent Masons and QMUL, 'International Arbitration Survey – Driving Efficiency in International Construction Disputes' (2019), available at <https://www.pinsentmasons.com/thinking/special-reports/international-arbitration-survey>.

263 Stipanowich (n 109 ch 2).

Hong Kong-UAE BITs, both signed in 2019, almost all discussion and initiatives until now have been focused on how to encourage disputing parties to try mediation in ISDS on a voluntary, opt-in basis. Below are the recent and current steps made towards increasing the use of mediation in ISDS through such a voluntary format.

3.3.3.1 IBA

In 2012, the IBA adopted Investor-State Mediation Rules, which was the 'first step in legitimising and normalising investor-state mediation'.[264] It was the first regulatory framework dedicated to specifically ISM. Despite this novel approach, ISM cases under IBA rules have been extremely rare. Two reasons are believed to have contributed to this.

Firstly, advance consent to mediation in IIAs is seldom found, especially in older generation BITs. Therefore, despite having a framework that establishes the procedural option for ISM, the incentive to resort to mediation is absent. This is very much in line with Coe's prediction above that without express consent to mediation in IIAs, this dispute resolution mechanism would remain underutilised.

Secondly, despite being provided with the procedural framework for mediation, the issue of non-enforceability of settlement agreements remained. Not having a procedure for mediation was never the main reason for its underutilisation. While the adoption of the IBA Mediation Rules was a step towards acknowledging mediation in ISDS, the real issue has always been the non-enforceability of settlement agreements. Therefore, voluntary, opt-in mediation rules, without an enforceability mechanism, were not enough for promoting ISM in ISDS.

On 14 April 2016, IAReporter announced the first known ISM case under the 2012 IBA Investor-State Mediation Rules.[265] A French engineering and consulting company, Systra SA, and its subsidiary company Systra Philippines Inc., had filed a notice of dispute in 2015 to the Republic of the Philippines under the 1994 France-Philippines BIT. The companies had been providing services for infrastructure projects to government agencies of the Philippines. The dispute

264 Franck, 'Using Investor–State Mediation Rules to Promote Conflict Management: An Introductory Guide' (n 1 in ch 1).

265 Luke Eric Peterson, 'In an Apparent First, Investor and Host-State Agree to Try Mediation Under IBA Rules to Resolve an Investment Treaty Dispute' (14 April 2016) IAReporter, available at <https://www.iareporter.com/articles/in-an-apparent-first-investor-and-hosssst-state-agree-to-try-mediation-under-iba-rules-to-resolve-an-investment-treaty-dispute/>.

is reported to concern overdue invoices for the performed work and services. Article 8 of the France-Philippines 1994 BIT divides the dispute resolution process into two steps. The first step is to attempt an amicable settlement during the six months cooling-off period. The second step follows the advance consent of the host state to conciliation or arbitration proceedings under the ICSID Convention.[266] This is only if and after amicable dispute settlement is unsuccessful, and the dispute is still ongoing between the parties. Before resorting to ICSID facilities, however, the disputants agreed to first attempt the resolution of their dispute through ISM in the ICC's ADR centre under the IBA ISM Rules.

Some commentators have questioned whether recourse to the IBA ISM Rules was allowed considering there was no prior consent to them in the relevant IIAs, and whether recourse to the IBA would then bar access to ICSID.[267] This ISM case illustrates how the IBA ISM Rules could work alongside the ICSID conciliation and arbitration rules that are already provided for in BITs.[268] The parties can resort to the IBA ISM Rules to attempt the settlement of their dispute before initiating the second step: ICSID conciliation or arbitration. This could be achieved by conducting the mediation proceedings during the predefined cooling-off periods that are already provided in IIAs. If the dispute remains unresolved, nothing precludes the parties from resorting to the pre-agreed ICSID dispute resolution mechanism.

3.3.3.2 International Investment Agreements

The increased presence of ISM can also be observed in the new generation of IIAs.[269] Progressively more IIAs have an express reference to mediation as part of their dispute resolution clause, which is generally quite atypical for older generation BITs and IIAs.[270] For example, section F – Resolution of investment disputes between investors and states of CETA between Canada and EU dedicates an individual Article 8.20 to (voluntary) mediation:

> 1. The disputing parties may at any time agree to have recourse to mediation.

266 Décret no 96–915 du 9 octobre 1996 portant publication de l'accord entre le Gouvernement de la République française et le Gouvernement de la République des Philippines sur l'encouragement et la protection réciproques des investissements (ensemble un protocole), signed 13 September 1994, entered into force 12 June 1996, art 8 (France-Philippines BIT).

267 Discussed in Chapter 4.

268 Frauke Nitschke, 'The IBA's Investor-State Mediation Rules and the ICSID Dispute Settlement Framework' (2014) 29(1) ICSID Review 112.

269 See above (n 21 in ch 1).

270 Titi (n 8 in ch 1).

2. Recourse to mediation is without prejudice to the legal position or rights of either disputing party under this Chapter and is governed by the rules agreed to by the disputing parties including, if available, the rules for mediation adopted by the Committee on Services and Investment pursuant to Article 8.44.3(c).
3. The mediator is appointed by agreement of the disputing parties. The disputing parties may also request that the Secretary General of ICSID appoint the mediator.
4. The disputing parties shall endeavour to reach a resolution of the dispute within 60 days from the appointment of the mediator.
5. If the disputing parties agree to have recourse to mediation, Articles 8.19.6 and 8.19.8 shall not apply from the date on which the disputing parties agreed to have recourse to mediation to the date on which either disputing party decides to terminate the mediation. A decision by a disputing party to terminate the mediation shall be transmitted by way of a letter to the mediator and the other disputing party.

The EU-Singapore Investment Protection Agreement 2018, which replaces 12 BITs between EU member states and Singapore, provides a whole annex dedicated to voluntary mediation between investors and states (Annex 6).[271]

Article 9.18 (1) of the Comprehensive and Progressive Agreement for Trans-Pacific Partnership (CPTPP) among Australia, Brunei, Canada, Chile, Japan, Malaysia, Mexico, New Zealand, Peru, Singapore, and Vietnam provides a voluntary conciliation and mediation step before arbitration:

> 1. In the event of an investment dispute, the claimant and the respondent should initially seek to resolve the dispute through consultation and negotiation, which may include the use of non-binding, third party procedures, such as good offices, conciliation or mediation.[272]

The article allocates six months for the dispute to be resolved through non-binding dispute resolution mechanisms. If the dispute is not resolved during this time, it can then be referred to arbitration.[273]

While multi-tier ISDS clauses with such an opt-in, voluntary ISM step are now becoming a common characteristic of new generation IIAs, references to

271 EU-Singapore IPA (n 21 in ch 1) annex 6.

272 Comprehensive and Progressive Agreement for Trans-Pacific Partnership (CPTPP) (n 21 in ch 1) art 9.18.

273 Ibid art 9.19(1); Claxton, Nottage and Ubilava (n 179); Claxton (n 2); Fan (n 26 in ch 1).

mandatory mediation as a pre-condition to arbitration remain extremely rare. Out of over 3000 IIAs, only two treaties in force, the Hong Kong-United Arab Emirates BIT (2019) and the IA-CEPA, provide for mandatory conciliation as a pre-condition to arbitration.[274] Both of these treaties, however, apply mandatory conciliation obligations to the claimant investor only.

The ISDS clause of the Hong Kong-United Arab Emirates BIT comprises a three-tier dispute resolution system. The first step is amicable settlement through consultations during the six-months cooling-off period. At the end of the six months, if the dispute is not settled amicably, disputants are provided with an additional six months for conciliation (Article 8(5)). Conciliation becomes mandatory for the claimant only when initiated by the respondent (the Contracting Party). Article 8(3) stipulates:

> When required by the Contracting Party, if the dispute cannot be settled amicably within six months from the date of receipt of the written notice, it shall be submitted to the competent authorities of that Contracting Party or arbitration centres thereof, for conciliation.

While this is a mandatory conciliation provision, the agreement to conciliate does not become binding for the claimant investor automatically and, unless initiated by the respondent state, nothing precludes the claimant from accessing arbitration directly after consultations. However, the international investment agreement does not seem to clarify whether the additional six months that was allowed for mandatory conciliation can be waived if it becomes obvious that settlement will not be reached. In particular, it may be evident from the beginning that the respondent never intended to engage in the conciliation process, but instead initiated it with the sole intent of gaining additional time before arbitration. This additional and unilaterally mandatory conciliation step further prolongs the total existing ISDS timeline by six months. This is because conciliation was not included in the cooling-off periods and instead represents an additional middle step in between the existing amicable settlement and consequent arbitration.

The IA-CEPA contains the other unconventional multi-tier ISDS clause, which is somewhat similar to that in the Hong Kong-United Arab Emirates

274 Hong Kong-UAE BIT (2019) (n 45); IA-CEPA (n 44); Ana Ubilava, 'Mandatory Investor-State Conciliation in New International Investment Treaties: Innovation and Interpretation' (5 September 2020) Kluwer Mediation Blog, availale at <http://mediationblog.kluwerarbitration.com/2020/09/05/mandatory-investor-state-conciliation-in-new-international-investment-treaties-innovation-and-interpretation/>.

BIT.[275] The ISDS clause of the IA-CEPA provides a unilaterally mandatory conciliation (mediation), which is a pre-condition to ISA.

> If the dispute cannot be resolved within 180 days from the date of receipt by the disputing Party of the written request for consultations, the disputing Party may initiate a conciliation process, which shall be mandatory for the disputing investor ...[276]

There are two scenarios in which the claimant can access ISA. If the consultations are unsuccessful, the claimant can proceed with arbitration after the 180-day cooling-off period ends but must wait another 90 days before the claim for arbitration can be submitted (in total 270 days). However, this is only if conciliation has not been initiated by either of the disputants. If the conciliation was initiated then to be allowed access to arbitration, the disputants are provided an additional 120 days for conciliation. Once this additional time is up, the claimant can proceed with arbitration only after 60 days. Therefore, conciliation too has to be unsuccessful for the claimant to then progress to ISA.[277] If the timeline of each of the steps is interpreted as cumulative, then mandatory conciliation increases the otherwise 270-day process to 360 days – from the date of notice of the dispute before ISA – which is an increase of approximately three months.[278] An alternative and also a plausible interpretation of these timelines is that if the notice of intent for arbitration can be given to the respondent during the consultations (180 days) or conciliation (120 days), then the waiting period for arbitration (60 or 90 days depending on whether there was a conciliation or not) could be counted within these times. The treaty language is not clear whether the stipulated times for consultations and conciliation need to end for the claimant to be permitted to issue the notice of arbitration, or whether these actions can overlap.[279] The interpretation adopted here is that these timelines are cumulative and not overlapping because, under the treaty, it is expressly stated that conciliation can be initiated during the cooling-off periods of consultations (Article 14.21). However, no such reference is made regarding the notice of intent for arbitration (Article 14.26). Regardless of the method of interpretation, conciliation increases the overall timeline by no more than 120 days. The IA-CEPA, similar to the Hong

275 IA-CEPA (n 44).
276 Ibid art 14.23.
277 Ubilava and Nottage (n 7 in ch 1).
278 IA-CEPA (n 44) art 14.23.
279 Ubilava (n 274).

Kong-United Arab Emirates BIT, is also silent on whether it is allowed to have the 120 days of mandatory conciliation waived for the claimant if settlement becomes less unlikely. Presumably, the best way forward would be to apply the reduced 60-day period before being allowed to submit an arbitration claim, not the 90 days mandated if conciliation has not been initiated.

The reference to mandatory conciliation in these IIAs, albeit unilateral, is a progressive and promising step towards normalising mandatory ADR mechanisms as a pre-condition to arbitration in ISDS. But the claimant investors might still try to bypass these ISDS clauses by invoking the MFN obligation under respective IIAs. Under the MFN obligation, states are required to treat investors and investments of the contracting state no less favourably than they treat the investors and investments of other states within their sovereign territory. Unless there is a specific ISDS carve-out in IIAs, the claimant investors of one treaty can have recourse to dispute resolution mechanisms of other (subsequent) treaties to which the respondent state is a contracting party, if they prove that the ISDS of the other treaty is more favourable. However, both the IA-CEPA (Article 14.21(3)) and the Hong Kong-United Arab Emirates BIT (Article 4(8)) have an express carve-out of ISDS from the MFN clause stating that the MFN obligation under the agreement does not extend to ISDS provisions. Thus, if, for example, Australia was to complete its current negotiations for an FTA with the UK,[280] which resulted in more conventional CPTPP-like ISDS provisions without mandatory ISM, an Australian investor into Indonesia could not invoke the MFN provision in the IA-CEPA to 'import' those standard ISDS provisions to bypass the mandatory ISM if invoked by Indonesia as the host state.

With the increasing instruments regulating the role of mediation in ISDS, more IIAs will contain express references to ISM in the future, providing for mediation on a voluntary or mandatory basis. This is especially true now that there is a new multilateral treaty aiming to ensure the universal enforceability of settlement agreements, as explained next.

3.3.3.3 Singapore Convention on Mediation

While recently, mediation has been promoted through individual treaties, a significant step towards further popularisation of mediation both in international commercial and investment dispute resolution platforms is the adoption of a multilateral convention – the Singapore Convention on Mediation.[281]

280 Australian Government Department of Foreign Affairs and Trade, 'Australia-United Kingdom Free Trade Agreement', FTAs under Negotiation, available at <https://www.dfat.gov.au/trade/agreements/negotiations/Pages/ftas-under-negotiation>.

281 Singapore Convention on Mediation (n 14 in ch 1).

The non-universal enforceability of cross-border settlement agreements deriving from mediation/conciliation proceedings has been deemed a principal setback for popularisation of ISM and other ADR mechanisms in ISDS.[282] After years of discussions, it was time to take actual steps towards implementing ISM. The first step was to address the enforceability issue of mediated settlement agreements on both international commercial and investor-state dispute resolution platforms. In 2014, the United States proposed to UNCITRAL to create a multilateral convention on the enforceability of international commercial mediation settlement agreements.[283] In the proposal, the United States noted that a convention would be able to eliminate variations in enforcement mechanisms of different states, which had not been achieved by the UNCITRAL Model Law on Conciliation.[284]

Two approaches could have been taken for the enforceability of the mediated settlement agreement.[285] One approach would have been for a mediated settlement agreement to follow the legislative requirements of the state in which enforcement was sought.[286] Only then would the settlement agreement qualify for universal enforceability. The second and preferred approach was for a future multilateral convention to lay down its own criteria for compliance by which a settlement agreement would automatically qualify for international enforceability.[287]

In 2014, UNCITRAL Working Group II was tasked with the creation and adoption of the first multilateral convention on the enforceability of settlement agreements deriving from mediation. Through the course of their work, it was often suggested to draft the multilateral mediation convention in the format of the New York Convention, which was also evident from multiple references to the latter during various sessions of Working Group II. Nevertheless, it was decided not to include 'recognition' as part of the convention, as this could trigger additional review and control mechanisms in the state of origin for the settlement agreements. Therefore, it was suggested to only include the phrase

282 Gary Born, 'A New Generation of International Adjudication' (2012) 61(4) Duke Law Journal 775; Edna Sussman, 'A Path Forward: A Convention for the Enforcement of Mediated Settlement Agreements' (2015) 12(6)Transnational Dispute Management, available at <https://www.transnational-dispute-management.com/article.asp?key=2295>.

283 UNCITRAL Working Group II, 'Planned and Possible Future Work – Part III Proposal by the Government of the United States of America: Future Work for Working Group II' (2 June 2014) 47th sess, UN Doc A/CN.9/822.

284 Ibid.

285 Deason (n 199 ch 2).

286 Ibid.

287 Ibid.

'binding and enforceable'.[288] In June 2018, after four years of work, UNCITRAL finalised the Singapore Convention on Mediation.[289] The Convention was opened for signature on 7 August 2019 in Singapore and came into force on 12 September 2020.[290]

Under the Singapore Convention on Mediation, disputants will no longer have to go through mediation-arbitration hybrid procedures (as outlined in Chapter 2 above) to try to transform their settlement agreements into consent awards for enforceability. Instead, those agreements will be universally enforceable without the need to be embedded into an arbitral award. This is a significant upgrade of the status of settlement agreements, that were previously treated as mere contracts. A mediated settlement agreement is enforced through the courts of a state where the enforcement is sought as long as it satisfies the requirements of the Singapore Convention on Mediation. Apart from the requirement to fall under the scope of Article 1, the party seeking enforcement should provide both an agreement signed by the parties and evidence that the settlement agreement resulted from mediation.[291] Article 1(1) stipulates that:

> This Convention applies to an agreement resulting from mediation and concluded in writing by parties to resolve a commercial dispute ("settlement agreement") which, at the time of its conclusion, is international …

The settlement agreement should result from mediation. The Singapore Convention on Mediation does not differentiate between mediation and conciliation or any other dispute resolution mechanism resulting in an amicable

288 UNCITRAL Working Group II, 'Report of Working Group II (Dispute Settlement) on the Work of its Sixty-Fifth Session' (Vienna, 12–23 September 2016), 50th sess, UN Doc A/CN.9/896.

289 Matthew Skinner et al, 'Update On The Singapore Mediation Convention' (28 January 2019) LEXOLOGY Newsfeed, available at <https://www.lexology.com/library/detail.aspx?g=818785ef-e7ab-4e41-9691-474886f84384>; Alexander (n 14 in ch 1); Singapore Convention on Mediation (n 14 in ch 1).

290 This marks the highest number of signatories on the first day in the history of UN trade conventions. See United Nations, 'List of Signatory States to the Singapore Convention on Mediation', available at <https://treaties.un.org/Pages/ViewDetails.aspx?src=TREATY&mtdsg_no=XXII-4&chapter=22&clang=_en>; Jalelah Abu Baker, 'A 'Powerful Statement' for Multilateralism, Says PM Lee as 46 Countries Ink Singapore Convention on Mediation' (7 August 2019) Channel News Asia, available at <https://www.channelnewsasia.com/news/singapore/singapore-convention-on-mediation-un-trade-disputes-pm-lee-11787744>.

291 Singapore Convention on Mediation (n 14 in ch 1) art 4.

settlement, as long as the procedure at hand complies with the definition of Article 2(3) cited above in Chapter 3.3.1.[292]

The settlement agreement should be made in writing, and it may be incorporated in one whole document, or consist of separate documents, or exist in other forms (for example digitally). According to Article 2(2):

> A settlement agreement is "in writing" if its content is recorded in any form. The requirement that a settlement agreement be in writing is met by an electronic communication if the information contained therein is accessible so as to be useable for subsequent reference.

As long as there is clear proof of the terms of the settlement, the requirement of being 'written' should be deemed to be complied with.

The settlement agreement should be commercial by nature. This has raised concerns among some commentators as to whether 'commercial' excludes the application of the Convention to investor-state disputes. What adds to the debate is that the term commercial is not defined under the Singapore Convention on Mediation. An analysis of the Convention, its travaux preparatoires, and other international instruments and organisations, suggests that the Convention will apply to investor-state disputes, as long as the dispute is broadly commercial by nature.[293] A wide definition of the term 'commercial', can be found in the Model Law developed also by UNICTRAL, could encompass at least some types of investor-state disputes (eg large-scale or complex transactions for the supply or exchange of goods or services; construction of works; consulting; engineering; licensing; investment; financing; banking; insurance; exploitation agreement or concession; joint venture and other forms of industrial or business cooperation).[294] The term 'commercial' was also provided as

292 Ibid.

293 Nitschke (n 1 in ch 1). UNCITRAL Working Group II, 'Settlement of commercial disputes: Enforceability of settlement agreements resulting from international commercial conciliation/mediation – Revision of the UNCITRAL Notes on Organizing Arbitral Proceedings' (Arbtiration and Conciliation), UN Doc A/CN.9/WG.II/WP.188; UNCITRAL Working Group II, 'Settlement of commercial disputes – International commercial conciliation: enforceability of settlement agreements' (Arbitration and Conciliation), UN Doc A/CN.9/WG.II/WP.195; UNCITRAL, Report of Working Group II (Arbitration and Conciliation) on the Work of its Sixty-Third Session (Vienna, 7–11 September 2015), UNCITRAL, 49th sess, UN Doc A/CN.9/861.

294 Shirlow (n 17 in ch 1); Schnabel (n 17 in ch 1); Mushegh Manukyan, 'Singapore Convention Series: A Call For A Broad Interpretation Of The Singapore Mediation Convention In The Context Of Investor-State Disputes' (10 July 2019) Kluwer Mediation Blog, available at

a reservation in the earlier New York Convention, which generally and in practice – apart from international commercial arbitration awards – also applies to ISA awards under the UNCITRAL Arbitration Rules. Further, the Singapore Convention on Mediation itself only excludes settlement agreements resolving personal, family or household matters, or relating to family, inheritance, or employment law. Moreover, parties to the Convention can make reservations under Article 8 declaring that the Convention will not apply settlements involving state entities. If such a reservation is made, the Convention shall still apply if the parties of a settlement agreement agree to opt-in. The fact that such reservations are considered under the Convention suggests that it applies to investor-state disputes unless reservations are made against it. For all these reasons, at least for certain types of transactions and/or treaty claim disputes, it is quite widely accepted that the Singapore Convention on Mediation applies to mediated settlement agreements resolving investor-state disputes.

The settlement agreement should be international at the time it is concluded. This means that it does not matter whether the mediation process was carrying the international element before the conclusion of the agreement. What matters is that the international element, as defined by the Singapore Convention on Mediation, is present at the time the parties concluded their settlement agreement. The settlement agreement acquires the international element from the disputants. It will be deemed to be international if, at the time of its conclusion, two or more parties to the agreement had their places of business in different countries. If the parties' places of business are in the same country, the settlement agreement may still carry the international element if their places of business differ from the country (a) which is closely connected to the subject matter of the agreement, or (b) wherein the main portion of the obligation is to be undertaken.

The Singapore Convention on Mediation also sets out a list of characteristics that would exclude settlement agreements from the scope of the Convention.[295] The Convention does not apply to (a) settlement agreements relating to consumer, family, inheritance or employment law; (b) settlement agreements that have resulted in the course of court proceedings, were approved by a court, or are enforceable as court judgements; and (c) settlement agreements that were embedded in arbitral awards and so can be enforced as consent awards.

While the Singapore Convention on Mediation provides a framework for the cross-border enforceability of settlement agreements, it does not offer

<http://mediationblog.kluwerarbitration.com/2019/06/10/singapore-convention-series-a-call-for-a-broad-interpretation-of-the-singapore-mediation-convention-in-the-context-of-investor-state-disputes/>.

295 Singapore Convention on Mediation (n 14 in ch 1) arts 2(2) and 2(3).

procedural rules for mediation proceedings. This gap can be filled by either the IBA Mediation Rules or the recent ICSID draft Mediation Rules.

3.3.3.4 ICSID Mediation Rules

On 2 August 2018, ICSID published its Working Paper 1, which comprised initial draft amendments to its rules.[296] The initial consultation and review process began in October of 2016. The Working Paper was open for public comment until 28 December 2018. The rules have been fully re-drafted in plain, modern, gender-neutral language, and reorganized in a user-friendly manner.

While the changes will not be to the ICSID Convention itself, they are still the most extensive amendments undertaken by ICSID to date. The announcement of Working Paper 1 generated an extensive body of comments and suggestions from states and the public (academics and practitioners) alike. These submissions were considered and incorporated into Working Paper 2, published in March 2019, Working Paper 3, published in August 2019, and Working Paper 4, published in February 2020.[297] Amendments were proposed to ICSID Convention Proceedings[298] and ICSID Additional Facility Proceedings.[299] Apart from amending the existing Rules, including the Conciliation Rules that were hardly ever used, ICSID also proposed a new set of free-standing rules – the ICSID Mediation Rules. They will apply to ISM proceedings and be accessible to member and non-member states and their investors. (By contrast, the ICSID Conciliation Rules are only available to disputes where the respondent, as well as the claimant's home state, are ICSID member-states. As for the ICSID AF Conciliation Rules, at least one of the relevant states must be an ICSID member state). Therefore, the ICSID Mediation Rules will not be limited by the membership status of a state or its investor and should appeal to a wider audience.

The ICSID Mediation Rules are designed mainly as a voluntary set of rules of an opt-in nature that the disputants can initiate at any time during their dispute. ISM under the ICSID Mediation Rules can be initiated on two grounds: (a) institution of mediation based on prior agreement (Rule 4); and (b) institution of mediation when there is no prior agreement to mediate (Rule 5). Currently,

296 ICSID WP1 – Consolidated Rules (n 19 in ch 1).

297 ICSID WP1 – Consolidated Rules, ICSID WP2 – Consolidated Rules, ICSID WP3, ICSID WP4 (n 19 in ch 1).

298 Administrative and Financial Regulations, Institution Rules, Arbitration Rules and Conciliation Rules.

299 Additional Facility Rules, Administrative and Financial Regulations, Arbitration Rules, Conciliation Rules, Fact-Finding Rules and Mediation Rules.

only a handful of IIAs in force provides for an agreement to mediate (voluntarily).[300] However, the ICSID Mediation Rules allow a party to initiate mediation proceedings despite the absence of the initial agreement to mediate, by seeking the consent of the other party through the Secretary-General of ICSID. This provision serves as a platform for promoting more ISM.[301]

Unlike the Singapore Convention on Mediation, ICSID recognises a difference between conciliation and mediation. In a mediation process, the mediator helps the parties come to an agreement. During a conciliation, however, the conciliation commission is more involved in the process of bringing the disputants to an agreement, which may also involve giving parties recommendations. Therefore, changes have also been made to the ICSID Conciliation Rules aiming to make the conciliation process more time- and cost-effective. The most interesting part is the amendments to the Report that the conciliator drafts at the end of conciliation proceedings. According to draft Conciliation Rule 34(2), parties to the conciliation proceedings are entitled to have their settlement agreement embedded in the Report in full.

> (2) The parties may provide the Commission with the complete and signed text of their settlement agreement and may request that the Commission embed such settlement in the Report.

The existing version of the Conciliation Rules does not have this type of provision even though parties have previously opted for having parts of their settlement agreement embedded in the Report, but not in full.

Neither the ICSID Conciliation Rules nor the ICSID Mediation Rules, address the issue of respective enforceability of the Report or the settlement agreement. ICSID's commentary on its proposed Rules in Working Paper 1, 2018 refers in this respect to the Singapore Convention on Mediation as a multilateral framework for the enforcement of mediated settlements that will apply to settlements reached in the context of investment disputes.[302]

---

300 James Claxton, 'Compelling Parties to Mediate Investor-State Disputes: No Pressure, No Diamonds?' (2020) 20(1) Pepperdine Dispute Resolution Law Journal 78. See also Comprehensive and Progressive Agreement for Trans-Pacific Partnership (CPTPP) (n 21 in ch 1) art 9.18; Comprehensive Economic and Trade Agreement (CETA) (n 9 in ch 1); Pappas (n 259 ch 2); EU-Vietnam FTA (n 9 in ch 1) art 3.31 and annex 10; EU-Singapore IPA (n 21 in ch 1) art 3.4 and annex 6.

301 Ubilava and Nottage (n 18 in ch 1).

302 ICSID WP1 – Synopsis, (n 18 in ch 1) 11.

> A new provision has been introduced to allow the parties' signed and complete settlement agreement to be embodied in a Report. This change allows parties in ICSID conciliation to benefit from the enforcement regime for mediated settlements contemplated in the draft Convention on Mediated Settlements (Singapore Mediation Convention) (CR 34(2); (AF)CR 42(2)).[303]

While reference to the enforcement route through the Singapore Convention on Mediation is not made in the subsequent working papers, it should be assumed that this approach is maintained. Therefore, the ICSID Conciliation and Mediation Rules rely on the enforcement instrument provided by the Singapore Convention on Mediation. This is achieved by both sets of Rules stipulating requirements for their Reports and settlement agreements similar to those provided in Article 4 of the Singapore Convention on Mediation, ensuring enforceability.

3.4 Conclusion

In recent years, the growing dissatisfaction with ISA has laid grounds for the idea of promoting more investor-state ADR mechanisms, in particular ISM. While mediation is rare in ISDS, therefore making it hard to forecast its benefits or trade-offs, it is at least expected to be, among other benefits, as time- and cost-efficient in ISDS as it is in domestic and international commercial dispute resolution spheres.

ISA needs a solution to remedy its shortcomings, which currently represent a considerable cause for concern among ISDS stakeholders. Inserting mediation in the ISDS regime can be a beneficial addition to the currently 'unruly' ISA process. Mediation promises to resolve investor-state disputes quickly, resulting in cheaper proceedings, and even if it is unsuccessful, it will not extend the overall ISDS timeline if integrated into the existing cooling-off periods. However, to achieve this, mediation needs to be fully and actively applied to investor-state disputes.

Currently, mediation is only offered in a voluntary opt-in framework, which is deemed sufficient for facilitating its future use. This sentiment is underpinned by the recent adoption of the Singapore Convention on Mediation, which many hope will ensure universal enforceability of settlement agreements.

303 Ibid.

Once mediated settlement agreements are enforceable, one view is that recourse to ISM and conciliation will grow considerably. Therefore, the need for a mandatory agreement to mediate disappears. However, inserting mediation into the ISDS regime in a voluntary format is not enough – even with the currently adopted Singapore Convention on Mediation, which promises universal enforceability of settlement agreements. Chances are that a voluntary ISM step will not be invoked by the claimants, or if initiated by the respondent, will most probably be turned down by the investor. The following Chapter 4 challenges the argument that enforceability of settlement agreements will be enough to warrant increased and adequate use of ISM in the current and foreseeable ISDS regime.

CHAPTER 4

Underutilisation of ADR in ISDS – A 'Fork in the Road'?

4.1 Introduction

Over time, it has become evident that arbitration is the preferred dispute resolution mechanism in ISDS. Hence, when it comes to the choice between arbitration and conciliation in ISDS, arbitration prevails considerably.[1] Since 1982, only twelve conciliation cases have been registered under the ICSID Conciliation Rules (and the Additional Facility (AF) Conciliation Rules) out of which 11 are contract-based investor-state disputes[2] and only one is a treaty-based investor-state conciliation.[3] However, the extent of recourse

---

1 Welsh and Schneider (n 24 in ch 1); Bottini and Lavista (n 22 in ch 1); Ucheora O. Onwuamaegbu, 'The Role of ADR in Investor-State Dispute Settlement: The ICSID Experience' (2007) 4(1) Transnational Dispute Management, available at <https://www.transnational-dispute-management.com/article.asp?key=964>.

2 *Xenofon Karagiannis v Republic of Albania* (*Pending*) (ICSID Conciliation Commission, Case No CONC/16/1, 16 May 2016) (*'Xenofon Karagiannis v Republic of Albania'*); *La Camerounaise des Eaux (CDE) v Republic of Cameroon and Cameroon Water Utilities Cooperation (CAMWATER)* (*Pending*) (ICSID Conciliation Commission, Case No CONC/19/1, 24 May 2019); *Société d'Energie et d'Eau du Gabon v Gabonese Republic* (*Report*) (ICSID Conciliation Commission, Case No CONC/19/1, 19 September 2018); *Republic of Equatorial Guinea v CMS Energy Corporation and others* (*Report*) (ICSID Conciliation Commission, Case No CONC (AF)/12/2, 12 May 2015); *Hess Equatorial Guinea, Inc. and Tullow Equatorial Guinea Limited v Republic of Equatorial Guinea* (*Pending*) (ICSID Conciliation Commission, Case No CONC (AF)/12/1, 15 May 2012); *RSM Production Corporation v Republic of Cameroon* (*Report*) (ICSID Conciliation Commission, Case No CONC/11/1, 11 June 2013); *Togo Electricité v Republic of Togo* (*Report*) (ICSID Conciliation Commission, Case No CONC/05/1, 6 April 2006); *TG World Petroleum Limited v Republic of Niger* (*Party Settlement*) (ICSID Conciliation Commission, Case No CONC/03/1, 8 April 2005); *SEDITEX Engineering Beratungsgesellschaft für dieTextilindustrie m.b.H. v Madagascar* (*Report*) (ICSID Conciliation Commission, Case No CONC/94/1, 19 July 1996); *Tesoro Petroleum Corporation v Trinidad and Tobago* (*Report*) (ICSID Conciliation Commission, Case No CONC/83/1, 27 November 1985); *SEDITEX Engineering Beratungsgesellschaft für die Textilindustrie m.b.H. v Democratic Republic of Madagascar* (*Party Settlement*) (ICSID Conciliation Commission, Case No CONC/82/1, 20 June 1983); *Shareholders of SESAM v Central African Republic* (*Report*) (ICSID Conciliation Commission, Case No CONC/07/1, 13 August 2008).

3 *Xenofon Karagiannis v Republic of Albania* (n 2). The most recent ICSID investor-State conciliation reported by IAReporter was between Barrick Niugini (and its subsidiary Zijin Mining Group) and Papua New Guinea. It has not yet been officially listed on the ICSID website but

 | DOI:10.1163/9789004532540_005

to investor-state conciliation under UNCITRAL Conciliation Rules is largely unknown.[4] The proceedings under UNCITRAL can be conducted on an ad hoc basis, meaning the parties are free to conduct conciliation proceedings under the UNCITRAL Conciliation Rules without registering their case with any of the dispute resolution institutions, unlike ICSID.[5]

The non-binding nature of ADR proceedings and the non-enforceability of settlement agreements are believed to be the principal causes for underutilisation of the ICSID Conciliation Rules (and AF Conciliation Rules) and the UNCITRAL Conciliation Rules.[6] Therefore, it is expected that the Singapore Convention on Mediation will ensure the enforcement of settlement agreements and be a contributing factor for increased utilisation of investor-state conciliation and mediation in the future. This, however, removes the necessity of inserting mediation as a mandatory pre-condition to arbitration in ISDS to ensure the full utilisation of multi-tier dispute resolution clauses.

A different approach or a hypothesis may be advanced when discussing the less favourable role of ADR in ISDS. Apart from the non-enforceability of settlement agreements, there may be an additional and, as a matter of fact, the principal cause for the underutilisation of conciliation in ISDS. The hypothesis is that the common wording of such clauses contributes to the incorrect interpretation of the choice between conciliation and arbitration, resulting in conciliation being rarely chosen.

The advance consent to dispute resolution under ICSID is usually provided in the ISDS clauses of treaties. The way these clauses are commonly formulated suggests that there is a choice between conciliation and arbitration. However, the extent and nature of such a choice seem to have conflicting interpretations. Anecdotal evidence, discussed later in this chapter, shows that there have been instances when claimants believed that the 'fork in the road' principle applied

is believed to have been initiated under the China-Papua New Guinea BIT (1991). See Daniel Charlotin, 'Barrick Puts Papua New Guinea on Notice of Dispute; Joint-Venture With Chinese Investors to Start Conciliation Proceedings at ICSID' (10 July 2020) IAReporter, available at <https://www-iareporter-com.ezproxy1.library.usyd.edu.au/articles/barrick-puts-papua-new-guinea-on-notice-of-dispute-joint-venture-with-chinese-investors-to-start-conciliation-proceedings-at-icsid/>.

4 Sanders (n 26 ch 2); Lew, Mistelis and Kröll (n 4 ch 2).

5 UNCITRAL Conciliation Rules, UN GAOR, 35th sess, Supp No 17, UN Doc A/35/17, 23 July 1980, art 8.

6 Titi (n 8 in ch 1); Edna Sussman, 'Investor-State Dispute Mediation: The Benefits and Obstacles' in Arthur W Rovine (ed), *Contemporary Issues in International Arbitration and Mediation: The Fordham Papers (2009)* (Brill Nijhoff 2010) 321; Stephen Schwebel, 'Is Mediation of Foreign Investment Disputes Plausible?' (2007) 22(2) ICSID Review 237.

to the choice between conciliation and arbitration. What this means is that parties have believed that recourse to conciliation, whether successful or not, would jeopardise their right to subsequent arbitration.

As for the advance consents for dispute resolution under the UNCITRAL Rules, they usually predominantly refer to the UNCITRAL Arbitration Rules only. This suggests that the absence of advance consent to the UNCITRAL Conciliation Rules could be the cause for their rare application in ISDS.

This chapter examines the forms of consent to ICSID to identify the conflicting interpretations of the choice between conciliation and arbitration. The forms of consent to the UNCITRAL Rules in IIAs should similarly be studied to confirm the absence of express reference to the UNCITRAL Conciliation Rules. It investigates the existing formulations of ISDS clauses and identifies the conflicting interpretations. It examines the three most common types of advance consent to ISDS to determine whether conciliation and arbitration are to the exclusion of one another. It employs the general rules of interpretation under the 1969 Vienna Convention on the Law of Treaties to determine the correct meaning assigned to the ISDS clauses of IIAs.[7] Finally, the discussion is followed by the possible ways forward to resolve the existing conflicting interpretations of advance consents to ISDS.

4.2 Formulation of ISDS Clauses and Problems with Interpretation

The process of initiating an ISDS is the following: a state gives its advance consent to ISDS through treaties, allowing a foreign investor to bring claims directly against that sovereign state without the involvement of the investor's home state. Such advance consents are usually incorporated in the ISDS clauses of IIAs such as BITs and FTAs. The ISDS clauses usually contain state consents to arbitration as the means for their dispute resolution, as well as to ADR mechanisms such as conciliation/mediation. However, express reference to conciliation in international investment treaties is relatively rare compared to advance consents to arbitration.[8]

The 1990s witnessed a dramatic increase in the treatification practices across the world. In particular, after the dissolution of the Eastern bloc and the

7 The Vienna Convention on the Law of Treaties, opened for signature 23 May 1969, 1155 UNTS 331, entered into force 27 January 1980 (The Vienna Convention on the Law of Treaties); Ana Ubilava, 'Underutilisation of ADR in ISDS: Resolving Treaty Interpretation Issues' (2022) 26 (2) UCLA Journal of International Law & Foreign Affairs 131.

8 Bottini and Lavista (n 22 in ch 1).

economic liberalisation of both Asian socialist and Latin American countries, these newly emerged economies wanted to be included in the international community as sovereign states and therefore they were very eager to engage in international investment markets.[9] As the number of new BITs and other multilateral IIAs increased in a short period, their texts and wordings shared significant similarities.[10] Generally speaking, international investment treaties have a varying level of consistency within their texts and formulations.[11] For example, the US and the UK seem to follow the treaty practices of their model templates, whereas Switzerland (another major outbound investor) seems to be more flexible and will adjust its model template in accordance with the terms of negotiation.[12] Unsurprisingly, developing and less developed economies have more diverse wordings in their pool of IIAs compared to developed states. This is mostly because developing countries, due to the power-imbalance on the international platform, tend to be rule-takers rather than rule-makers.[13] Rule-takers have little negotiating power against their developed counterparts, and this is reflected on their diverse pool of international treaties.[14] State practices also differ in their treaty updating methods. For example, while the UK has maintained its treaty template with no major changes over several decades, the US and Canada have made significant amendments to their existing treaty

9 See generally Poulsen (n 25 in ch 3); Henry Veltmeyer, 'Liberalisation and Structural Adjustment in Latin America: In Search of an Alternative' (1993) 28(39) Economic and Political Weekly 2080.

10 Noah Rubins, 'Comments To Jack C. Coe Jr's Article on Conciliation' (2007) 4(1) Transnational Dispute Management, available at <https://www.transnational-dispute-management.com/article.asp?key=962>.

11 Tomer Broude, Yoram Z Haftel and Alexander Thompson, 'The Trans-Pacific Partnership and Regulatory Space: A Comparison of Treaty Texts' (2017) 20(2) Journal of International Economic Law 391; Wolfgang Alschner and Dmitriy Skougarevskiy, 'Mapping the Universe of International Investment Agreements' (2016) 19(3) Journal of International Economic Law 561; Shotaro Hamamoto and Luke Nottage, 'Foreign Investment In and Out of Japan: Economic Backdrop, Domestic Law, and International Treaty-based Investor-State Dispute Resolution' (2011) 8(5) Transnational Dispute Management, available at <https://www.transnational-dispute-management.com/article.asp?key=1766>.

12 Alschner and Skougarevskiy (n 11). Japan is similarly flexible, as seen especially in its earlier BITs, Luke Nottage and Shotaro Hamamoto, 'Japan' in Chester Brown (ed), *Commentaries on Selected Model Investment Treaties* (Oxford University Press 2013) 347.

13 Poulsen (n 25 in ch 3). Cf (especially in recent years) Luke Nottage, Julien Chaisse and Sakda Thanitcul, 'International Investment Treaties and Arbitration Across Asia: A Bird's Eye View' in Julien Chaisse and Luke Nottage (eds), *International Investment Treaties and Arbitration Across Asia* (Brill Nijhoff 2018) 1.

14 Alschner and Skougarevskiy (n 11). But see Poulsen (n 25 in ch 3) 64 for when Romania was directly pushing the UK to conclude a BIT.

templates. Whereas EU member states have experimented with treaty wording, particularly during the earlier stages of forming their BITs.[15] Such variety in treaty drafting practices also somewhat impact the diverse language found in ISDS clauses and, in particular, how consents to arbitration and conciliation are worded and formulated. However, despite the abovementioned inconsistency in the wording of provisions, the outline of an ISDS clause is relatively similar in most IIAs from the 1990s to the 2000s. ISDS clauses in IIAs typically consist of a multi-tiered dispute resolution process:

> (1) Any dispute arising out of an investment, between a Contracting Party and an investor of the other Contracting Party shall, as far as possible, be settled amicably between the parties to the dispute.
>
> (2) If a dispute according to paragraph (1) cannot be settled within three months of a written notification of a sufficiently detailed claim, the dispute shall upon the request of the Contracting Party or of the investor of the other Contracting Party be submitted for conciliation or arbitration to the International Centre for Settlement of Investment Disputes ...[16]

Therefore, the dispute resolution process can be divided into two stages: the first stage is the stage of an amicable settlement when a dispute is still going through ADR channels such as negotiation and consultations, which takes place before recourse to ICSID or UNCITRAL dispute resolution mechanisms. The second stage is a formal phase when ICSID or UNCITRAL dispute resolution mechanisms come into play through advance consent already provided in the ISDS clause such as arbitration and conciliation.

4.2.1 *The First Stage*

This is the stage of the early days of a dispute. It begins with one party notifying the other of a dispute and ends right before the formal dispute resolution proceedings such as, for example, arbitration and conciliation are initiated. The ISDS clauses of international treaties usually provide a multi-step dispute resolution process where the parties are encouraged to first resolve their disputes amicably through negotiations and consultations during the 'cooling-off

15 Alschner and Skougarevskiy (n 11).

16 Agreement Between the Republic of Korea and the Republic of Austria for the Encouragment and Protection of Investments, signed 14 March 1991, entered into force 1 November 1991, art 8 (Korea-Austria BIT).

periods'.[17] Cooling-off periods are stipulated periods of time, mostly three or six months (sometimes more), to allow parties to attempt settlement before initiating the arbitration.[18] Regardless of which dispute resolution mechanism the parties choose in this stage, having recourse to ADR does not jeopardise the right of the party to initiate ISA. The issue of conflicting interpretations is raised later.

There are four main types of references to ADR that can easily be distinguished. The first type, also usually characteristic of older BITs, is an open-ended reference made to amicable settlements.[19] This is when parties are encouraged to try and settle their disputes amicably but without reference to any particular ADR mechanisms. An example of an open-ended reference to amicable settlements is the Germany-Lebanon BIT 1997. Article 9(1) provides for amicable settlement as the first step towards conflict resolution but does not mention any specific ADR mechanism:

> For the purpose of solving disputes with respect to investments between a Contracting Party and an investor of the other Contracting Party, the parties to the dispute will try to solve the case, as far as possible, amicably. [20]

The second type of reference is when the amicable settlement mechanism is specified but usually made to negotiations and consultations only, for example, Article 18(4) of the Japan-Ukraine BIT 2015. This clause refers parties to consultations only and does not mention any other third-party facilitated ADR mechanisms, before directing the dispute to arbitration:

> If the investment dispute cannot be settled through such consultations within six months from the date on which the disputing investor requested in writing the disputing Party for consultations, the disputing investor may, subject to subparagraph 7(a), submit the investment dispute to one of the following international arbitrations ...[21]

---

17 UNCTAD, 'Dispute Settlement: Investor-State', UNCTAD Series on Issues in International Investment Agreements, UNCTAD/ITE/IIT/30, 26 July 2003; Investor–State Disputes: Prevention and Alternatives to Arbitration (n 10 in ch 1).

18 Investor–State Disputes: Prevention and Alternatives to Arbitration (n 10 in ch 1). Ubilava (n 7).

19 Anna Joubin-Bret and Barton Legum, 'A Set of Rules Dedicated to Investor–State Mediation: The IBA Investor–State Mediation Rules' (2014) 29(1) ICSID Review 17.

20 Lebanon-Germany BIT (n 130 in ch 3) art 9(1).

21 Agreement Between Japan and Ukraine for the Promotion and Protection of Investment, signed 5 February 2015, entered into force 26 November 2015 (Japan-Ukraine BIT).

The third type of reference is when an ISDS clause in addition to negotiations and consultations also encourages parties to settle disputes through third-party procedures such as mediation and conciliation. The Turkey-US (1985) BIT is a good example that has an additional reference to third-party procedures if negotiations are unsuccessful. However, this treaty does not further clarify which procedural rules or institutions are to govern such procedures:

> 2. In the event of an investment dispute between a Party and a national or company of the other party, the parties to the dispute should initially seek a resolution through **consultations and negotiations** in good faith. If such consultations and negotiations are unsuccessful, the dispute may be settled through the use of a **non-binding third party procedures** upon which such national or company and the Party mutually agree. If the dispute cannot be resolved through the foregoing procedures, the dispute shall be submitted for settlement in accordance with any previously agreed, applicable dispute settlement procedures. [22]

Another practice, similar to the one above, but not different enough to put in a separate category, is a combination of negotiations and consultations with non-binding third-party procedures, but again without further clarification. This trend can be observed in the US Model BIT 2012 in Section B, Article 23, which is titled 'Consultation and Negotiation':

> In the event of an investment dispute, the claimant and the respondent should initially seek to resolve the dispute through consultation and negotiation, which may include the use of non-binding, third-party procedures.

The fourth type of reference is when an ISDS clause, on top of what was included in the third reference type, also specifies certain procedures to follow for mediation or conciliation processes, but this is a relatively rare occurrence.[23] Most treaties and especially BITs are silent on which mediation or conciliation rules to use and what procedures to follow.[24] Article 26 of the Japan-Colombia BIT (2011) is an example of the fourth type of reference. Here,

22 Treaty Between the United States of America and the Republic of Turkey Concerning the Reciprocal Encouragement and Protection of Investments, signed 3 December 1985, entered into force 18 May 1990 art VI (US-Turkey BIT) (emphasis added).

23 Comprehensive Economic and Trade Agreement (CETA) (n 9 in ch 1) ch 8 s F art 8.19.

24 Salacuse (n 12 in ch 1).

the ISDS clause provides for all types of ADR mechanisms, including third-party facilitated conciliation, and stipulates the procedure for such conciliation the ICSID Conciliation Rules:[25]

> 1. In the event of an investment dispute, the disputing parties shall, as far as possible, settle the dispute amicably through **consultations and negotiations** which may include the use of **non-binding and third-party procedures.** The proceeding for consultations and negotiations shall begin with a request in writing delivered to the competent authority of the disputing Party set out in Article 41. The request shall be accompanied by a brief summary of the factual and legal basis of the investment dispute sufficient to present the problem clearly. Such request shall be delivered to the disputing Party before the submission of the 'notice of intent' to the disputing Party referred to in paragraph 3 of Article 27.
> 2. Consultations and negotiations shall be carried out at least during six months.
> 3. As **one of the** non-binding and third-party procedures referred to in paragraph 1, the disputing **parties may agree** to submit the investment dispute to conciliation procedure under the ICSID Convention or under the ICSID Additional Facility Rules.[26]

While the abovementioned ISDS clause provides for conciliation independently, separate from the arbitration phase, the BIT remains unclear as to whether recourse to conciliation in the First Stage precludes consequent recourse to arbitration. This is because, according to Article 27(5) of the Japan-Colombia BIT, parties will be allowed to proceed with arbitration if the dispute cannot be settled through the consultations and negotiations referred to in Article 26, although Article 27(5) is silent on what happens if the conciliation procedures are attempted but unsuccessful:

> If the investment dispute cannot be settled within seven months and fifteen days from the date on which the disputing investor requested the disputing Party in writing for consultations and negotiations referred to

25 Agreement Between Japan and the Republic of Colombia for the Liberalization, Promotion and Protection of Investment, signed 12 September 2011, entered into force 11 September 2015 (Japan-Colombia BIT).

26 Ibid (emphasis added).

> in Article 26, the disputing investor may submit a claim referred to in paragraph 2 to one of the following arbitrations: [27]

In such circumstances, it would be logical to look for some interpretative clarifications in the ICSID Convention or in its Arbitration and Conciliation Rules on the question of whether conciliation would be to the exclusion of arbitration and vice versa. However, no such answer can be found in the abovementioned instruments. In fact, this ambiguity extends to the interpretation of the ICSID Convention itself.

Interestingly, the reference to a voluntary ADR mechanism in an ISDS clause quite often can be interpreted as mandatory by various ISDS stakeholders and commentators.[28] For example, Bonnitcha et al classify Article 8.20 of the CETA as providing for compulsory mediation before arbitration.[29] Yet according to Article 8.20 of the CETA, '[t]he disputing parties may at any time agree to have recourse to mediation', which is clearly an option provided to the parties, considering the word 'may'. This formulation, in fact, does not provide for a mandatory mediation clause.

Overall, across IIAs, the wordings of the cooling-off periods have been non-uniform and have had a rather general formulation. Consequently, this has been reflected in inconsistent tribunal decisions on the matter.[30] For example, some tribunals have found that non-compliance with the requirements of the cooling-off period was a bar to the jurisdiction of the ensuing ISA tribunal. The tribunals in *Salini v Morocco*,[31] *AMT v Zaire*[32] and *Azurix v Argentine*[33] had to

27 Ibid art 27.

28 UNCTAD, 'Investment Policy Hub' (n 2 in ch 1).

29 Bonnitcha, Poulsen and Waibel (n 26 in ch 3).

30 UNCTAD (n 222 ch 3) 58.

31 *Salini Costruttori S.p.A. and Italstrade S.p.A. v Kingdom of Morocco (Decision on Jurisdiction)* (ICSID Arbitral Tribunal, Case No ARB/00/4, 31 July 2001). The tribunal had to determine whether the claimant had complied with the requirement of the Agreement between Italy and Morocco for the Promotion and Protection of Investment, signed 18 July 1990, entered into force 7 April 2000 (Italy-Morocco BIT) to try to resolve the dispute amicably within the cooling-off period by examining the communications of the parties.

32 *American Manufacturing & Trading, Inc. v Republic of Zaire (Award)* (ICSID Arbitral Tribunal, Case No ARB/93/1, 21 February 1997). The tribunal found that the claimant's unsuccessful attempt to negotiate still constituted compliance with the art VII(2) requirement of the Treaty Between United States of America and the Argentine Republic Concerning the Reciprocal Encouragement and Protection of Investment, signed 14 November 1991, entered into force 20 October 1994.

33 *Azurix Corp. v The Argentine Republic (Award)* (ICSID Arbitral Tribunal, Case No ARB/01/12, 14 July 2006). The tribunal found that despite the claimant's unsuccessful attempt

examine the pre-arbitration communications and attempts of the claimants to settle amicably in order to determine whether the corresponding requirements have been complied with and hence whether the tribunals had jurisdiction over the cases.[34] Tribunals in *Western NIS Enterprise Fund v Ukraine,*[35] *Burlington v Ecuador,*[36] *Murphy v Ecuador*[37] and *Almasryia v Kuwait*[38] found that cooling-off periods represented a mandatory requirement that had to be complied with. Moreover, in *Wintershall v Argentina*, the tribunal declined jurisdiction when it found that the pre-arbitration requirement had not been met.[39]

By contrast, tribunals in other cases (such as in *Ethyl Corporation v Canada,*[40] *SGS v Pakistan,*[41] *Occidental v Ecuador*[42] and *Olin Holdings Limited v Libya*)[43] have treated cooling-off periods as procedural issues and directory by nature, meaning they did not constitute a mandatory pre-condition and do not bar the jurisdiction of the relevant ISA tribunals.[44]

Therefore, according to the existing practice observed through case law, the disputing parties will be deemed to have complied with the requirements of the first stage of the dispute resolution by simply initiating negotiations or consultations.

---

to settle amicably through negotiations, it had complied with the requirements of the BIT text.

34 Christoph Schreuer, 'Travelling the BIT Route: of Waiting Periods, Umbrella Clauses and Forks in the Road' (2004) 5(2) Journal of World Investment & Trade 231.

35 *Western NIS Enterprise Fund v Ukraine (Order)* (ICSID Arbitral Tribunal, Case No ARB/04/2, 16 March 2006).

36 *Burlington Resources Inc. v Republic of Ecuador (Decision on Jurisdiction)* (ICSID Arbitral Tribunal, Case No ARB/08/5, 2 June 2010).

37 *Murphy Exploration and Production Company International v Republic of Ecuador (Award on Jurisdiction)* (ICSID Arbitral Tribunal, Case No ARB/08/4, 15 December 2010).

38 *Almasryia for Operating & Maintaining Touristic Construction Co. L.L.C. v State of Kuwait (Award)* (ICSID Arbitral Tribunal, Case No ARB/18/2, 1 November 2019).

39 *Wintershall Aktiengesellschaft v Argentine Republic (Award)* (ICSID Arbitral Tribunal, Case No ARB/04/14, 8 December 2008).

40 *Ethyl Corporation v The Government of Canada (Award on Jurisdiction)* (24 June 1998).

41 *SGS Société Générale de Surveillance S.A. v Islamic Republic of Pakistan (Decision on Jurisdiction)* (ICSID Arbitral Tribunal, Case No ARB/01/13, 6 August 2003).

42 *Occidental Petroleum Corporation and Occidental Exploration and Production Company v The Republic of Ecuador (Decision on Jurisdiction)* (ICSID Arbitral Tribunal, Case No ARB/06/11, 9 September 2008).

43 *Olin Holdings Limited v State of Libya (Award on Jurisdiction)* (ICC, Case No 20355/MCP, 28 June 2016).

44 Schreuer (n 34); UNCTAD (n 222 in ch 3) 59.

This, however, is not the same for third-party neutral dispute resolution mechanisms such as conciliation and mediation. Despite the fact that mediation can be initiated at any point in time throughout the ISDS process unless mediation is provided in a mandatory format as a pre-condition to arbitration, it is very unlikely for the disputants to agree on yet another step before arbitration once the negotiations and consultations fail. To date, it is very rare for treaties to include a mandatory reference to mediation or conciliation as a prerequisite to arbitration. For example, according to Article 9 of the Sweden-India BIT (2000), the investor is required to either exhaust local remedies (or other previously agreed means of dispute resolution) or initiate ICSID Conciliation before being allowed to have recourse to arbitration:[45]

> 1) Any dispute between an Investor of one Contracting Party and the other Contracting Party in relation to an investment of the former under this Agreement shall, as far as possible, be settled amicably through negotiations between the parties to the dispute.
> 2) If such a dispute has not been amicably settled within a period of six months the Investor that is party to the dispute may submit the dispute for resolution according to the ***following options***:
>   (a) to the courts or administrative tribunals of the Contracting Party that is party to the dispute; ***or***
>   (b) in accordance with any applicable, previously agreed dispute settlement procedure; ***or***
>   (c) to international conciliation under the Rules of the United Nations Commission on
>   International Trade Law (hereinafter referred to as 'UNCITRAL').
> 3. Should the investor fail to exercise the options in paragraph 2 (a) and (b) of this Article or where the conciliation proceedings under Article 2 (c) of this paragraph are terminated other than by the signing of a settlement agreement, the dispute shall be referred to binding international arbitration ...[46]

As stipulated above, conciliation is not the only mandatory pre-condition to arbitration, but rather one of the few options. Therefore, it could be bypassed

45 Rubins (n 10) (emphasis added).

46 Agreement Between the Government of the Kingdom of Sweden and the Government of the Republic of India for the Promotion and Reciprocal Protection of Investments, signed 4 July 2000, terminated 22 March 2017, entered into force 1 April 2001, art 9 (Sweden-India BIT).

if the claimant opted for exhausting local remedies (courts or administrative tribunals) or other previously agreed mechanisms.

Two, relatively recent, treaties, the IA-CEPA and the Hong Kong-United Arab Emirates BIT (HK-UAE BIT), have an unconventional multi-step ISDS clause.[47] The uniqueness of their ISDS provisions lies in the mandatory conciliation (mediation) as a prerequisite to arbitration. When initiated, conciliation becomes mandatory only for the claimant investor and therefore it is a unilaterally mandatory pre-condition.[48] Both treaties, the IA-CEPA and the HK-UAE, offer a three-tier dispute resolution process: standard consultations during cooling-off periods, an additional conciliation step before arbitration and, lastly, arbitration through either ICSID or UNCITRAL Arbitration Rules (or the Stockholm Chamber of Commerce in the case of the HK-UAE).

Article 14.23 of IA-CEPA stipulates: 'If the dispute cannot be resolved within 180 days from the date of receipt by the disputing Party of the written request for consultations, the disputing Party may initiate a conciliation process, which shall be mandatory for the disputing investor …'[49]

Therefore, under IA-CEPA there are two possible options for the claimant to proceed to arbitration: (1) variant one, when no conciliation has been initiated, then the claimant can proceed from consultations (after 180 days) straight to arbitration; (2) variant two, when conciliation has been initiated, in this case the claimant would have to go through consultations, followed by a conciliation proceeding and if the latter is unsuccessful only then the claimant can gain access to arbitration.[50] Under IA-CEPA, conciliation proceedings are allocated an additional 120 days in the ISDS timeline.[51]

Similarly, under the HK-UAE BIT, the claimant has two ways to reach the arbitration. If the respondent state (referred to as the Contracting Party in the Article) does not initiate conciliation, then the claimant can proceed directly to arbitration once the cooling-off period for consultations ends. Article 8 reads:

> (1) Any dispute between an investor of one Contracting Party and the other Contracting Party concerning an investment of the investor covered by this Agreement shall, as far as possible, be settled amicably through consultation between the parties to the dispute …
>
> (3) When required by the Contracting Party, if the dispute cannot be settled amicably within six months from the date of receipt of the

47 IA-CEPA (n 44 in ch 3) art 14.24; HK-UAE BIT (2019) (n 45 in ch 3) art 8.
48 Ubilava (n 274 in ch 3).
49 IA-CEPA (n 44 in ch 3) art 14.24.
50 Ubilava and Nottage (n 7 in ch 1).
51 IA-CEPA (n 44 in ch 3) art 14.24.

written notice, it shall be submitted to the competent authorities of that Contracting Party or arbitration centres thereof, for conciliation ...

(5) If the dispute cannot be settled amicably within six months from the date of receipt of the written notice or from the start of the conciliation referred to in paragraph (3) of this Article, the dispute shall upon the request of the investor be settled by arbitration by submitting the dispute to [arbitration].[52]

However, according to paragraph 3, when the conciliation is initiated by the respondent state, it becomes mandatory for the claimant to participate in order to preserve access to subsequent arbitration (in those cases where the conciliation has been unsuccessful). Conciliation is allocated six months, which is a little longer than what is provided under the IA-CEPA.

Similar provisions of mandatory mediation and conciliation step are also found in the four treaties concluded by the United Arab Emirates: Armenia-UAE BIT (2017), Serbia-UAE BIT (2014), Estonia-UAE BIT and Jordan-UAE BIT (2010).[53] However, the Jordan-UAE BIT, unlike the remaining three above, does not have a unilaterally mandatory provision. Instead, mediation and conciliation are compulsory automatic steps for the disputants, which represents the first step of the ISDS process. While the original text of the treaty is only available in the Arabic language, an English translation of the ISDS provision is quoted in an award of the *Itisaluna Iraq LLC and others v Republic of Iraq* case:

I. Settlement of any dispute arising from an investment between a Contracting Party and an investor of the other Contracting Party shall be resolved by way of the amicable means of mediation and conciliation.

II. If such a dispute cannot thus be settled in accordance with item (First) above, and means of internal review have been exhausted within (180) one hundred and eighty days after the submission of a written application for resolution, either of the parties to the dispute may submit the dispute to:

a) to the competent courts of the Contracting Party in whose territory the investment was made;

52 HK-UAE BIT (2019) (n 45 in ch 3).

53 Armenia-UAE BIT (2017) (n 45 in ch 3) art 10; Serbia-UAE BIT (2014) (n 45 in ch 3) art 9; Estonia-UAE BIT (n 45 in ch 3) art 9; Jordan-UAE BIT (2010) (n 45 in ch 3) art 9.

b) the International Centre for Settlement of Investment Disputes (ICSID) (hereinafter referred to as "the Centre"), established pursuant to the Convention on the Settlement of Investment Disputes between States and nationals of other States signed in Washington, D.C., on 18 March 1965 if the Contracting Parties are both parties thereto;[54]

This type of ISDS clause, which sets out mediation and conciliation as an automatic pre-condition to arbitration, is unique to the best of my knowledge and is not found in any other existing treaty.

4.2.2 *The Second Stage*

This stage, or the formal dispute resolution, begins if the dispute has not been resolved amicably in the first stage of ISDS. This is when IIAs allow the parties to have recourse to arbitration and conciliation, by referring them to specific arbitration and conciliation rules and corresponding facilities, which had previously been agreed by the host and home-states. In most IIAs, these rules are either the ICSID Convention and Rules or the UNCITRAL Arbitration Rules.[55] The problem in the second stage relates to the way advance consents are formulated:

1) For ICSID: when the party to the dispute is choosing between ICSID conciliation and arbitration and considers one to be in exclusion of the other.
2) For UNCITRAL: when the consent is only explicitly given to the UNCITRAL Arbitration Rules, but not to the UNCITRAL Conciliation Rules.

The formulation and wordings of the formal dispute resolution phase (or the second stage) are not uniform either. Consents to ICSID in the second stage can be grouped into three categories.

Consents that fall under the first category would be when an ISDS clause contains consent to both conciliation and arbitration. This is the most common and widely found formulation; however, it appears that these types of consents provide a choice between conciliation and arbitration.[56] This is because most IIAs use the phrase 'conciliation ***or*** arbitration', indicating a choice between

54 *Itisaluna Iraq LLC and others v Republic of Iraq* (n 46 in ch 3).

55 In the minority of cases, an investor-state dispute under the UNCITRAL Arbitration Rules may, with the agreement of the parties, be administered by the LCIA or PCA (as described in Alschner and Skougarevskiy's (n 11) empirical study).

56 August Reinisch, 'Dispute Settlement-2.2 Selecting the Appropriate Forum' (2003) UNCTAD, UN Doc UNCTAD/EDM/Misc.232/Add.1.

the two processes. For example, Article 10 (4) of the Albania-Greece BIT (1991) provides for conciliation or arbitration:

> In case both Contracting Parties have become members of the Convention of 18 March 1965 on the Settlement of Investment Disputes between States and Nationals of the Other States, disputes between either Contracting Party and the investor of the other Contracting Party under the first paragraph of this Article shall be submitted for settlement by **conciliation or arbitration** to the International Centre for the Settlement of Investment Disputes.[57]

This type of formulation has caused controversy, both in terms of interpretation and practice, and rightly so.[58] The root of the problem is that with this type of ISDS clause, conciliation is usually not provided for in the first stage. Instead, conciliation is only offered after the amicable phase is over, the dispute has been progressed to a formal dispute resolution phase, the second stage, and conciliation is provided as an alternative to arbitration. Expectedly, this has caused uncertainty as to whether the choice of conciliation, if the dispute were still unresolved, would then preclude the claimant to proceed with arbitration. In other words, the party is put to a one-off initial election between options. According to UNCTAD's report in 2003, '… if one party opts for conciliation … the other party is prevented from instituting or ultimately insisting on arbitral proceedings unless it is clearly provided for that unsuccessful conciliation is followed by arbitration at some stage'.[59] Therefore, unless an ISDS clause explicitly allows for arbitration after an unsuccessful conciliation, this view suggests that conciliation is to the exclusion of arbitration. However, such clear-cut wording for the choice between conciliation and arbitration is rare in IIAs. Nevertheless, this is only one interpretation of the phrase 'conciliation or arbitration' out of several other contradictory interpretations, which will be discussed in detail below.

The second type of consent, also commonly found in IIAs, is when consent is given explicitly and only to arbitration under the ICSID Convention. Article 26 of the ICSID Convention states that the 'Consent of the parties to arbitration under this Convention shall unless otherwise stated, be deemed consent

57 Agreement Between the Government of the Hellenic Republic and the Government of the Republic of Albania for the Encouragement and Reciprocal Protection of Investments, signed 1 August 1991, entered into force 4 January 1995 (Greece-Albania BIT) (emphasis added).

58 Bottini and Lavista (n 22 in ch 1). Ubilava (n 7).

59 Reinisch (n 56) 13.

to such arbitration to the exclusion of any other remedy'.[60] One interpretation of this clause is that this exclusion, apart from local remedies, also includes conciliation.[61] Accordingly, if an IIA dispute settlement clause only contains consent to arbitration under the ICSID Convention, this excludes the right of the claimant to have recourse to conciliation. However, this is a controversial and erroneous assumption. For example, Article 9 of the Georgia-Finland BIT (2006) specifies arbitration under ICSID and UNCITRAL and does not mention conciliation.[62] However, an in-depth analysis, presented later, shows that advance consent to arbitration does not exclude conciliation before or even during (in parallel to) arbitration proceedings, and that recourse to conciliation does not then jeopardise the claimant's access to arbitration.

The third type of consent is when the ISDS clause refers to the ICSID Convention in general. For example, Article 8 of the Lebanon-Slovakia BIT (2009) provides a reference to the ICSID Convention:

> 2. ... the investor shall be entitled to submit the case ... to:
>
> b) the International Centre for Settlement of Investment Disputes (ICSID) established pursuant to the applicable provisions of the Convention on the Settlement of Investment Disputes between States and Nationals of other States opened for signature at Washington D.C. on 18 March 1965;[63]

General consent to the ICSID Convention without specifying the ICSID Arbitration or Conciliation Rules has generally been understood as consent to both, since the ICSID Convention encompasses both, a view reinforced by Article 25 of the ICSID Convention. In the case of *SPP v Egypt*, the Tribunal held that consent to the jurisdiction of the Centre (ICSID) meant that the investor could make a choice from the dispute resolution mechanisms that the Centre offered; that is, either conciliation or arbitration.[64] The EU-Singapore Investment Protection Agreement (2018) provides for comprehensive procedures for the

60 The ICSID Convention (n 6 in ch 1) art 26.

61 Bottini and Lavista (n 22 ch 1); Christoph Schreuer, *The ICSID Convention: A Commentary* (Cambridge University Press 2009) 348.

62 Agreement Between the Government of the Republic of Finland and the Government of Georgia on the Promotion and Protection of Investments, signed 24 November 2006, entered into force 30 December 2007 (Georgia-Finland BIT).

63 Agreement Between the Lebanese Republic and the Slovak Republic for the Promotion and reciprocal Protection of Investments, signed 20 February 2009, entered into force 22 May 2010, art 8 (Lebanon-Slovakia BIT).

64 *Southern Pacific Properties (Middle East) Limited v Arab Republic of Egypt (Award)* (ICSID Arbitral Tribunal, Case No ARB/84/3, 20 May 1992).

first stage – consultations, followed by a separate article on mediation and ADR mechanisms before initiating arbitration. According to Article 3.4, subclause 2: 'Recourse to mediation is voluntary and without prejudice to the legal position of either disputing party'.[65] Despite the obvious intention of the parties to the FTA to encourage mediation prior to arbitration, by providing an additional explanatory provision, this still does not guarantee that recourse to ICSID Conciliation would not jeopardise the right to proceed with arbitration since it does not make a reference to conciliation. This is because the second stage of the dispute resolution process provided in Article 3.6 of the FTA refers parties to the ICSID Convention in general. However, the ICSID Convention does not offer a clear and direct interpretative tool to determine whether having initial recourse to conciliation under ICSID would be a bar to arbitration.

The problem of interpretation applies to each of the three types of consents listed above. While in the first category, there is ambiguity with the conjunction 'or', in the second category, advance consent is given to arbitration only, leaving it open to interpretation whether conciliation could still be used at any stage, without barring arbitration. As for the third category of consents, while the case law suggests that consent to the ICSID Convention means to consent to all the dispute resolution mechanisms provided by it, it is unclear whether recourse to conciliation first would impede the right to subsequent arbitration, an interpretation issue similar to the consents of the second category.

The formulation of ISDS clauses that reference UNCITRAL is different to those that refer to ICSID. The most common reference to UNCITRAL in IIAs is a reference to the UNCITRAL Arbitration Rules.[66] In contrast, express consent to the UNCITRAL Conciliation Rules is quite rare.[67] For example, while Article 6.21(3)(b) of the India-Singapore CECA (2005) specifically mentions both conciliation and arbitration under ICSID, the following Article 6.21(3)(c) only contains consent to arbitration under UNCITRAL:

> 3. … the investor may submit the dispute to:
>   (a) the courts or administrative tribunals of the disputing Party;

65 EU-Singapore IPA (n 21 in ch 1).

66 According to the UNCTAD investment policy website (n 2 in ch 1), out of over 2500 mapped international investment agreements, 1632 IIAs carried an ISDS clause. Apart from the IIAs already examined in this paper, I also chose IIAs on a random basis to observe common trends of reference to UNCITRAL in IIAs. I picked three to five IIAs, each from America, Europe, and Asia, with 24 IIAs total for the periods 1982–1987, 1988–1993, 1994–1999, 2000–2005, 2006–2011, 2012–2017, and 2018–2019 (listed in Bibliography).

67 Out of all the IIAs examined in this paper, only the Sweden-India BIT (n 46) contains an explicit reference to the UNCITRAL Conciliation Rules.

(b) the International Centre for Settlement of Investment Disputes (ICSID) for conciliation or arbitration pursuant to Articles 28 or 36 of the Convention ...; or
(c) arbitration under the rules of the United Nations Commission on International Trade Law (UNCITRAL).

Article 1 of the UNCITRAL Conciliation Rules stipulates that consent to the Rules must be explicitly provided for by the parties in order for the Rules to apply:

> (1) These Rules apply to conciliation of disputes arising out of or relating to a contractual or other legal relationship where the parties seeking an amicable settlement of their dispute have agreed that the UNCITRAL Conciliation Rules apply.

Article 1 should not be understood as a requirement for the parties to have advance consent provided to conciliation in the treaties, but rather as a statement that parties are free to agree on UNCITRAL Conciliation proceedings at any time before or during their dispute. Therefore, the absence of prior express consent to the UNCITRAL Conciliation Rules does not preclude the parties from initiating conciliation proceedings for the settlement of their disputes at any stage of the ISDS process. However, it is questionable whether this option (or opportunity) is clear to the disputants unless it is explicitly mentioned in the respective ISDS clause of a treaty. Moreover, it is highly unlikely for the disputing parties to an unsuccessful first stage to agree on having another non-binding dispute resolution mechanism as an additional step before arbitration unless such a step is made mandatory.

The problem with the contradictory interpretation of the choice between the ICSID Conciliation and Arbitration Rules could explain the rare occurrence of conciliation proceedings under ICSID. The rare use of the UNCITRAL Conciliation Rules, however, is not necessarily only connected with the way consent is formulated in ISDS clauses. An additional reason could be that there is simply not enough information on disputes that settle through conciliation because they are not registered under any institutional dispute resolution body.

4.3 Choosing between Conciliation and Arbitration

Three types of consents to ICSID, as provided under ISDS clauses, will be discussed in detail below. These are: (1) consent to conciliation and arbitration but written with a common phrase 'conciliation or arbitration', (2) consent to ICSID

Arbitration Rules only, and (2) a general consent to the ICSID Convention. The goal, for the first category of consents, is to determine what the conjunction 'or' as used in the phrase 'conciliation or arbitration' entails in the first category of consents, and whether choice of conciliation by a claimant is to the exclusion of arbitration.

When reference is made to ICSID Arbitration only, second category, consent is deemed to be given only to arbitration.[68] This interpretation initially seems relatively straightforward. However, according to ICSID, consent to the jurisdiction of ICSID can be given via IIAs before the dispute arises, or (more rarely in practice) after a dispute has arisen.[69] This includes consent to conciliation proceedings under ICSID. Therefore, even when an ISDS clause provides consent to arbitration only, it should not preclude the claimant from initiating conciliation prior to arbitration. The other question, however, is whether initiating conciliation first would bar access to arbitration. This leads us to the third category of consents.

When a consent is provided to the ICSID Convention, it is deemed to be given to all the dispute resolution mechanisms under the Convention. Therefore, according to this interpretation, the claimant has access to both conciliation and arbitration. However, it is unclear whether the ICSID Convention requires a separate agreement between the parties to first initiate conciliation and then arbitration, or whether the claimant is free to proceed with conciliation first without the need to have prior consent from the respondent.

It becomes obvious that consents to ICSID Arbitration only (second category) and to the ICSID Convention (third category) are somewhat linked to the issue of the first type of consent (conciliation or arbitration). This is because all three types of references lead to the same question, which calls for the need to determine whether conciliation can be initiated before arbitration without jeopardising the rights of the parties to the arbitration.

One interpretation defines the phrase 'conciliation or arbitration' as conciliation in exclusion of arbitration. This means if conciliation is initiated first, the claimant will be barred from accessing arbitration regardless of the outcome of the conciliation.

The other view is that conciliation is to the exclusion of arbitration only if it is successful and therefore there is no more dispute to be resolved between the parties. This corresponds with the general requirement of ISDS clauses that there should be an existing dispute for the parties to initiate any type of

68 Schreuer (n 34).

69 The ICSID Convention (n 6 in ch 1) s V-Jurisdiction of the Centre.

dispute resolution mechanism, arbitration in particular. Therefore, it is essential to establish the correct interpretation of ISDS clauses in BITS with the following wording – 'conciliation or arbitration'. The goal here is to determine whether the conjunction 'or' used in such sentences carries the meaning of 'instead'.

This can be achieved by employing the general rules of interpretation provided in the Vienna Convention on the Law of Treaties. The rules of interpretation provided in Articles 31 and 32 of the Vienna Convention are accepted by states to reflect customary international law upheld by the International Court of Justice as well as other international courts.[70]

1. A treaty shall be interpreted in good faith in accordance with the ordinary meaning to be given to the terms of the treaty in their context and in the light of its object and purpose.
2. The context for the purpose of the interpretation of a treaty shall comprise, in addition to the text, including its preamble and annexes:
   (a) any agreement relating to the treaty which was made between all the parties in connexion with the conclusion of the treaty;
   (b) any instrument which was made by one or more parties in connexion with the conclusion of the treaty and accepted by the other parties as an instrument related to the treaty.
3. There shall be taken into account, together with the context:
   (a) any subsequent agreement between the parties regarding the interpretation of the treaty or the application of its provisions;
   (b) any subsequent practice in the application of the treaty which establishes the agreement of the parties regarding its interpretation;
   (c) any relevant rules of international law applicable in the relations between the parties.
4. A special meaning shall be given to a term if it is established that the parties so intended.[71]

70 *Application of the Convention on the Prevention and Punishment of the Crime of Genocide (Croatia v Serbia)* (*Judgment*) [2015] ICJ Rep 3, 64 [138]; *Pulp Mills on the River Uruguay (Argentina v Uruguay)* (*Judgment*) [2010] ICJ Rep 14, 46 [65]; *Sovereignty over Pulau Ligitan and Pulau Sipadan (Indonesia/Malaysia)* (*Judgment*) [2002] ICJ Rep 625, 645–646 [37]-[38]; Appellate Body Report, *United States – Countervailing Duties on Certain Corrosion-Resistant Carbon Steel Flat Products from Germany*, WTO Doc WT/DS213/AB/R (28 November 2002) [61].

71 The Vienna Convention on the Law of Treaties (n 7) art 31.

Article 31(1) is the most widely applied rule of interpretation by the various dispute resolution tribunals compared to the rest of its subclauses.[72] It offers four tests that should be applied when interpreting a treaty or its provisions: (a) good faith, (b) ordinary meaning, (c) context, and (d) object and purpose. Article 31(2) further extends the scope of 'context' by encompassing the preamble, annexes, and conclusion texts of the treaty that is to be interpreted. Article 31(3) provides for the opportunity to engage subsequent agreements and practices related to the treaty in question, as well as the corresponding rules of international law that can be used for interpretative purposes. Article 31(4) discusses the possibility of a special meaning given to the terms of the treaty by the parties. It can be used instead of, or in conjunction with, the 'ordinary meaning' test provided in Article 31(1).

As the treaties are assumed to have been drafted in good faith, the ordinary meaning test provided by Article 31(1) of the Vienna Convention will be the next step in the process of interpretation. The ordinary meaning is the 'current and normal, regular and usual meaning' attributed to a particular term of the treaty by the parties.[73] In the case of the phrase 'conciliation or arbitration', the usual meaning of the term 'or' needs to be defined. According to the Oxford Dictionary, the conjunction 'or' is 'used to link alternatives'.[74] Therefore, placing the conjunction 'or' between the words conciliation and arbitration suggests that they are alternatives of one another. It is, however, debatable whether being alternatives also implies that they are exclusive of one another. For example, Article 11(1) of the Sweden-Hungary BIT stipulates a very clear intention of the drafters to provide for a choice between two alternatives. According to Article 11(1):

> Each Contracting Party hereby consents to submit to the International Centre for the Settlement of Investment Disputes for settlement by conciliation or arbitration ... If the parties to such a dispute have different opinions as to whether conciliations or arbitration is the more appropriate method of settlement, the **investor shall have the right to choose.**[75]

72 Romesh Weeramantry, *Treaty Interpretation in Investment Arbitration* (Oxford University Press 2012) 40.

73 Mark Villiger, 'Part II Interpretation of Treaties, 6 The Rules on Interpretation: Misgivings, Misunderstandings, Miscarriage? The 'Crucible' Intended by the International Law Commission' in Enzo Cannizzaro (ed), *The Law of Treaties Beyond the Vienna Convention* (Oxford University Press, 2011) 109.

74 Oxford English Dictionary (online at 28 January 2021) 'or'.

75 Agreement Between the Government of the Kingdom of Sweden and the Government of the Hungarian People's Republic for the Promotion and Reciprocal Protection of

Yet it remains unclear whether there in a mutually exclusive choice between conciliation and arbitration, raising the issue if the 'fork in the road' principle, similar to, for example, an exclusive choice between local courts and arbitration. Examining the ordinary meaning of the word 'or' does not provide a definitive answer to the question at hand and therefore it needs to be interpreted in conjunction with other interpretative tools provided by Article 31 of the Vienna Convention.[76]

According to Article 31(4) of the Vienna Convention, a term should be interpreted in accordance with its ordinary meaning unless it is established that the parties have intentionally attributed a special meaning to it. In our case, this would be whether a special meaning is usually assigned to the word 'or' in the texts of treaties that have the phrase 'conciliation or arbitration' in their ISDS clauses. None of the BITs that have the 'conciliation or arbitration' wording appear to have defined the term 'or' differently from its usual definition or given it a special meaning in the text. The interpretative tool provided by Article 31 is required and employed because the treaty in question has not assigned a special meaning to the term in the first place. Weeramantry, for example, suggests that Article 31(4) of the Vienna Convention is 'likely to assume relevance when the special meaning is able to be derived from materials or circumstances external' to the treaty in question.[77] Such external materials directly relevant to the text of a treaty, to help provide a special meaning to the phrase 'conciliation or arbitration', would be the ICSID Convention and ICSID Arbitration and Conciliation Rules.

The need to incorporate the ICSID Convention and Rules into the interpretation process also becomes evident when applying the 'object and purpose' test to treaties and ISDS clauses.[78] While the objectives of IIAs may differ from treaty to treaty, the primary goal is usually to encourage economic cooperation between states. This is achieved by ensuring that the standards of treatment for foreign investments are met and warranted through ISDS clauses. The phrase 'conciliation or arbitration' is usually encountered in ISDS clauses that refer parties to the ICSID Convention and Rules. Quoting Prosper Weil from *Tokios Tokeles v Ukraine*, 'it is not for the Parties [to a BIT] to extend the jurisdiction of ICSID beyond what the Convention provides for. It is the Convention

Investments, signed and entered into force 21 April 1987 (Sweden-Hungary BIT) (emphasis added).

76 *Aguas Del Tunari, S.A., v Republic of Bolivia (Decision on Jurisdiction)* (ICSID Arbitral Tribunal, Case No ARB/02/3, 21 October 2005) [226]; Weeramantry (n 72) 49.

77 Weeramantry (n 72).

78 The Vienna Convention on the Law of Treaties (n 7) art 31(1).

that determines the jurisdiction of ICSID ....'[79] However, neither the ICSID Convention, nor its rules, offer any clear indication on how the choice between conciliation and arbitration should be interpreted through the Convention.

This leads to the test of 'context' in which the phrase 'conciliation or arbitration' could have been used in treaties. The context could be determined with the help of similar or identical phrases provided in other provisions of the same treaty.[80] A similar formulation to the phrase 'conciliation or arbitration', is often found in the ISDS clauses when referring to the choice between two ADR mechanisms (usually in the first stage). This is when the parties are encouraged to settle their disputes, for example, through negotiations and consultations. An interesting trend can be observed in some of the BITs that have these types of references. The choice between consultations and negotiation is sometimes worded with the conjunction 'and', but at other times with the conjunction 'or'.[81] However, when it comes to the second stage (albeit in the same article and same treaty), the choice between conciliation and arbitration is almost always formulated with the conjunction 'or'. Unlike the duo of conciliation and arbitration where only arbitration renders a binding outcome, both the negotiations and consultations are non-binding and amicable by nature. The claimant is always free to choose between negotiations and consultations, or in fact initiate both consecutively and even concurrently, as long as there is an ongoing dispute between the parties. However, in the case of conciliation and arbitration, arbitration does not entail an amicable process, and yields outcomes very different from the former. Therefore, the intention of the drafters could have been to purposefully differentiate the type of choice between negotiations and consultations from the choice between conciliation 'or' arbitration by using conjunctions that carry different meanings. But this is not the case; the conjunctions 'and' and 'or' are both used for negotiations and consultations, without having any special intention assigned to them.

---

79 *Tokios Tokeles v Ukraine (Dissenting Opinion)* (ICSID Arbitral Tribunal, Case No ARB/02/18, 29 April 2004). Also quoted in Weeramantry (n 72) 97.

80 Weeramantry (n 72) 59 lists several tribunals that employed the same approach to interpretation as the one used above. In particular, the tribunals observed how a similar or identical term to the one they were interpreting was used in other articles of the same treaty. See *Loewen Group, Inc. and Raymond L. Loewen v United States of America (Award on Jurisdiction)* (ICSID Arbitral Tribunal, Case No ARB(AF)/98/3, 5 January 2001) [40]; *ADF Group Inc. v United States of America (Award)* (ICSID Arbitral Tribunal, Case No ARB(AF)/00/1, 9 January 2003) [164]-[165].

81 Sweden-India BIT (n 46) art 6.21(1); Agreement Between the Republic of Austria and Georgia for the Promotion and Protection of Investments, signed 18 October 2001, entered into force 1 March 2004, art 12(1) (Austria-Georgia BIT).

The terms of the treaty do not exist in isolation; instead, they are closely linked with the other treaty provisions, as well as external sources. While IIAs provide the wording 'conciliation or arbitration', no further contextual definition is provided. Here, the context needs to be analysed in conjunction with Articles 31(3)(b) and (c) of the Vienna Convention.[82] In order to interpret the meaning of the phrase 'conciliation or arbitration' in its context, it is necessary to go beyond the limits of the text of such treaties and examine possible interpretations from the ICSID Convention and Rules. The ICSID Convention and Rules do not provide a straightforward answer to the question posed. Yet analysing the meaning and context of these dispute resolution mechanisms within ICSID can still shed some light on the questions at hand.

According to the Preamble of the ICSID Convention, '[a]ttaching particular importance to the availability of facilities for international conciliation or arbitration to which Contracting States and nationals of other Contracting States may submit disputes if they so desire'.[83] While it is clear from the text of the Preamble that ICSID provides both dispute resolution options for the disputing parties, the choice between conciliation and arbitration is worded with the conjunction 'or'. This is identical to the ISDS clauses of IIAs that result in conflicting interpretations. But, later in the text of the ICSID Convention, conciliation and arbitration are referred to with the conjunction 'and'. Considering this seemingly trivial but arguably crucial difference, it seems as if the drafters did not give much meaning to the difference between 'and' and 'or'. The version of the Preamble that uses the conjunction 'or' could have been simply copied into the texts of treaties without much thought, which consequently spread amongst the states during the increased treatification, especially from the 1990s onwards. Article 26 of the ICSID Convention poses the potential risk of conflicting interpretations:

> Consent of the parties to arbitration under this Convention shall, unless otherwise stated, be deemed consent to such arbitration to the exclusion of any other remedy. A Contracting State may require the exhaustion of any other remedy.

According to Schreuer, 'the better view appears to be that the exclusion of any other remedy would go beyond judicial proceedings'.[84] However, it is questionable whether going beyond judicial proceedings also includes conciliation.

82 The Vienna Convention on the Law of Treaties (n 7).

83 The ICSID Convention (n 6 in ch 1).

84 Schreuer (n 34) 402.

While Article 26 limits consent to arbitration, it does not mean that the same restriction applies to conciliation; that is, consent to conciliation does not bar the right to arbitration. If that were the case, a similar provision to Article 26 would exist for conciliation in the text of the ICSID Convention.[85] Additionally, Article 35 of the ICSID Convention also seems to consider the possibility of arbitration after conciliation. It states that information acquired during conciliation will not be used during subsequent arbitration. Article 28(2) (Request for Conciliation) stipulates:

> The request shall contain the information concerning the issues in dispute, the identity of the parties and their consent to conciliation in accordance with the rules of procedure for the institution of conciliation and arbitration proceedings.

Article 36(2) (Request for Arbitration) of the ICSID Convention contains an identical provision, but about arbitration.[86]

Conciliation does not seem to bar a party from access to the procedural rules of both conciliation and arbitration. The same goes for the consent to arbitration, which does not seem to preclude a claimant from having access to both the conciliation and arbitration procedural rules. If drafters had a contrary intention, then logically consent to one would not automatically give access to the rules of procedure of both dispute resolution mechanisms, as it does now. In that were the case, Article 28(2) would then read: '[t]he request shall contain ... their consent to conciliation in accordance with the rules of procedure for the institution of conciliation proceedings'. And for Article 36(2), the wording would be: '[t]he request shall contain ... their consent to arbitration in accordance with the rules of procedure for the institution of arbitration proceedings'. Interestingly, Ginkel makes the following observation:

> [I]f the claimant (first) chooses conciliation under Article 28 of the Convention, the theory is that the other party may well be prevented from instituting arbitral proceedings, – unless it has been clearly provided (in the investment agreement, the applicable bilateral investment agreement or other document in which the State has given its consent to

85 Rubins (n 10) 4.

86 '[t]he request shall contain the information concerning the issues in dispute, the identity of the parties and their consent to arbitration in accordance with the rules of procedure for the institution of conciliation and arbitration proceedings'.

ICSID dispute resolution) that a conciliation proceeding not resulting in a settlement may be followed by arbitration.[87]

However, Ginkel further suggests that nothing precludes arbitration and conciliation running concurrently or even staying the arbitration proceedings while engaging in conciliation. Parties may initiate conciliation any time before or during the arbitral proceedings if there is an existing dispute to conciliate.

Moreover, adopting a restrictive interpretation of the words 'conciliation or arbitration' 'would be contrary to the consensual nature of conciliation and would unnecessarily limit the parties in their search for an efficient and mutually acceptable resolution of their dispute' according to Rubins.[88] If the initial intention of such wording was to, in fact, limit the choice to either conciliation or arbitration, nobody would choose conciliation because it yields a non-binding outcome. Yet parties, in general, are always free to initiate non-binding third-party assisted procedures without limiting their access to arbitration (similar to first stage references to ADR proceedings such as negotiations and consultations, which are not a bar to subsequent arbitration during the Second Stage). Hence, interpreting a consensual non-binding mechanism as a choice that excludes binding arbitration would not be reasonably justifiable.

An exception to the common wording of ISDS provisions providing a choice between conciliation or arbitration is found in the Guatemala-Israel BIT (2006). It lists four dispute resolution mechanisms including conciliation, however choosing one of these mechanisms will be to the exclusion of any other. Article 8 stipulates:

> 2. If a dispute under paragraph 1 of this Article cannot be settled within six (6) months of a written notification of this dispute, it shall be on the request of the Investor settled as follows:
>   (a) by a competent court of the Host Contracting Party; or
>   (b) **by conciliation**; or
>   (c) by arbitration by the International Center for the Settlement of Investment Disputes (ICSID) ...
>   (e) by an ad hoc arbitration tribunal, which is to be established under the Arbitration Rules of the United Nations Commission on International Trade Law (UNCITRAL) ...

---

87 Eric van Ginkel, 'Toward Mandatory ICSID Conciliation?-Reflections on Professor Coe's Article on Investor-State Conciliation' (2007) 4(1) Transnational Dispute Management, available at <https://www.transnational-dispute-management.com/article.asp?key=961>.

88 Rubins (n 10).

4. **The choice of one dispute settlement mechanism will exclude any other.** Notwithstanding the above, an investor who has submitted the dispute to national jurisdiction may have recourse to the arbitral tribunals mentioned in paragraph 2 of this Article so long as a judgment has not been delivered on the subject matter of the dispute by a national court.[89]

The intention of the drafters seems to be quite straightforward, in that they wanted the 'fork in the road' principle to apply to courts, conciliation, and arbitration under ICSID and UNCITRAL. As already stated, conciliation is a non-binding dispute resolution mechanism that could precede or be used concurrently with arbitration – especially if a settlement has not been reached by the parties and there is an existing dispute between the parties. Yet the first sentence of Article 8(4) above suggests that if conciliation is initiated, it bars access to courts and arbitration, which seems an odd thing to have in an ISDS provision. What is even more intriguing is the second sentence of Article 8(4), according to which it seems like the 'fork in the road' principle applies to courts and arbitration only. This strongly suggests that conciliation fell under the general exclusion by. This is because paragraph 4 provides for a reservation to the exclusion. It considers the possibility of proceeding to arbitration even when a dispute has already been submitted to local courts, but only before the court judgment has been issued. If the drafters had intentionally included conciliation in the exclusion list, then a similar reservation would also apply to cases in which conciliation was unsuccessful. For example, this is the case with Article 9 of the India-Israel BIT (1996):

(1) Any dispute between an investor of one Contracting Party and the other Contracting Party in relation to an investment of the former under this Agreement shall, as far as possible, be settled amicably through negotiations between the parties to the dispute.
(2) Any such dispute which has not been amicably settled within a period of six months may, if both parties agree, be submitted:
    (a) for resolution in accordance with the law of the Contracting Party which has admitted the investment to that Contracting Party's competent judicial or administrative bodies: or
    (b) to international conciliation.

89 Agreement Between the Government of the State of Israel and the Government of the Republic of Guatemala for the Reciprocal Promotion and Protection of Investments, signed 7 November 2006, entered into force 15 January 2009, art 8 (Guatemala-Israel BIT) (emphasis added).

(3) Should the Parties fail to agree on a dispute settlement procedure provided under paragraph 2 of this Article or where a dispute is referred to conciliation but conciliation proceedings are terminated other than by signing of a settlement agreement, the dispute may be referred to Arbitration.

What also adds to the uncertainty as to whether conciliation may have been unintentionally included in the exclusion in the Guatemala-Israel BIT (2006) is that no other BIT concluded by Israel[90] and Guatemala[91] with other states apply the 'fork in the road' principle to conciliation. For example, a nearly identical provision to Article 8 of the Guatemala-Israel BIT (2006) is found in Article 10 of the Guatemala-Trinidad and Tobago BIT (2013) and BLEU (Belgium-Luxembourg Economic Union)-Guatemala BIT (2005). In both cases, however, conciliation is not included in the list of dispute settlement mechanisms that are in exclusion of one another.

In order to eliminate any remaining ambiguities or doubts regarding the nonexclusive nature of the phrase 'conciliation or arbitration' in IIAs, a supplementary interpretative tool can be used in the form of Article 32 of the Vienna Convention:

> Article 32 Supplementary means of interpretation
>
> Recourse may be had to supplementary means of interpretation, including the preparatory work of the treaty and the circumstances of

90 Israel has concluded 36 BITs in total (listed in Bibliography).

91 The remaining BITs concluded by Guatemala that were available in English did not have conciliation and/or a limitation to one forum: Agreement Between the Government of the Republic of Guatemala and the Government of the Russian Federation on Promotion and Reciprocal Protection of Investments, signed 27 November 2013, not yet in force (Guatemala-Russian Federation BIT); Agreement Between the Republic of Austria and the Republic of Guatemala for the Promotion and Protection of Investments, signed 16 January 2006, entered into force 1 December 2012 (Austria-Guatemala BIT); Agreement Between the Government of the Republic of Finland and the Government of the Republic of Guatemala on the Promotion and Protection of Investments, signed 14 April 2005, entered into force 6 January 2007 (Finland-Guatemala BIT); Agreement Between the Republic of Guatemala and the Czech Republic for the Promotion and Reciprocal Protection of Investments, signed 8 July 2003, entered into force 29 April 2005 (Czech Republic-Guatemala BIT); Agreement Between the Republic of Guatemala and the Kingdom of the Netherlands on the Promotion and Reciprocal Protection of Investments, signed 18 May 2001, entered into force 1 September 2002 (Guatemala-Netherlands BIT); Agreement Between the Government of the Republic of Korea and the Government of the Republic of Guatemala for the Promotion and Protection of Investments, signed 1 August 2000, entered into force 17 August 2002 (Korea-Guatemala BIT).

its conclusion, in order to confirm the meaning resulting from the application of article 31, or to determine the meaning when the interpretation according to article 31:

(a) leaves the meaning ambiguous or obscure; or
(b) leads to a result which is manifestly absurd or unreasonable.

Due to its non-mandatory character, this interpretation test has not been used as often as Article 31 – the general rule of interpretation. While Article 32 includes 'preparatory work of the treaty', it does not limit 'supplementary means of interpretation' to certain types of documents. As Weeramantry points out, 'the canvas of potentially applicable Article 32 interpretative aids or guidelines thus remains large'.[92] There have been cases where the International Court of Justice examined other treaties with the same subject matter or even with a similar provision in order to clarify an ambiguous provision in a treaty.[93] For example, according to Mbengue, 'other treaties on the same subject matter may be considered as supplementary means of interpretation in the sense of Article 32'.[94] Therefore, an interpretative guide of one treaty can be applied to determine the interpretation of the phrase 'conciliation or arbitration' in another.

The 2016 Guide on Investment Mediation issued by the Secretariat of the Energy Charter Mediation seems to be the only document providing a direct interpretation of the phrase 'conciliation or arbitration'.[95] The Guide is a voluntary instrument to facilitate the amicable settlement of investment disputes through mediation that can be used by governments and companies willing to engage in such dispute resolution proceedings. The aim of the Guide is to provide the option of mediation as part of the amicable settlement stipulated under Article 26 of ECT and to explain the mediation process in general. Like many other treaties, Article 26 of the ECT gives the claimant a choice to provide

92 Weeramantry (n 72) 102.

93 *Case concerning rights of nationals of the United States of America in Morocco (Judgment)* [1952] ICJ Rep 176 (examining the similar words: renounces claiming in two Declarations); *Constitution of the Maritime Safety Committee of the Inter-Governmental Maritime Consultative Organization (Advisory Opinion)* [1960] ICJ Rep 150 (examining the provisions by looking at other Conventions dealing with a similar subject matter); *Interpretation of the Agreement of 25 March 1951 between the WHO and Egypt (Advisory Opinion)* [1980] ICJ Rep 73 (examining other various types of agreements that provided similar terms); *Oil Platforms (Preliminary Objection Judgment)* [1996] ICJ Rep 803 (examining other treaties with a similar provision).

94 Anthony Aust, *Modern Treaty Law and Practice* (Cambridge University Press 2013) 220.

95 The Energy Charter Conference, *Guide on Investment Mediation* (2016).

unconditional consent to ICSID Conciliation, among other options.[96] This is where the direct interpretation on the choice between ICSID conciliation and arbitration provided by the Guide proves useful. Article 26 (Settlement of Disputes Between an Investor and a Contracting Party) stipulates:

> (1) Disputes between a Contracting Party and an Investor of another Contracting Party relating to an Investment of the latter in the Area of the former, which concern an alleged breach of an obligation of the former under Part III shall, if possible, be settled amicably.
> (2) If such disputes cannot be settled according to the provisions of paragraph (1) within a period of three months from the date on which either party to the dispute requested amicable settlement, the Investor party to the dispute may choose to submit it for resolution:
> (a) to the courts or administrative tribunals of the Contracting Party [party] to the dispute;
> (3) (a) Subject only to subparagraphs (b) and (c), each Contracting Party hereby gives its unconditional consent to the submission of a dispute to international **arbitration or conciliation** in accordance with the provisions of this Article.

It appears that the ambiguity surrounding the choice between conciliation and arbitration has existed since 1992, when, during the negotiations on the Basic Agreement draft 10, the Australian delegation stated that 'it will be necessary to find wording to ensure that going to conciliation does not prevent a party then seeking arbitration'.[97] The Guide, however, states that the 'fork in the road' clause only refers to domestic proceedings and that the restriction does not apply to conciliation:

> [E]ven if an investor starts international arbitration under Art. 26.4 ECT or under the agreement of the parties after the dispute arises, there is still a possibility of staying the proceedings and attempting to resolve the dispute through conciliation.[98]

Indeed, the Guide not only interprets the wording of 'conciliation or arbitration' as the right to first initiate conciliation and then pursue arbitration, but it

96 ECT (n 59 in ch 3).

97 Annex 5 to Basic Agreement 10 of 19 March 1992, quoted in Energy Charter Secretariat, Conflict Prevention and Dispute Resolution: Main Provisions and Instruments (2016) 114.

98 The Energy Charter Conference (n 95) s 2.2(iv).

also states that even when arbitration is being initiated first, under the ICSID Convention, the parties are always free to conciliate by staying the arbitration proceedings. Therefore, if the wording of ECT Article 26 is interpreted as a choice between conciliation and arbitration without the exclusion of either, then it could also very well serve as a basis for interpreting the wording of IIAs signed by ECT Member States containing an identical phrase.

Compared to earlier standalone BITS, FTAS now usually include a more comprehensive ISDS procedure for the first stage of the dispute resolution process. In particular, individual articles and provisions are dedicated to providing a detailed description of what the early consultations/negotiations or conciliation/mediation process should entail. These initiatives are a positive step toward promoting more ADR in ISDS. However, the second stage of the dispute resolution remains the same: recourse to ICSID in general, only to ICSID Arbitration Rules, or a choice between ICSID Conciliation and Arbitration Rules. It seems like the drafters of IIAs put in extra effort by defining ADR procedures but relied on the ICSID Convention for interpretation without providing further clarification as to the wording of their own IIAs. In its present form, the ICSID Convention does not provide such clarification. Despite the scale of the recently proposed amendments by ICSID, such amendments only cover the ICSID Rules and do not extend to the ICSID Convention.[99] However, neither the proposed amendment of the ICSID Conciliation Rules nor of the ICSID Arbitration Rules addresses the question of whether the choice between conciliation and arbitration is in exclusion of one another. As Ginkel and Rubins pointed out, the phrase 'conciliation or arbitration' stipulated in IIAs most probably does not limit the choice of the claimant. Instead, when IIAs refer to conciliation and arbitration, such wording expands the choice to both dispute resolution mechanisms. This interpretation is also supported by the text of the ICSID Convention.

Therefore, if conciliation is not explicitly stipulated to be in exclusion of arbitration in the relevant treaty, then such proceedings should be deemed to be allowed by the ICSID Convention. In fact, even when there is a provision that states that conciliation is in exclusion of any other remedy (as in the rare case of the Guatemala-Israel BIT 2006), it should not be read as a singular sentence. If that statement is not supported by the rest of the text of the IIA, then there is room to believe that the 'fork in the road' principle was unintentionally imposed on conciliation.

---

99 Ubilava and Nottage (n 18 in ch 1).

The use of conciliation during the second stage is rare. Thus, case law cannot assist with how the choice between conciliation and arbitration is to be made. The first known treaty-based investor-State conciliation initiated under ICSID is *Xenofon Karagiannis v Republic of Albania* and invokes the Albania-Greece BIT (1991). The text of that BIT provides for 'conciliation or arbitration': the wording which has caused so much of the ambiguity in interpretation thus far.[100] The same question applies to the most recent investor-state conciliation case under ICSID, between Barrick Niugini and subsidiary Zijin Mining Group, and Papua New Guinea.[101] Article 7 of the China-Papua New Guinea BIT, which is believed to be the underlying treaty of this conciliation case, also incorporates the phrase 'conciliation or arbitration'. It will therefore be interesting to observe what happens once the Commission is constituted, that is, whether the foreign investor retains its right to proceed with an ICSID Arbitration after the conclusion of conciliation proceedings – if the conciliation proves unsuccessful.

4.4 Possible Solutions

The following conclusions can be drawn from this analysis concerning the conflicting interpretations of the choice between conciliation and arbitration.

Consent to conciliation was not intended to be in exclusion of arbitration by the drafters of the ICSID Convention. Therefore, the phrase 'conciliation or arbitration' provided in the ISDS provisions of IIAs should not be perceived as a bar to arbitration as long as there is an existing dispute between the parties that was not resolved by conciliation.

Consent to the ICSID Arbitration Rules in the ISDS provisions of IIAs should not be interpreted as excluding conciliation. Arbitration as a binding dispute resolution mechanism yields final awards. The objective of Article 26 of the ICSID Convention was not to exclude conciliation. Instead, its purpose was to ensure that claimants would not take their already resolved dispute, in which there was a binding and final award, to domestic courts or vice versa. When analysing other parts of the ICSID Convention and Rules, as well as the nature of conciliation and supplementary means of interpretation such as the ECT, it becomes obvious that consent to arbitration does not preclude a party from initiating conciliation. Moreover, in a case where conciliation is initiated first,

100 *Xenofon Karagiannis v Republic of Albania* (n 2).
101 Charlotin (n 3).

if the dispute between the parties was not settled, they would still have access to arbitration.

Consent to the ICSID Convention, in general, should be interpreted as consent to all the dispute resolution mechanisms under the auspices of ICSID. This is because there is nothing in the ICSID Convention or its Rules that denies the parties access to both the conciliation and arbitration rules of procedure.

It is possible to eliminate the ambiguities associated with the use of the ICSID Conciliation Rules by amending relevant areas of international investment law. There are two ways to do so:

(1) make relevant changes to the ICSID Convention and Rules; and/or
(2) make relevant changes to the wording of ISDS clauses in individual IIAS.

4.4.1 *Making Changes to the Convention and Rules*

Amendments to the ICSID Convention could entail two approaches. One is inserting some additional language within Article 26 of the ICSID Convention, which would clarify that arbitration is not in exclusion of conciliation and/or other amicable dispute resolution mechanisms. This is to also take into consideration the new ICSID Mediation Rules, which the parties of the dispute are entitled to have access to at any time before or during arbitration proceedings. The updated Article 26 would read as follows:

> Consent of the parties to arbitration under this Convention shall, unless otherwise stated, be deemed consent to such arbitration to the exclusion of any other remedy ***except for conciliation and other amicable dispute resolution mechanisms.*** A Contracting State may require the exhaustion of local administrative or judicial remedies as a condition of its consent to arbitration under this Convention.

The second area of amendment could be the addition of a new article to of the ICSID Convention (which concerns conciliation), or the addition of a sentence to Chapter 3 any of the existing articles in that chapter. The sentence, or the article, would clearly state that recourse to conciliation before or during arbitration is not a bar to subsequent arbitration if the conciliation proceedings are unsuccessful and the dispute is not resolved. It would be necessary to make an identical or similar addition to Chapter 4 of the ICSID Convention, which concerns arbitration.

The problem with amending the ICSID Convention, however, is that a majority of two-thirds of its member States is required for any change to be adopted.[102] Even after having the support of the majority, the amendment would need to be ratified, accepted, or approved, conditional upon the individual regulations of each of the Contracting States.

A less complex procedure is required to make amendments to the ICSID Arbitration and Conciliation Rules. Additional provisions could be added to the Rules, which could clarify that conciliation is not in exclusion of arbitration and vice versa. The only possible downfall of amending the Rules is that the controversy associated with Article 26 of the ICSID Convention may remain. This is because, on the one hand, the new articles of both the Arbitration and Conciliation Rules would state that they are not in exclusion of one another unless the dispute has been successfully resolved. Yet, on the other hand, Article 26 of the ICSID Convention would still mandate the same: that consent to arbitration would be deemed in exclusion of any other remedy. However, even with the existing wording of both the Convention and Rules, it can be argued that conciliation is most likely not included in the exclusive list of 'any other remedy'. Moreover, if the Rules specifically stipulate that arbitration is not in exclusion of conciliation as well as other amicable dispute resolution mechanisms, then both Article 26 of the Convention and the new amended Rules could be read and interpreted as one. By doing this, the Rules would fill the gap in Article 26 of the ICSID Convention. Therefore, making changes to the ICSID Rules would only produce positive results, with less hassle. However, amending the ICSID Convention along with the Rules would need the involvement of multiple States. And ensuring such involvement would require a colossal effort.

As determined by this study, consent to the UNCITRAL Arbitration Rules in IIAs does not pose actual interpretation problems. This is stipulated in Article 1 of the UNCITRAL Conciliation Rules:

> (1) These Rules apply to conciliation of disputes arising out of or relating to a contractual or other legal relationship where the parties seeking an amicable settlement of their dispute have agreed that the UNCITRAL Conciliation Rules apply.

Even when there is no explicit consent to the UNCITRAL Conciliation Rules, nothing precludes the parties from commencing conciliation proceedings at any time during their dispute, if the parties agree. Therefore, amendments to the UNCITRAL Rules would not be necessary.

---

102 The ICSID Convention (n 6 in ch 1) art 66.

4.4.2 *Making Changes to IIAs*

Another way to eliminate the issues associated with conciliation would be to clarify the correlation between conciliation and arbitration in ISDS clauses that provide consent to ICSID and UNCITRAL dispute settlement mechanisms. This could be achieved by adding relevant explanatory paragraphs to the ISDS clauses, such as:

(1) nothing precludes the parties from initiating conciliation or any other ADR mechanism at any time during the dispute; and/or
(2) choosing one of conciliation and arbitration does not exclude the other as long as the dispute remains unresolved.

This process would only require the involvement of two States at a time. Reaching agreements on this matter would probably be easier between two States compared to negotiations between multiple member States, in the case of ICSID. Nevertheless, it would require renegotiation of over three thousand existing BITs. This would be massive in scale, and it could take years for all of them to be updated and ultimately impact the ISDS process. More on possible ways forward is presented in Chapter 6.

The issue of conflicting interpretations of ISDS clauses in IIAs will take time to resolve. It may be years before a unified approach is put in place by those wishing to remove any remaining obstacles to investor-state conciliation. Meanwhile, the Singapore Convention on Mediation is a promising step towards encouraging more ADR in ISDS. Recent incentives of ICSID are also directed towards facilitation of the increased use of mediation in investor-state disputes. Once implemented in practice, both developments may, indeed, prove to be successful in promoting increased use of mediation and conciliation in investor-state disputes. But it is also possible for the rate of recourse to investor-state conciliation to remain low unless the source for conflicting interpretations of the choice between conciliation and arbitration is eliminated, despite the prospect of enforceability of settlement agreements promised by the Singapore Convention on Mediation.

4.5 Conclusion

Over the decades, it has been believed that investor-state conciliation was underutilised due to the non-enforceability of any resulting settlement agreement. This belief has now extended to the argument that having relevant procedural rules in place and improving enforceability for settlement agreements will be enough to warrant the popularisation of ISM – therefore, the need for mandatory ISM disappears. This chapter challenged that argument by instead advancing a hypothesis that the reason for the underutilisation of investor-state conciliation is embedded in the wording of advance consents to ISDS that are incorporated into various treaties. The current common ISDS formulation may mistakenly suggest that there is a 'fork in the road' when it comes to the choice between conciliation and arbitration, with one being to the exclusion of the other. This interpretation has consequently resulted in the obvious preference of arbitration over conciliation. Therefore, it is fair to assume that such ambiguously worded advance consents will continue to have a negative impact on the prospects of conciliation in ISDS regardless of recent incentives for promoting more ADR mechanisms.

Nevertheless, the preference for arbitration over conciliation (and other ADR mechanisms) is not solely caused by the advantage arbitral awards have over settlement agreements by being enforceable, nor the attribution of the 'fork in the road' principle to the choice between conciliation and arbitration. There exist some common arguments, or rather misconceptions, that settlement agreements reached through ADR proceedings are less attractive compared to arbitral awards.[103] The validity of these arguments will be examined in the following chapter.

103 Ubilava (n 274 in ch 3).

CHAPTER 5

Empirical Analysis of the Validity of Arguments against Mandatory ISM

5.1 Introduction

There are many arguments against mandatory ISM as a pre-condition to ISA, and they are widely accepted as valid among most legal commentators and practitioners. Some of these arguments, while plausible in theory, lack any empirical support. The fact is that the misconceptions applied to mediation can also be attributed to any dispute resolution mechanism which results in a settlement agreement, including, for example, negotiation, consultation, and conciliation. Yet, these critiques are mostly set forward as arguments against mandatory ISM.

According to one set of arguments (or misconceptions) against mandatory ISM, not all disputes can be settled through dispute resolution mechanisms that conclude with a settlement agreement instead of an award or a court decision. These critiques are predominantly representative of a respondent state's perspective and difficulties associated with settlements from such a state's viewpoint:

- the unwillingness of a respondent state to look weak if they settle and the fear of being accused of admitting guilt;
- the difficulty with determining an authority to settle on behalf of a sovereign state;
- reluctance of state representatives to be responsible for the terms of settlement agreements and therefore accountable to the public;
- the lack of understanding how disputes with non-monetary claims can be settled between a foreign investor and a sovereign state.

Another set of common misconceptions applies to the nature of settlements, such as, for example, arguments that settlements pay less compared to what claimants would be awarded if they had won the case, or that settlements are used with sinister intentions-to avoid the transparency requirements of arbitration and keep disputes secret. Consequently, mediation is not seen as an appropriate dispute resolution mechanism for mandatory application in the ISDS regime, for which transparency and public accountability are key.

For some readers, the idea of mandatory mediation could also raise the question of the party autonomy and whether this fundamental tenet of mediation

 | DOI:10.1163/9789004532540_006

would be lost if it became a mandatory pre-condition to arbitration.[1] However, this is the least concerning argument against mandatory ISM. This is because, the party autonomy can be maintained even in the compulsory setting, similarly to ISA. In their agreement to mediate, which can be a separate agreement or be part of an ISDS clause in an IIA, parties can still preserve flexibility by choosing, in advance, the mediation forum and mediation rules as well as an agreed list of mediators. Moreover, mandatory format of ISM does not mean the parties will be forced into settlement and give up the consensual nature of mediation.[2] The compulsory element applies to the initiation and engagement in mediation as a prerequisite to arbitration. This said, the final outcome of the mediation process and the decision to settle (or not to settle) would still fully belong to the parties. Therefore, the risk of sacrificing party autonomy for mandatory ISM is considerably low.

Unlike the critiques of ISA that have been supported by an extensive body of empirical studies, arguments against mandatory ISM, while plausibly valid, are only hypothetical by nature. They are largely based on anecdotes and the subjective assumptions of various commentators and lack empirical evidence. This is because very little is known about investor-state disputes that resolve through ADR mechanisms such as mediation and conciliation. Mediated investor-state disputes are not recorded in any repository and mostly take place behind closed doors. While most ISA cases become known once registered, one can only speculate on mediated investor-state disputes that never escalated to arbitration because they were resolved amicably. Besides, it is also interesting and, indeed, intriguing to know how many disputes that eventually end up in ISA have initially been unsuccessfully mediated.[3] The lack of information on mediated investor-state disputes has prompted subjective assumptions against its prospective mandatory inclusion in ISDS among certain segments of legal scholars and practitioners, but these theories have not been tested, and therefore are not necessarily empirically justified.

The only dataset that can be used to empirically examine investor-state disputes that settle through ADR mechanisms is that of disputes that have already been registered for arbitration but settled before the tribunal rendered its final

1 James Peter, 'Med-Arb in International Arbitration' (1997) 8 *American Review of International Arbitration* 83.

2 Dorcas Quek Anderson, 'Supporting party autonomy in the enforcement of cross-border mediated settlement agreements: A brave new world or unchartered territory?' (2018) Max Planck Institute Luxembourg Summer School-International Association of Procedural Law Summer School.

3 Salacuse (n 12 in ch 1).

award.[4] Not all ISA cases are concluded with win-lose outcomes. In fact, a case can be concluded through a settlement agreement or be discontinued without reaching a settlement. Such cases can be examined to determine the validity of common critiques against mandatory ISM. Critics claim that due to certain characteristics of ISM, this dispute resolution mechanism would not be compatible with ISDS in a mandatory format. Mediation shares these heavily criticised characteristics with other ADR dispute resolution mechanisms that also result in settlement agreements (negotiations, consultations, and conciliation). Hence, the problem is not as much with mediation itself as it is with dispute resolution mechanisms that result in settlement agreements. Therefore, regardless of which dispute resolution mechanism was used by the parties to reach settlement agreements during ongoing arbitration proceedings, examining such settlements can provide insight into how the abovementioned characteristics apply to actual investment disputes.

Four research questions are examined here that correspond with the major critiques of ISM (or, more broadly, critiques of ADR mechanisms that result in settlement agreements in ISDS): (1) Would mandatory ISM be futile because certain types of investor-state disputes cannot be resolved through settlement agreements? (2) Would mandatory ISM contribute to secret outcomes because amicable settlements impede transparency? (3) Would mandatory ISM be a waste of time because settlements pay less compared to what investors are awarded when they win? (4) Has the non-enforceability of settlement agreements been a problem in practice? Each research question is examined separately, first through a descriptive analysis of the relevant data, then by a more involved econometric regression method.

The findings offer important contributions to the literature on empirical analysis of ISM. The research approach used in this empirical analysis could serve as a platform for regaining trust in the ADR mechanism in ISDS and promoting mandatory ISM as a pre-condition to ISA.[5]

This chapter provides a review of similar empirical methodologies of previous studies in the field, albeit noting that those studies focus on ISA, not mediation. It also presents the data and methodology used for the empirical analysis. The chapter then examines the four arguments against mandatory

4 A dispute also becomes public knowledge when it is registered under the ICSID Conciliation Rules. However, due to the insufficient number of such conciliated cases – 12 cases so far – empirically analysing them would not provide reliable results.

5 Nancy Welsh, 'Mandatory Mediation and Its Variations' in Susan Franck and Anna Joubin-Bret (eds), *Investor-State Disputes: Prevention and Alternatives to Arbitration II* (UNCTAD 2011) 108.

ISM and discusses the key findings of the empirical analysis for each research question followed by a conclusion.

5.2 Previous Empirical Studies

While much has been discussed about mandatory ISM and its applicability to investment disputes given the many peculiarities of those disputes, very few of these discussions have been based on empirical evidence. In fact, due to the limited access to information on mediated investment disputes, any arguments are either based on narrow empirical analyses, such as questionnaires disseminated in limited circles, or on opinions of commentators without further empirical support.[6]

A more sizable body of empirical studies is dedicated to (1) the outcomes of investment disputes (more generalised); and (2) certain aspects of investment arbitration outcomes (more specific). None of the studies, however, applies rigorous empirical analysis to evaluate whether the many critiques posed against ADR mechanisms in ISDS are supported by the data.

It has not been long since an empirical approach was first applied to investment disputes. Franck was one of the first scholars to employ empirical analysis of investor-state disputes and awards.[7] The 2007 study examined publicly available awards of treaty-based investor-state disputes before 1 June 2006 to determine the validity of seven claims about ISA. While this was the first empirical study of its kind, it was limited to only 52 final awards. That number did not include discontinued and settled outcomes. Franck's approach is very similar to the one used in this analysis, which examines four research questions and evaluates their validity. However, unlike the empirical analysis conducted by Franck, the empirical analysis presented in this chapter investigates claims against ISM instead of claims against ISA, and also employs econometric regression models in addition to descriptive statistics.

In 2014, another descriptive analysis was conducted with a similar aim but different focus: to evaluate whether legitimacy critiques against ISA were supported empirically.[8] The study analysed a bigger sample, consisting of 147 known, treaty-based ISA cases that were fully or partially resolved between

6 Chew, Reed and Thomas (n 28 in ch 1).

7 Franck (n 84 in ch 3). See also Susan Franck, 'Development and Outcomes of Investment Treaty Arbitration' (2009) 50(2) Harvard International Law Journal 435.

8 Daniel Behn, 'Legitimacy, Evolution, and Growth in Investment Treaty Arbitration: Empirically Evaluating the State-of-the-Art' (2015) 46(2) Georgetown Journal of International Law 389.

September 2011 and 2014. While Behn's research did not exclude from analysis discontinued and settled cases, it did not address the critiques of ISM, because its focus was ISA rather than ISM.[9] However, in evaluating the critiques of investment treaty arbitration, the majority of the variables that Behn examined data against correspond with those used in the current empirical analysis; for example the average length of the dispute resolution process, distribution of outcomes per industry, the size of awarded amounts, the impact of the disputants' development status on the outcomes, and questions regarding transparency. Therefore, while the aim of Behn's study does not align with that of the present study, the approach of evaluating critiques through empirical analysis is similar.

Also relevant is a 2015 paper by Franck and Wylie.[10] Compared to Franck's previous empirical works, this paper was a more comprehensive empirical analysis of international investment arbitration outcomes. The study examined win/loss outcomes and averages of claimed and awarded amounts using a descriptive analysis. It then used regression analysis to predict outcomes of investment treaty arbitrations. While this study included settled and discontinued outcomes in its database, these outcomes were not analysed individually against the many critiques of ADR mechanisms in ISDS. This is because the focus of Franck and Wylie's research was not on ADR, but rather on investment treaty arbitration.

In a 2017 study, Remmer investigated the outcomes of investment treaty arbitrations through econometric analysis.[11] Remmer's study examined five hypotheses to reassess the factors impacting the outcomes of investment disputes. Out of these five hypotheses, only one referred to settlements: whether disputes in certain industries were more likely to be concluded through settlements rather than through other outcomes. The findings of the study suggested that disputes with infrastructural investments were more likely to be settled whereas oil, gas and mining had no significant impact on outcomes.

Two very similar empirical studies researched a specific area of investment arbitration outcomes – secrecy. The 2016 article by Hafner-Burton, Steinert-Threlkeld, and Victor uses a rigorous econometric analysis to examine

9 Ibid.

10 Susan Franck and Lindsey Wylie, 'Predicting Outcomes in Investment Treaty Arbitration' (2015) 65(3) Duke Law Journal 494.

11 Karen Remmer, 'The Outcomes of Investment Treaty Arbitration: A Reassessmen' in Lisa E Sachs, Lise Johnson and Columbia Center on Sustainable Investment (CCSI) (eds), *Yearbook on International Investment Law and Policy 2015–2016* (8th ed, Oxford University Press, 2017) 144.

transparency and patterns of secrecy in international investment arbitration.[12] Their study focused on undisclosed arbitration awards and pre-award settlements with the goal of identifying the factors that may have influenced disputants' decisions to keep their outcomes secret. The study found that (a) investment disputes in industries that were coded as long-lived (for example construction, mining and electricity) were more likely to be kept secret compared to disputes in short-lived investments (for example finances, telecom and tourism); and (b) previous public losses had an impact on a state's decision to keep their ongoing cases secret. The study, however, was limited to outcomes (awards and settlements) that were undisclosed; the empirical analysis did not include outcomes that were not secret. Yet including such outcomes could have provided a broader picture on whether the independent variables the authors examined had a similar impact on outcomes that were public. Moreover, the study was limited to treaty-based disputes under ICSID, which further narrowed the sample of the analysis.

A 2017 empirical study by Hafner-Burton, Puig and Victor with an even narrower scope of inquiry examined the secrecy of settled investment disputes.[13] This further reduced the sample of investment disputes. They found that factors influencing secrecy also influenced settlements. According to their study, the majority of all ICSID cases with undisclosed outcomes were settlements. However, when examining the dependent variable (secret), they did not include settlement as one of the independent variables. Doing so would have provided information on whether settlements influence secrecy instead of arriving at this conclusion indirectly – the factors influencing secrecy were somewhat similar to the factors influencing settlements. Therefore, the findings of this study may not be enough to make an undisputed empirical claim that settlements are directly associated with undisclosed outcomes.

For the past decade, academics have tried to tackle the many critiques of ISA through empirical studies, whether by means of simple descriptive analysis or using more rigorous econometric methods. The focus of empirical research on ISA is understandable since treaty-based arbitration has been under the spotlight for the past decade. Now, as the focus is shifting to the subject of ISM and, more generally, towards the role and applicability of ADR mechanisms in ISDS, it becomes possible, and indeed highly desirable, to examine some of the pressing questions through similar empirical tools.

12 Emilie M Hafner-Burton, Zachary C Steinert-Threlkeld and David G Victor, 'Predictability Versus Flexibility: Secrecy in International Investment Arbitration' (2016) 68(3) World Politics 413.

13 Hafner-Burton, Puig and Victor (n 144 in ch 3).

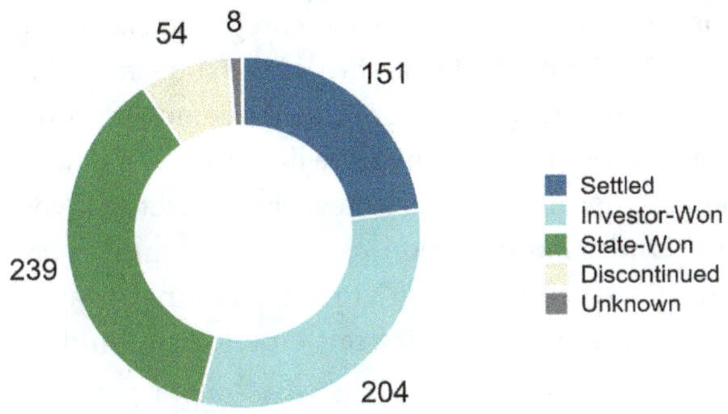

FIGURE 3 Outcomes of concluded investor-state arbitration cases

5.3 Data and Methodology

This chapter presents the analysis of 656 registered, treaty-based ISA cases that were concluded by 31 December 2019. The data used for conducting the empirical study were collected from several sources, such ICSID's database, the UNCTAD database, IAReporter, and italaw.[14] The data suggest that parties have been settling investor-state disputes more often than is commonly believed.[15] By the end of 2019, almost a quarter of concluded ISA cases had been amicably settled (see Figure 3). The finding that settlements are not rare in ISDS indicates that dispute resolution mechanisms that result in settlements are normally applicable to investor-state disputes, as they are to arbitration.[16] While it is unknown which ADR mechanism the parties used to reach settlement agreements – they may have used direct negotiations or even employed the services of a neutral third-party such as a mediator – the fact remains that a concluded settlement agreement was deemed acceptable by the disputants to resolve their investor-state dispute.

The cases presented in the data include the following outcomes: investor-won (204), state-won (239), settled (151), discontinued (54), and unknown

14 ICSID, 'Search Cases', available at <https://icsid.worldbank.org/cases/case-database>; UNCTAD, 'Investment Policy Hub' (n 2 in ch 1); IAReporter, 'News Headlines', available at <https://www.iareporter.com/>; Italaw, 'Newly Posted Awards, Decisions & Materials', available at <https://www.italaw.com/>.

15 Mark Clodfelter, 'Why Aren't More Investor-state Treaty Disputes Settled Amicably?' in Susan Franck and Anna Joubin-Bret (eds), *Investor-State Disputes: Prevention and Alternatives to Arbitration II* (UNCTAD 2011) 38.

16 Ibid.

outcomes (8). For the purposes of this analysis, a case is categorised as won by an investor when the final award determines the liability of the state, regardless of the amount of damages awarded to the investor. A case is deemed as won by a state when the arbitral tribunal does not find the state liable, as well as when it is dismissed on jurisdictional grounds. A case is categorised as settled when the arbitral proceedings are terminated based on party settlement.[17] A case is categorised as discontinued pursuant to a failure to act, a failure to pay the arbitration, or when there is no evidence of party settlement as grounds for termination.[18]

Based on their common economic characteristics, cases are grouped into five industry sectors: resources, infrastructure, manufacturing, finance, and other (Table 2).[19] They are further grouped into two broader categories – short-lived and long-lived – depending on the type of investment. For the purposes of this analysis, the short-lived industry group consists of economic sectors provided under the finance, manufacturing, and other industry groups.[20] The long-lived industry group consists of economic sectors with a 'long-term investment interest'. What constitutes such an interest is determined by how difficult it would be for an investor to retrieve all or a significant portion of its sunk costs. For example, when an investment is made in the infrastructure industry, removing material improvements may not be an easy task. The same goes for the resources industry, which may require the installation of special equipment for purposes such as mining or quarrying.[21] It also reflects on whether investors had long-term or short-term interests attributed to their investment to maintain their existing investment relationship with the state.

Each of the four research questions are first assessed using descriptive statistics followed by a regression-based analysis of the data. The descriptive analysis provides a brief summary of the data and a general overview of the

17 ICSID Arbitration Rules (n 107 in ch 3) rr 43 and 44; ICSID Additional Facility Rules (n 142 in ch 3) arts 49 and 50; UNCITRAL Arbitration Rules (n 108 in ch 3) art 34(1); UNCITRAL Arbitration Rules (2010) (n 139 in ch 3) art 36(1).

18 See the corresponding articles of the ICSID Arbitration Rules (n 107 in ch 3), ICSID Administrative and Financial Regulations (n 141 in ch 3), and UNCITRAL Arbitration Rules (2010) (n 139 in ch 3). Cases in which the proceedings were terminated under r 44 of the ICSID Arbitration Rules (n 107 in ch 3), but for which there was no indication of the party settlement, were individually coded as Discontinued.

19 Table 2 uses classifications based on the list of economic sectors and their codes provided in International Standard Industrial Classification of All Economic Activities (ISIC), UN Doc ST/ESA/STAT/SER.M/4/Rev.4, 2008.

20 Hafner-Burton, Steinert-Threlkeld and Victor (n 12).

21 Ibid; Remmer (n 11); Behn (n 8); Sergio Puig and Anton Strezhnev, 'The David Effect and ISDS' (2017) 28(3) European Journal of International Law 731.

patterns. The regression analysis further examines the possible relationship between the variables of interest by controlling multiple impacting factors and thereby leading to more accurate findings.

TABLE 2 Economic sectors and industry groups

Industry group/name	Economic sector	Sector code
Long-lived investments		
Resources	Agriculture	A
	Mining and quarrying	B
Infrastructure	Electricity, gas, steam and air conditioning supply	D
	Water supply; sewerage, waste management and remediation activities	E
	Construction	F
	Transportation and storage	H
	Information communication	J
Short-Lived Investments		
Manufacturing	Manufacturing	C
Finance	Financial and insurance activities	K
Other	Wholesale and retail trade; repair of motor vehicles and motorcycles	G
	Accommodation and food service activities	I
	Real estate activities	L
	Professional, scientific and technical activities	M
	Administrative and support service activities	N
	Public administration and defence, compulsory social security	O
	Human health and social work activities	Q
	Arts, entertainment and recreation	R

Note: Industries P (Education), S (Other services and activities) and T (Activities of households as employers; undifferentiated goods- and services-providing activities of household for own use) had zero known ISA cases from the database.

Research question 1 investigates whether patterns can be identified in ISA cases that would suggest that disputes with certain characteristics make them unsuitable to be settled amicably. The binary dependent variable here is *Settlement,* which indicates whether an ISA was settled or concluded through other outcomes.

Research question 2 examines whether amicable settlements impede transparency. This research question is addressed with two regression models. In the first model, the binary dependent variable takes on one when the case transparency status is given as *Public*. That is, when both the final award/settlement agreement *and* the awarded/settled amounts are disclosed. Therefore, this regression model groups the disclosure of outcomes into general categories of fully public versus fully confidential cases. In the second model, the binary dependent variable takes on one when the case transparency status is either *Public* or *Partly Confidential.* This includes fully disclosed outcomes as well as outcomes that were not fully public but had the relevant awarded/settled amounts publicly disclosed. This approach ensures that cases in which the final awarded and settled amounts were made public are differentiated from cases in which sometimes even benchmark information was kept confidential.

Research question 3 examines whether settled outcomes pay less compared to the awarded amounts in investor-won cases. The dependent variable in the regression model is *Pay-out,* measured in billion USD. It represents the dollar value of the amount that a claimant eventually received by either an award or through settlement.

Research question 4 investigates whether the empirical evidence supports the common opinion that non-enforceability of settlement agreements has been problematic. The analysis focuses on how the disputants tackled the non-enforceability of their agreements, which represent simple contracts rather than universally enforceable awards. The expected results of the analysis were that parties would use the opportunity of having an on-going arbitration and have their arbitral awards embody their settlement agreements. The binary dependent variable here takes on one if the settlement agreement is *Not Embedded.* It refers to settlement agreements that were not embedded into arbitral awards, despite the opportunity to be attributed with the enforceability mechanism of arbitral awards.

In all instances, the regression models include the following five independent variables that could affect the dependent variables of interest:

- *Long-Lived Investments:* Often the scale of damage can be determined by the industry, for example, if the initial investment were a short-lived or long-lived investment.[22] Whether an investment is short-lived or long-lived can also be somewhat reflective of the short- or long-term interest an investor may have in maintaining their investment relationship with a respondent state. This variable, coded as a binary variable, comprises infrastructure and resources industry groups.
- *Developing* (*Respondent*) *and Developing* (*Claimant*)*:* The power imbalance between the development levels of an investor's home state and the respondent state can be crucial. State development profiles are grouped into developed and developing economies. The term *Developing* is attributed to countries that belong to low income, lower middle income, or upper middle-income economies, based on the World Bank's classification of countries. High income economies are considered as developed countries.[23]
- *ICSID Rule:* It is of interest to determine whether being part of the ICSID Convention has a different impact on the dependent variable as opposed to other non-ICSID rules, eg. the ICSID AF Rules or UNCITRAL Arbitration Rules. Apart from the different enforcement routes that awards take through ICSID and non-ICSID proceedings, while cases under the ICSID Rules benefit from formal institutional arbitration proceedings, cases under the UNCITRAL Arbitration Rules are commonly conducted through ad hoc proceedings independent from formal institutions. This can constitute a significant impact factor on the dependent variables in each regression model provided in this analysis.
- *Claimed Amount:* The size of the claimed amount can play an important role in the parties' decisions to settle, and to disclose the details of their case. Moreover, there should be a direct relationship between the claimed amount and the pay-out.

Other factors, not included in the regression models, could also be related to the dependent variables in consideration. For example, a certain political climate in a respondent state, or the extent of public interest in a particular case, could impact the progression of a dispute, which although extremely intriguing, would be hard to test for across the 656 ISA cases in the data set. Alternatively, the effect of FDI flows to the respondent state could be considered. Notwithstanding inconclusive and often controversial information

22 Hafner-Burton, Steinert-Threlkeld and Victor (n 12).

23 ICC Moot, 'World Bank List of Economies (June 2017)', available at <http://iccmoot.com/wp-content/uploads/2017/07/World-Bank-List-of-Economies.pdf>.

on FDI,[24] this is an important area of research that goes beyond the scope of this book.

The results of econometric regressions, for four models each associated with the research question posed above, are displayed in Table 3. The subsequent section presents an in-depth empirical analysis of each research question, based on descriptive statistics of the relevant data and the associated regression results provided in this table.

5.4 Common Critiques of Investor-State Mediation – Findings and Discussion

It has been argued that mediation is a voluntary process, and that transforming it into a compulsory automatic step in ISDS would undermine its whole core concept. Besides, the principal argument of mandatory ISM's opponents is that not all investor-state disputes can be mediated. This opinion builds on the fact that, unlike domestic and international commercial disputes, in investment disputes one party is always a state, which implies certain peculiarities.[25] While some disputes may be more suitable for mediation and hence trigger less of its problematic aspects, others may not. Accordingly, the argument is that mediation is not a one-size-fits-all type of dispute resolution mechanism and should not be incorporated as a compulsory, automatic step before arbitration for all investor-state disputes. The purpose of this section is to determine whether this assumption is supported empirically.

5.4.1 *Would Mandatory Investor-State Mediation Be Futile Because Amicable Dispute Settlement Mechanisms Are Unsuitable for Certain Types of Investor-State Disputes?*

In order to address this question, several possible impacting factors of investor-state disputes are analysed empirically. This is to determine whether a pattern can be identified that would support the statement that certain types of investor-state disputes may not be suitable for amicable settlement through mediation. If the findings of the analysis suggest that certain characteristics of a dispute have a negative impact on settlement outcomes, then it could be argued that mediation in a mandatory framework would not be applicable to

24 Armstrong and Nottage (n 197 in ch 3).

25 Reisman (n 27 in ch 1); James Allsop, 'Commercial and Investor-state Arbitrations: the Importance of Recognising their Differences' (16 April 2018) Opening Keynote Address, ICCA Congress Sydney.

TABLE 3 Results of the regression analysis

	Model (1)	Model (2)		Model (3)	Model (4)
Dependent variable	Settled	Transparency		Pay-out	Settled cases that are not embedded
		(a) Public	(b) Public and partly confidential		
Settled		-0.549***	-0.544***	-0.197	
		(0.143)	(0.149)	(0.196)	
Claimed Amount	0.068***	-0.034	0.028	0.383***	
	(0.010)	(0.025)	(0.017)	(0.041)	
Long-lived Investments	0.061*	0.125***	0.061*	-0.068	0.144
	(0.033)	(0.047)	(0.032)	(0.046)	(0.118)
Developing (Respondent)	0.085***	-0.126**	0.020	-0.096	0.048
	(0.032)	(0.053)	(0.035)	(0.088)	(0.113)
Developing (Claimant)	0.021	-0.250***	-0.001	-0.053	-0.189
	(0.055)	(0.071)	(0.039)	(0.102)	(0.138)
ICSID Rule	0.012	0.108**	-0.001	-0.120	0.469***
	(0.035)	(0.046)	(0.028)	(0.118)	(0.085)
Claim×Developing (Respondent)	-0.068***	0.039	-0.027	0.035	
	(0.010)	(0.025)	(0.017)	(0.041)	
Settled×Claimed Amount		0.026	0.043***	0.062*	
		(0.020)	(0.011)	(0.033)	
Settled×Long-lived		-0.098	0.086	0.004	
		(0.117)	(0.129)	(0.104)	
Settled×Developing (Respondent)		-0.022	0.257*	0.140	
		(0.120)	(0.137)	(0.119)	
Settled×Developing (Claimant)		0.091	-0.195	-0.121	
		(0.100)	(0.143)	(0.149)	
Settled×ICSID Rule		0.017	-0.256**	0.108	
		(0.097)	(0.104)	(0.139)	
Number of Obs.	513	513	513	213	95
R^2	0.26	0.75	0.89	0.97	0.81

Note: The pay-out and claimed amounts are in billion USD. In each model, year fixed effects are estimated, but not reported here. The observations are weighted by the number of cases in that year. Heteroscedasticity consistent standard errors are in parentheses. * p<0.1, ** p<0.05, and *** p<0.01.

all investor-state disputes. However, if the analysis does not find a significantly negative impact of any of the examined factors on settlement outcomes, then this would challenge the critique of mandatory ISM.

5.4.1.1 Settling a Case Would Make a State Look Weak and Indicate an Admission of Guilt

Various studies have referred to settlement as an admission of guilt or a sign of weakness from the state's perspective. Initiating mediation or accepting mediation could send the wrong signal to the claimant, suggesting that the respondent state does not have a strong case if the dispute were to then go to arbitration. Consequently, it is argued that countries would not want to look weak or admit to any wrongdoing and, therefore, making ISM mandatory would not serve any good purpose in ISDS. For example, in their article, Welsh and Schneider write:

> While a state can frame an adverse arbitral award as an unfortunate loss that nonetheless requires adherence due to treaty obligations, the state's voluntary settlement that *acknowledges the commission of a wrong* and payment of a substantial sum to the investor has the potential to be a much harder political decision to sell to constituents.[26]

However, it is arguable whether being open to settlement is always seen as an indicator of admitting guilt or having a weak case to argue in arbitration. For example, after amicably settling an ISA case in May 2017, having agreed to pay USD23 million instead of the originally claimed compensation of USD85.5 million, the Bolivian government explained:[27]

> This demonstrates, once again, the willingness of the government of President Morales to fulfill absolutely all its international commitments and to send a signal, also, to the international community that in Bolivia, investors will have absolute security, with absolute transparency and with the best working conditions in order to be able to invest in the country.[28]

---

26 Welsh and Schneider (n 24 in ch 1) 86–87 (emphasis added).

27 *Abertis Infraestructuras SA v Bolivia* (*Settlement Agreement*) (PCA, Case No 2011–14, 11 May 2017).

28 Damien Charlotin and Luke Eric Peterson, 'Bolivia: an Update on Three Investment Treaty Arbitrations (Glencore, Abertis and Quiborax)' (12 May 2017) IA Reporter, available at <https://www-iareporter-com.ezproxy1.library.usyd.edu.au/articles/bolivia-an-update-on-three-investment-treaty-arbitrations/>.

Another example of settlement projecting the exact opposite sentiment to what has been commonly assigned to it is the case of the settlement agreement between Egypt and ArcelorMittal.[29] The Deputy Justice Minister for Arbitration and International Disputes, and the Commissioner of the High Council for International Arbitration of Egypt, noted that 'no party comes out as a loser' when reaching settlement agreements.[30] So this statement against settlement might be a product of personal opinion rather than affirmation of a widespread reality.

Interestingly, this type of interpretation of a state's position only arises when opponents argue against settlement agreements reached via conciliation or mediation. In fact, no such argument has been advanced when disputes are resolved through negotiation/consultations during the first stage of dispute resolution (during the cooling-off periods: from notice of dispute before initiating arbitration). This seems odd considering settlements reached through any of these ADR mechanisms remove the dispute from arbitral proceedings. Besides, if mediation, in a voluntary format, is associated with the abovementioned problematic signals, then making mediation an automatic and integral step of ISDS as a mandatory pre-condition to arbitration could remove such negative connotations. If mediation were a mandatory pre-condition to arbitration, taking part in it would be a compulsory step for both parties if they wished to progress to arbitration – this way states could avoid any further speculation on their decision to participate in such mediation.

5.4.1.2 Difficulty Determining an Authority to Settle on Behalf of a State

Opponents of mandatory mediation argue that it would be problematic for states to determine an authority directly entitled to conclude settlements on their behalf.[31] This difficulty is associated with the layers of bureaucracy and departmentalisation of different bodies of a state.[32] Yet this assumption is not

29 Morosini and Badin (n 192 in ch 3).

30 'Coffee with Moustafa El Bahabety, Deputy Justice Minister for Arbitration and International Disputes and the Commissioner of the High Council for International Arbitration' (10 November 2016) Enterprise, available at <https://enterprise.press/stories/2016/11/10/coffee-with-moustafa-el-bahabety-deputy-justice-minister-for-arbitration-and-international-disputes-and-the-commissioner-of-the-high-council-for-international-arbitration/>.

31 Silvia Constain, 'Mediation in Investor–State Dispute Settlement: Government Policy and the Changing Landscape' (2014) 29(1) ICSID Review 25; Coe (n 235 in ch 3); Reisman (n 27 in ch 1).

32 Welsh and Schneider (n 24 in ch 1).

necessarily based on the actual experience of states, but rather the similar bureaucratic problems that big corporations faced when settling commercial disputes.[33]

Practice shows that several states have adopted regulations that determine representatives with the authority to conclude amicable settlements on the state's behalf regardless of the subject matter.[34] For example, countries like Guatemala and Colombia have begun identifying responsible government agencies whose actions may affect international investment rights protected under IIAs.[35] For their part, the Republic of Korea and the Kingdom of Morocco have both established an investment ombudsmen and specific institutions responsible for settlement through procedures between the foreign investor and the government.[36] Brazil recently concluded Cooperation and Investment Facilitation Agreements (CIFAS); even though the Agreements do not contain an ISDS clause, they provide risk mitigating measures by identifying the state representative with the authority to de-escalate disputes.[37] This is achieved through two channels: an ombudsman institution whose responsibility it is to 'act directly to prevent disputes and to facilitate their resolution in coordination with the competent government authorities and in collaboration with the appropriate private entities'; and by Joint Committees that 'seek consensus and resolve amicably any questions or conflicts regarding the investments of the Parties'.[38]

At an institutional level, the ICSID Mediation Rules require states to nominate the authority to settle a dispute on their behalf. Article 18(4) states that:

> (4) At the first session or within any other period as the mediator may determine, each party shall:
> (a) identify a representative who is authorized to settle the dispute on its behalf; and

33 Reisman (n 27 in ch 1); Titi (n 8 in ch 1).

34 Rodrigo Polanco Lazo, 'Systems of Legal Defence Used by Latin American Countries in Investment Disputes' (2016) 17(4) Journal of World Investment & Trade 562; Nguyen and Vu (n 194 in ch 3).

35 Investor–State Disputes: Prevention and Alternatives to Arbitration (n 10 in ch 1).

36 Ibid.

37 Morosini and Badin (n 192 in ch 3). Cf Geraldo Vidigal and Beatriz Stevens, 'Brazil's New Model of Dispute Settlement for Investment: Return to the Past or Alternative for the Future?' (2018) 19(3) Journal of World Investment & Trade 475.

38 Brazil – Mozambique CIFA (n 193 in ch 3) arts 4(v) and 5; Brazil-Angola CIFA (n 193 in ch 3); Kawharu (n 193 in ch 3).

(b) describe the process that would be followed to implement a settlement.[39]

Just how many states will accept these Rules is unclear, but Article 18(4) is a welcome incentive that could provide a solution to the problem of not having a previously identified authorised representative to amicably settle cases on behalf of a sovereign state.

Thus, while not all countries may have in place appropriate regulations for determining state authority for settlements, it is easily achievable for those who wish to promote settlements, especially though ISM. Moreover, one-fourth of known ISA cases have been resolved based on party settlement, which indicates that countries can and do determine representatives with the authority to settle. This further undermines concerns expressed by some commentators who argued against mandatory ISM, claiming that reaching settlement would be difficult for governments due to the difficulty associated with assigning settlement authority to their representatives. The anecdotal evidence discussed above suggests that some countries have already laid down relevant rules for determining state authority to settle. The ICSID Mediation Rules also indicates an expectation that states should be able to have an identified authority designated for the settlement on its behalf. The quantitative evidence presented further suggests that settlements are certainly quite widely capable of being reached and that in practice a range of government officials have made it possible to agree on settlement terms on behalf of their states. Despite these necessarily general observations, for many countries there may be structural problems for officials to settle – especially for developing countries with political uncertainties, weaker rule of law and higher levels of corruption. Therefore, we might assume that settlement rates should be lower for developing countries[40] However, according to the findings of this study, developing countries in fact have higher settlement rates compared to developed economies (as detailed in the following section). This suggests that the problem may not be as serious as some anticipate. Moreover, in-depth country studies would be needed to draw a more comprehensive picture regarding this matter, which goes beyond the scope of this book.

39 ICSID WP1 – Consolidated Rules (n 19 in ch 1).

40 Reisman (n 27 in ch 1); Titi (n 8 in ch 1) 26; Shirlow (n 17 in ch 1).

5.4.1.3 Shifting the Blame to an Arbitrator Rather than Being Accountable for Settlement Terms

Some commentators contend that the responsibility to amicably settle matters of public importance on behalf of the state can prove to be too burdensome for individual government officials.[41] Due to the sovereign nature of one party to the dispute, making decisions to settle could be difficult for government authorities trying to balance factors such as national security, political accountability, and the economy.[42] When a dispute is resolved by adjudication, the responsibility for the decision is easily shifted to the adjudicator. Thus, government officials taking part in the dispute settlement process can shift the blame to arbitrators for rendering unfavourable awards. Yet, when a state amicably settles a dispute by agreeing on certain terms with a foreign investor, the individual government official, or group of representatives with the authority to settle, may be made personally liable under domestic law for corruption, bribery, or other offences.[43]

For example, at a 2017 ICSID conference titled "Investor-State Mediation: Perspectives from states, Mediators & Practitioners", panellists discussed the results of a survey listing the drawbacks of ISM. According to the conference report, the survey showed that the most prominent drawback for amicable settlements was 'a desire to avoid being seen as voluntarily accepting the responsibility for a potential liability (versus having an external third party impose that liability)'.[44] Another example is the 2017 survey on obstacles of settlements conducted by the National University of Singapore's Centre for International Law, which found that states prefer to shift responsibility for the final decision to an arbitrator rather than be accountable to the public for a voluntary outcome such as amicable settlement.[45]

Assuming this finding is correct, one would expect that personal liability issues of public officials would be more common in developing countries than in countries with better democracies and the rule of law. This is because developing countries, unlike developed economies, have more frequent and drastic changes in their ruling powers. Sometimes, new governments in power prosecute former governments on the basis of alleged unlawful activity or

41 Welsh and Schneider (n 24 in ch 1); Reisman (n 27 in ch 1).

42 Reed (n 27 in ch 1).

43 Salacuse (n 12 in ch 1); Sussman (n 233 in ch 3).

44 ICSID, 'ICSID Hosts Half-Day Event, "Investor-State Mediation: Perspectives from States, Mediators & Practitioners" on June 15' (14 July 2017) News Releases, available at <https://icsid.worldbank.org/en/Pages/News.aspx?CID=243>.

45 Chew, Reed and Thomas (n 28 in ch 1).

corruption. Such unlawful conduct may include settlements that were cumbersome for the state or were (allegedly) concluded by the previous government for private gain. However, not all developing states prosecute their previous government officials, and not all developed economies are immune to corruption. Accordingly, if the fear of personal liability and reluctance to take responsibility were significant impediments to mediation, then one would expect a considerably small number of cases of investor-state settlements in ISDS, especially where the respondent is a developing country.

However, this is not the case. While the exact details of mediated investor-state disputes are unknown, data show that one fourth of 656 known concluded treaty-based ISA cases between the years 1990–2017 were terminated prematurely due to party settlement.[46] In fact, the data suggest that developing states settled approximately 25% of their ISA cases, whereas the settlement rate for developed states was only 17%.[47] Settlements between investors and state governments require: (a) a state representative with the authority to settle; and (b) the responsible state official agreeing to the terms of settlement without shifting blame for the final decision to an arbitrator. And settlements between investors and state governments are not necessarily uncommon. Therefore, the fear regarding political responsibility and public accountability for the terms of a settlement is not an impediment to settlements or ISM.

Because these three critiques are more opinion-based rather than data-driven arguments, examining them would require a detailed analysis of sufficient anecdotal evidence, which falls outside the scope of this empirical study. What can be examined empirically, however, is whether certain characteristics of investor-state disputes make them less suitable for amicable settlement mechanisms. This can be achieved by analysing the existing cases that have been amicably settled and comparing them with the rest of the concluded ISA cases that concluded with outcomes other than settlements.

The first characteristic to examine is the industry in which the investment was made. The industry group can suggest whether cases with long-term investment interests – resources and infrastructure – are more prone to settlement than cases with short-term investment industries (Manufacturing, Finance, and Other). This is because maintaining continuous business relationships may be more beneficial for the disputants than winning the case, which would prematurely disrupt investment relationships. The findings

46 This does not include ISA cases that were discontinued based on grounds other than settlement. The findings are based on the author's own calculations.

47 Based on the author's own calculations.

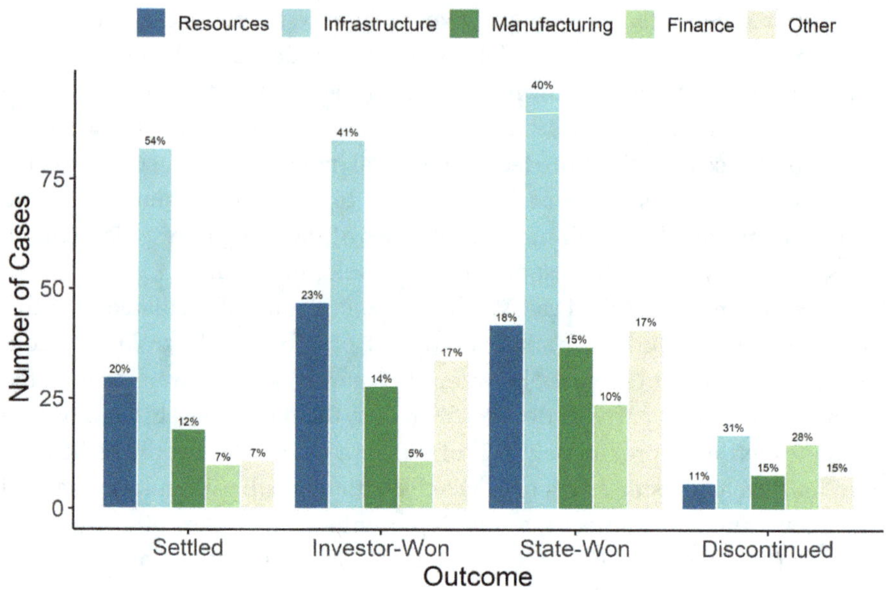

FIGURE 4 Distribution of industries per outcome

could suggest whether the long-lived or short-lived investment interests have an impact on settlement rates. Figure 4 illustrates that every industry group had an ISA case that concluded with party settlement prior to the final arbitral award. Moreover, looking at long- and short-lived investments and their corresponding economic sectors, the data suggest that more than 70% of settled ISA cases took place in long-lived investment industry groups (Resources and Infrastructure).[48]

Another characteristic of a case that could make it incompatible with dispute settlement mechanisms resulting in settlements is the size of the claimed amount. It could help determine whether cases involving higher claims are being settled at lower rates than cases involving smaller claims. The higher the claimed amount, the more the respondent has to offer in order to satisfy the claimant and reach the settlement agreement. This also means that the weight of the decision (size of settlement amount) lies with the state instead of shifting 'blame' for the awarded amount to the tribunal.

As illustrated in Table 4, the data suggest that the average claimed amount for cases that were settled is higher than the average claimed amount for cases that were state-won or discontinued. The average of the claimed amounts

48 Cf Remmer (n 11).

in cases that concluded with settlement is USD1089 million, compared to USD535 million for state-won and discontinued cases. However, the average of the claimed amounts in cases that were won by an investor is slightly higher, at USD1230 million. In addition, I report the median values of the aforementioned. The advantage of median values is that, unlike average values, they are robust to the presence of ISA cases with extremely high claimed amounts, which skews the results. The median claimed amount is more than three times higher for cases that have been settled than for cases that had other outcomes. The median claimed amount for settled cases across all industry groups is USD335 million. The median claimed amount for the 185 investor-won cases analysed is USD118 million, and USD100 million for the 241 state-won and discontinued cases.

The results of the regression model (1) in Table 3 suggest that the bigger the claimed amount, the higher the probability of a settlement outcome when the respondent is a state with a strong economy. More specifically, a USD one billion increase in the claimed amount results in a seven-percentage point increase in the probability of settlement of cases against developed states. However, the effect is largely non-existent for cases against developing states. Therefore, the data suggest that developing countries settle cases with smaller claims more often than developed countries. More specifically, disputes with larger claims (in particular those exceeding USD1.25 billion) are settled by developed respondents more often than developing respondents.

These findings could be explained by two factors. One is the financial factor: as developed economies have better financial capacity; it is no surprise that they settle disputes with large claims more often than their less financially fortunate developing country counterparts. Therefore, for them, it is easier to conclude settlement agreements in disputes that have large claims. The second factor relates to the rule of law and corruption levels: developed economies have a stronger rule of law as well as lower rates of corruption compared to developing countries. This could suggest that state representatives of developed economies with the authority to settle do not have to fear personal or political liability for the legitimacy of the terms of the settlement they conclude on behalf of their governments. Developing respondent states, however, may prefer shifting the 'blame' for the final outcome to independent arbitral tribunals instead of taking responsibility for the terms and size of settlement amounts especially for disputes with significantly larger claims.

Similarly, to Remmer's study, which found that disputes with infrastructure investments increased the likelihood of settlement, the results of this analysis suggest that long-lived investments (which include infrastructure – see Table 2) increase the probability of settlement by approximately six percentage points.

TABLE 4 The rates of claimed amounts in settled vs other outcomes

		Settled	Investor-Won	State-Won & Discontinued
Claimed amounts	Number of cases analysed	94	185	241
	Median claimed amount (USD)	335M	118M	100M
	Average claimed amount (USD)	1089M	1230M	535M
Awarded/ Settled amounts	Number of cases analysed	42	192	
	Median awarded amount (USD)	84M	20M	
	Average awarded amount (USD)	418M	436M	
Ratio between claimed and awarded/ settled amounts	Number of cases analysed	35	178	
	Median award-to-claimed ratio	0.26	0.25	
	Average award-to-claimed ratio	0.31	0.34	

However, Remmer differentiated between the industry sectors and grouped infrastructure separate from oil, gas, and mining due to which this effect was absent for disputes in the latter industry sector.[49] This empirical analysis, however, groups infrastructure together with oil, gas, and mining under long-lived investments. The findings of this study suggest that settling a case may indeed be the preferred route for resolving a dispute where the disputants have long-term investment interests and are keen to preserve ongoing relationships.

5.4.1.4 Mediation Not Suitable for Disputes with Non-pecuniary Claims

Some commentators argue that mandatory ISM would be unsuitable for investor-state disputes with non-monetary claims because settling on

49 Ibid.

non-pecuniary terms would be difficult.[50] These are disputes where the clamant requires the respondent to take legislative, policy, or other action not directly connected to monetary compensation.[51] For example, an authority determined by a state to conclude settlement agreements may not be authorised to agree on certain non-monetary issues that are the prerogative of another branch or body of the government.[52] Yet, curiously, this concern does not seem to bother critics when investor-state disputes without monetary claims are amicably settled in the First Stage through negotiations and consultations.[53] This leaves the impression of targeted criticism aimed against mediation only. Yet mediation may be more appropriate for disputes where claimants seek specific actions from states, instead of compensation.[54] This is because arbitral tribunals are less likely to intervene in the domestic issues of a state and order a respondent to perform certain actions, such as, for example, withdrawing certain legislation or issuing particular licenses. Whereas during a mediation process, parties have more flexibility and a better opportunity to agree on matters that go beyond monetary compensation.[55]

During negotiations for the Singapore Convention on Mediation, the question was raised whether the Convention should only cover mediated settlement agreements with monetary obligations instead of extending to non-pecuniary matters.[56] Imposing restrictions of this nature could have resulted in limiting the innovative approaches and creative solutions to resolving individual disputes. This would have been contrary to the whole essence of mediation. Therefore, the suggestion to exclude mediated settlement agreements with non-pecuniary obligations from the scope of the Convention and to limit that scope to monetary relief was rejected. This decision of UNCITRAL Working Group II demonstrates that mediation is equally suitable for disputes with both monetary and non-monetary relief, and that enforcement of settlement agreements with non-monetary terms is possible.

---

50 Chew, Reed and Thomas (n 28 in ch 1).

51 Reed (n 27 in ch 1).

52 Sussman (n 233 in ch 3); Barton Legum, 'The Difficulties of Conciliation in Investment Treaty Cases: A Comment on Professor Jack J. Coe's "Toward A Complementary Use Of Conciliation In Investor-State Disputes-A Preliminary Sketch"' (2007) 4(1) Transnational Dispute Management, available at <https://www.transnational-dispute-management.com/article.asp?key=963>.

53 The period during which parties are encouraged to settle their dispute amicably before registering that dispute for arbitration proceedings: see Chapter 4.

54 Titi (n 8 in ch 1).

55 Ibid.

56 Schnabel (n 17 in ch 1).

If non-monetary claims were to be an obstacle to successful mediation, then there should be no ISDS agreements on non-pecuniary terms. However, the findings of the empirical analysis suggest not only that settlement agreements have been reached on non-pecuniary terms, but also that such agreements were reached for disputes that initially claimed monetary compensation.

In the dataset, only two cases claimed non-pecuniary relief, and both were won by states. It is, however, different for cases that were concluded on non-pecuniary terms. Specifically, 22 cases in the dataset were concluded on non-monetary terms. Of these, only one was won by an investor; the rest were amicably settled by the parties. Of these 21 amicably settled cases, 17 cases had amounts indicated in their initial claims. That is, even though the initial claimed amount was monetary, the parties agreed on non-pecuniary settlement terms.

5.4.2 *Would Mandatory Investor-State Mediation Contribute to Secret Outcomes Because Amicable Settlements Impede Transparency?*

Over the years, ISA awards have helped shape international standards of treatment by interpreting and refining international law-making generally. This has been achieved through transparent interpretations of the law, which is crucial for investor-state dispute settlement.[57] Relevant reforms have been made to ensure that appropriate levels of transparency are maintained in ISDS. In 2014, the UNCITRAL Rules on Transparency in Treaty-Based investor-state arbitration entered into force. They were followed by the UN Convention on Transparency in Treaty-Based Investor-State Arbitration (the Mauritius Convention on Transparency) in force from 2017. Transparency in ISDS is important not only as a contributor to the formation and development of international investment law but also because of the public interest involved. By contrast, confidentiality is a primary characteristic of mediation, and often its selling point in international commercial dispute resolution. Due to this tension, commentators fear that when marrying these two phenomena into ISM, two things could happen: (1) loss of the principal characteristic that defines mediation and/or (2) sacrifice of the all-important principle of transparency, to maintain confidentiality.[58]

The main argument against settlement in ISDS is that states will use this platform to bypass public scrutiny, retain their reputation, and keep their

57 Reisman (n 27 in ch 1).

58 The International Bar Association (IBA) Investor-State Mediation Rules 2012, for example, prevent ex parte communications. See Micah Burch, Luke Nottage and Brett Williams, 'Appropriate treaty-based dispute resolution for Asia-Pacific commerce in the 21st century' (2012) 35(3) University of New South Wales Law Journal 1013.

allegedly wrongful treatment of foreign investors in the shadows.[59] In practice, things are not quite as the critics would suggest. There is no database that would record the exact or even approximate number of investor-state disputes that have been settled before they reached arbitral institutions. Therefore, hypothetically, for every known, registered, treaty-based ISA case, there may be two or more investor-state disputes that have been settled before escalating to arbitration. The question is: how much do these unknown cases contribute to the development of international investment law and how do we ensure transparency?

There is, in fact, no way of accessing and regulating this area of ISDS as such settlements happen behind closed doors. Yet there is a way to introduce some level of transparency and regulation to such ADR practices. Significant steps have already been taken towards making ISM more attractive to the parties, including procedural rules provided by the ICSID Mediation Rules and the enforcement mechanism warranted by the Singapore Convention on Mediation. But for the disputants to benefit from these instruments, they will have to conduct their mediation process in the open. While the terms of their settlement may remain undisclosed if the parties so choose, the fact of ISM would become known to the public. Therefore, while ISM allows the parties to maintain confidentiality of their settlement terms, promoting and encouraging it through formal steps could provide further insight into this dispute resolution mechanism.

For the purposes of this empirical study, transparency is divided into three categories. This allows differentiation between the varying levels of disclosure of information during the dispute resolution process:[60]

1. *Confidential*: Merits, final award/settlement agreement and amounts are confidential, only the outcome is public; [61]
2. *Partly Confidential*: Merits and final award/settlement agreement are confidential, only outcome and amounts are public; and
3. *Public*: merits, final award/settlement agreement, outcome and amounts are public.

---

59 Hafner-Burton, Puig and Victor (n 144 in ch 3).

60 The term 'transparency' refers to the disclosure status of the (a) final award or settlement agreement and (b) award or settlement amount. For this reason, the analysis does not differentiate between more categories of transparency and confidentiality based on individual procedural steps, as this falls outside the scope of the book.

61 The term 'outcome' in this context refers to the outcome of the case; whether the case was won by an investor or a state, whether it was settled by the parties, or whether it was discontinued.

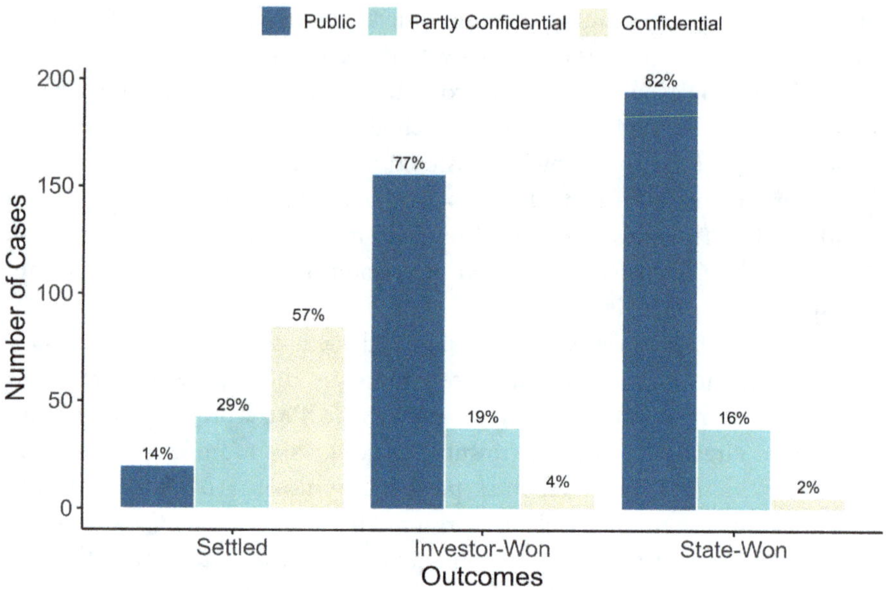

FIGURE 5 Transparency of outcomes

The data, as illustrated in Figure 5, suggest that in 43% of settled cases, the final outcome and settlement amounts were disclosed (*Partly Confidential* and *Public* cases).

Notably, 14% of settled outcomes were fully public. In 29% of cases, dispute proceedings were kept confidential, but the settlement outcome and the settlement amount were public. This figure is considerably lower compared to investor-won and state-won cases where awarded amounts are typically disclosed (96% and 98%, respectively). While it is clear that settled cases have high rates of undisclosed proceedings – 57% remain fully confidential – ISM is not the only dispute resolution mechanism through which parties can keep the details (for example awarded amount) of their dispute confidential. Approximately 23% of investor-won and 18% of state-won cases remained confidential. While these cases had varying levels of confidentiality, the merits and the text of the final award were kept undisclosed.

It is also important to note that while the rates of settlement and confidential outcomes had been decreasing over the past decade or so, since 2013, the trajectory of confidential outcomes has changed, widening the gap between settled cases and confidential cases (see Figure 6). This suggests that the outcomes of ISA cases continue to be undisclosed without necessarily being concluded with settlements.

This somewhat disproves the argument that mediation is a threat to transparency. Even in ISA cases, confidentiality can be maintained by the parties to some degree. The same could apply to ISM cases. If the disputants know that mediation is an inevitable step at some stage of their dispute, they will not waste their time mediating behind closed doors and will instead employ the benefits of either the ICSID Mediation Rules or the Singapore Convention on Mediation through mandatory mediation. Therefore, mandating mediation as a pre-condition to arbitration could extract amicable settlements from a confidential setting and place them in a formally regulated public sphere.

In this section, the research question was tackled with two regression models (see Table 3, Model 2(a) and 2(b)). Both regression models examine whether and to what extent certain factors impact the probability of the disclosure of ISA outcomes but differentiate between the disclosure categories. Two versions of the dependent variable were considered: (a) *Public*, which takes on a value of one if the awards/settlement agreement and the awarded/settlement amounts of a case were public, and zero otherwise; and (b) *Public and Partly Confidential*, which takes on a value of one if on top of fully public cases the awarded/settlement amounts of a case (otherwise confidential) are also known, and zero otherwise.

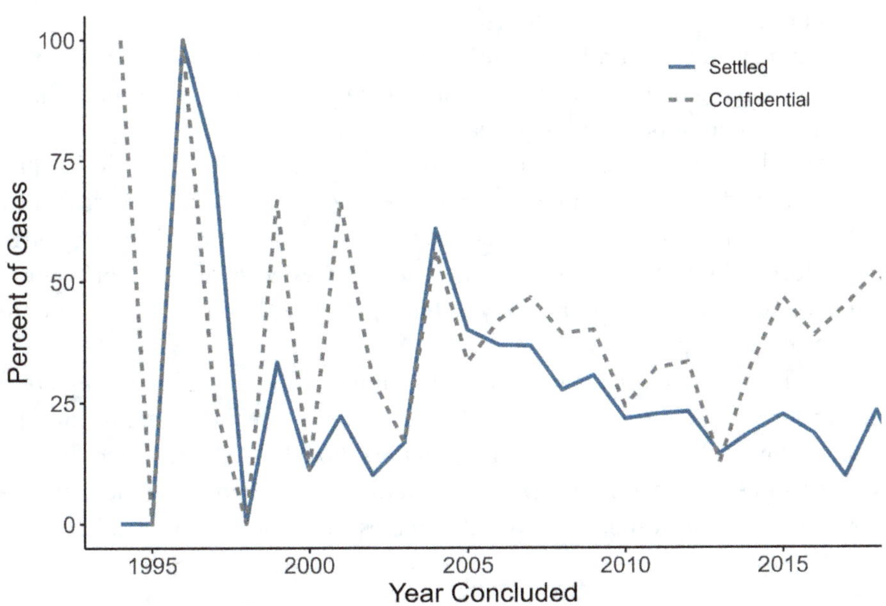

FIGURE 6 Settled and confidential outcomes in timeline

The findings of model 2(a) indicate that cases that settle are 55% less likely to be made public compared to non-settled cases. This accords with the findings of the descriptive analysis presented earlier.

The regression results further illustrate that ISA outcomes are 13% less likely to be disclosed when the respondent is a developing economy rather than a developed economy. Thus, low- and middle-income countries are more inclined to keep information about investment disputes confidential. This suggests that it is not so much about which dispute resolution mechanism determined the secrecy of the outcome, but rather more about the identity of the disputants.

The empirical analysis also found that cases in long-lived investments that are not settled have higher disclosure rates compared to those involving short-lived investments. Specifically, when an award is rendered for a case with long-lived investments, there is a 13-percentage point higher probability of a fully public award compared to a case with short-lived investments. This effect is largely mitigated for cases that are settled. Therefore, while the relevant industry does not have a significant impact on disclosure rates when disputes are settled, it does affect transparency of other outcomes. This finding goes against the results of the 2016 study by Hafner-Burton, Steinert-Threlkeld and Victor, discussed earlier in Section B of this Chapter, which found that investment disputes in long-lived industries were more likely to be kept secret compared to disputes in short-lived industries.[62] However, the latter study was limited to investor-state disputes under ICSID only.

As expected, cases under ICSID increase the probability of public awards/settlement agreements by almost 11 percentage points. The size of the claimed amount had no impact on the probability of disclosure.

In model 2(b), the results show that settled cases reduce the probability of public settlement amounts by 55 percentage points, which decreases by a further 26 percentage points if such settlements are reached under ICSID. Therefore, while settlements increase the chances of confidentiality, settlements under ICSID are more likely to be kept secret than ICSID AF and non-ICSID settlements.

The findings regarding the impact of claimed amounts and the interaction effect with the economic power of the respondent state are different from the previous model. This is because the previous model (2)(a) examined full disclosure rates, where both the awards/settlement agreements and the amounts were publicly disclosed. However, this regression model examines both: the

62 Hafner-Burton, Steinert-Threlkeld and Victor (n 12).

fully public outcomes and those outcomes where only the awarded/settled amounts were disclosed. Based on the results of this model, a larger claim amount (a positive USD one billion change in claimed amounts) increases the probability of disclosure of the awarded/settled amounts by 26 percentage points when the respondent is a developed state. In other words, developed countries tend to keep disputes with larger claims public compared to developing countries and compared to disputes with smaller claims. Again, this could be caused by the fact that disputes with large claims attract more public scrutiny, and thus state accountability. By contrast, low profile disputes tend to be less noticeable, and so do not require state accountability and therefore remain undisclosed.

5.4.3 *Would Mandatory Investor-State Mediation Be a Waste of Time Because Settlements Pay Less Compared to What Investors Are Awarded When They Win?*

There is a common misconception that settlements pay less compared to what an investor would get if it had won the arbitration. For example, according to Wells, investors rejected every effort of the Indonesian Ministry of State Owned Enterprises and the United States embassy to mediate in the Indonesian Electric Power Case because '[c]onciliation would have meant a smaller award, it appeared, and the investor would have had to continue with a project that is apparently no longer consistent with its new business strategy'.[63] Therefore, opposing the idea of mandatory mediation as a pre-condition to arbitration seems like a reasonable reaction – that is, if the assumption that settlements pay less is true. But looking at the bigger picture, even when investor-state disputes are decided in favour of investors, they rarely live up to the expectations of the claimants. Not only do the claimants not receive the amount they claimed, but they also lose or considerably infringe the benefits of their existing investment.[64] Similarly for the state, even when winning, the procedures are costly and time-consuming and can have a negative impact on reputation.[65]

It is not just the awarded amounts that need to be considered, but tribunal and party expenses also contribute to the excessive costs of ISA. A 2017 study showed that average claimant costs reached USD6,019,000, and average respondent costs totalled USD4,855,000 (see Table 1 in Chapter 3).[66] Mediation and conciliation, on the contrary, cost much less. Therefore, judging only

63 Wells (n 24 in ch 1).
64 Wälde (n 152 in ch 2).
65 Braun (n 244 in ch 3).
66 Hodgson and Campbell (Table 1, n c).

from a costs and expenses perspective, mediation is cheaper than arbitration. Further, when comparing the ratio of awarded-to-claimed amounts with settled-to-claimed amounts, it turns out that settlements do not pay less compared to awarded amounts (Figure 7).

While the assumption that settlements pay less than awards is commonly relied upon when arguing against the necessity of mandatory ISM, it is unclear whether this assumption is supported by empirical evidence. In fact, the assumption is usually either a commentator's personal opinion, or based on one, unique investment dispute. Further, there are hundreds of other investment disputes which could potentially provide contradictory information about the compensation rates of settled-to-claimed amounts versus awarded-to-claimed amounts. Therefore, without the relevant empirical research, the common belief that settlements pay less than awards should not be relied on.

A descriptive analysis of the data suggests that settlement amounts are not in any significant way smaller than awarded amounts. The findings further indicate that settled-to-claimed compensation rates and awarded-to-claimed compensation rates are very similar. Specifically, on average, investors are awarded 31% of their original claim. However, during settlements, investors are on average awarded 34% of their original claim (Figure 7). The medians are quite similar as well: the settled-to-claimed ratio is 26%, and the awarded-to-claimed ratio is 25% for investor-won outcomes (refer to Table 4). Therefore, it can be argued that the assumption that settlements pay less is not supported empirically.

A comparison of the awarded-to-claimed amount rates for investor-won cases and the settled-to-claimed amount rates for settled cases across all five industry groups is revealing. For investor-won cases, on average claimant investors are awarded the most in the finance sector, receiving more than 60% of their originally claimed amount. For settled cases, claimants are paid the most in the manufacturing sector, receiving a little over 56% of their originally claimed amount (Figure 8).

The results of the regression Model (3) (see Table 3) suggest, as expected, that pay-outs are closely linked to the claimed amounts – a positive USD one billion change in the claimed amount is associated with an increase of almost USD0.4 billion in the pay-out. None of the other factors considered appears to have a significant impact on pay-outs.

The robustness checks performed in this empirical analysis take into account the Argentina effect (Annex II). The results of the regression analysis omitting cases against Argentina show little difference from those presented in Table 3, apart from the results of Model 3 (*Pay-Out*). When ISA cases with larger claims are settled, their pay-outs are 14 percentage points lower than

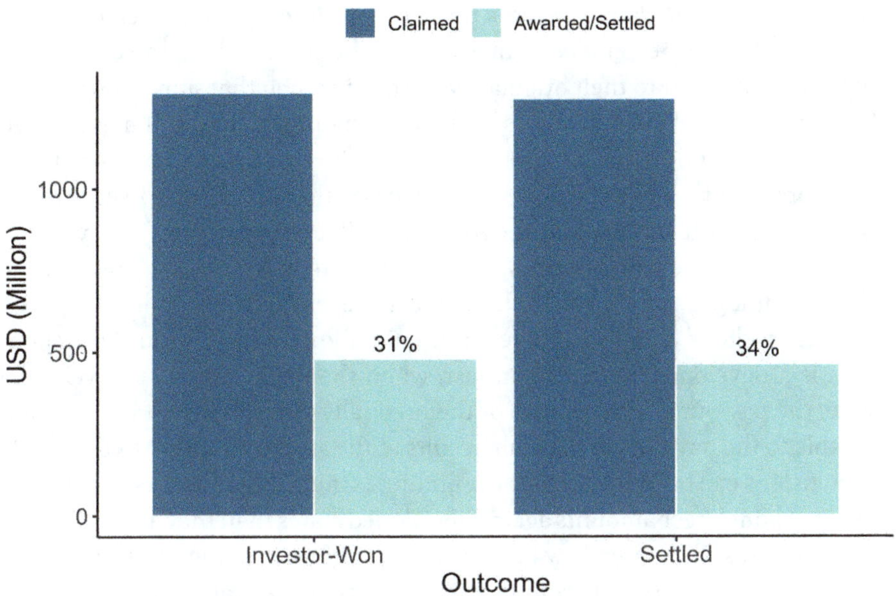

FIGURE 7 The average ratio of awarded/settled-to-claimed amounts

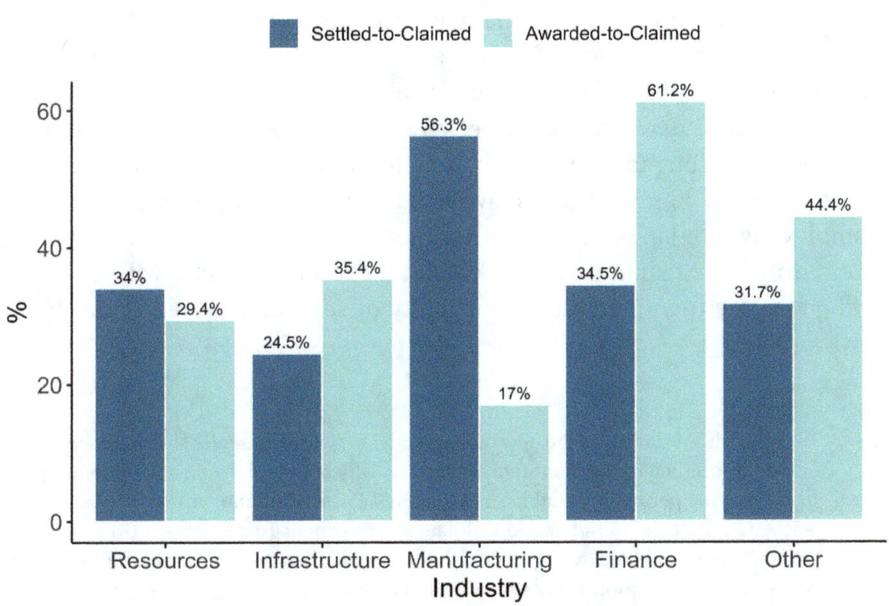

FIGURE 8 The average ratio of awarded/settled-to-claimed amounts per industry group

cases with smaller claims or cases that do not settle. This can mean some of the following: (a) respondent states seem to be more willing to compensate the claimant closer to their original claimed sum when that sum is low; (b) the larger the original claim, the less likely the respondent state will make a high ratio pay-out; and (c) when cases with large claims are won by investors, those investors receive higher pay-outs than in cases that settle. The divergence in the findings with and without the Argentina effect suggests that it may be too early to determine with accuracy whether settlements in fact pay less.

Other findings of Annex II show that for every USD one billion claimed amount, there is an approximately USD0.6 billion pay-out when the respondent is a developed state. By contrast, when the respondent is a developing state, the pay-out is around 40% of the originally claimed sum, which is comparable to the pay-outs in the main results of the study in Table 3. Two possible conclusions can be drawn from these findings. One is that investors (claimants) tend to claim larger amounts against developed states than they are entitled to, as such states will more likely be able to pay compared to their less financially fortunate developing state counterparts. The second is that arbitrators tend to spare developing economies by awarding smaller pay-outs than what would be awarded against stronger economies.

5.4.4 *Has the Non-enforceability of Settlement Agreements Been a Problem in Practice?*

The non-enforceability of settlement agreements was deemed to be the main reason for underutilisation of ADR mechanisms in ISDS, including investor-state conciliation and now mediation.[67] Settlement agreements take the form of a contract, a new agreement between the parties, and parties are often unable or unwilling to comply with the relevant terms. Non-compliance with those terms could give rise to new disputes that would prolong the already complex investor-state dispute settlement process.[68] With the new Singapore Convention on Mediation, it is believed that recourse to ISM will grow as it will guarantee the universal enforceability of settlement agreements.[69] This

---

67 Schwebel (n 6 in ch 4).

68 For example, according to the new Indian Model BIT, local remedies should be exhausted before proceeding to investor-State arbitration, which, overall, could add up to five years to the waiting period. See Prabhash Ranjan and Pushkar Anand, 'Investor State Dispute Settlement in the 2016 Indian Model Bilateral Investment Treaty: Does it Go Too Far?' in Julien Chaisse and Luke Nottage (eds), *International Investment Treaties and Arbitration Across Asia* (Brill Nijhoff 2018) 579; Rubins (n 10 ch 4).

69 Alexander (n 14 in ch 1).

is believed to be enough to promote ISM without the need to have it incorporated as a mandatory pre-condition to arbitration to ensure its use.

This study examines trends relating to how parties to ISA addressed the issue of enforceability of their settlement agreements before the adoption of the Singapore Convention on Mediation. It is impossible to establish whether the risk of non-compliance and non-universal enforceability was a significant concern for parties to a settlement at the time they were concluding their settlement agreements. However, it is possible to examine whether this concern had manifested in practice by observing how often settlement agreements were embedded into arbitral awards. The only way to attribute universal enforceability to a settlement agreement would be to transform it into an arbitral award. Interestingly, however, the data suggest otherwise.

Out of 151 settled cases in the dataset, 22 cases were embedded, 92 cases were not embedded, and the status of the remaining 37 cases was unknown. Even if it is assumed that all the unknown cases were indeed embedded into arbitral awards, at least 61% of the total known settled ISA cases were not embedded into arbitral awards (Table 5).

Figure 9 illustrates that there has been an upward trend of settled agreements not being embedded into arbitral awards. Since 2001, more than 50% of settlement agreements have not been embedded into an arbitral award in all but four years (2004, 2007, 2011, and 2014). The share of not embedded settlement agreements has been noticeably high from 2015 onwards.

Results of the regression model (4) (see Table 3) indicate that settlement agreements under ICSID are significantly less likely to be embedded compared to settlement agreements reached during non-ICSID arbitration proceedings.

It was expected that settlement agreements for cases in long-lived investments and against developing states would have been embedded into arbitral awards more often. This is because, in a case with a long-lived investment, the relationship between a foreign investor and a state carries relatively long-term investment interests compared to short-lived investments. Therefore, when such cases settle, it is the assumption of this study that both parties would warrant the enforceability of their settlement agreements by having them embedded into arbitral awards. Another expectation was that settlements reached with developing states would pose a higher risk of non-compliance than settlements with developed states, and hence would show higher rates of settlement agreements as consent awards. Contrary to this, the findings did not suggest that either long-lived investments or the developing status of a respondent state had a significant impact on the embodiment of settlement agreements.

TABLE 5 Settlement agreements embedded and not embedded into arbitral awards

Total number of amicably settled cases	**151**
Number of Settlement Agreements Embedded into Arbitral Awards	22
Number of Settlement Agreements Not Embedded into Arbitral Awards	92
Unknown Status of Embodiment	37

While this methodology does not directly estimate the rate of compliance with the terms of settlement agreements, the findings illustrate that a significant share of such agreements were not embedded despite the absence of any other external enforceability mechanism. Moreover, the findings do not give a definitive answer as to whether enforceability was a major impediment to conciliation and the reason for conciliation's underuse in ISDS. However, they

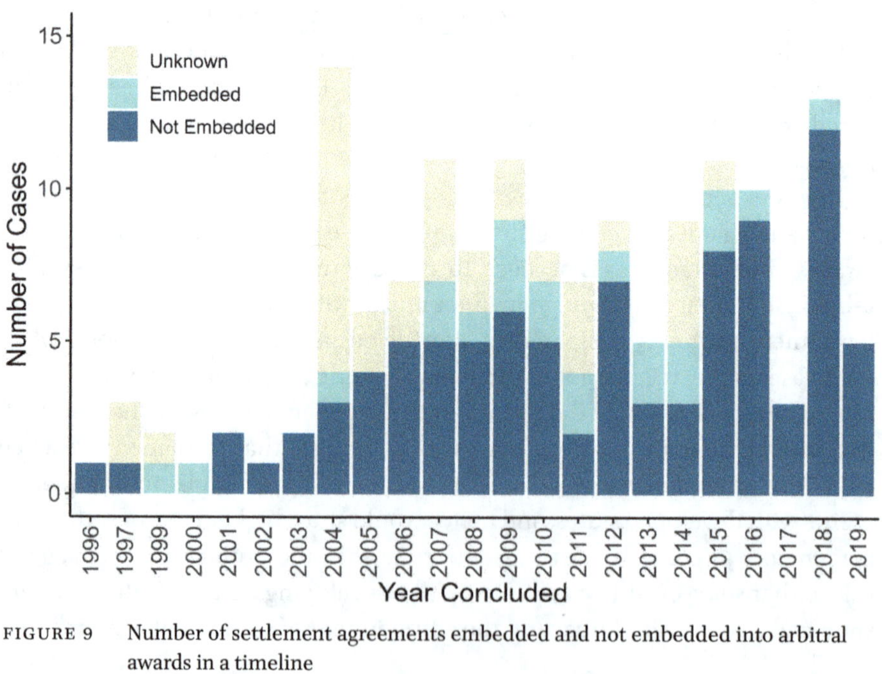

FIGURE 9 Number of settlement agreements embedded and not embedded into arbitral awards in a timeline

suggest that once a settlement has been reached between the disputants, the problem of non-enforceability of settlement agreements largely ceases.

To sum up, the findings suggest that the non-enforceability of settlement agreements was probably not as problematic in practice as has been described in the literature. If this is the case, then the Singapore Convention on Mediation will not be enough to facilitate increased use of ISM or conciliation in the future. Moreover, as discussed in Chapter 4, limited use of investor-state conciliation is likely to be caused by conflicting interpretations of advance consent to conciliation and arbitration. This affirms the argument that current incentives are not enough to guarantee full and complete use of ADR mechanisms in ISDS; those mechanisms need to be inserted into the ISDS process as mandatory steps before arbitration.

5.5 Conclusion

The unprecedented growth in the number of ISA cases has triggered discussion on the increased role of ISM, its voluntary or mandatory format, and the compatibility of ADR mechanisms with ISDS. This empirical analysis suggests that much of the criticism of ISM (in its mandatory format) has been hypothetical and largely lacks empirical evidence.

The argument that mandatory ISM will not be compatible with ISDS has not been supported empirically. The empirical analysis presented in this chapter examined whether certain types of arbitration cases were never concluded on settlement terms, which could suggest that including mandatory ISM in ISDS would be futile. The following observations can be made based on the empirical analysis:

Every industry group had at least one ISA case that had been settled. This suggests that investor-state disputes with investments in any industry group are suitable for mediation and therefore mandatory mediation would normally apply to them without exception.

Disputes with long-term investment interests (long-lived industries) showed higher settlement rates compared to disputes in short-lived industries. This finding is in line with the position that those dispute resolution mechanisms that result in settlements preserve investment relationships while still being able to provide a win-win outcome for the parties.

Settlements can also be reached on non-pecuniary terms, even when the initial claim is monetary. Therefore, the argument that mandatory ISM would be an unsuitable dispute settlement mechanism for disputes with non-monetary claims is not accurate.

The size of the claims in the dispute does not impede settlement outcomes. In fact, in high-profile cases (with claims exceeding USD1.25 billion), developed respondents seem to be settling disputes more often than developing respondents. However, overall, the economic development of the respondents showed no negative impact on settlement rates of disputes. State representatives seem to be settling disputes of various sizes and investment types regardless of the respondent state's economic development level. Therefore, the argument that mandatory ISM would not be suitable for all investor-state disputes because some state representatives may prefer to avoid responsibility and shift blame for the final outcome to an arbitrator does not well justify opposition towards mandatory ISM.

Cases that settle are more likely to have settlement agreements and settlement amounts undisclosed than cases that conclude with an arbitral award. Despite the finding that settlements increase the probability of confidentiality, it is worth noting that there are cases that remain undisclosed regardless of their outcome. While the settlement rate of disputes has been declining annually, the rate of confidential cases has been increasing. The data indicate that only approximately half of all settled outcomes remain undisclosed. In relation to the other half, either the whole settlement agreement was made public or at least the settlement amount was disclosed. It is more likely that most confidential settlements happen during arrangements and negotiations that take place 'behind closed doors' before such disputes are even registered for arbitration. There is no information on such disputes and therefore no available data on the rates of the associated confidential settlements. Making ISM a mandatory pre-condition to arbitration would warrant at least some level of transparency about those settlements, for example the fact that the parties initiated the process.

The argument that claimants receive less compensation through settlements than by winning has not been fully supported empirically. Statistically, the compensation received by claimants in both cases (settled or investor-won) amounts to, on average, 32% of their original claims. However, unlike investor-won cases, settled outcomes usually take less time, which, in turn, saves arbitral and party costs while still yielding the same compensation results as investor-won disputes. To speculate, on average, settlements are a better option for claimants than winning an arbitration case. In addition, settlements also help preserve functional ongoing or future investment relationships between the investor and the respondent state.

The primary argument against mandatory ISM is the non-enforceability of settlement agreements. At first glance, this may no longer be a pressing issue, considering the gradual adoption of the multilateral Singapore Convention on

Mediation. Nevertheless, the data have provided an opportunity to test this argument and the findings are interesting. If the non-enforceability of settlement agreements were in fact problematic for disputants, the data would indicate higher rates of consent awards, where settlement agreements are embedded into arbitral awards. The study found that in 61% of cases, settlement agreements were not embedded into arbitral awards. Moreover, the developing economic status of a respondent state had no significant impact on the embodiment status of settlement agreements. Similarly, long-term investment interest had no impact on the rates of embodiment. It is possible that the non-binding nature of a settlement agreement is actually less concerning to the parties once settlement is reached.

Therefore, while the incentives of UNCITRAL and the adoption of the Singapore Convention on Mediation are significant steps towards popularisation of ADR in ISDS, eliminating the enforceability issue may not be enough for promoting ISM/conciliation because enforceability may well not be as much of an impediment to ADR in ISDS as has been widely assumed. Consequently, the reasons for the underutilisation of, for example, conciliation in ISDS may lie elsewhere, beyond the issue of enforceability, as discussed in an earlier chapter.[70]

This empirical study is not without caveats. To the extent that no comprehensive data are available on amicable settlements of investor-state disputes before arbitration commences, possible selection issues are inevitable. It could be argued that these cases never reached the arbitration stage because they were settled amicably, so the dispute was eliminated during an earlier stage. Therefore, it is possible that current findings relating to settlement rates are biased downward. While the lack of information on disputes that settle amicably before registering for arbitration remains a significant caveat of this study, it is indeed an interesting avenue for future (possibly more qualitative) empirical research. According to Franck, '[e]mpirical legal scholarship can and should aid the examination of the current system to test conventional wisdom, dispel myths, and provide data that can promote efficient conflict management'.[71]

70 An alternative hypothesis about the underuse of ICSID Conciliation is provided in Chapter 4.

71 Franck (n 94 in ch 3).

CHAPTER 6

General Conclusions and Recommendations

6.1 Three Key Findings

The general arguments presented against mandatory ISM revolve around the entrenched belief that this and other similar dispute resolution mechanisms should remain purely voluntary and that the traditional mechanisms should not be changed (for example by foreign investors and states committing in advance to attempt mediation before arbitration). However, a dispute resolution mechanism is what the drafters and disputants make of it. And just because mediation was indeed originally a voluntary dispute resolution mechanism, dating back to the days of Plato and Cicero, this does not mean it cannot be remodelled and fitted into modern-day ISDS after due consideration of current and foreseeable need.[1] Moreover, the reason why mediation has recently been proposed as a tool for tackling costs, delays and other problematic aspects of ISDS is not only due to its purely voluntary nature. In fact, the attractiveness of mediation does not lie in how it is initiated – whether agreed to in advance or only after the dispute has arisen, or whether initiated automatically or as an opt-in step – but rather in how it is concluded (settlement agreement) and how quickly it reaches an outcome (time efficiency). Unlike arbitration, a settlement agreement that is actually concluded through a mediation process is an instrument that fully reflects the current interests of all disputants. It represents a win-win result, as opposed to the win-lose outcome of arbitral awards. Accordingly, making ISM mandatory should guarantee its full use by the parties, and any outcome will reflect the disputants' mutually agreed terms – be it a successful settlement or an absence of settlement.

This book made three original and important contributions to the field of international investment law and ISDS in particular. First, it highlighted a general trend of scepticism and resistance towards every significant update to already established dispute resolution practices. However, in hindsight, arguments did not prevail in practice when (a) presented against the inclusion of mandatory mediation in domestic judicial systems; and (b) those against mediation in multi-tier dispute resolution clauses in international commercial dispute resolution platforms. On the contrary, mediation has come to be

1 Barrett and Barrett (n 1 in ch 2).

 | DOI:10.1163/9789004532540_007

successfully incorporated and utilised in these dispute resolution systems. Through this historical analogy, it can similarly be speculated that none of the general arguments against ISM, which often migrate from international commercial dispute resolution into the field of ISDS, will prove overwhelming once mandatory ISM is fully implemented and utilised. It also identified and analysed the existing problems contributing to the need to incorporate mediation into ISDS, contrasting the various shortcomings of ISA with the benefits of ISM.

Second, and more specifically, this book challenged an existing misconception that there is no need to promote mediation in a mandatory format in ISDS. This view asserts that once new procedural rules (such as the proposed ICSID Mediation Rules) and a new enforcement mechanism (especially the Singapore Convention on Mediation) are in place, recourse to voluntary opt-in ISM will significantly increase. When conciliation in ISDS is provided as an option to investors rather than a requirement, it has been seldom used over the decades despite the existence of relevant procedural rules such as the ICSID Conciliation Rules, and more recently the IBA ISM Rules. Part of the blame for these Rules' underuse is often attributed to the non-binding and non-enforceable outcome of any settlement reached. But while the current proposal to add new ICSID Mediation Rules is undoubtedly a positive step towards the promotion of ADR in ISDS, in its current voluntary (opt-in) format, it remains doubtful that ISM will be used to its full potential.

Indeed, there may be an additional or even a primary cause for the underuse of conciliation and mediation in ISDS, and it may not necessarily be the non-enforceability of a settlement agreement. A thorough and original doctrinal analysis showed that the existing usual formulations of ISDS clauses, which contain the advance consent of a state to ICSID dispute resolution mechanisms, often mistakenly lead parties and their legal advisors to believe that the choice of conciliation or arbitration is to the exclusion of the other. Following that interpretation, it is not surprising that arbitration (generating a binding, final and enforceable award) is almost always chosen over conciliation (with its potentially non-binding, non-enforceable, and therefore not final outcome). Unless more clarity is provided regarding the choice between conciliation and arbitration, either by ICSID or by individual states when concluding future IIAs, it is unlikely that this ADR mechanism (conciliation) will be used more than it currently is. On this view, it also becomes incorrect to assume that the non-enforceability of settlement agreements is the principal reason for the underutilisation of ADR mechanisms like mediation. Relatedly, assuming that improvements in the enforceability of settlement agreements will result in significantly increased use of voluntary ISM is also questionable. And importantly, this empirical study seems to show that the non-enforceability of settlement agreements has not been as problematic in practice as the literature would suggest, which leads to the third major contribution made by this book.

As investigated, there exist further misconceptions regarding settling investor-state disputes through ADR (including conciliation as well as mediation). A pioneering empirical analysis discussed here debunked arguments against the compatibility of mandatory ISM with ISDS by empirically analysing the existing ISA cases that terminate based on party settlement before the arbitration award is rendered. Descriptive statistics highlighted a surprising proportion of settlements where the parties did not embody their agreement in a consent award, even though this would have facilitated enforceability. In addition, the findings suggest that ISA disputes that concluded with awards (be those investor-won or state-won outcomes) did not have special characteristics that other cases that concluded with settlements did not share. This implies that investor-state disputes are as much suitable to be settled through dispute resolution mechanisms that result in settlement agreements (like mediation) as they are to be concluded through arbitration awards. Specifically, making mediation mandatory for investor-state disputes would seem to be compatible with all types of investor-state disputes, regardless of, amongst other things, the economic sector of a dispute, the size of the claimed amount, and the fact that it may be a dispute with a non-monetary claim.

The empirical analysis also challenged the view that mandatory mediation would contribute significantly to increased secrecy through settlement agreements. Instead, settlements happen even before disputes reach the arbitration phase, so when settlement agreements are concluded they remain unknown to the public. Making participation in mediation mandatory would in fact remove such settlements from the realm of the unknown because, at the very least, the use of mediation would become known to the public. In addition, the empirical analysis found that while the number of settlements has been decreasing annually, the number of outcomes of investor-state disputes that are kept confidential has been rising. This suggests that the blame for transparency concerns should not fall on mediation or settlement agreements overall. Disputes remain undisclosed even when they are concluded with arbitration awards.

Lastly, the analysis challenged arguments commonly raised against promoting mediation, such as not having a defined authority to settle or looking weak when settling an investment dispute, by reference to more qualitative evidence. It can, therefore, be concluded that nothing precludes mediation being made an automatic mandatory pre-condition to ISA and being integrated as such into the ISDS regime, to help address the latter's costs, delays, and other problems.

Moreover, incorporating ISM as a mandatory pre-condition to ISA has significant potential benefits. Settlements can indeed be prompted anyway by the possibility of arbitration, but it seems more plausible (especially considering the experience with international commercial arbitration and litigation) that skilled mediators will further prompt settlement in those disputes that do not generate settlements 'in the shadow' of just arbitration. The empirical analysis of 656 concluded treaty-based ISA cases found (as shown in Figure 2) that 46% of the total settled ISA cases from the database (70 out of 151) had settled before the award on jurisdiction was rendered, or when there was no jurisdiction phase – before the parties exchanged their first memorials and counter memorials. In fact, 16% of the disputes were settled as early as before the constitution of the tribunal. This suggests that the pressure of a looming arbitration forced the disputants (back) to the negotiation table, helping to generate a settlement agreement without the need for full arbitral intervention. Accordingly, it can be conservatively speculated that at least approximately 10% of concluded ISA cases (70 cases out of 656 cases from the database) would have been resolved amicably if there were appropriate ISM proceedings in place prior to the disputants initiating arbitration proceedings. As for those cases in which ISM is unsuccessful, the disputants would still have the same unrestricted access to subsequent ISA. As more mandatory mediation occurs as a pre-condition to arbitration under new treaties or through relevant other instruments, it will be possible to undertake quantitative analysis to determine whether settlement rates increase due solely to mediation. However, considering the current information deficit regarding mediated settlements, it is too early to do so yet.

6.2 Three Avenues for ISM Reform

It remains to be determined how to insert ISM effectively as a mandatory pre-condition to arbitration in the existing ISDS regime. The challenge is that the regime involves more than 3000 IIAs, alongside well-established procedural rules (mainly the ICSID and UNCITRAL Arbitration Rules). The question on implementation and promotion of ADR in ISDS has also been set for future consideration by the UNCITRAL Working Group III, which would be due in the next couple of years.[2] However, as of today, no definitive action plan has been

2 UNCITRAL Working Group III, 'Possible reform of investor-State dispute settlement (ISDS) – Dispute prevention and mitigation – Means of alternative dispute resolution' A/CN.9/WG.

put forward. Nevertheless, three possible options can be considered to reform the current ISDS regime and promote more ISM.

6.2.1 *Mandatory Mediation in Multi-tier Dispute Resolution Clauses for New IIAs*

Mediation in a mandatory form could be provided through multi-tiered dispute resolution clauses in IIAs, similar to those that became – after initial scepticism – widespread in international commercial contracts.[3] Under this scenario, mandatory ISM can be agreed to by the states when concluding new IIAs. The exact wording of the ISDS clauses with mandatory mediation/conciliation would largely depend on the individual needs and interests of the relevant contracting parties. However, below are some of the key points that such multi-tier dispute resolution clauses should consider for future treaties.

6.2.1.1 The Unilaterally Mandatory Mediation Step

For multi-tiered dispute resolution clauses in IIAs, the obligation to first engage in mediation before proceeding to arbitration might be imposed only on the claimant (foreign investor). On this approach, the decision of the respondent (host state) not to invoke mediation would not breach the requirement of mandatory ISM. The logic is that the respondent would most likely welcome the opportunity to sit at the negotiating table and attempt further amicable settlement of a dispute before it proceeds to costly, lengthy, and increasingly public arbitration. This sort of one-sided ISM provision can already be found as an innovation in the IA-CEPA and the Hong Kong-United Arab Emirates BIT, both signed in 2019 (discussed in Chapter 4). Each mandates conciliation as a pre-condition to arbitration only for the claimant investor, and only once it has been initiated (presumably by the respondent state).[4]

However, these treaties are missing other necessary regulatory provisions that are preferable for mandatory ADR clauses in ISDS. For example, under these treaties, conciliation only becomes mandatory if and when initiated by the respondent. Therefore, if not so initiated, the claimant could proceed with arbitration directly after the cooling-off periods. Instead, mandatory mediation should be initiated automatically, regardless of whether it is invoked by the parties or not. This way the claimant will only have one expectation, and factor in all the mandatory steps (including mediation) before reaching ISA. Moreover, when a dispute arises, the parties will be less likely to waste their

---

III/WP.190.

3 Kumberg (n 24 in ch 1).

4 *IA-CEPA* (n 44 in ch 3).

time negotiating and mediating separately, behind closed doors, if they know they will have to mediate anyway. This could facilitate a significant portion of otherwise undisclosed investor-state disputes being made known to the public, regardless of whether the final settlement agreement is disclosed or kept confidential.

6.2.1.2 Integrating Mandatory Mediation into the Existing Cooling-Off Periods

One of the principal concerns about a multi-tier ISDS clause involving mandatory mediation is that it would extend the timeline of the whole dispute resolution process. For example, the IA-CEPA arguably increases the overall ISDS timeline by up to 120 days, whereas the Hong Kong-United Arab Emirates BIT increases it by six months. Therefore, instead of adding mandatory mediation as an additional step in between amicable settlement (promoted with cooling-off periods) and arbitration, as is done in those two treaties, the mandatory mediation step should be integrated within the cooling-off periods that are provided in the majority of, if not all, IIAs.[5] This would ensure that the overall ISDS timeline remains unchanged and that the cooling-off periods are utilised to their full potential. This does not mean that the negotiations and consultations phase would be swallowed up by the mandatory mediation provision. The former two amicable settlement methods would remain within the cooling-off periods, but as voluntary steps. It would then be up to the claimants whether they would use negotiations or consultations and what portion of time they would allocate to those processes before progressing to mandatory mediation.

Those treaties that do not integrate mandatory mediation (conciliation) into cooling-off periods, but instead allocate additional time for conciliation (such as the IA-CEPA), should factor in certain conditions that would allow the claimant to waive the said timeframe. Importantly, this should not be by waiver of mandatory mediation, but by cutting down the time for such proceedings in certain circumstances. As discussed earlier, in treaties that allocate additional time for conciliation (mediation), mandatory mediation is triggered once it is initiated by the respondent and does not commence automatically. There is a risk that respondents might use the additional time provided for mandatory mediation only to delay arbitration. The respondent may refuse to participate altogether or take part but without any intention of exploring the possibility of settlement. In such cases, the treaty should expressly provide for the claimant to have the opportunity to cut down the added time that was intended for

5 Coe (n 235 in ch 3); Salacuse (n 12 in ch 1).

mandatory mediation and proceed directly to ISA. The mediator/conciliator could attest to the fact that the respondent did not participate or that they clearly had no genuine intention to settle. Thus, the claimant could argue a right to waiver based on the mediator's statement, while the final decision on whether the arbitral tribunal has jurisdiction without completion of the mandatory ISM step would lie with the tribunal.

6.2.1.3 Detailed Provisions for Mandatory Mediation Procedures

Article 8(3) of the Hong Kong-United Arab Emirates BIT stipulates that the dispute will be submitted to 'the competent authorities of that Contracting Party or arbitration centres thereof, for conciliation'. Yet it fails to specify what is meant under 'competent authorities' or under the 'arbitration centres thereof'. It may be that conciliation proceedings under this provision are meant to be conducted through the respondent state's domestic dispute resolution channels or arbitration centres. This is problematic for a number of reasons. First, efficiency may be questionable for the competent authority or a domestic arbitration centre of the contracting party – in this case, the respondent state – when catering for investor-state conciliation proceedings (for example, appropriate industry-specific expertise of the conciliator). Second, domestic routes may not be appropriate due to the risk of bias and concerns about impartiality. Third, the claimant may not trust the process or feel comfortable, which again would not result in anything meaningful. All of the above would generate fruitless conciliation proceedings, especially during an ongoing dispute, which already entails distrust and disconnection between the parties.

The best way forward would be to choose one of two possible types of references. The first is an open-ended reference to mediation procedural rules and dispute resolution centres in general, without specification. The second is a reference to specific mediation rules and dispute resolution centres, but those that are international and independent from the influence of either the respondent or the claimant and its home state, combined with a reference to any other centre that might be mutually agreed after the dispute is filed.

Under the first type of (open-ended) reference, the difficulty would arise once the disputing parties were faced with the need to decide. They would have to decide and agree on mediation rules and dispute resolution centres whilst being in the middle of an ongoing dispute. However, unlike the reference contained in Article 8(3) of the Hong Kong-United Arab Emirates BIT above, this type of generalised consent provides an abundance of options instead of limiting the claimant to the (perhaps domestic) dispute resolution venues of a respondent state.

The second type is a reference to specific mediation rules and dispute resolution centres, but unlike domestic channels, these dispute resolution procedures would be impartial and, similar to the consent provided for arbitration, go beyond the sovereign borders of any state. These could be the existing 2012 IBA Rules for Investor-State Mediation or the most recent ICSID Mediation Rules for investor-state disputes. ICSID has been working on Investor-State Mediation Rules since 2018, when it first announced an initial draft. Since then, ICSID has received several rounds of comments and suggestions from various experts and countries for the improvement of these Rules. By the time the Rules are adopted, they will most probably be the instrument best reflecting the current needs of the international investment regime and the role of ISM.

6.2.1.4 MFN Clause with ISDS Carve-Out

Initially, the integration of mandatory ISM into IIAs will not happen all at once. This means that while some treaties may have mandatory ISM, others may still choose to conclude treaties with traditional, purely voluntary mediation proceedings involving neutral third parties. This could prove to be an issue because the claimant could potentially invoke the MFN clause in order to import more favourable ISDS provisions from other treaties (to which the respondent state is the party) and therefore bypass the mandatory mediation step (discussed in Chapter 4). Accordingly, in order to ensure that the mandatory mediation provision applies to the contracting state and the investor of the other contracting party, the MFN clause of the original treaty should have a specific carve-out concerning ISDS provisions. This way, the claimant investor will not be able to access dispute resolution processes not provided for in the treaty between the investor's home state and the host state (respondent).

The above analysis, including four recommendations for treaty drafters, is focused on ISM provisions being added to new treaties. For existing BITs and IIAs, countries could renegotiate the ISDS clauses, but this would require the renegotiation of thousands of existing IIAs. Even if this were feasible, it would not happen overnight. One way forward in this respect is to integrate the mandatory ISM step into regional investment treaties (eg multilateral IIAs, such as those involving ASEAN or the CPTPP) covering multiple states at once. However, the provisions of new treaties would have to take priority over, or simply replace, the existing IIAs of individual states.[6] This may require a shift in state practice. So far for Australia, for example, although when concluding

6 Luke Nottage, 'Submission for DFAT Review of Australia's Bilateral Investment Treaties' (13 September 2020) available at <https://erga-omnes.sydney.edu.au/wp-content/uploads/2020/09/2020_DFATreviewBITs_Nottage_LN03-1.pdf>.

an FTA, the practice is usually to mutually agree to terminate any BIT, there are exceptions (for example with China, although the FTA envisages a work program to deal with the BIT that remains in force). More significantly, even when Australia concludes a regional treaty, it leaves any bilateral and/or other regional FTA in place. Thus, the investor can choose which FTA to invoke, and indeed potentially invoke several in parallel or in succession to obtain maximum compensation for loss suffered.[7]

6.2.2 *Amendments to ICSID with Additional Mandatory Mediation Step for All Types of Investor-State Arbitration Cases*

Apart from renegotiating individual treaties, possibly in conjunction with concluding wider regional treaties, another but perhaps less feasible way forward would be making mediation a mandatory pre-condition to arbitration under ICSID. The changes would need to be made to Article 26 of the ICSID Convention, which stipulates that consent of parties to arbitration is deemed to be to the exclusion of other remedies. Such advance consents are nowadays mostly incorporated into IIAs. There are typically three types of consent: to dispute resolution under the ICSID Convention, to the ICSID Arbitration Rules, or to both conciliation and arbitration under the ICSID Rules. But the focus of this discussion is consent to the ICSID Convention and the ICSID Arbitration Rules, and not to ICSID conciliation, because mandatory ISM would have to be attached as an automatic pre-step to arbitration under ICSID. Consent to the ICSID Convention is deemed to encompass all dispute resolution mechanisms offered by ICSID. Hypothetically, if new ICSID Mediation Rules were approved, and if they were to be made a mandatory pre-condition to arbitration by making relevant changes to the Convention, then consent to the ICSID Convention in treaties would automatically qualify as consent to those Mediation Rules as well as the ICSID Arbitration Rules. By contrast, when consent in treaties is given expressly and only to the ICSID Arbitration Rules, then the question arises whether changes to the Convention that require mediation before arbitration would suffice to extend this consent to mediation as well. Additional consent to mediation may still be necessary in individual treaties.

7 For example, Australia has a 2003 FTA with Singapore (amended in 2017), the 2018 CPTPP between Australia, Singapore and five other nations, and the 2010 ASEAN+ treaty. See Luke Nottage, 'Clive Palmer Versus (Western) Australia. He Could Survive a High Court Loss if His Company is Found to be "Foreign"' (10 September 2020) The Conversation, available at <https://theconversation.com/clive-palmer-versus-western-australia-he-could-survive-a-high-court-loss-if-his-company-is-found-to-be-foreign-145334>.

The following changes to the formulation of Article 26 of the ICSID Convention could be enough to avoid having to integrate additional consent to mediation in IIAs. For example, a new Article 26 could read that consent to arbitration is deemed to be to the exclusion of other remedies except for mandatory ISM, which is to be conducted under the relevant ICSID Mediation Rules. But even if such amendments were to be proposed to the Secretary-General by a member state, under Article 66 of the ICSID Convention, a majority of two-thirds of the Administrative Council (comprising 163 Member States) would be required for the amendments to become effective.

The fastest way to inject mandatory ISM into the existing ISDS regime would be to incorporate it into the ICSID Convention. As the associated ICSID Arbitration Rules are the most used in ISDS, the impact would be remarkable. However, it would require a tremendous effort to make the relevant and necessary changes to the ICSID Convention. Further, additional advance consents would probably still be required through IIAs. Finally, incorporation would not cover treaties where the only dispute resolution option uses a non- ICSID procedure, notably the UNCITRAL Arbitration Rules.

6.2.3 *Mauritius Convention Style Multilateral Treaty*

The best way forward, therefore, is to incorporate mandatory ISM into ISDS by using a similar method to that employed by the 2014 United Nations Convention on Transparency in Treaty-based Investor-State Arbitration (Mauritius Convention on Transparency).[8] In 2014, UNCITRAL adopted Rules on Transparency, but these only applied to ISAs conducted under the UNCITRAL Arbitration Rules that arose from IIAs concluded on or after 1 April 2014. However, the application of these Rules was extended to investor-state disputes arising out of treaties concluded even before 2014, through the Mauritius Convention on Transparency.[9] This is a unique multilateral instrument adopted by UNCITRAL that was created with the sole purpose of ensuring that the 2014 UNCITRAL Rules on Transparency could be retrofitted to disputes arising out of treaties concluded before 2014. Moreover, through the Mauritius Convention, the application of the UNCITRAL Rules on Transparency is not limited to investor-state disputes conducted under the UNCITRAL Arbitration Rules. In fact, the Rules on Transparency can apply to arbitrations conducted under any rules (for example under ICSID, ICC, SCC, etc).[10] This occurs

8 Mauritius Convention on Transparency (n 32 in ch 1).

9 Ubilava and Nottage (n 7 in ch 1).

10 Stephan Schill, 'Editorial: The Mauritius Convention on Transparency' (2015) 16(2) Journal of World Investment & Trade 201.

when both home and host states have acceded to the Mauritius Convention. Alternatively, the Rules on Transparency can also apply to an investor-state dispute with the claimant investor's consent (even if its home state has not acceded to the Mauritius Convention). This unique combination allows for the fast, efficient, and wide-reaching incorporation of investment treaty reforms.[11]

A similar style of convention could be adopted by UNCITRAL for ISM, perhaps in conjunction with other reforms for ISDS currently being debated under the auspices of UNCITRAL (for example for clarification of the 'fork in the road' issue discussed in Chapter 4). This way, multi-tier dispute resolution clauses with mandatory ISM could be integrated into old- and new-generation IIAs alike and apply to any treaty-based investor-state dispute, without the need to renegotiate over 3000 treaties. This would ensure wide-reaching, rapid, and efficient investment treaty reform.

A more difficult question is how to incentivise states to actively adopt the prospect of mediation, be it through their future bilateral and multilateral treaties or preparing their national legislations for ISM. The latter would seem to be more difficult considering there are diverse national legislative systems of different states with varying levels of legislative readiness and capacity for ISM. Answering this question seems to be empirically impossible with current data or the lack of it. However, as the discussions on exploring the ways to implement ISM increase, especially on global platforms such as UNCITRAL, the prospects of ISM seem to be promising.

11 Kaufmann-Kohler and Potestà (n 217 in ch 3).

Annexes

ANNEX 1 Results of the regression analysis (2000–2019 concluded cases)

	Model (1)	Model (2)		Model (3)	Model (4)
Dependent Variable	**Settled**	**Transparency**		**Pay-out**	**Settled cases that are not embedded**
		(a) Public	**(b) Public and partly confidential**		
Settled		-0.554***	-0.546***	-0.225	
		(0.136)	(0.152)	(0.184)	
Claimed Amount	0.072***	-0.038	0.022	0.398***	
	(0.010)	(0.024)	(0.017)	(0.040)	
Long-lived	0.076**	0.123***	0.059**	-0.063	0.140
Investment	(0.032)	(0.042)	(0.029)	(0.039)	(0.120)
Developing	0.084**	-0.110**	0.013	-0.063	0.079
(Respondent)	(0.034)	(0.046)	(0.032)	(0.065)	(0.111)
Developing	-0.008	-0.211***	-0.038	-0.054	-0.194
(Claimant)	(0.052)	(0.066)	(0.047)	(0.081)	(0.142)
ICSID Rule	-0.002	0.127***	-0.010	-0.100	0.512***
	(0.035)	(0.040)	(0.025)	(0.098)	(0.085)
Claim×Developing	-0.072***	0.043*	-0.022	0.022	
(Respondent)	(0.010)	(0.024)	(0.017)	(0.038)	
Settled×Claimed		0.024	0.044***	0.054	
Amount		(0.020)	(0.012)	(0.035)	
Settled×Long-lived		-0.076	0.115	0.022	
		(0.101)	(0.128)	(0.098)	
Settled×Developing		-0.076	0.220	0.139	
(Respondent)		(0.123)	(0.148)	(0.116)	
Settled×Developing		0.077	-0.132	-0.192	
(Claimant)		(0.093)	(0.141)	(0.156)	

 | DOI:10.1163/9789004532540_008

ANNEX 1 Results of the regression analysis (2000–2019 concluded cases) (*cont.*)

	Model (1)	Model (2)		Model (3)	Model (4)
Settled×ICSID Rule		0.012	-0.280***	0.104	
		(0.087)	(0.100)	(0.116)	
Number of Obs.	500	500	500	205	90
R^2	0.29	0.78	0.89	0.97	0.80

Note: The pay-out and claimed amounts are in billion USD. In each model, year fixed effects are estimated, but not reported here. Heteroscedasticity consistent standard errors are in parentheses. * p<0.1, ** p<0.05, and *** p<0.01.

ANNEX 2 Results of the regression analysis (without Argentina)

	Model (1)	Model (2)		Model (3)	Model (4)
Dependent variable	**Settled**	**Transparency**		**Pay-out**	**Settled cases that are not embedded**
		(a) Public	(b) Public and partly confidential		
Settled		-0.551***	-0.607***	-0.216	
		(0.153)	(0.158)	(0.193)	
Claimed Amount	0.070***	-0.005	0.030	0.580***	
	(0.011)	(0.018)	(0.019)	(0.066)	
Long-lived	0.060*	0.113**	0.049	-0.083	0.068
Investment	(0.033)	(0.049)	(0.030)	(0.055)	(0.121)
Developing	0.082**	-0.115**	0.036	-0.068	0.018
(Respondent)	(0.032)	(0.053)	(0.035)	(0.096)	(0.123)
Developing	0.025	-0.255***	-0.011	-0.055	-0.216*
(Claimant)	(0.056)	(0.069)	(0.038)	(0.105)	(0.123)
ICSID Rule	-0.015	0.127***	0.023	-0.145	0.437***
	(0.035)	(0.047)	(0.027)	(0.141)	(0.091)
Claim×Developing	-0.071***	0.010	-0.030	-0.161**	
(Respondent)	(0.011)	(0.018)	(0.018)	(0.065)	

ANNEX 2 Results of the regression analysis (without Argentina) (*cont.*)

	Model (1)	Model (2)		Model (3)	Model (4)
Settled×Claimed		-0.009	0.032***	-0.138**	
Amount		(0.010)	(0.013)	(0.061)	
Settled×Long-lived		-0.045	0.172	0.073	
		(0.122)	(0.135)	(0.108)	
Settled×Developing		-0.034	0.281**	0.181	
(Respondent)		(0.121)	(0.140)	(0.112)	
Settled×Developing		0.156*	-0.233	-0.104	
(Claimant)		(0.094)	(0.164)	(0.113)	
Settled×ICSID Rule		-0.041	-0.211*	0.244	
		(0.107)	(0.112)	(0.162)	
Number of Obs.	469	469	500	191	80
R^2	0.25	0.76	0.90	0.97	0.82

Note: The pay-out and claimed amounts are in billion USD. In each model, year fixed effects are estimated, but not reported here. The observations are weighted by the number of cases in that year. Heteroscedasticity consistent standard errors are in parentheses. * p<0.1, ** p<0.05, and *** p<0.01.

Bibliography

Books, Journal Articles

Abramson H, 'New Singapore Convention on Cross-Border Mediated Settlements: Key Choices' in Catharine Titi and Katia Fach Gómez (eds), *Mediation in International Commercial and Investment Disputes* (Oxford University Press 2019) 360.

Aggestam K, 'Quasi-informal Mediation in the Oslo Channel: Larsen and Holst as Individual Mediators' in Jacob Bercovitch (ed), *Studies in International Mediation: Essays in Honor of Jeffrey Z. Rubin* (Palgrave Macmillan 2002) 58.

Allee T and Peinhardt C, 'Contingent Credibility: The Impact of Investment Treaty Violations on Foreign Direct Investment' (2011) 65(3) International Organization 401.

Alschner W and Skougarevskiy D, 'Mapping the Universe of International Investment Agreements' (2016) 19(3) Journal of International Economic Law 561.

Alschner W and Skougarevskiy D, 'The New Gold Standard? Empirically Situating the Trans-Pacific Partnership in the Investment Treaty Universe' (2016) 17(3) Journal of World Investment & Trade 339.

American Society of International Law, 'Thailand and United States: Treaty of Amity and Economic Relations' (1966) 5(5) International Legal Materials 876.

Anderson D, 'Supporting party autonomy in the enforcement of cross-border mediated settlement agreements: A brave new world or unchartered territory?' (2018) Max Planck Institute Luxembourg Summer School-International Association of Procedural Law Summer School.

Arato J, Brown C and Ortino F, 'Parsing and Managing Inconsistency in Investor-State Dispute Settlement' (2020) 21(2–3) Journal of World Investment & Trade 336.

Astor H and Chinkin C, *Dispute resolution in Australia* (LexisNexis Butterworths 2002).

Aust A, *Modern Treaty Law and Practice* (Cambridge University Press 2013).

Barker J, 'International Mediation-A Better Alternative for the Resolution of Commercial Disputes: Guidelines for a US Negotiator Involved in an International Commercial Mediation with Mexicans' (1996) 19(1) Loyola of Los Angeles International and Comparative Law Journal 1.

Barr M, 'Mandatory arbitration in consumer finance and investor contracts' (2015) 11(4) New York University Journal of Law and Business 793.

Barrett J and Barrett J, *A History of Alternative Dispute Resolution: The Story of a Political, Social, and Cultural Movement* (John Wiley & Sons 2004).

Bartel B, 'Med-Arb as a Distinct Method of Dispute Resolution: History, Analysis, and Potential' (1991) 27(3) Willamette Law Review 661.

Bath V and Nottage L, 'The ASEAN Comprehensive Investment Agreement and 'ASEAN Plus'–The Australia-New Zealand Free Trade Area (AANZFTA) and the PRC-ASEAN

Investment Agreement' in M. Bungenberg et al (eds), *International Investment Law: A Handbook* (Nomos Verlagsgellschaft 2015) 283.

Bathurst T, 'The Role of the Courts in the Changing Dispute Resolution Landscape' (2012) 35(3) University of New South Wales Law Journal 870.

Behn D, 'Legitimacy, Evolution, and Growth in Investment Treaty Arbitration: Empirically Evaluating the State-of-the-Art' (2015) 46(2) Georgetown Journal of International Law 389.

Benson B, 'An exploration of the impact of modern arbitration statutes on the development of arbitration in the United States' (1995) 11(2) Journal of Law, Economics, & Organization 479.

Bercovitch J, 'Mediation in International Conflict: An Overview of Theory, a Review of Practice' in I William Zartman and J Lewis Rasmussen (eds), *Peacemaking in International Conflict: Methods and Techniques* (United States Institute of Peace Press 1997) 125.

Bercovitch J, *Studies in International Mediation* (Macmillan 2002).

Besch M, 'Typical Questions Arising within Negotiations' in Marc Bungenberg et al (eds), *International Investment Law* (1st ed, Nomos Verlagsgesellschaft mbH & Co KG 2015) 93.

Bishop D, Reisman M and Crawford J, *Foreign Investment Disputes: Cases, Materials and Commentary* (Kluwer International 2005).

Bjorklund A, 'NAFTA's Contributions to Investor-State Dispute Settlement' in Marc Bungenberg et al (eds), *International Investment Law* (1st ed, Nomos Verlagsgesellschaft mbH & Co KG 2015) 261.

Böckstiegel K, 'The Future of International Investment Law–Substantive Protection and Dispute Settlement' in Marc Bungenberg et al (eds), *International Investment Law* (Nomos Verlagsgesellschaft mbH & Co KG 2015) 1863.

Bonnitcha J, Poulsen L and Waibel M, *The Political Economy of the Investment Treaty Regime* (Oxford University Press 2017).

Born G, 'A New Generation of International Adjudication' (2012) 61(4) Duke Law Journal 775.

Born G, *International Commercial Arbitration*, vol. 1 (Kluwer Law International 2009).

Bottini G and Lavista V, 'Conciliation And BITs' in Arthur W Rovine (ed), *Contemporary Issues in International Arbitration and Mediation: The Fordham Papers (2009)* (Brill Nijhoff 2010) 358.

Boulle L, 'International Enforceability of Mediated Settlement Agreements: Developing the Conceptual Framework' (2014) 7(1) Contemporary Asia Arbitration Journal 35.

Boulle L, *Mediation: Principles, Process, Practice* (3rd ed, LexisNexis Butterworths 2011).

Braun T, 'Investor-State Mediation: Is There A Future?' in Arthur W Rovine (ed), *Contemporary Issues in International Arbitration and Mediation: The Fordham Papers (2009)* (Brill Nijhoff 2010) 374.

Broude T, Haftel Y and Thompson A, 'The Trans-Pacific Partnership and Regulatory Space: A Comparison of Treaty Texts' (2017) 20(2) Journal of International Economic Law 391.

Brown C and Winch P, 'The Confidentiality and Transparency Debate in Commercial and Investment Mediation' in Catharine Titi and Katia Fach Gómez (eds), *Mediation in International Commercial and Investment Disputes* (Oxford University Press 2019).

Brown C, 'Introduction: The Development and Importance of the Model Bilateral Investment Treaty' in Chester Brown (ed), *Commentaries on Selected Model Investment Treaties* (Oxford University Press 2013).

Brown C, 'The End of the Affair? Hulley Enterprises Ltd (Cyprus) v Russian Federation; Yukos Universal Ltd (Isle of Man) v Russian Federation; Veteran Petroleum Ltd (Cyprus) v Russian Federation, UNCITRAL, PCA Nos AA 226, 227, 228, Final Awards, 18 July 2014 (Yves Fortier, Charles Poncet, Stephen Schwebel)' (2016) 17(1) *Journal of World Investment & Trade* 126.

Brown C, 'The Evolution of the Regime of International Investment Agreements: History, Economics and Politics' in Marc Bungenberg et al (eds), *International Investment Law* (1st ed, Nomos Verlagsgesellschaft mbH & Co KG 2015) 153.

Bu Y and Huo X, 'The Revival of ADR in China: The Path to Rule of Law or the Turn Against Law?' in Carlos Esplugues and Louis Marquis (eds), *New Developments in Civil and Commercial Mediation* (Springer 2015).

Bühler M, 'Awarding Costs in International Commercial Arbitration: An Overview (1/2)' (2004) 22(2) ASA Bulletin 249.

Bungenberg M and Titi C, 'Precedents in International Investment Law' in Marc Bungenberg et al (eds), *International Investment Law* (Nomos Verlagsgesellschaft mbH & Co. KG 2015) 1505.

Burch M, Nottage L and Williams B, 'Appropriate treaty-based dispute resolution for Asia-Pacific commerce in the 21st century' (2012) 35(3) University of New South Wales Law Journal 1013.

Bush R, 'Substituting Mediation for Arbitration: The Growing Market for Evaluative Mediation, and What it Means for the ADR Field' (2002) 3(1) Pepperdine Dispute Resolution Law Journal 111.

Buth R, 'Limits to the Quantitative Data on Court-Connected Mediation in the Federal Courts of Australia' (2009) 20(4) Australasian Dispute Resolution Journal 229.

Caron D and Caplan L, *The UNCITRAL Arbitration Rules: a Commentary* (Oxford University Press 2013).

Carrington P, 'ADR and the Future of Adjudication: A Primer on Dispute Resolution' (1996) 15(1) Review of Litigation 485.

Cheng T, 'Reflections on Culture in Med-Arb' in Arthur W Rovine (ed), *Contemporary Issues in International Arbitration and Mediation: The Fordham Papers (2009)* (Brill Nijhoff 2010) 419.

Chern C, *International Commercial Mediation* (Informa Law from Routledge 2008).

Chern C, *The Commercial Mediator's Handbook* (CRC Press 2014).

Chesterman S, 'Asia's Ambivalence about International Law and Institutions: Past, Present and Futures' (2016) 27(4) European Journal of International Law 945.

Chong A and Steffek F, 'Enforcement of International Settlement Agreements Resulting from Mediation under the Singapore Convention: Private International Law Issues in Perspective' (2019) 31(1) Singapore Academy of Law Journal 448.

Claxton J, 'Compelling Parties to Mediate Investor-State Disputes: No Pressure, No Diamonds?' (2020) 20(1) Pepperdine Dispute Resolution Law Journal 78.

Claxton J, Nottage L and Teramura N, 'Disruption as a Catalyst for International Dispute Services in Japan: No Longer Business as Usual?' in Luke Nottage et al (eds), *New Frontiers in Asia-Pacific International Arbitration and Dispute Resolution* (Wolters Kluwer 2021) 237.

Claxton J, Nottage L and Ubilava A, 'Mandatory Investor-State Conciliation Before Arbitration in Asia-Pacific Treaties: New Developments and Implications for India and Australia', (2021) 3 Indian Journal of International Economic 209.

Clodfelter M, 'The Future Direction of Investment Agreements in the European Union' (2013) 12(1) Santa Clara Journal of International Law 159.

Clodfelter M, 'Why Aren't More Investor-state Treaty Disputes Settled Amicably?' in Susan Franck and Anna Joubin-Bret (eds), *Investor-State Disputes: Prevention and Alternatives to Arbitration II* (UNCTAD 2011) 38.

Coe J, 'Settlement of Investor-State Disputes through Mediation-Preliminary Remarks on Processes, Problems and Prospects' in R Doak Bishop (ed), *Enforcement of Arbitral Awards Against Sovereigns* (Juris Publishers 2009) 73.

Coe J, 'Should Mediation of Investment Disputes Be Encouraged, and, If So, by Whom and How?' in Arthur W Rovine (ed), *Contemporary Issues in International Arbitration and Mediation: The Fordham Papers (2009)* (Brill Nijhoff 2010) 339.

Coe J, 'Toward a Complementary Use of Conciliation in Investor-State Disputes-A Preliminary Sketch' (2005) 12(1) UC Davis Journal of International Law & Policy 7.

Cohen J, 'Barnacles, Aristocracy and Truth Denial: Three Not So Beautiful Aspects of Contemporary Mediation' (2014) 16(3) Cardozo Journal of Conflict Resolution 779.

Commission J and Moloo R, *Procedural Issues in International Investment Arbitration* (Oxford University Press 2018).

Constain S, 'Mediation in Investor–State Dispute Settlement: Government Policy and the Changing Landscape' (2014) 29(1) ICSID Review 25.

Costantino C and Merchant C, *Designing Conflict Management Systems: A Guide to Creating Productive and Healthy Organizations* (Jossey-Bass 1996).

Crawford J, 'Continuity and Discontinuity in International Dispute Settlement: An Inaugural Lecture' (2009) 1(1) Journal of International Dispute Settlement 801.

Crespo M, 'From Paper to People: Building Conflict Resolution Capacity and Frameworks for Sustainable Implementation of IIAs to Increase Investor-State Satisfaction' in Susan Franck and Anna Joubin-Bret (eds), *Investor-State Disputes: Prevention and Alternatives to Arbitration II* (UNCTAD 2011) 55.

Crockett A, 'Indonesia's Bilateral Investment Treaties: Between Generations?' (2015) 30(2) ICSID Review 437.

David R, *Arbitration in International Trade* (Kluwer Law and Taxation Publishers 1985).

De Ly F, Friedman M and Di Brozolo L, 'International Law Association International Commercial Arbitration Committee's Report and Recommendations on 'Confidentiality in International Commercial Arbitration'' (2012) 28(3) Arbitration International 355.

De Vera C, 'Arbitrating Harmony: Med-Arb and the Confluence of Culture and Rule of Law in the Resolution of International Commercial Disputes in China' (2004) 18(1) Columbia Journal of Asian Law 149.

Deason E, 'Enforcement of Settlement Agreements in International Commercial Mediation: A New Legal Framework' (2015) 22(1) Dispute Resolution Magazine 32.

Drahozal C, 'Empirical Findings on International Arbitration: An Overview' in Thomas Schultz and Federico Ortino (eds), *The Oxford Handbook on International Arbitration* (Oxford University Press 2020) 643.

Dupont C, Thomas Schultz and Merih Angin, 'Political Risk and Investment Arbitration: An Empirical Study' (2016) 7(1) Journal of International Dispute Settlement 136.

Dzung N and Trang N, 'International Investment Dispute Resolution in Vietnam: Opportunities and Challenges' in Julien Chaisse and Luke Nottage (eds), *International Investment Treaties and Arbitration Across Asia* (Brill Nijhoff 2018) 280.

Echandi R and Kher P, 'Can International Investor-State Disputes be Prevented? Empirical Evidence from Settlements in ICSID Arbitration' (2014) 29(1) ICSID Review 41.

Emerson F, 'History of Arbitration Practice and Law' (1970) 19(1) Cleveland State Law Review 1585.

Esplugues C and Marquis L, *New Developments in Civil and Commercial Mediation* (Springer 2015).

Esplugues C, *New Developments in Civil and Commercial Mediation: Global Comparative Perspectives*, vol 6 (Springer International Publishing 2015) 1199.

Evans P and Moens G, 'Reflections on the Role of Mediators and Arbitrators Can a Good Mediator Also Be a Good Arbitrator' (2009) 6(1) Macquarie Journal of Business Law 265.

Fan K, 'An Empirical Study of Arbitrators Acting as Mediators in China' (2014) 15(3) Cardozo Journal of Conflict Resolution 777.

Fan K, 'Mediation of Investor-State Disputes: A Treaty Survey', (2020) 2 Journal of Dispute Resolution 327.

Fan K, 'The Risks of Apparent Bias When an Arbitrator Act as a Mediator-Remarks on Hong Kong Court's Decision in Gao Haiyan' in Andrea Bonomi and Gian Paolo Romano (eds), *Yearbook of Private International Law Volume XIII* (Sellier European Law Publishers 2011) 535.

Ficks E, 'Models of General Court-Connected Conciliation and Mediation for Commercial Disputes in Sweden, Australia and Japan' (2008) 13(25) Journal of Japanese Law 131.

Franck S and Joubin-Bret A, 'Investor–State Mediation: A Simulation' (2014) 29(1) ICSID Review 90.

Franck S and Wylie L, 'Predicting Outcomes in Investment Treaty Arbitration' (2015) 65(3) Duke Law Journal 494.

Franck S, 'Development and Outcomes of Investment Treaty Arbitration' (2009) 50(2) Harvard International Law Journal 435.

Franck S, 'Empirically Evaluating Claims About Investment Treaty Arbitration' (2007) 86(1) North Carolina Law Review 1.

Franck S, 'Rationalising Costs in Investment Treaty Arbitration' (2011) 88(4) Washington University Law Review 769.

Franck S, 'The Legitimacy Crisis in Investment Treaty Arbitration: Privatizing Public International Law through Inconsistent Decisions' (2004) 73(4) Fordham Law Review 1521.

Franck S, 'Using Investor–State Mediation Rules to Promote Conflict Management: An Introductory Guide' (2014) 29(1) ICSID Review 66.

Franck S, *Arbitration Costs: Myths and Realities in Investment Treaty Arbitration* (Oxford University Press 2019).

Gaffney J and Akçay Z, 'European Bilateral Approaches' in Marc Bungenberg et al (eds), *International Investment Law* (1st ed, Nomos Verlagsgesellschaft mbH & Co KG 2015) 186.

Garnett R, 'The Hague Choice of Court Convention: Magnum Opus or Much Ado About Nothing?' (2009) 5(1) Journal of Private International Law 161.

Gaudet M, 'Overcoming regional differences' (1988) 5(4) Journal of International Arbitration 67.

Gerbay R, 'Is the End Nigh Again? An Empirical Assessment of the 'Judicialization' of International Arbitration' (2014) 24(2) American Journal of International Arbitration 223.

Giogetti C, 'Is the Truth in the Eyes of the Beholder-The Perils and Benefits of Empirical Research in International Investment Arbitration' (2013) 12(1) Santa Clara Journal of International Law 263.

Goodrich M, 'Arb-Med: Ideal Solution or Dangerous Heresy' (2012) 15(1) International Arbitration Law Review 12.

Gotanda J, 'Consistently Inconsistent: The Need for Predictability in Awarding Costs and Fees in Investment Treaty Arbitrations' (2013) 28(2) ICSID Review 420.

Greenwood L, 'A Window of Opportunity? Building a Short Period of Time into Arbitral Rules in Order for Parties to Explore Settlement' (2011) 27(2) Arbitration International 199.

Griffith G and Mitchell A, 'Contractual Dispute Resolution in International Trade: The UNCITRAL Arbitration Rules (1976) and the UNCITRAL Conciliation Rules (1980)' (2002) 3(1) Melbourne Journal of International Law 184.

Hafner-Burton E, Puig S and Victor D, 'Against Secrecy: The Social Cost of International Dispute Settlement' (2017) 42(2) Yale Journal of International Law 279.

Hafner-Burton E, Steinert-Threlkeld Z and Victor D, 'Predictability Versus Flexibility: Secrecy in International Investment Arbitration' (2016) 68(3) World Politics 413.

Hamilton J, Omar E Garcia-Bolivar and Hernando Otero, *Latin American Investment Protections: Comparative Perspectives on Laws, Treaties, and Disputes for Investors, States and Counsel* (Martinus Nijhoff Publishers 2012) 71.

Happ R, 'The Energy Charter Treaty' in Marc Bungenberg et al (eds), *International Investment Law* (1st ed, Nomos Verlagsgesellschaft mbH & Co KG 2015) 240.

Henckels C, 'Protecting Regulatory Autonomy Through Greater Precision in Investment Treaties: the TPP, CETA, and TTIP' (2016) 19(1) Journal of International Economic Law 27.

Henderson D, *The MAI affair: A Story and its Lessons* (Royal Institute of International Affairs 1999).

Hensler D, 'Our Courts, Ourselves: How the Alternative Dispute Resolution Movement Is Re-Shaping Our Legal System' (2017) 122(1) Dickinson Law Review 349.

Hensler D, 'Suppose It's Not True: Challenging Mediation Ideology' (2002) 1 Journal of Dispute Resolution 81.

Hensler D, 'What We Know and Don't Know About Court-Administered Arbitration' (1985) 69(5) Judicature 270.

Herbert W et al, 'International Commercial Mediation' (2011) 45(1) The International Lawyer 111.

Hess B and Pelzer N, 'Mediation in Germany: Finding the Right Balance between Regulation and Self-Regulation' in Carlos Esplugues and Louis Marquis (eds), *New Developments in Civil and Commercial Mediation*, (Springer 2015) 291.

Hobér K, 'Does Investment Arbitration have a Future?' in Marc Bungenberg et al (eds), *International Investment Law: A Handbook* (1st ed, Nomos Verlagsgesellschaft mbH & Co KG 2015) 1873.

Hollingdale M, 'Mediation in the Resources Sector:'Alternative' Dispute Resolution or Now the Norm?' in Gabriël A Moens and Philip Evans (eds), *Arbitration and Dispute Resolution in the Resources Sector* (Springer 2015) 101.

Holmes M and Brown C, *The International Arbitration Act 1974: A Commentary* (3rd ed, LexisNexis Butterworths Australia 2018).

Hu D and Nottage L, 'The International Arbitration Act Matters in Australia: Where to Litigate and Why (Not)' (2016) 35(1) The Arbitrator and Mediator 91.

Huber S and Trachte-Huber W, 'Top Ten Developments in Arbitration in the 1990s' (2000) 55(4) Dispute Resolution Journal 24.

Hwang M and Lee S, 'Survey of South East Asian Nations on the Application of the New York Convention' (2008) 25(6) Journal of International Arbitration 873.

Idei N, 'The Nuclear Damage Claim Dispute Resolution Center' (2012) Japan Commercial Arbitration Association Newsletter 1.

Irie H, 'An Overview on the Current Status of Japanese Private Dispute Resolution – Small Impact of the ADR Act and it's still at the Early Stage' (2010) The Japan Commercial Arbitration Association.

Jolles A, 'Consequences of Multi-tier Arbitration Clauses: Issues of Enforcement' (2006) 72(4) Arbitration: The International Journal of Arbitration, Mediation and Dispute Management 329.

Joubin-Bret A and Legum B, 'A Set of Rules Dedicated to Investor–State Mediation: The IBA Investor–State Mediation Rules' (2014) 29(1) ICSID Review 17.

Kakiuchi S, 'Regulating Mediation in Japan: Latest Development and Its Background' in Carlos Esplugues and Louis Marquis (eds), *New Developments in Civil and Commercial Mediation* (Springer 2015).

Karl J, 'The Negotiations on the OECD Multilateral Agreement on Investment' in Marc Bungenberg et al (eds), *International Investment Law* (1st ed, Nomos Verlagsgesellschaft mbH & Co KG 2015) 342.

Kaufmann–Kohler G and Fan K, 'Integrating Mediation into Arbitration: Why It Works in China' (2008) 25(4) Journal of International Arbitration 479.

Kaufmann–Kohler G, 'When Arbitrators Facilitate Settlement: Towards a Transnational Standard: Clayton Utz/University of Sydney International Arbitration Lecture' (2009) 25(2) Arbitration International 187.

Kawharu A and Nottage L, 'Foreign Investment Regulation and Treaty Practice in New Zealand and Australia: Getting it Together in the Asia-Pacific?' in Julien Chaisse and Luke Nottage (eds), *International Investment Treaties and Arbitration Across Asia* (Brill Nijhoff 2018) 443.

Kawharu A and Nottage L, 'Models for Investment Treaties in the Asian Region: An Underview' (2017) 34(3) Arizona Journal of International and Comparative Law 461.

Kawharu A, 'Punctuated Equilibrium: The Potential Role of FTA Trade Commissions in the Evolution of International Investment Law' (2017) 20(1) Journal of International Economic Law 87.

Kelly M, 'No Case Too Big to Mediate' (2016) 892(1) LawTalk 28.

Kinnear M and Fischer G, *Building International Investment Law: The First 50 Years of ICSID* (Kluwer Law International BV 2015).

Kiser R, *How Leading Lawyers Think: Expert Insights Into Judgment and Advocacy* (Springer Science & Business Media 2011).

Kleinheisterkamp J and Poulsen L, 'Investment Protection in TTIP: Three Feasible Proposals' in Marc Bungenberg et al (eds), *European Yearbook of International Economic Law* (Springer International Publishing 2016) 527.

Koch C, 'Is There a Default Principle of Cost Allocation in International Arbitration?' (2014) 31(4) Journal of International Arbitration 485.

Kronke H, *Recognition and Enforcement of Foreign Arbitral Awards: A Global Commentary on the New York Convention* (Kluwer Law International 2010).

Kurtz J and Nottage L, 'Investment Treaty Arbitration 'Down Under': Policy and Politics in Australia' (2015) 30(2) ICSID Review-Foreign Investment Law Journal 465.

Kurtz J, 'A General Investment Agreement in the WTO? Lessons from Chapter 11 of NAFTA and the OECD Multilateral Agreement on Investment' (2002) 23(4) University of Pennsylvania Journal of International Economic Law 713.

Lack J, 'Appropriate Dispute Resolution (ADR): the Spectrum of Hybrid Techniques Available to the Parties' in Arnold Ingen-Housz (ed), *ADR in Business Practice and Issues across Countries and Cultures* (Kluwer Law International 2011) 339.

Lamm C, Pham H and Bay A, 'Consent and Due Process in Multiparty Investor-State Arbitrations' in Christina Binder et al (eds), *International Investment Law for the 21st Century: Essays in Honour of Christoph Schreuer* (Oxford University Press 2009) 54.

Lande J and Wohl R, 'Listening to Experienced Users: Improving Quality and Use of Commercial Mediation' (2007) 13(3) Dispute Resolution Magazine 18.

Langford M, Behn D and Létourneau-Tremblay L, 'Empirical Perspectives on Investment Arbitration: What Do We Know? Does It Matter?' (2020) 21(2–3) Journal of World Investment & Trade 188.

Lazo R, 'Systems of Legal Defence Used by Latin American Countries in Investment Disputes' (2016) 17(4) Journal of World Investment & Trade 562.

Lee J, 'Introduction of an Appellate Review Mechanism for International Investment Disputes: Expected Benefits and Remaining Tasks' in Jean E Kalicki and Anna Joubin-Bret (eds), *Reshaping the Investor-State Dispute Settlement System Journeys for the 21st Century* (Brill Nijhoff 2015) 474.

Lee J, 'Mending the Wound or Pulling It Apart: New Proposals for International Investment Courts and Fragmentation of International Investment Law' (2018) 39(1) Northwestern Journal of International Law & Business 1.

Lee J, 'Settling Investment Disputes Through Mediation' in Mahdev Mohan and Chester Brown (eds), *The Asian Turn in Foreign Investment* (Cambridge University Press 2021).

Lew J, Mistelis L and Kröll S, *Comparative International Commercial Arbitration* (Kluwer Law International 2003).

Limbury A, 'Getting the Best of Both Worlds with Med-Arb' (2010) 48(8) Law Society Journal 62.

Lipsky D and Seeber R, 'The Appropriate Resolution of Corporate Disputes: A Report on the Growing Use of ADR by US Corporations' (1998) 4 Martin and Laurie Scheinman Institute on Conflict Resolution.

Lowenfeld A, 'The ICSID Convention: Origins and Transformation' (2009) 38(1) Georgia Journal of International and Comparative Law 47.

Lubman S, 'Mao and Mediation: Politics and Dispute Resolution in Communist China' (1967) 55(5) California Law Review 1284.

Martin T, 'International Mediation: An Evolving Market' in Arthur W Rovine (ed), *Contemporary Issues in International Arbitration and Mediation: the Fordham Papers 2010* (Brill Nijhoff 2010) 404.

Mau S, 'Arbitration to Mediation to Arbitration With the Same Parties in the Same International Commercial Dispute Before the Same Neutral: Innovative Evolution or Recipe for Disaster?' (2015) 31(8) Construction Law Journal 429.

McEwen C and Wissler R, 'Finding Out if It Is True: Comparing Mediation and Negotiation Through Research' (2002) 1 Journal of Dispute Resolution 131.

McIlwrath M and Savage J, *International Arbitration and Mediation: A Practical Guide* (Kluwer Law International BV 2010).

Miles K, *The Origins of International Investment Law: Empire, Environment, and the Safeguarding of Capital,* vol 99 (Cambridge University Press 2013) 22.

Mistelis Land Baltag C, 'Trends and Challenges in International Arbitration: Two Surveys of In-House Counsel of Major Corporations' (2008) 2(5) World Arbitration and Mediation Review 83.

Montanes M, 'Bolivia's Denunciation of the Convention on the Settlement of Investment Disputes between States and Nationals of Other States' (2007) 46(5) International Legal Materials 969.

Montanes M, 'Introductory Note to Bolivia's Denunciation of the Convention on the Settlement of Investment Disputes between States and Nationals of Other States' (2007) 46(5) International Legal Materials 969.

Morosini F and Sanchez Badin M, 'The Brazilian Agreement on Cooperation and Facilitation of Investments (ACFI): A New Formula for International Investment Agreements' (2015) 6(3) Investment Treaty News 3.

Morris G, 'From Anecdote to Evidence: The New Zealand Commercial Mediation Market' (2016) 22(1) New Zealand Business Law Quarterly 10.

Moser M, 'CIETAC Arbitration: A Success Story', (1998) 15(1) Journal of International Arbitration 27.

Moses M, *The Principles and Practice of International Commercial Arbitration* (Cambridge University Press 2017).

Najar J, 'Inside Out: A User's Perspective on Challenges in International Arbitration' (2009) 25(4) Arbitration International 515.

Newcombe A and Paradell L, *Law and Practice of Investment Treaties: Standards of Treatment* (Wolters Kluwer Law & Business 2009).

Newcombe A, 'The Americas' in Marc Bungenberg et al (eds), *International Investment Law* (1st ed, Nomos Verlagsgesellschaft mbH & Co KG 2015) 202.

Newmark C and Hill R, 'Can a Mediated Settlement Become an Enforceable Arbitration Award?' (2014) 16(1) Arbitration International 81.

Nigmatullina D, 'The Combined Use of Mediation and Arbitration in Commercial Dispute Resolution: Results from an International Study' (2016) 33(1) Journal of International Arbitration 37.

Nitschke F, 'The IBA's Investor-State Mediation Rules and the ICSID Dispute Settlement Framework' (2014) 29(1) ICSID Review 112.

Nitschke F, 'The ICSID Conciliation Rules in Practice' in Catharine Titi and Katia Fach Gómez (eds), *Mediation in International Commercial and Investment Disputes*, (Oxford University Press, 2019) 121.

Nolan-Haley J, 'Mediation: the new arbitration' (2012) 17(1) Harvard Negotiation Law Review 61.

Nottage L and Garnett R (eds), *International Arbitration in Australia* (The Federation Press 2010).

Nottage L and Garnett R, 'The Australian Centre for International Commercial Arbitration' in Helene Ruiz Fabri (ed), *Max Planck Encyclopedia of International Procedural Law* (Oxford University Press 2019) 1–18.

Nottage L and Garnett R, 'Top 20 Things to Change in or Around Australia's International Arbitration Act' (2010) 6(1) Asian International Arbitration Journal 1.

Nottage L and Hamamoto S, 'Japan' in Chester Brown (ed), *Commentaries on Selected Model Investment Treaties* (Oxford University Press 2013) 347.

Nottage L and Jetin B, 'New Frontiers in Asia-Pacific Trade, Investment and International Business Dispute Resolution' in Luke Nottage et al (eds), *New Frontiers in Asia-Pacific International Arbitration and Dispute Resolution* (Wolters Kluwer 2021) 1.

Nottage L, 'A Weather Map for International Arbitration: Mainly Sunny, Some Clouds, Possible Thunderstorms' (2015) 26(4) American Review of International Arbitration 495.

Nottage L, 'Confidentiality and Transparency in International Arbitration: Asia-Pacific Tensions and Expectations' (2020) 16(1) Asian International Arbitration Journal 1.

Nottage L, 'In/formalisation and Glocalisation of International Commercial Arbitration and Investment Treaty Arbitration in Asia' in Joachim Zekoll, Moritz Bälz, and Iwo Amelung (eds), *Formalisation and Flexibilisation in Dispute Resolution* (Brill 2014) 211.

Nottage L, 'International Arbitration and Society at Large' in A Bjorklund, F Ferrari and S Kroell (eds), *Cambridge Compendium of International Commercial and Investment Arbitration* (Cambridge University Press 2022) forthcoming.

Nottage L, 'International Commercial Arbitration in Australia: What's New and What's Next?' (2013) 30(5) Journal of International Arbitration 465.

Nottage L, 'Investor-State Arbitration Policy and Practice after *Philip Morris Asia v Australia*' in Leon Trakman and Nicola Ranieri (eds), *Regionalism in International Investment Law* (Oxford University Press 2013) 452.

Nottage L, 'Investor-State Arbitration Policy and Practice in Australia' in Armand De Mestral (ed), *Second Thoughts: Investor-State Arbitration Between Developed Democracies* (Centre for International Governance Innovation 2017) 377.

Nottage L, 'Is (International) Commercial Arbitration ADR?' (2002) 4(1) The Arbitrator and Mediator 83.

Nottage L, 'Rebalancing Investment Treaties and Investor-State Arbitration: Two Approaches' (2016) Journal of World Investment & Trade 1015.

Nottage L, Chaisse J and Thanitcul S, 'International Investment Treaties and Arbitration Across Asia: A Bird's Eye View' in Julien Chaisse and Luke Nottage (eds), *International Investment Treaties and Arbitration Across Asia* (Brill Nijhoff 2018) 1.

Nottage L, *International Commercial and Investor-State Arbitration: Australia and Japan in Regional and Global Contexts* (Edward Elgar Publishing 2021).

Nussbaum A, 'Arbitration Between the Lena Goldfields Ltd. and the Soviet Government' (1950) 36(1) Cornell Law Quarterly 31.

Oghigian H, 'The Mediation/Arbitration Hybrid' (2003) 20(1) Journal of International Arbitration 75.

Pappas B, 'Med-Arb and the Legalization of Alternative Dispute Resolution' (2015) 20(1) Harvard Negotiation Law Review 157.

Park E, 'Appellate Review in Investor-State Arbitration' in Jean E Kalicki and Anna Joubin-Bret (eds), *Reshaping the Investor-State Dispute Settlement System* (Brill Nijhoff 2015) 443.

Peter J, 'Med-Arb in International Arbitration' (1997) 8 *American Review of International Arbitration* 83.

Phillips G, 'Same-Neutral Med-Arb: What does the Future Hold?' (2005) 60(2) Dispute Resolution Journal 24.

Poulsen L and Aisbett E, 'Diplomats Want Treaties: Diplomatic Agendas and Perks in the Investment Regime' (2016) 7(1) Journal of International Dispute Settlement 72.

Poulsen L, *Bounded Rationality and Economic Diplomacy: The Politics of Investment Treaties in Developing Countries* (Cambridge University Press 2015).

Press A, 'International Trends in Dispute Resolution a US Perspective' (2000) 3(2) ADR Bulletin 1.

Pryles M, *Dispute Resolution in Asia* (Kluwer Law International 2006) 109.

Puig S and Strezhnev A, 'The David Effect and ISDS' (2017) 28(3) European Journal of International Law 731.

Raghavan V, 'New Horizons for Alternative Dispute Resolution in India-The New Arbitration Law of 1996' (1996) 13(4) Journal of International Arbitration 5.

Rana R and Sanson M, 'International Commercial Arbitration' (2011) 6(4) Construction Law International 39.

Ranjan P and Anand P, 'Investor State Dispute Settlement in the 2016 Indian Model Bilateral Investment Treaty: Does it Go Too Far?' in Julien Chaisse and Luke Nottage (eds), *International Investment Treaties and Arbitration Across Asia* (Brill Nijhoff 2018) 579.

Ranjan P, 'India and Bilateral Investment Treaties: From Rejection to Embracement to Hesitance?' in Srinivas Burra and R Rajesh Babu (eds), *Locating India in the Contemporary International Legal Order* (Springer 2018) 101.

Rastegar K, 'Denouncing ICSID' in Christina Binder et al (eds), *International Investment Law for the 21st Century: Essays in Honour of Christoph Schreuer* (Oxford University Press 2009) 278.

Reed L, 'Allocation of Costs in International Arbitration' (2011) 26(1) ICSID Review 76.

Reed L, 'Great Expectations: Where Does the Proliferation of International Dispute Resolution Tribunals Leave International Law?' (2002) 96(1) Proceedings of the Annual Meeting (American Society of International Law) 219.

Reed L, 'Synopsis of Closing Remarks' in Susan Franck and Anna Joubin-Bret (eds), *Investor-State Disputes: Prevention and Alternatives to Arbitration II* (UNCTAD 2011) 30.

Reif L, 'Conciliation As A Mechanism For The Resolution Of International Economic And Business Disputes' (1990) 14(3) Fordham International Law Journal 578.

Reif L, 'The Use of Conciliation or Mediation for the Resolution of International Commercial Disputes' (2007) 45(1) Canadian Business Law Journal 20.

Reinisch A, 'The European Union and Investor-State Dispute Settlement: from Investor-State Arbitration to a Permanent Investment Court' in Armand De Mestral (ed), *Second Thoughts: Investor-State Arbitration between Developed Democracies* (McGill-Queen's University Press 2017) 333.

Reinisch A, 'The Future of Investment Arbitration' in Christina Binder et al (eds), *International Investment Law for the 21st Century: Essays in Honour of Christoph Schreuer* (Oxford University Press 2009) 894.

Reinstein E, 'Finding a Happy Ending for Foreign Investors: The Enforcement of Arbitration Awards in the People's Republic of China' (2005) 16(1) Indiana International & Comparative Law Review 37.

Reisman M and Richardson B, 'Tribunals and Courts: An Interpretation of the Architecture of International Commercial Arbitration' in Albert Jan van den Berg (ed), *Arbitration-The Next Fifty Years* (Kluwer Law International 2012) 21.

Reisman M, 'International Investment Arbitration and ADR: Married but Best Living Apart' (2009) 24(1) ICSID Review 185.

Remmer K, 'The Outcomes of Investment Treaty Arbitration: A Reassessmen' in Lisa E Sachs, Lise Johnson and Columbia Center on Sustainable Investment (CCSI) (eds), *Yearbook on International Investment Law and Policy 2015–2016* (8th ed, Oxford University Press, 2017) 144.

Risse J, 'Ten Drastic Proposals for Saving Time and Costs in Arbitral Proceedings' (2013) 29(3) Arbitration International 466.

Risse J, 'Thinking Ahead: Dispute Resolution after the Corona Crisis' (2020) 18(4) German Arbitration Journal (SchiedsVZ) 165.

Roberts A, 'State-to-State Investment Treaty Arbitration: A Hybrid Theory of Interdependent Rights and Shared Interpretive Authority' (2014) 55(1) Harvard International Law Journal 1.

Roebuck D and de Loynes de Fumichon B, *Roman arbitration* (Holo Books 2004).

Roebuck D, 'Cleopatra Compromised: Arbitration in Egypt in the First Century BC' (2008) 74(3) Arbitration: the Journal of the Chartered Institute of Arbitrators 263.

Roebuck D, 'Cultural Differences and Mediation: An Introduction' (2002) 4(2) Asian Dispute Review 135.

Roebuck D, 'Sources for the History of Arbitration: A Bibliographical Introduction' (1998) 14(3) Arbitration international 237.

Roebuck D, *Ancient Greek Arbitration* (Holo Books 2001).

Rosoff J, 'Hybrid Efficiency in Arbitration: Waiving Potential Conflicts for Dual Role Arbitrators in Med–Arb and Arb–Med Proceedings' (2009) 26(1) Journal of International Arbitration 89.

Ross D, 'Med-Arb/Arb-Med: A More Efficient ADR Process or an Invitation to a Potential Ethical Disaster?' in Arthur W Rovine (ed), *Contemporary Issues in International Arbitration and Mediation: The Fordham Papers (2012)* (Brill Nijhoff 2013) 352.

Rubins N, 'The Allocation of Costs and Attorney's Fees in Investor-State Arbitration' (2003) 18(1) ICSID Review 109.

Salacuse J, 'Is There a Better Way? Alternative Methods of Treaty-Based, Investor-State Dispute Resolution' (2007) 31(1) Fordham International Law Journal 138.

Salacuse J, *The Law of Investment Treaties* (OUP Oxford 2015).

Salacuse J, 'Towards a Global Treaty on Foreign Investment: the Search for a Grand Bargain' in Norbert Horn and Stefan Kroll (eds), *Arbitrating Foreign Investment Disputes* (Kluwer Law International 2004) 51.

Sanders P, 'The History of the New York Convention' in Albert Jan van den Berg (ed), *Improving the Efficiency of Arbitration Agreements and Awards: 40 Years of Application of the New York Convention* (Kluwer Law International 1999) 11.

Sanders P, 'Procedures and Practices under the UNCITRAL Rules' (1979) 27(2–3) American Journal of Comparative Law 453.

Sanders P, 'UNCITRAL's Model Law on International Commercial Conciliation' (2007) 23(1) Arbitration International 105.

Sauve P, 'Multilateral Rules on Investment: Is Forward Movement Possible?' (2006) 9(2) Journal of International Economic Law 325.

Schaefer J, 'Leaving the Colonial Arbitration Laws Behind: Southeast Asia's Move into the International Arbitration Arena' (2000) 16(3) Arbitration International 297.

Schill S, 'Editorial: The Mauritius Convention on Transparency' (2015) 16(2) Journal of World Investment & Trade 201.

Schill S, 'Reforming Investor–State Dispute Settlement: A (Comparative and International) Constitutional Law Framework' (2017) 20(3) Journal of International Economic Law 649.

Schnabel T, 'The Singapore Convention on Mediation: A Framework for the Cross-Border Recognition and Enforcement of Mediated Settlements' (2019) 19(1) Pepperdine Dispute Resolution Law Journal 1.

Schreuer C, 'The Future of International Investment Law' in Marc Bungenberg et al (eds), *International Investment Law* (1st ed, Nomos Verlagsgesellschaft mbH & Co KG 2015) 1904.

Schreuer C, *The ICSID Convention: A Commentary* (Cambridge University Press 2009) 348.

Schreuer C, 'Travelling the BIT Route: of Waiting Periods, Umbrella Clauses and Forks in the Road' (2004) 5(2) Journal of World Investment & Trade 231.

Schwebel S, 'Is Mediation of Foreign Investment Disputes Plausible?' (2007) 22(2) ICSID Review 237.

Scott K and Wilson C, 'Questions Clients Have About Whether (and How) to Mediate and How Counsel Should Answer Them' (2008) 63(2) Dispute Resolution Journal 26.

Sekolec J and Getty M, 'The UMA and the UNCITRAL Model Rule: An Emerging Consensus on Mediation and Conciliation', (2003) 1 Journal of Dispute Resolution 175.

Senft L and Savage C, 'ADR in the Courts: Progress, Problems, and Possibilities' (2003) 108(1) Penn State Law Review 327.

Shalakany A, 'Arbitration and the Third World: A Plea for Reassessing Bias Under the Specter of Neoliberalism' (2000) 41(2) Harvard International Law Journal 419.

Shirlow E, 'The Promises and Pitfalls of Investor-State Mediation' in Lisa E Sachs, Lise Johnson and Jesse Coleman (eds), *Yearbook on International Investment Law and Policy 2019* (Oxford University Press 2021), 461.

Singh J, 'Indian Investment Treaty Practice: Qualitatively and Quantitatively Assessing Recent Developments' in Luke Nottage et al (eds), *New Frontiers in Asia-Pacific International Arbitration and Dispute Resolution* (Wolters Kluwer 2021) 287.

Slate W, 'UNCITRAL (United Nations Commission on International Trade Law) Its Workings in International Arbitration and a New Model Conciliation Law' (2004) 6(1) Cardozo Journal of Conflict Resolution 73.

Smit R and Robinson T, 'Cost Awards in International Commercial Arbitration: Proposed Guidelines for Promoting Time and Cost Efficiency' (2010) 20(3) The American Review of International Arbitration (ARIA) 267.

Sornarajah M, 'The Climate of International Arbitration', (1991) 8 (2) Journal of International Arbitration 47.

Sourdin T, *Alternative Dispute Resolution* (5th ed, Thomson Reuters Professional Australia Pty Limited 2016).

Spain A, 'Integration Matters: Rethinking the Architecture of International Dispute Resolution' (2010) 32(1) University of Pennsylvania Journal of International Law 1.

Spencer D and Brogan M, *Mediation Law and Practice* (Cambridge University Press 2006).

Spencer D, 'The Decline of the Trial in Australia' (2011) The Arbitrator and Mediator 1.

Steele B, 'Enforcing International Commercial Mediation Agreements as Arbitral Awards Under the New York Convention' (2006) 54(5) UCLA Law Review 1385.

Stipanowich T and Lamare R, 'Living with ADR: Evolving Perceptions and Use of Mediation, Arbitration, and Conflict Management in Fortune 1000 Corporations' (2014) 19(1) Harvard Negotiation Law Review 1.

Stipanowich T, 'Arbitration: The New Litigation' (2010) 1 University of Illinois Law Review 1.

Stipanowich T, 'Beyond Arbitration: Innovation and Evolution in the United States Construction Industry' (1996) 31(1) Wake Forest Law Review 65.

Stipanowich T, 'The International Evolution of Mediation: A Call for Dialogue and Deliberation' (2015) 46(4) Victoria University of Wellington Law Review 1191.

Strong S, 'Beyond International Commercial Arbitration-The Promise of International Commercial Mediation' (2014) 45(1) Washington University Journal of Law and Policy 10.

Strong S, 'Realizing Rationality: An Empirical Assessment of International Commercial Mediation' (2016) 73(4) Washington and Lee Law Review 1973.

Strong S, 'Recognition and Enforcement of Foreign Judgements in US Courts: Problems and Possibilities' (2014) 33(1) The Review of Litigation 45.

Strong S, 'The Role of Empirical Research and Dispute System Design in Proposing and Developing International Treaties: A Case Study of the Singapore Convention on Mediation' (2018) 20(4) Cardozo Journal of Conflict Resolution 1103.

Sussman E, 'Combinations and Permutations of Arbitration and Mediation: Issues and Solutions' in Arnold Ingen-Housz (ed), *ADR in Business Practice and Issues across Countries and Cultures* (Kluwer Law International 2011) 381.

Sussman E, 'Investor-State Dispute Mediation: The Benefits and Obstacles' in Arthur W Rovine (ed), *Contemporary Issues in International Arbitration and Mediation: The Fordham Papers (2009)* (Brill Nijhoff 2010) 321.

Sussman E, 'Med-Arb: An Argument for Favoring Ex Parte Communications in the Mediation Phase' (2013) 7(2) World Arbitration and Mediation Review 421.

Sussman E, 'The New York Convention Through a Mediation Prism' (2009) 15(4) Dispute Resolution Magazine 10.

Taelman P and Voet S, 'Mediation in Belgium: A Long and Winding Road' in Carlos Esplugues and Louis Marquis (eds), *New Developments in Civil and Commercial Mediation* (Springer 2015).

Thomas C, 'Reflections on article 1105 of NAFTA: History, State Practice and the Influence of Commentators' (2002) 17(1) ICSID Review 21.

Titi C, 'Mediation and the Settlement of Investment Disputes: Between Utopia and Realism' in Catharine Titi and Katia Fach Gómez (eds), *Mediation in International Commercial and Investment Disputes* (Oxford University Press 2019) 21.

Trakman L and Musayelyan D, 'The Repudiation of Investor–Sate Arbitration and Subsequent Treaty Practice: the Resurgence of Qualified Investor–State Arbitration' (2016) 31(1) ICSID Review-Foreign Investment Law Journal 194.

Ubilava A and Nottage L, 'Novel and Noteworthy Aspects of Australia's Recent Investment Agreements and ISDS Policy: The CPTPP, Hong Kong, Indonesia and Mauritius Transparency Treaties' in Luke Nottage et al (eds), *New Frontiers in Asia-Pacific International Arbitration and Dispute Resolution* (Wolters Kluwer 2021) 115.

Ubilava A, 'Amicable Settlements in Investor-State Disputes: Empirical Analysis of Patterns and Perceived Problems' (2020) 21(4) Journal of World Investment and Trade 528.

Ubilava A, 'Underutilisation of ADR in ISDS: Resolving Treaty Interpretation Issues' (2022) 26(2) UCLA Journal of International Law & Foreign Affairs 131.

Van den Berg A and Haag T, *The New York Arbitration Convention of 1958: Towards a Uniform Judicial Interpretation* (Kluwer law and taxation Deventer 1981).

van Ginkel E, 'The UNCITRAL Model Law on International Commercial Conciliation' (2004) 21(1) Journal of International Arbitration 1.

Van Harten G and Loughlin M, 'Investment Treaty Arbitration as a Species of Global Administrative Law' (2006) 17(1) European Journal of International Law 121.

Vandevelde K, 'A Brief History of International Investment Agreements' (2005) 12(1) UC Davis Journal of International Law & Policy 157.

Vandevelde K, 'Of Politics and Markets: The Shifting Ideology of the BITs' (1993) 11(2) International Tax & Business Lawyer 159.

Vandevelde K, *The First Bilateral Investment Treaties: U.S. Postwar Friendship, Commerce, and Navigation Treaties* (Oxford University Press 2017).

Vanoverbeke D, *Community and State in the Japanese Farm Village: Farm Tenancy Conciliation (1924–1938)*, vol 29 (Leuven University Press 2004).

Veltmeyer H, 'Liberalisation and Structural Adjustment in Latin America: In Search of an Alternative' (1993) 28(39) Economic and Political Weekly 2080.

Vidigal G and Stevens G, 'Brazil's New Model of Dispute Settlement for Investment: Return to the Past or Alternative for the Future?' (2018) 19(3) Journal of World Investment & Trade 475.

Villiger M, 'Part II Interpretation of Treaties, 6 The Rules on Interpretation: Misgivings, Misunderstandings, Miscarriage? The 'Crucible' Intended by the International Law Commission' in Enzo Cannizzaro (ed), *The Law of Treaties Beyond the Vienna Convention* (Oxford University Press, 2011) 109.

von Kumberg W, 'Making Mediation Mainstream: An Application for Investment Treaty Disputes' in Susan Franck and Anna Joubin-Bret (eds), *Investor-State Disputes: Prevention and Alternatives to Arbitration II* (UNCTAD 2011) 71.

von Kumberg W, Lack J and Leathes M, 'Enabling Early Settlement in Investor–State Arbitration: The Time to Introduce Mediation Has Come' (2014) 29(1) ICSID Review 133.

von Walter A, 'Investor-State Contracts in the Context of International Investment Law' in Marc Bungenberg et al (eds), *International Investment Law* (1st ed, Nomos Verlagsgesellschaft mbH & Co KG 2015) 80.

Wälde T, 'Efficient Management of Transnational Disputes: Mutual Gain by Mediation or Joint Loss in Litigation' (2006) 22(2) Arbitration International 205.

Ward E, 'Mandatory Court-Annexed Alternative Dispute Resolution in the United States Federal Courts: Panacea or Pandemic' (2007) 81(1) St. John's Law Review 77.

Webster T, 'Efficiency in Investment Arbitration: Recent Decisions on Preliminary and Costs Issues' (2009) 25(4) Arbitration International 469.

Weeramantry R, *Treaty Interpretation in Investment Arbitration* (Oxford University Press 2012) 40.

Welsh N and Schneider A, 'Becoming Investor-State Mediation'(2012) 1(1) Penn State Journal of Law and International Affairs 86.

Welsh N and Schneider A, 'The Thoughtful Integration of Mediation into Bilateral Investment Treaty Arbitration' (2013) 18(1) Harvard Negotiation Law Review 71.

Welsh N, 'Mandatory Mediation and Its Variations' in Susan Franck and Anna Joubin-Bret (eds), *Investor-State Disputes: Prevention and Alternatives to Arbitration II* (UNCTAD 2011) 108.

Welsh N, 'The Thinning Vision of Self-Determination in Court-Connected Mediation: The Inevitable Price of Institutionalization' (2001) 6(1) Harvard Negotiation Law Review 1.

Wilson T, 'Setting Boundaries Rather than Imposing Bans: Is it Possible to Regulate Consumer Arbitration Clauses to Achieve Fairness for Consumers?' (2016) 39(3) Journal of Consumer Policy 349.

Wissler R, 'Court-Connected Mediation in General Civil Cases: What We Know from Empirical Research' (2002) 17(3) Ohio State Journal on Dispute Resolution 641.

Wolski B, 'ARB-MED-ARB (and MSAs): A Whole Which Is Less than, Not Greater than, the Sum of Its Parts' (2013) 6(2) Contemporary Asia Arbitration Journal 249.

Wolski B, 'Enforcing Mediated Settlement Agreements (MSAs): Critical Questions and Directions for Future Research' (2014) 7(1) Contemporary Asia Arbitration Journal 87.

Yackee J, 'The First Investor-State Arbitration: The Suez Canal Company v Egypt (1864)' (2016) 17(3) Journal of World Investment & Trade 401.

Yeo A and Menon S, 'Indonesia-Arbitrating with Foreign Parties: A Closer Look at Indonesia's Approach to Investor-State Dispute Settlement' (2016) 18(3) Asian Dispute Review 124.

Online Journals, Blog Posts

Alexander N, 'Brexit and EU mediation' (18 July 2016) Kluwer Mediation Blog, available at <http://mediationblog.kluwerarbitration.com/2016/07/18/brexit-and-london-as-a-mediation-venue/>.

Alexander N, 'It's DONE: The Singapore Convention on Mediation' (9 August 2019) Kluwer Mediation Blog, available at <http://mediationblog.kluwerarbitration.com/2019/08/09/its-done-the-singapore-convention-on-mediation/>.

Anderson D, Alexander N and Howard A, 'UNCITRAL and the Enforceability of iMSAs: the Debate Heats Up – Part 3' (22 September 2016) Kluwer Mediation Blog, available at <http://mediationblog.kluwerarbitration.com/2016/09/22/uncitral-and-the-enforceability-of-imsas-the-debate-heats-up-part-3/>.

Armstrong S and Nottage L, 'The Impact of Investment Treaties and ISDS Provisions on Foreign Direct Investment: A Baseline Econometric Analysis' (2016) Research Paper No 16/74, Sydney Law School, available at <https://papers.ssrn.com/sol3/papers.cfm?abstract_id=2824090>.

Arthur H, 'Where do We Stand? Where Should We Go? An Assessment of Recent Costs Allocation Trends in International Commercial and Investment Arbitration' (2015) 12(6) Transnational Dispute Management, available at <https://www.transnational-dispute-management.com/article.asp?key=2279>.

Baertlein L, 'Starbucks to Pay $2.76 Billion in Kraft Grocery Rift' (13 November 2013) Reuters, available at <https://www.reuters.com/article/us-starbucks-kraft-idUSBRE9AB17920131112>.

Baker J, 'A 'Powerful Statement' for Multilateralism, Says PM Lee as 46 Countries Ink Singapore Convention on Mediation' (7 August 2019) Channel News Asia, available at <https://www.channelnewsasia.com/news/singapore/singapore-convention-on-mediation-un-trade-disputes-pm-lee-11787744>.

Barbière C, 'France and Germany to Form United Front Against ISDS' (15 January 2015) EURACTIV, available at <http://www.euractiv.com/section/trade-society/news/france-and-germany-to-form-united-front-against-isds/>.

Behn D and Daza A, 'The Defense Burden in Investment Arbitration' (2019) PluriCourts Working Paper.

Bernasconi-Osterwalder N and Rosert D, 'Investment Treaty Arbitration: Opportunities to reform arbitral rules and processes' (12 March 2014) International Institute for Sustainable Development, available at <https://www.iisd.org/publications/investment-treaty-arbitration-opportunities-reform-arbitral-rules-and-processes>.

Bollyky T, 'TPP Tobacco Exception Proves the New Rule in Trade' (4 February 2016) Expert Brief, available at <https://www.cfr.org/expert-brief/tpp-tobacco-exception-proves-new-rule-trade>.

Bond G, 'Who Should Be Promoting Mediation and Why? Mediation in Germany: The Poor Cousin to the Courts?' (24 November 2016) Kluwer Mediation Blog, available at <http://mediationblog.kluwerarbitration.com/2016/11/24/who-should-be-promoting-mediation-and-why-mediation-in-germany-the-poor-cousin-to-the-courts/>.

Cappiello B, 'ISDS in European International Agreements: Alternative Justice or Alternative to Justice?' (2016) 13(1) Transnational Dispute Management, available at <https://www.transnational-dispute-management.com/article.asp?key=2314>.

Charlotin D and Peterson L, 'Bolivia: an Update on Three Investment Treaty Arbitrations (Glencore, Abertis and Quiborax)' (12 May 2017) IA Reporter, available at <https://www-iareporter-com.ezproxy1.library.usyd.edu.au/articles/bolivia-an-update-on-three-investment-treaty-arbitrations/>.

Charlotin D, 'Barrick Puts Papua New Guinea on Notice of Dispute; Joint-Venture With Chinese Investors to Start Conciliation Proceedings at ICSID' (10 July 2020) IAReporter, available at <https://www-iareporter-com.ezproxy1.library.usyd.edu.au/articles/barrick-puts-papua-new-guinea-on-notice-of-dispute-joint-venture-with-chinese-investors-to-start-conciliation-proceedings-at-icsid/>.

Chew S, Reed L and Thomas C, 'Report: Survey on Obstacles to Settlement of Investor-State Disputes' (2018) National University of Singapore Working Paper, available at <https://papers.ssrn.com/sol3/papers.cfm?abstract_id=3247492>.

Chua A, 'Law Passed to Boost Framework for Commercial Mediation in S'pore' (11 January 2017) Today, available at <https://www.todayonline.com/singapore/law-passed-boost-framework-commerical-mediation-spore>.

Claxton J, 'Faithful Friend and Flattering Foe: How Investment Treaties Both Facilitate and Discourage Investor-State Mediation' (2 November 2020) SSRN, available at <https://papers.ssrn.com/sol3/papers.cfm?abstract_id=3690682>.

Claxton J, Nottage L and Ubilava A, 'Pioneering Mandatory Investor-State Conciliation Before Arbitration in Asia-Pacific Treaties: IA-CEPA and HK-UAE BIT' (5 September 2020) Kluwer Arbitration Blog, available at <http://arbitrationblog.kluwerarbitration.com/2020/09/05/pioneering-mandatory-investor-state-conciliation-before-arbitration-in-asia-pacific-treaties-ia-cepa-and-hk-uae-bit/>.

Connerty A, 'Alternative Dispute Resolution' (2007) 4(5) Transnational Dispute Management, availabe at <https://www.transnational-dispute-management.com/about-author-a-z-profile.asp?key=1088>.

De Palo G, D'Urso L, Trevor M, Branon B, Canessa R, Cawyer B and Florence L, 'Rebooting the Mediation Directive: Assessing the Limited Impact of its Implementation and Proposing Measures to Increase the Number of Mediations in the EU' (2014) Directorate General for Intenrational Policies, Policy Department C: Citizens' Rights and Constitutional Affairs 162, available at <https://www.europarl.europa.eu/thinktank/en/document/IPOL-JURI_ET(2014)493042>.

Douglas D, '19th International Arbitration Lecture: A Response to DFAT's Review of Australia's Bilateral Investment Treaties' (14 October 2020,)online lecture, available at <https://youtu.be/bwhUcDyBWlY>.

Ewing-Chow Mand Losari J, 'Indonesia is Letting its Bilateral Treaties Lapse so as to Renegotiate Better Ones' (15 April 2014) Centre for International Law-National University of Singapore, available at <https://cil.nus.edu.sg/wp-content/uploads/2010/12/Ewing-Chow+Losari-FT-Article-Indonesia-is-letting-its-bilateral-treaties-lapse-15Apr2014.pdf>.

Hainbach P, 'The EU's Approach to Investor-State Arbitration in the Comprehensive Economic and Trade Agreement (CETA)' (2016) 13(1) Transnational Dispute Management, available at <https://www.transnational-dispute-management.com/article.asp?key=2315>.

Hamamoto S and Nottage L, 'Foreign Investment In and Out of Japan: Economic Backdrop, Domestic Law, and International Treaty-based Investor-State Dispute Resolution' (2011) 8(5) Transnational Dispute Management, available at <https://www.transnational-dispute-management.com/article.asp?key=1766>.

Hamida B, 'Cost Issue in Investor-State Arbitration Decisions Rendered Against the Investor: a Synthetic Table' (2005) 2(5) Transnational Dispute Management, available at <https://www.transnational-dispute-management.com/article.asp?key=606>.

Harrison J, 'Recent Developments to Promote Transparency and Public Participation in Investment Treaty Arbitration' Working Paper No 2011/01, University of Edinburgh School of Law, available at <https://papers.ssrn.com/sol3/papers.cfm?abstract_id =1739181>.

Hepburn J and Huber M, 'An Assessment of Australia's Parliamentary Report on ISDS in the TPP' (5 January 2017) Kluwer Arbitration Blog, available at <http://kluwer arbitrationblog.com/2017/01/05/reserved-an-assessment-of-australias-parliament ary-report-on-isds-in-the-tpp/>.

Hesseldahl A, 'The Intel-AMD Settlement: A Play-by-Play' (16 November 2009) Bloomberg, available at <https://www.bloomberg.com/news/articles/2009-11-15 /the-intel-amd-settlement-a-play-by-play>.

Hindelang S, 'Study on Investor-State Dispute Settlement (ISDS) and Alternatives to Dispute Resolution in International Investment Law' (2016) 13(1) Transnational Dispute Management, available at <https://www.transnational-dispute-manage ment.com/article.asp?key=2313>.

Hodgson M and Campbell A, 'Damages and Costs in Investment Treaty Arbitration Revisited' (14 December 2017) Global Arbitration Review, available at <https:// globalarbitrationreview.com/damages-and-costs-in-investment-treaty-arbitration -revisited>.

Hodgson M, 'Costs in Investment Treaty Arbitration: The Case for Reform' (2014) 11(1) Transnational Dispute Management, available at <https://www.transnational-dis pute-management.com/article.asp?key=2088>.

Hutchens G, 'Trans-Pacific Partnership Makes Australia Vulnerable to Court Challenges, Report Claims' (25 October 2016,) International Trade News, available at <https:// www.theguardian.com/business/2016/oct/25/trans-pacific-partnership-makes -australia-vulnerable-to-court-challenges-report-claims>.

Johnson L and Bernasconi-Osterwalder N, 'New UNCITRAL Arbitration Rules on Transparency: Application, Content and Next Steps' (18 September 2013) Investment Treaty News, available at <https://www.iisd.org/itn/2013/09/18/new-uncitral-arbi tration-rules-on-transparency-application-content-and-next-steps-2/>.

Joubin-Bret A, 'Why We Need a Global Appellate Mechanism for International Investment Law' (27 April 2015) Columbia FDI Perspectives No 146, Columbia Centre on Sustainable Development.

Kamminga P, 'Overcoming Barriers to Using Mediation in Multi-Party Disputes' (27 July 2013) SSRN, available at <https://papers.ssrn.com/sol3/papers.cfm?abstract _id=2298874>.

Kapoor S, 'Singapore Convention Series: How Does The Singapore Mediation Convention Affect International Dispute Resolution? ISDS Perspective' (15 November 2019) Kluwer Mediation Blog, available at <http://mediationblog.kluwerarbitration.com/2019/11/15/singapore-convention-series-how-does-the-singapore-mediation-convention-affect-international-dispute-resolution-isds-perspective/>.

Kaufmann-Kohler G and Potestà M, 'Can the Mauritius Convention Serve as a Model for the Reform of Investor-State Arbitration in Connection with the Introduction of a Permanent Investment Tribunal or an Appeal Mechanism?' (3 June 2016) Research Paper, UNCITRAL, available at <https://www.uncitral.org/pdf/english/CIDS_Research_Paper_Mauritius.pdf>.

Kichaven J, 'A Tool for Multi-Party Insurance Litigation Mediation with "Additional Insureds"' (2008) Mediate.com, available at <https://www.mediate.com/articles/kichavenJ15.cfm>.

Lai A and Suen m, 'Background Paper for Session 1 – Overcoming Challenges to the Use of Mediation in ISDS' (9 November 2020) Virtual Pre-Intersessional Meeting on the Use of Mediation in ISDS, available at <https://aail.org/uncitral-wgiii-virtual-pre-intersessional/>.

Lavranos N, 'The Deafening Silence of the Anti-ISDS Groups After the Philip Morris Decision' (24 February 2016) Kluwer Arbitration Blog, available at <http://arbitrationblog.kluwerarbitration.com/2016/02/24/the-deafening-silence-of-the-anti-isds-groups-after-the-philip-morris-decision/>.

Lavranos N, 'The First Steps Towards a Multilateral Investment Court (MIC)' (13 July 2017) EFILA BLOG, available at <https://efilablog.org/2017/07/19/the-first-steps-towards-a-multilateral-investment-court-mic/>.

Lazo R and Di Benedetto F, 'Recent Developments in the Most Controversial Aspects of EU International Investment Agreements: Portfolio Investments and Investor-State Dispute Settlement', (2016) 13(1) Transnational Dispute Management, available at <https://www.transnational-dispute-management.com/article.asp?key=2317>.

Legum B, 'Appellate Mechanisms for Investment Arbitration: Worth a Second Look for the Trans-Pacific Partnership and the Proposed EU-US FTA?' (2014) 11(1) Transnational Dispute Management, available at <https://www.transnational-dispute-management.com/article.asp?key=2073>.

Loh D, 'Two Bills Passed to Boost Singapore's Position as Dispute Resolution Hub' (11 January 2017) Channel News Asia, available at <https://www.channelnewsasia.com/news/singapore/two-bills-passed-to-boost-singapore-s-position-as-dispute/3428178.html>.

Maniruzzaman M, 'A Rethink of Investor-State Dispute Settlement' (30 May 2013,) Kluwer Arbitration Blog, available at <http://arbitrationblog.kluwerarbitration.com/2013/05/30/a-rethink-of-investor-state-dispute-settlement/>.

Manukyan M, 'Singapore Convention Series: A Call For A Broad Interpretation Of The Singapore Mediation Convention In The Context Of Investor-State Disputes' (10 July 2019) Kluwer Mediation Blog, available at <http://mediationblog.kluwerarbitration.com/2019/06/10/singapore-convention-series-a-call-for-a-broad-interpretation-of-the-singapore-mediation-convention-in-the-context-of-investor-state-disputes/>.

Merritt C, 'Mediation in NSW Supreme Court works: Spigelman' (1 October 2010) The Australian, available at <www.theaustralian.com.au>.

Nappert S, Nottage L and Campbell C, 'Assessing Treaty-based Investor-State Dispute Settlement: Abandon, Retain or Reform?' (2014) 11(1) Transnational Dispute Management, available at <https://www.transnational-dispute-management.com/article.asp?key=2024>.

Ng D, 'Background Paper for Session 4 – "The Way Forward for Mediation as a Reform Option for ISDS"' (9 November 2020) Virtual Pre-Intersessional Meeting on the Use of Mediation in ISDS, available at <https://aail.org/wp-content/uploads/2020/11/2020_UNCITRAL_WGIII_Background_Paper_Session_4.pd>f.

Nguyen T and Vu T, 'Investor-State Dispute Settlement from the Perspective of Vietnam: Looking for a "Post-Honeymoon" Reform' (2014) 11(1) Transnational Dispute Management, available at <https://www.transnational-dispute-management.com/article.asp?key=2041>.

Nottage L, 'Are US Investors Exceptionally Litigious with ISDS Claims?' (14 November 2016) Kluwer Arbitration Blog, available at <http://kluwerarbitrationblog.com/2016/11/14/are-us-investors-exceptionally-litigious-with-isds-claims/>.

Nottage L, 'Clive Palmer Versus (Western) Australia. He Could Survive a High Court Loss if His Company is Found to be "Foreign"' (10 September 2020) The Conversation, available at <https://theconversation.com/clive-palmer-versus-western-australia-he-could-survive-a-high-court-loss-if-his-company-is-found-to-be-foreign-145334>.

Nottage L, 'Do Many of Australia's Bilateral Treaties Really Not Provide Full Advance Consent to Investor-State Arbitration? Analysis of Planet Mining v Indonesia and Regional Implications' (2015) 12(1) Transnational Dispute Management available at <https://www.transnational-dispute-management.com/article.asp?key=2177>.

Nottage L, 'Submission for DFAT Review of Australia's Bilateral Investment Treaties' (13 September 2020) available at <https://erga-omnes.sydney.edu.au/wp-content/uploads/2020/09/2020_DFATreviewBITs_Nottage_LN03-1.pdf>.

Nottage L, 'Will Privately-Supplied ADR Keep Growing in Japan?' (17 March 2010) Japanese Law And The Asia-Pacific, available at <https://japaneselaw.sydney.edu.au/2010/03/will-privately-supplied-adr-keep-growing-in-japan/>.

Onwuamaegbu U, 'The Role of ADR in Investor-State Dispute Settlement: The ICSID Experience' (2007) 4(1) Transnational Dispute Management, available at <https://www.transnational-dispute-management.com/article.asp?key=964>.

Paliashvili I, Burger E and Lewis M, 'Resolution of Commercial Disputes in Russia and Ukraine: is Mediation a Viable Option?' (2004) 1(3) Transnational Dispute Management, available at <https://www.transnational-dispute-management.com/article.asp?key=249>.

Papadimos N and King S, 'Australian Arbitration Week Recap: Re-assessing Australia's Bilateral Investment Treaty Practices' (29 October 2020) Kluwer Arbitration Blog, available at <http://arbitrationblog.kluwerarbitration.com/2020/10/29/australian-arbitration-week-recap-re-assessing-australias-bilateral-investment-treaty-practices/>.

Parra A, 'Advancing Reform at ICSID' (2014) 11(1) Transnational Dispute Management, available at <https://www.transnational-dispute-management.com/article.asp?key=2031>.

Pelc K, 'Does the International Investment Regime Induce Frivolous Litigation?' (10 May 2016) SSRN, available at <https://papers.ssrn.com/sol3/papers.cfm?abstract_id=2778056>.

Pernt V and Lukic S, 'Mediation on the Heels of Arbitration – Competition or Peaceful Coexistence?' (6 October 2016) Kluwer Arbitration Blog, available at <http://arbitrationblog.kluwerarbitration.com/2016/10/06/mediation-on-the-heels-of-arbitration-competition-or-peaceful-coexistence/>.

Peterson L, 'In an Apparent First, Investor and Host-State Agree to Try Mediation Under IBA Rules to Resolve an Investment Treaty Dispute' (14 April 2016) IAReporter, available at <https://www.iareporter.com/articles/in-an-apparent-first-investor-and-hossssst-state-agree-to-try-mediation-under-iba-rules-to-resolve-an-investment-treaty-dispute/>.

Peterson L, 'In-Depth: Arbitrators in Crystallex Case Sidestep Debate Over Lawful vs Unlawful Expropriation, and Accept Validity of Two of Four Damages Valuation Methods' (9 April 2016) IAReporter, available at <https://www-iareporter-com.ezproxy1.library.usyd.edu.au/articles/24957/>.

Polanco R, 'Is there a life for Latin American countries after denouncing the ICSID convention?' (2014) 11(1) Transnational Dispute Management, available at <https://www.transnational-dispute-management.com/article.asp?key=2037>.

Poole C, 'The Future of Mediation' (2015) Mediate.com, available at <https://www.mediate.com/articles/PooleFutures.cfm>.

Pouget S, 'Arbitrating and Mediating Disputes: Benchmarking Arbitration and Mediation Regimes for Commercial Disputes Related to Foreign Direct Investment' (1 October 2013) The World Bank, available at <https://openknowledge.worldbank.org/handle/10986/16849>.

Press Association, 'Corby Council Agrees Compensation for Birth Defects in Toxic Waste Case' (17 April 2010) The Guardian, available at <https://www.theguardian.com/environment/2010/apr/16/corby-compensation-birth-defects-toxic-steel>.

Ranald P, 'When Even Winning is Losing. The Surprising Cost of Defeating Philip Morris Over Plain Packaging' (27 March 2019) The Conversation, available at <https://theconversation.com/when-even-winning-is-losing-the-surprising-cost-of-defeating-philip-morris-over-plain-packaging-114279>.

Rheuben J and Nottage L, 'Resolving Claims from the Fukushima Nuclear Disaster' (26 Janaury 2015) Japanese Law And The Asia-Pacific (Japanese Law in Asia-Pacific Socio-Economic Context), available at <https://japaneselaw.sydney.edu.au/2015/01/resolving-claims-from-the-fukushima-nuclear-disaster/>.

Roberts A and Bouraoui Z, 'UNCITRAL and ISDS Reforms: Concerns about Costs, Transparency, Third Party Funding and Counterclaims' (6 June 2018) EJIL:TALK! Blog of the European Journal of International Law, available at <https://www.ejiltalk.org/uncitral-and-isds-reforms-concerns-about-costs-transparency-third-party-funding-and-counterclaims/>.

Roberts A and St. John T, 'UNCITRAL and ISDS Reforms: The Divided West and the Battle by and for the Rest' (30 April 2019) EJIL:TALK! Blog of the European Journal of International Law, available at <https://www.ejiltalk.org/uncitral-and-isds-reforms-the-divided-west-and-the-battle-by-and-for-the-rest/>.

Rubins R, 'Comments To Jack C. Coe Jr's Article on Conciliation' (2007) 4(1) Transnational Dispute Management, available at <https://www.transnational-dispute-management.com/article.asp?key=962>.

Sanderson C, 'Billion-dollar Odebrecht dispute settled through mediation' (2020) Global Arbitration Review, available at <https://globalarbitrationreview.com/settlements/billion-dollar-odebrecht-dispute-settled-through-mediation>.

Schill S, 'The TTIP Negotiations: US versus EU Leadership in Global Investment Governance' (4 March 2016) Kluwer Arbitration Blog, available at <http://arbitrationblog.kluwerarbitration.com/2016/03/05/the-ttip-negotiations-us-versus-eu-leadership-in-global-investment-governance/>.

Schneider M, 'Combining Arbitration with Conciliation' (2004) 1(1) Transnational Dispute Management, available at <https://www.transnational-dispute-management.com/article.asp?key=35>.

Skinner M et al, 'Update On The Singapore Mediation Convention' (28 January 2019) LEXOLOGY Newsfeed, available at <https://www.lexology.com/library/detail.aspx?g=818785ef-e7ab-4e41-9691-474886f84384>.

Sussman E, 'A Path Forward: A Convention for the Enforcement of Mediated Settlement Agreements' (2015) 12(6) Transnational Dispute Management, available at <https://www.transnational-dispute-management.com/article.asp?key=2295>.

Sussman E, 'Developing an Effective Med-arb/Arb-med Process' (2010) 7(1) Transnational Dispute Management, available at <https://www.transnational-dispute-management.com/article.asp?key=1592>.

Sussman E, 'The Advantages of Mediation and the Special Challenges to its Utilization in Investor State Disputes' (2014) 11(1) Transnational Dispute Management, available at <https://www.transnational-dispute-management.com/article.asp?key=2081>.

Tavernise S, 'Tobacco Firms' Strategy Limits Poorer Nations' Smoking Laws' (13 December 2013) The New York Times, available at <http://www.nytimes.com/2013/12/13/health/tobacco-industry-tactics-limit-poorer-nations-smoking-laws.html>.

Torres A and Otero H, 'Commercial Mediation in the Americas' (2016) 13(1) Transnational Dispute Management, available at <https://www.transnational-dispute-management.com/article.asp?key=2334>.

Ubilava A and Nottage L, 'ICSID's New Mediation Rules: A Small but Positive Step Forward' (17 October 2018) ICSID, available at <https://icsid.worldbank.org/sites/default/files/amendments/public-input/Ubilava_Notage_10.17.2018.pdf>.

Ubilava A, 'Mandatory Investor-State Conciliation in New International Investment Treaties: Innovation and Interpretation' (5 September 2020) Kluwer Mediation Blog, availale at <http://mediationblog.kluwerarbitration.com/2020/09/05/mandatory-investor-state-conciliation-in-new-international-investment-treaties-innovation-and-interpretation/>.

Uchkunova I and Temnikov O, 'Allocation of Costs in ICSID Arbitration' (3 December 2014) Kluwer Arbitration Blog, available at <http://arbitrationblog.kluwerarbitration.com/2014/12/03/allocation-of-costs-in-icsid-arbitration/>.

van Ginkel E, 'Toward Mandatory ICSID Conciliation?-Reflections on Professor Coe's Article on Investor-State Conciliation' (2007) 4(1) Transnational Dispute Management, available at <https://www.transnational-dispute-management.com/article.asp?key=961>.

Wells L, 'Investor State Conciliation – A Comment', (2005) 2(5) Transnational Dispute Management, available at <https://www.transnational-dispute-management.com/article.asp?key=678>.

Woods L, 'Fit for purpose? The EU's Investment Court System' (23 March 2016) Kluwer Arbitration Blog, available at <http://arbitrationblog.kluwerarbitration.com/2016/03/23/to-be-decided/>.

Cases

Abertis Infraestructuras S.A. v Government of Bolivia (PCA, Case No 2011–14, 11 May 2017).

Abertis Infraestructuras SA v Bolivia (Settlement Agreement) (PCA, Case No 2011–14, 11 May 2017).

ADC Affiliate Limited and ADC & ADMC Management Limited v The Republic of Hungary (Final Award) (ICSID Arbitral Tribunal, Case No ARB/03/16, 27 September 2006) [531]-[533].

ADF Group Inc. v United States of America (Award) (ICSID Arbitral Tribunal, Case No ARB(AF)/00/1, 9 January 2003) [164]-[165].

Aguas Del Tunari, S.A., v Republic of Bolivia (Decision on Jurisdiction) (ICSID Arbitral Tribunal, Case No ARB/02/3, 21 October 2005) [226].

Air BP S.A. v Plurinational State of Bolivia (Pending); *Guaracachi America, Inc. and Rurelec PLC v The Plurinational State of Bolivia (Final Award)* (PCA, Case No 2011–17, 31 January 2014).

Albacora S.A. v Republic of Ecuador (Final Award) (PCA, Case No 2016–11, 12 July 2017).

Almasryia for Operating & Maintaining Touristic Construction Co. L.L.C. v State of Kuwait (Award) (ICSID Arbitral Tribunal, Case No ARB/18/2, 1 November 2019).

American Manufacturing & Trading, Inc. v Republic of Zaire (Award) (ICSID Arbitral Tribunal, Case No ARB/93/1, 21 February 1997).

Amkor Technology v Tessera 5:14-cv-03604, ND Cal, 2014.

Appellate Body Report, *United States – Countervailing Duties on Certain Corrosion-Resistant Carbon Steel Flat Products from Germany*, WTO Doc WT/DS213/AB/R (28 November 2002) [61].

Application of the Convention on the Prevention and Punishment of the Crime of Genocide (Croatia v Serbia) (Judgment) [2015] ICJ Rep 3, 64 [138].

Azurix Corp. v The Argentine Republic (Award) (ICSID Arbitral Tribunal, Case No ARB/01/12, 14 July 2006).

Banco Bilbao Vizcaya Argentaria S.A. v Plurinational State of Bolivia (ICSID Arbitral Tribunal, Case No ARB(AF)/18/5, Pending).

Burlington Resources Inc. v Republic of Ecuador (Decision on Jurisdiction) (ICSID Arbitral Tribunal, Case No ARB/08/5, 2 June 2010).

Case concerning rights of nationals of the United States of America in Morocco (Judgment) [1952] ICJ Rep 176.

CME Czech Republic B.V. v The Czech Republic (UNCITRAL, Dissenting opinion of the Arbitrator JUDr Jaroslav Hándl against the Partial Arbitration Award, 13 September 2001).

CME Czech Republic B.V. v The Czech Republic (UNCITRAL, Partial Award, 13 September 2001).

Constitution of the Maritime Safety Committee of the Inter-Governmental Maritime Consultative Organization (Advisory Opinion) [1960] ICJ Rep 150.

Copper Mesa Mining Corporation v Republic of Ecuador (Final Award) (PCA, Case No 2012–2, 15 March 2016).

Crystallex International Corporation v Bolivarian Republic of Venezuela (Award) (ICSID Arbitral Tribunal, Case No ARB(AF)/11/2, 2 April 2016).

Deutsche Telekom v India (PCA, Case No 2014–10, 2 September 2013).

E.T.I. Euro Telecom International N.V. v Republic of Bolivia (II) (PCA, Settled).

Enron Corporation and Ponderosa Assets, L.P. v Argentine Republic (Award) (ICSID Arbitral Tribunal, Case No ARB/01/3, 22 May 2007).

Ethyl Corporation v The Government of Canada (Award on Jurisdiction) (24 June 1998).

Gao Haiyan and Xie Heping v Keeneye Holdings Limited and New Purple Golden Resources Development Limited, Hong Kong, Court of First Instance, Decision No HCCT 41/2010, 12 April 2011.

Gemplus, S.A., SLP, S.A., and Gemplus Industrial S.A. de C.V. v United Mexican States (Award) (ICSID Arbitral Tribunal, Case No ARB(AF)/04/3, 16 June 2010).

Glencore Finance (Bermuda) Ltd. v Plurinational State of Bolivia (PCA, Case No 2016–39, Pending).

GS Société Générale de Surveillance S.A. v Republic of the Philippines (Decision on Jurisdiction) (ICSID Arbitral Tribunal, Case No ARB/02/6, 29 January 2004).

Hess Equatorial Guinea, Inc. and Tullow Equatorial Guinea Limited v Republic of Equatorial Guinea (Pending) (ICSID Conciliation Commission, Case No CONC(AF)/12/1, 15 May 2012).

Holiday Inns S.A. and others v Morocco (Discontinued) (ICSID Arbitral Tribunal, Case No ARB/72/1, 17 October 1978).

Hulley Enterprises Limited (Cyprus) v The Russian Federation (Final Award) (PCA, Case No 2005-03/AA226, 18 July 2014).

Iberdrola, S.A. and Iberdrola Energía, S.A.U. v Plurinational State of Bolivia (PCA, Case No 2015-05, 16 February 2016).

International Research Corp PLC v Lufthansa Systems Asia Pacific Pte Ltd and another [2013] SGCA 55, 130.

Interpretation of the Agreement of 25 March 1951 between the WHO and Egypt (Advisory Opinion) [1980] ICJ Rep 73.

Itisaluna Iraq LLC and others v Republic of Iraq (Award), (ICSID Arbitral Tribunal, Case No. ARB/17/10, 3 April 2020, 60.

Julio Miguel Orlandini-Ágreda and Compañía Minera Orlandini Ltda. v Plurinational State of Bolivia (PCA, Case No 2018–39, Pending).

La Camerounaise des Eaux (CDE) v Republic of Cameroon and Cameroon Water Utilities Cooperation (CAMWATER) (Pending) (ICSID Conciliation Commission, Case No CONC/19/1, 24 May 2019).

LG&E Energy Corp, LG&E Capital Corp and LG&E International Inc v Argentine Republic (Decision on Liability) (ICSID Arbitral Tribunal, Case No ARB/02/1, 3 October 2006).

Loewen Group, Inc. and Raymond L. Loewen v United States of America (Award on Jurisdiction) (ICSID Arbitral Tribunal, Case No ARB(AF)/98/3, 5 January 2001) [40].

Mantenimientos, Ayuda a la Explotación y Servicios S.A. and Sociedad Española de Montajes Industriales S.A. (formerly Consorcio GLP) v Republic of Ecuador (Award on Jurisdiction) (ICC, 21 December 2018).

Merck Sharpe & Dohme (I.A.) Corporation v The Republic of Ecuador (Partial Final Award) (PCA, Case 2012–10, 25 January 2018).

Metalclad Corporation v The United Mexican States (Award) (ICSID Arbitral Tribunal, Case No ARB(AF)/97/1, 30 August 2000).

Methanex Corporation v United States of America (Final Award), 7 August 2005, Part IV Ch B [18] and [22].

Murphy Exploration & Production Company – International v The Republic of Ecuador (II) (Final Award) (PCA, Case No 2012–16, 10 February 2017).

Murphy Exploration and Production Company International v Republic of Ecuador (Award on Jurisdiction) (ICSID Arbitral Tribunal, Case No ARB/08/4, 15 December 2010).

Occidental Petroleum Corporation and Occidental Exploration and Production Company v The Republic of Ecuador (Decision on Jurisdiction) (ICSID Arbitral Tribunal, Case No ARB/06/11, 9 September 2008).

Oil Platforms (Preliminary Objection Judgment) [1996] ICJ Rep 803

Oiltanking GmbH, Graña Montero S.A. and Graña Montero S.A.A. v Bolivia (PCA, Settled).

Olin Holdings Limited v State of Libya (Award on Jurisdiction) (ICC, Case No 20355/MCP, 28 June 2016).

Pan American Energy LLC v Plurinational State of Bolivia (ICSID Arbitral Tribunal, Case No ARB/10/8, 24 February 2014).

Paz Holdings Ltd. v Plurinational State of Bolivia (11 November 2015).

Pope & Talbot Inc. v The Government of Canada (Award on the Merits of Phase II), 10 April 2001, [79].

Pulp Mills on the River Uruguay (Argentina v Uruguay) (Judgment) [2010] ICJ Rep 14, 46 [65].

Red Eléctrica Internacional S.A.U. v Plurinational State of Bolivia (13 November 2014).

Republic of Equatorial Guinea v CMS Energy Corporation and others (Report) (ICSID Conciliation Commission, Case No CONC(AF)/12/2, 12 May 2015).

Republic of Equatorial Guinea v CMS Energy Corporation and others (Report) (ICSID Arbitral Tribunal, Case No CONC(AF)/12/2, 12 May 2015).

RSM Production Corporation v Republic of Cameroon (Report) (ICSID Conciliation Commission, Case No CONC/11/1, 11 June 2013).

Salini Costruttori S.p.A. and Italstrade S.p.A. v Kingdom of Morocco (Decision on Jurisdiction) (ICSID Arbitral Tribunal, Case No ARB/00/4, 31 July 2001).

SEDITEX Engineering Beratungsgesellschaft für die Textilindustrie m.b.H. v Democratic Republic of Madagascar (Party Settlement) (ICSID Conciliation Commission, Case No CONC/82/1, 20 June 1983).

SEDITEX Engineering Beratungsgesellschaft für dieTextilindustrie m.b.H. v Madagascar (Report) (ICSID Conciliation Commission, Case No CONC/94/1, 19 July 1996).

Sempra Energy Internationa v The Argentine Republic (*Award*) (ICSID Arbitral Tribunal, Case No ARB/02/16, 28 September 2007).

SGS Société Générale de Surveillance S.A. v Islamic Republic of Pakistan (*Decision on Jurisdiction*) (ICSID Arbitral Tribunal, Case No ARB/01/13, 6 August 2003).

SGS Société Générale de Surveillance S.A. v Islamic Republic of Pakistan (*Decision on Jurisdiction*) (ICSID Arbitral Tribunal, Case No ARB/01/13, 6 August 2003).

Shareholders of SESAM v Central African Republic (*Report*) (ICSID Conciliation Commission, Case No CONC/07/1, 13 August 2008).

Société d'Energie et d'Eau du Gabon v Gabonese Republic (*Report*) (ICSID Conciliation Commission, Case No CONC/19/1, 19 September 2018).

South American Silver Limited v The Plurinational State of Bolivia (*Final Award*) (PCA, Case No 2013–15, 30 August 2018).

Southern Pacific Properties (Middle East) Limited v Arab Republic of Egypt (*Award*) (ICSID Arbitral Tribunal, Case No ARB/84/3, 20 May 1992).

Sovereignty over Pulau Ligitan and Pulau Sipadan (Indonesia/Malaysia) (*Judgment*) [2002] ICJ Rep 625, 645–646 [37]-[38].

Tesoro Petroleum Corporation v Trinidad and Tobago (*Report*) (ICSID Conciliation Commission, Case No CONC/83/1, 27 November 1985).

Tethyan Copper Company Pty Limited v Islamic Republic of Pakistan (*Award*) (ICSID Arbitral Tribunal, Case No ARB/12/1, 12 July 2019).

TG World Petroleum Limited v Republic of Niger (*Party Settlement*) (ICSID Conciliation Commission, Case No CONC/03/1, 8 April 2005).

The Odebrecht-Tecnimont-Estrella consortium v Corporación Dominicana de Empresas Eléctricas Estatales (*CDEEE*) (March 2020) Mediated Settlement Agreement, International *ADR* Center of the International Chamber of Commerce (*ICC*).

Togo Electricité v Republic of Togo (*Report*) (ICSID Conciliation Commission, Case No CONC/05/1, 6 April 2006).

Tokios Tokeles v Ukraine (*Dissenting Opinion*) (ICSID Arbitral Tribunal, Case No ARB/02/18, 29 April 2004).

Veteran Petroleum Limited (Cyprus) v The Russian Federation (*Final Award*) (PCA, Case No 2005-05/AA228, 18 July 2014).

Victor Pey Casado and President Allende Foundation v Republic of Chile (*Award*) (ICSID Arbitral Tribunal, Case No ARB/98/2, 2 May 2008).

Vodafone International Holdings BV v Government of India [*I*] (PCA, Case No 2016–35, 17 April 2014).

Western NIS Enterprise Fund v Ukraine (*Order*) (ICSID Arbitral Tribunal, Case No ARB/04/2, 16 March 2006).

White Industries Australia Limited v The Republic of India (UNCITRAL, Final Award, 30 November 2011).

Wintershall Aktiengesellschaft v Argentine Republic (Award) (ICSID Arbitral Tribunal, Case No ARB/04/14, 8 December 2008).

WorleyParsons International, Inc. v Republic of Ecuador (UNCITRAL, Pending).

Xenofon Karagiannis v Republic of Albania (Pending) (ICSID Conciliation Commission, Case No CONC/16/1, 16 May 2016) (*'Xenofon Karagiannis v Republic of Albania'*).

Yukos Universal Limited (Isle of Man) v The Russian Federation (Final Award) (PCA, Case No 2005–04/AA227, 18 July 2014).

Treaties

Additional Protocol Concerning the Reciprocal Encouragement and Protection of Investment, United States of America-The Czech Republic-Czech and Slovak Federal Republic, signed 22 October 1991, entered into force 19 December 1992 (Czech Republic-United States of America BIT).

Agreement Between Bosnia and Herzegovina and the Government of the Italian Republic on the Promotion and Protection of Investments, signed 19 May 2000, entered into force 10 February 2005, expired.

Agreement between Italy and Morocco for the Promotion and Protection of Investment, signed 18 July 1990, entered into force 7 April 2000 (Italy-Morocco BIT).

Agreement Between Japan and the Republic of Colombia for the Liberalization, Promotion and Protection of Investment, signed 12 September 2011, entered into force 11 September 2015 (Japan-Colombia BIT).

Agreement Between Japan and Ukraine for the Promotion and Protection of Investment, signed 5 February 2015, entered into force 26 November 2015 (Japan-Ukraine BIT).

Agreement Between Serbia and Montenegro and the State of Israel on Reciprocal Promotion and Protection of Investments, signed 28 July 2004, entered into force 7 February 2006.

Agreement Between the Government of Australia and the Government of the Republic of India on the Promotion and Protection of Investments, signed 26 February 1999, terminated 23 March 2017, entered into force 4 May 2000 (Australia-India BIT).

Agreement Between the Government of Canada and the Government of the Union of Soviet Socialist Republics for the Promotion and Reciprocal Protection of Investment, signed 20 November 1989, entered into force 27 June 1991.

Agreement Between the Government of Hong Kong and the Government of Australia for the Promotion and Protection of Investments, signed 15 September 1993, entered into force 15 October 1993, terminated 17 January 2020).

Agreement Between the Government of Montenegro and the Government of the Republic of Moldova on Promotion and Reciprocal Protection of Investments, signed 20 June 2014, entered into force 23 June 2015.

Agreement Between the Government of the Czech Republic and the Government of the State of Israel for the Reciprocal Promotion and Protection of Investments, signed 23 September 1997, entered into force 16 March 1999.

Agreement Between the Government of the Federal Democratic Republic of Ethiopia and the Government of the State of Israel for the Reciprocal Promotion and Protection of Investment, signed 26 November 2003, entered into force 15 February 2006.

Agreement Between the Government of the Hellenic Republic and the Government of the Republic of Albania for the Encouragement and Reciprocal Protection of Investments, signed 1 August 1991, entered into force 4 January 1995 (Greece-Albania BIT).

Agreement Between the Government of the Hong Kong Special Administrative Region of the People's Republic of China and the Government of The United Arab Emirates for the Promotion and Reciprocal Protection of Investments, signed and entered into force 6 March 2020 (Hong Kong-UAE BIT).

Agreement Between the Government of the Kingdom of Sweden and the Government of the Hungarian People's Republic for the Promotion and Reciprocal Protection of Investments, signed and entered into force 21 April 1987 (Sweden-Hungary BIT).

Agreement Between the Government of the Kingdom of Sweden and the Government of the Republic of India for the Promotion and Reciprocal Protection of Investments, signed 4 July 2000, terminated 22 March 2017, entered into force 1 April 2001, art 9 (Sweden-India BIT).

Agreement Between the Government of the Kingdom of Sweden and the Government of the Republic of Estonia on the Promotion and Reciprocal Protection of Investments, signed 31 March 1992, entered into force 20 May 1992.

Agreement Between the Government of the Kingdom of Thailand and the Government of the State of Israel for the Reciprocal Promotion and Protection of Investments, signed 18 February 2000, entered into force 28 August 2003.

Agreement Between the Government of the People's Republic of China and the Government of the State of Kuwait for the Promotion and Protection of Investments, singed 23 November 1985, entered into force 24 December 1986.

Agreement Between the Government of the People's Republic of Bulgaria and The Government of the Republic of Cyprus on Mutual Encouragement and Protection of Investments, signed 12 November 1987, entered into force 18 May 1988.

Agreement between the Government of the People's Republic of China and the Government of the State of Israel for the Promotion and Reciprocal Protection of Investments, signed 10 April 1995, entered into force 13 January 2009.

Agreement Between the Government of the Republic of Armenia and the Government of The United Arab Emirates for the Promotion and Reciprocal Protection of Investments, signed 22 July 2016, entered into force 21 November 2017 (Armenia-UAE BIT).

Agreement Between the Government of The Republic of Bulgaria and The Government of The State of Israel for the Promotion and Reciprocal Protection of Investments, signed 6 December 1993, entered into force 17 December 1996.

Agreement Between the Government of the Republic of Croatia and the Government of the State of Israel for the Reciprocal Promotion and Protection of Investments, signed 1 August 2000, entered into force 18 July 2003.

Agreement Between the Government of the Republic of Estonia and the Government of The United Arab Emirates for the Promotion and Reciprocal Protection of Investments, signed 20 April 2011, entered into force 21 March 2012 (Estonia-UAE BIT).

Agreement Between the Government of the Republic of Estonia and the State of Israel for the Promotion and Reciprocal Protection of Investments, signed 14 March 1994, entered into force 23 May 1995.

Agreement Between the Government of the Republic of Finland and the Government of the Republic of Guatemala on the Promotion and Protection of Investments, signed 14 April 2005, entered into force 6 January 2007 (Finland-Guatemala BIT).

Agreement Between the Government of the Republic of Finland and the Government of Georgia on the Promotion and Protection of Investments, signed 24 November 2006, entered into force 30 December 2007 (Georgia-Finland BIT).

Agreement Between the Government of the Republic of Guatemala and the Government of the Russian Federation on Promotion and Reciprocal Protection of Investments, signed 27 November 2013, not yet in force (Guatemala-Russian Federation BIT).

Agreement Between the Government of the Republic of India and the Government of Malaysia for the Promotion and Protection of Investments, signed 17 January 2011, entered into force 1 July 2011.

Agreement between the Government of the Republic of Kazakhstan and the Government of the United Arab Emirates on Promotion and Reciprocal Protection of Investments, signed 24 March 2018, not yet in force, art 10 (Kazakhstan-United Arab Emirates BIT).

Agreement Between the Government of the Republic of Korea and the Government of the State of Israel for the Reciprocal Promotion and Protection of Investments, signed 7 February 1999, entered into force 19 June 2003.

Agreement Between the Government of the Republic of Korea and the Government of the Republic of Guatemala for the Promotion and Protection of Investments, signed 1 August 2000, entered into force 17 August 2002 (Korea-Guatemala BIT).

Agreement Between the Government of the Republic of Korea and the Government of the Republic of Uzbekistan for the Promotion and Reciprocal Protection of Investments, signed 17 June 1992, entered into force 20 November 1992.

Agreement Between the Government of the Republic of Latvia and the Government of the State of Israel for the Promotion and Reciprocal Protection of Investments, signed 27 February 1994, entered into force 9 May 1995.

Agreement between the Government of the Republic of Lithuania and the Government of Ukraine for the promotion and reciprocal protection of investments, signed 8 February 1994, entered into force 6 March 1995.

Agreement Between the Government of the Republic of Paraguay and the Government of the Republic of Cuba on the Promotion and Reciprocal Protection of Investments, signed 21 November 2000, entered into force 6 December 2002.

Agreement Between the Government of the Republic of Serbia and the Government of The United Arab Emirates for the Promotion and Reciprocal Protection of Investments, signed 17 February 2013, entered into force 25 December 2014 (Serbia-UAE BIT).

Agreement Between the Government of the Republic of South Africa and the Government of the State of Israel for the Reciprocal Promotion and Protection of Investments, signed 20 July 2004, not yet in force.

Agreement Between the Government of the Republic of South Africa and the Government of the Republic of Zimbabwe, signed 27 November 2009, entered into force 15 September 2010.

Agreement between the Government of the Republic of Turkey and the Government of Romania on the reciprocal promotion and protection of investments, signed 3 March 2008, entered into force 8 July 2010.

Agreement Between the Government of the Slovak Republic and the Government of the State of Israel for the Promotion and Reciprocal Protection of Investments, signed 8 September 1999, entered into force 24 June 2003.

Agreement between the Government of the State of Israel and the Government of the Republic of the Union of Myanmar for the Reciprocal Promotion and Protection of Investments, signed 5 October 2014, entered into force 5 September 2017.

Agreement Between the Government of the State of Israel and the Government of the Republic of Azerbaijan for the Reciprocal Promotion and Protection of Investments, signed 20 February 2007, entered into force 5 September 2009.

Agreement Between the Government of the State of Israel and the Government of Mongolia for the Reciprocal Promotion and Protection of Investments, signed 25 November 2003, entered into force 2 September 2004.

Agreement Between the Government of the State of Israel and the Government of the Republic of Belarus for the Reciprocal Promotion and Protection of Investments, signed 11 April 2000, entered into force 14 August 2003.

Agreement Between the Government of the State of Israel and the Government of the Republic of El Salvador for the Reciprocal Promotion and Protection of Investments, signed 3 April 2000, entered into force 7 July 2003.

Agreement Between the Government of the State of Israel and the Government of the Republic of Armenia for the Promotion and Reciprocal Protection of Investments, signed 19 January 2000, entered into force 25 June 2003.

Agreement Between the Government of the State of Israel and the Government of the Republic of Cyprus for the Reciprocal Promotion and Protection of Investments, signed 13 October 1998, entered into force 17 June 2003.

Agreement Between the Government of the State of Israel and the Government of Romania for the Promotion and Reciprocal Protection of Investments, signed 3 August 1998, entered into force 27 July 2003.

Agreement Between the Government of the State of Israel and the Government of the Republic of Slovenia for the Reciprocal Promotion and Protection of Investments, signed 13 May 1998, entered into force 2 October 1999.

Agreement Between the Government of the State of Israel and the Government of the Oriental Republic of Uruguay for the Reciprocal Promotion and Protection of Investments, signed 30 March 1998, entered into force 7 October 2004.

Agreement Between the Government of the State of Israel and the Government of the Republic of Moldova for the Reciprocal Promotion and Protection of Investments, signed 22 June 1997, entered into force 16 March 1999.

Agreement Between the Government of the State of Israel and the Government of the Republic of Turkey for the Reciprocal Promotion and Protection of Investments, signed 14 March 1996, entered into force 27 August 1998.

Agreement Between the Government of the State of Israel and the Government of the Republic of Albania for the Promotion and Reciprocal Protection of Investments, signed 29 January 1996, entered into force 18 February 1997.

Agreement between the Government of the State of Israel and the Government of the Republic of Kazakhstan for the promotion and reciprocal protection of investments, signed 27 December 1995, entered into force 19 February 1997.

Agreement Between the Government of the State of Israel and the Government of the Republic of Argentina for the Promotion and Reciprocal Protection of Investments, signed 2 July 1995, entered into force 10 April 1997.

Agreement Between the Government of the State of Israel and the Government of the Republic of Georgia for the Promotion and Reciprocal Protection of Investments, signed 19 June, entered into force 18 February 1997.

Agreement Between the Government of the State of Israel and the Government of Turkmenistan for the Promotion and Reciprocal Protection of Investments, signed 24 May 1995, entered into force 18 February 1997.

Agreement Between the Government of the State of Israel and the Government of the Republic of Lithuania for the Promotion and Reciprocal Protection of Investments, signed 2 October 1994, entered into force 11 July 1996.

Agreement Between the Government of the State of Israel and the Government of the Republic of Uzbekistan for the Promotion and Reciprocal Protection of Investments, signed 4 July 1994, entered into force 18 February 1997.

Agreement Between the Government of the State of Israel and the Government of Ukraine for the Reciprocal Promotion and Protection of Investments, signed 24 November 2010, entered into force 20 November 2012.

Agreement Between the Government of the State of Israel and the Government of the Republic of Poland for the Promotion and Reciprocal Protection of Investments, signed 22 May 1991, entered into force 6 May 1992.

Agreement Between the Government of the State of Israel and the Government of the Republic of Guatemala for the Reciprocal Promotion and Protection of Investments, signed 7 November 2006, entered into force 15 January 2009, art 8 (Guatemala-Israel BIT).

Agreement Between the Government of the United Kingdom of Great Britain and Northern Ireland and the Government of the Republic of Panama for the Promotion and Protection of Investments, signed 7 October 1983, entered into force 7 November 1985.

Agreement Between the Government of the United Mexican States and the Government of the Republic of Belarus on the Promotion and Reciprocal Protection of Investments, signed 4 September 2008, entered into force 27 August 2009.

Agreement Between the Hashemite Kingdom of Jordan and the United Arab Emirates for the Promotion and Reciprocal Protection of Investments, signed 15 April 2009, entered into force 12 February 2010 (Jordan-UAE BIT).

Agreement Between the Lebanese Republic and the Federal Republic of Germany on the Promotion and Reciprocal Protection of Investments, signed 18 March 1997, entered into force 25 March 1999 (Lebanon-Germany BIT).

Agreement Between the Lebanese Republic and the Slovak Republic for the Promotion and reciprocal Protection of Investments, signed 20 February 2009, entered into force 22 May 2010, art 8 (Lebanon-Slovakia BIT).

Agreement Between the Republic of Austria and Georgia for the Promotion and Protection of Investments, signed 18 October 2001, entered into force 1 March 2004, art 12(1) (Austria-Georgia BIT).

Agreement Between the Republic of Austria and the Republic of Guatemala for the Promotion and Protection of Investments, signed 16 January 2006, entered into force 1 December 2012 (Austria-Guatemala BIT).

Agreement Between the Republic of Chad and the Republic of Italy to Protect and Promote Investment Capital, signed 11 June 1969, entered into force 11 June 1969, art 7 (Chad-Italy BIT).

Agreement Between the Republic of Guatemala and the Czech Republic for the Promotion and Reciprocal Protection of Investments, signed 8 July 2003, entered into force 29 April 2005 (Czech Republic-Guatemala BIT).

Agreement Between the Republic of Guatemala and the Kingdom of the Netherlands on the Promotion and Reciprocal Protection of Investments, signed 18 May 2001, entered into force 1 September 2002 (Guatemala-Netherlands BIT).

Agreement Between the Republic of Korea and the Republic of Austria for the Encouragment and Protection of Investments, signed 14 March 1991, entered into force 1 November 1991, art 8 (Korea-Austria BIT).

Agreement Between the Slovak Republic and the Republic of Moldova for the Promotion and Reciprocal Protection of Investments, signed 7 April 2008, entered into force 15 November 2009.

Agreement Between the State of Israel and Japan for the Liberalization, Promotion and Protection of Investment, signed 1 February 2017, entered into force 5 October 2017.

Agreement Between the State of Israel and Serbia and Montenegro for the Reciprocal Promotion and Protection of Investments, signed 28 July 2004, entered into force 7 February 2006.

Agreement between the United States of America, the United Mexican States, and Canada, signed and entered into force 1 July 2020 (USMCA).

Agreement for the Reciprocal Promotion and Protection of Investments Between the Argentine Republic and the United Arab Emirates, signed 16 April 2018, not yet in force, art 20 (Argentina-UAE BIT).

ASEAN Comprehensive Investment Agreement, signed 26 February 2009, entered into force 24 February 2012.

ASEAN-Australia-New Zealand Free Trade Agreement, signed 27 February 2009, entered into force 1 January 2010 (AANZFTA).

Comprehensive and Progressive Agreement for Trans-Pacific Partnership (CPTPP), opened for signature 8 March 2018, entered into force 30 December 2018.

Comprehensive Economic and Trade Agreement (CETA), signed 20 October 2016, entered into force provisionally 21 September 2017 (Comprehensive Economic and Trade Agreement (CETA).

Comprehensive Economic Cooperation Agreement Between the Republic of India and the Republic of Singapore, signed 29 June 2005, entered into force 1 August 2005.

Convention for the Pacific Settlement of International Disputes (Hague Convention I), signed 29 July 1899, entered into force 4 September 1900.

Convention for the Pacific Settlement of International Disputes (Hague Convention II), signed 18 October 1907, entered into force 26 January 1910.

Convention on Jurisdiction and the Enforcement of Judgements in Civil and Commercial Matters, opened for signature 27 September 1968, entered into force 1 February 1973 (Brussels Convention).

Convention on the Recognition and Enforcement of Foreign Arbitral Awards, opened for signature 10 June 1958, 330 UNTS 3, entered into force 7 June 1959 (The New York Convention).

Convention on the Settlement of Investment Disputes between States and Nationals of Other States, opened for signature 18 March 1965, 575 UNTS 159, entered into force 14 October 1966 (The ICSID Convention).

Cooperation and Investment Facilitation Agreement between the Government of the Federative Republic of Brazil and the Government of the Republic of Mozambique, signed 30 March 2015, not yet in force (Brazil-Mozambique CIFA).

Cooperation and Investment Facilitation Agreement between the Government of the Federative Republic of Brazil and the Government of the Republic of Angola, signed 1 April 2015, entered into force 28 July 2017 (Brazil-Angola CIFA).

Décret no 96–915 du 9 octobre 1996 portant publication de l'accord entre le Gouvernement de la République française et le Gouvernement de la République des Philippines sur l'encouragement et la protection réciproques des investissements (ensemble un protocole), signed 13 September 1994, entered into force 12 June 1996, art 8 (France-Philippines BIT).

Free Trade Agreement between the Government of the Republic of Korea and the Government of the Socialist Republic of Vietnam, signed 5 May 2015, entered into force 20 December 2015.

Free Trade Agreement between the Republic of Korea and the Republics of Central America, signed 21 February 2018, entered into force 1 November 2019, art 9.16 (Free Trade Agreement between the Republic of Korea and the Republics of Central America).

Geneva Convention on the Execution of Foreign Arbitral Awards, opened for signature 26 September 1927, 92 LNTS 301, entered into force 25 July 1929 (Geneva Convention on the Execution of Foreign Arbitral Awards).

Geneva Protocol on Arbitration Clauses, opened for signature 24 September 1923, 27 LNTS 157, entered into force 28 July 1924 (Geneva Protocol on Arbitration Clauses).

Indonesia-Australia Comprehensive Economic Partnership Agreement, signed 4 March 2019, entered into force 5 July 2020 (IA-CEPA).

Investment Protection Agreement, signed 19 October 2018, not yet in force, annex 6 (EU-Singapore IPA).

NAFTA, Agreement Between the United States of America, the United Mexican States, and Canada 7/1/20.

Netherlands and Indonesia Agreement on Economic Cooperation, signed 7 July 1968, entered into force 7 July 1971, art 11 (Indonesia-Netherlands BIT).

Peru-Australia Free Trade Agreement, signed and entered into force 11 February 2020, art 8.19 (Peru-Australia Free Trade Agreement).

The Energy Charter Treaty (ECT), opened for signature December 1994, entered into force April 1998.

The Multilateral Agreement on Investment: Commentary to the Consolidated Text, DAFFE/MAI(98)8/REV1.

The Multilateral Agreement on Investment: Draft Consolidated Text, DAFFE/MAI(98)7/ REV1.

The Vienna Convention on the Law of Treaties, opened for signature 23 May 1969, 1155 UNTS 331, entered into force 27 January 1980.

Trade Agreement and an Investment Protection Agreement, signed 30 June 2019, trade agreement entered into force 1 August 2020, investment protection agreement not yet in force (EU-Vietnam FTA).

Treaty Between the Federal Republic of Germany and the State of Israel Concerning the Encouragement and Reciprocal Protection of Investments, signed 24 June 1976, not yet in force.

Treaty Between the United States of America and Jamaica Concerning the Reciprocal Encouragement and Protection of Investment, signed 4 February 1994, entered into force 7 March 1997.

Treaty Between the United States of America and the Republic of Turkey Concerning the Reciprocal Encouragement and Protection of Investments, signed 3 December 1985, entered into force 18 May 1990 art VI (US-Turkey BIT).

Treaty Between United States of America and the Argentine Republic Concerning the Reciprocal Encouragement and Protection of Investment, signed 14 November 1991, entered into force 20 October 1994.

United Nations Convention on International Settlement Agreements Resulting from Mediation, opened for signature 7 August 2019, entered into force 12 September 2020 (Singapore Convention on Mediation).

United Nations Convention on Transparency in Treaty-based Investor-State Arbitration, opened for signature 10 December 2014, entered into force 18 October 2017 (Mauritius Convention on Transparency).

Legislation

Arbitration Act 1996 (UK).

Civil Procedure Act 2005 (NSW) No 28, s 26(1).

Commercial Arbitration Act 2010 (NSW.

Federal Court of Australia Act 1976 (Cth).

International Arbitration Act (Chapter 143A) 1994 (Singapore).

Model Text for the Indian Bilateral Investment Treaty 2015 (India) (India Model BIT).

New Hong Kong Arbitration Ordinance 2010.

Other Material

'AMD and Intel Announce Settlement of All Antitrust and IP Disputes' (12 November 2009) Intel Newsroom, available at <https://www.intel.com/pressroom/archive/releases/2009/20091112corp_a.htm>.

'Coffee with Moustafa El Bahabety, Deputy Justice Minister for Arbitration and International Disputes and the Commissioner of the High Council for International Arbitration' (10 November 2016) Enterprise, available at <https://enterprise.press/stories/2016/11/10/coffee-with-moustafa-el-bahabety-deputy-justice-minister-for-arbitration-and-international-disputes-and-the-commissioner-of-the-high-council-for-international-arbitration/>.

'How Users View the Proposal for a UN Convention on the Enforcement of Mediated Settlements', International Mediation Institute, available at <https://www.imimediation.org/wp-content/uploads/2018/06/IMI-UN-Convention-on-Enforcement-Survey-Summary-final-27.11.14.pdf>.

'IBA Mediation Committee Reports on UNCITRAL Model Law Regarding Conciliation', International Bar Association, available at <https://www.ibanet.org/ENews_Archive/IBA_November_2007_ENews_MediationSummary.aspx>.

'ICC 2014 Mediation Guidance Notes', International Chamber of Commerce (ICC).

'ICC Celebrates Case Milestone, Announces Record Figures for 2019', International Chamber of Commence, available at <https://iccwbo.org/media-wall/news-speeches/icc-celebrates-25000th-case-milestone-and-announces-record-figures-for-2019/>.

'ICC releases 2019 Dispute Resolution statistics' (15 July 2020) ICC News, available at <https://iccwbo.org/media-wall/news-speeches/icc-releases-2019-dispute-resolution-statistics/>.

'Measuring the Costs of Delays in Dispute Resolution: Arbitration is Faster to Resolution than Court – and the Difference Can be Assessed Monetarily' American Arbitration Association, available at <https://go.adr.org/impactsofdelay.html>.

'Statistics', China International Economic and Trade Arbitration Commission, available at <http://www.cietac.org/index.php?m=Page&a=index&id=40&l=en>.

'Statistics', Hong Kong International Arbitration Centre, available at <https://www.hkiac.org/about-us/statistics>.

'Status: UNCITRAL Model Law on International Commercial Conciliation (2002)', UNCITRAL, available at <https://uncitral.un.org/en/texts/arbitration/modellaw/commercial_conciliation/status>.

2014 Annual Review, Supreme Court of New South Wales, 34 (2014 Annual Review).

Academic Forum on ISDS – Working Group 2, 'Duration of ISDS Proceedings', Concept Papers Project: Matching Concerns and Reform Options, Geneva Center for International Dispute Settlement, available at <https://www.cids.ch/images/Documents/Academic-Forum/2_Duration_-_WG2.pdf>.

Allsop J, 'Commercial and Investor-state Arbitrations: the Importance of Recognising their Differences' (16 April 2018) Opening Keynote Address, ICCA Congress Sydney.

American Arbitration Association, 'Drafting Dispute Resolution Clauses A Practical Guide' (2013) 16.

Asian Academy of International Law, 'UNCITRAL Working Group III Virtual Pre-Intersessional Meeting (Afternoon Session)' (15 November 2020) virtual conference, Youtube, available at <https://www.youtube.com/watch?v=AEjp_ASQfj8>.

Australian Disputes Centre, available at <https://www.disputescentre.com.au/history>.

Australian Government Attorney General's Department, available at <https://www.ag.gov.au/LegalSystem/AlternateDisputeResolution/Pages/default.aspx>.

Australian Government Department of Foreign Affairs and Trade, 'Australia-United Kingdom Free Trade Agreement', FTAs under Negotiation, available at <https://www.dfat.gov.au/trade/agreements/negotiations/Pages/ftas-under-negotiation>.

Australian Government Productivity Commission, 'Access to Justice Arrangements: Overview' (2014) Inquiry Report No. 72.

Centre for Effective Dispute Resolution, 'CEDR Commission on Settlement in International Arbitration' (2009).

Centre for Effective Dispute Resolution, 'The Seventh Mediation Audit A survey of commercial mediator attitudes and experience' (2016) CEDR, available at <https://www.cedr.com/wp-content/uploads/2020/01/The_Seventh_Mediation_Audit_2016-1.pdf>.

Council of the European Union, 'Parliamentary Debates, on certain aspects of mediation in civil and commercial matters' European Parliament, Directive 2008/52/EC.

CPR International Institute for Conflict Preservation & Resolution, 'Attitudes Toward ADR In the Asia-Pacific Region: A CPR Survey' (2013).

Energy Charter Secretariat, 'Decision of the Energy Charter Conference', 2016.

Energy Charter Secretariat, 'The International Energy Charter Consolidated Energy Charter Treaty', 2016.

Energy Charter Secretariat, Conflict Prevention and Dispute Resolution: Main Provisions and Instruments (2016).

European Commission, 'Commission Proposes New Investment Court System for TTIP and Other EU Trade and Investment Negotiations' (16 September 2015) News Archive, available at <http://trade.ec.europa.eu/doclib/press/index.cfm?id=1364>.

European Commission, 'EU Negotiating Texts in TTIP' (14 July 2016) News Archive, available at <http://trade.ec.europa.eu/doclib/press/index.cfm?id=1230>.

European Commission, 'EU-Singapore Trade and Investment Agreements' (18 April 2018) News Archive, available at <http://trade.ec.europa.eu/doclib/press/index.cfm?id=961>.

European Commission, 'The EU and Vietnam finalise landmark trade deal' (2 December 2015) News Archive, available at <http://trade.ec.europa.eu/doclib/press/index.cfm?id=1409>.

IAReporter, 'News Headlines', available at <https://www.iareporter.com/>.

ICC Moot, 'World Bank List of Economies (June 2017)', available at <http://iccmoot.com/wp-content/uploads/2017/07/World-Bank-List-of-Economies.pdf>.

ICSID Case Database in December 2020 'ICSID Caseload Database', available at <https://icsid.worldbank.org/en/Pages/cases/AdvancedSearch.aspx>.

ICSID, 'ICSID Hosts Half-Day Event, "Investor-State Mediation: Perspectives from States, Mediators & Practitioners" on June 15' (14 July 2017) News Releases, available at <https://icsid.worldbank.org/en/Pages/News.aspx?CID=243>.

ICSID, 'Search Cases', available at <https://icsid.worldbank.org/cases/case-database>.

ICSID, Additional Facility Rules (2006) (ICSID Additional Facility Rules).

ICSID, Administrative and Financial Regulations (2006) (ICSID Administrative and Financial Regulations).

ICSID, 'Model ICSID Arbitration Clauses', available at <http://icsidfiles.worldbank.org/icsid/icsid/staticfiles/model-clauses-en/main-eng.htm>.

ICSID, Proposals for Amendment of the ICSID Rules, Working Paper No 1, Synopsis, 3 August 2018, (ICSID WP1 – Synopsis).

ICSID, Proposals for Amendment of the ICSID Rules, Working Paper No 1, Consolidated Rules, 3 August 2018, (ICSID WP1 – Consolidated Rules).

ICSID, Proposals for Amendment of the ICSID Rules, Working Paper No 2, Consolidated Rules, 15 March 2019, (ICSID WP2 – Consolidated Rules).

ICSID, Proposals for Amendment of the ICSID Rules, Working Paper No 3, 16 August 2019, (ICSID WP3).

ICSID, Proposals for Amendment of the ICSID Rules, Working Paper No 4, 28 February 2020, (ICSID WP4).

ICSID, Rules of Procedure for Arbitration Proceedings (Arbitration Rules) (2006) (ICSID Arbitration Rules).

ICSID, Rules of Procedure for Conciliation Proceedings (Conciliation Rules) (2006).

International Chamber of Commerce Commission Report, 'Controlling Time and Costs in Arbitration' (2018) ICC Publication 861–2 ENG.

International Energy Charter, 'List of Cases', available at <https://www.energychartertreaty.org/cases/list-of-cases/>.

International Standard Industrial Classification of All Economic Activities (ISIC), UN Doc ST/ESA/STAT/SER.M/4/Rev.4, 2008.

Investment Policy Responses to the Covid-19 Pandemic, UN Doc Special Issue No.2, UNCTAD, 4 May 2020.

Italaw, 'Newly Posted Awards, Decisions & Materials', available at <https://www.italaw.com/>.

Joint Standing Committee on Treaties (JSCOT), Report 165 Trans-Pacific Partnership Agreement (Report No 165, 2016).

LCIA, 'Director General's Report 2008', available at <https://www.lcia.org/LCIA/reports.aspx.

LCIA, 'Director General's Report 2009', available at <https://www.lcia.org/LCIA/reports.aspx.

LCIA, 'Director General's Report 2010', available at <https://www.lcia.org/LCIA/reports.aspx>.

LCIA, 'Registrar's Report 2015', available at <https://www.lcia.org/LCIA/reports.aspx>.

Model Law on International Commercial Arbitration, GA Res 40/72, UN Doc A/40/17, Annex I, 21 June 1985, art 30 (1).

Model Law on International Commercial Conciliation, GA Res 57/18, UN Doc A/RES/57/18, 24 January 2003 (Model Law on International Commercial Conciliation).

Model Law on International Commercial Mediation and International Settlement Agreements Resulting from Mediation, GA Res 73/199, UN Doc A/RES/73/199, 3 January 2019, adopted 20 December 2018.

OECD Database, available at <http://www1.oecd.org.ezproxy.library.sydney.edu.au/daf/mai/index.htm.

Official Records of the General Assembly, Seventy-second Session, Supplement No. 17 (A/72/17).

Pinsent Masons and QMUL, 'International Arbitration Survey – Driving Efficiency in International Construction Disputes' (2019), available at <https://www.pinsentmasons.com/thinking/special-reports/international-arbitration-survey>.

Productivity Commission, 'Bilateral and Regional Trade Agreements', Productivity Commission Research Report, Australian Government.

Queen Mary University London (QMUL) and Corporate Counsel International Arbitration Group (CCIAG), QMUL-CCIAG Survey: Investors' Perceptions of ISDS (2020).

Queen Mary University London (QMUL), 'Corporate choices in International Arbitration: Industry perspectives' (2013).

Queen Mary University London (QMUL), 'International Arbitration Survey: Improvements and Innovations in International Arbitration', 2015.

Queen Mary University London (QMUL), 'International Arbitration Survey: The Evolution of International Arbitration', 2018.

RCEP draft (leaked) <https://www.keionline.org/23065>.

Reinisch A, 'Dispute Settlement-2.2 Selecting the Appropriate Forum' (2003) UNCTAD, UN Doc UNCTAD/EDM/Misc.232/Add.1.

Settlement of Commercial Disputes – Enforcement of Settlement Agreements Resulting from International Commercial Conciliation/Mediation – Compilation of Comments by Governments, 48th sess, UN Doc A/CN.9/846/Add.2, 22 April 2015.

Submission from the European Union and its member States (A/CN.9/WG.III/WP.159/Add.1,).

Submission from the Government of Brazil (A/CN.9/WG.III/WP.171).

Submission from the Government of China (A/CN.9/WG.III/WP.177).

Submission from the Government of Indonesia (A/CN.9/WG.III/WP.156).

Submission from the Government of Mali (A/CN.9/WG.III/WP.181).

Submission from the Government of Morocco (A/CN.9/WG.III/WP.161).

Submission from the Government of South Africa (A/CN.9/WG.III/WP.176).

Submission from the Government of Thailand (A/CN.9/WG.III/WP.162).

Submission from the Government of the Republic of Korea (A/CN.9/WG.III/WP.179).

Submission from the Governments of Chile, Israel, and Japan (A/CN.9/WG.III/WP.163).

Submission from the Governments of Chile, Israel, Japan, Mexico, and Peru (A/CN.9/WG.III/WP.182).

Talpis J, 'Recent Developments Relating to the Use of Mediation to Resolve International Disputes in Canada' (28 August 2015) Advisory Committee on Private Commercial Disputes (Article 2022, NAFTA) Conference Paper.

The Energy Charter Conference, *Guide on Investment Mediation* (2016).

The Institute of Arbitrators & Mediators Australia, available at <https://www.iama.org.au/about-us>.

UNCIRAL Working Group III, available at <https://uncitral.un.org/en/working_groups/3/investor-state>.

UNCITRAL Arbitration Rules (as revised in 2010), GA Res 65/22, UN Doc A/RES/65/22 (10 January 2011, adopted 6 December 2010) art 34(5) (UNCITRAL Arbitration Rules).

UNCITRAL Arbitration Rules, GA Res 31/98, UN GAOR, 31st sess, 99th plen mtg, Supp No 39, adopted 15 December 1976 (UNCITRAL Arbitration Rules).

UNCITRAL Conciliation Rules, UN GAOR, 35th sess, Supp No 17, UN Doc A/35/17, 23 July 1980.

UNCITRAL Working Group II, 'Planned and Possible Future Work – Part III Proposal by the Government of the United States of America: Future Work for Working Group II' (2 June 2014) 47th sess, UN Doc A/CN.9/822.

UNCITRAL Working Group II, 'Report of Working Group II (Arbitration and Conciliation) on the Work of its Sixty-Third Session' (Vienna, 7–11 September 2015), UNCITRAL, 49th sess, UN Doc A/CN.9/861.

UNCITRAL Working Group II, 'Report of Working Group II (Dispute Settlement) on the Work of its Sixty-Fifth Session' (Vienna, 12–23 September 2016), 50th sess, UN Doc A/CN.9/896.

UNCITRAL Working Group II, 'Settlement of commercial disputes – International commercial conciliation: enforceability of settlement agreements' (Arbitration and Conciliation), UN Doc A/CN.9/WG.II/WP.195.

UNCITRAL Working Group II, 'Settlement of commercial disputes: Enforceability of settlement agreements resulting from international commercial conciliation/ mediation – Revision of the UNCITRAL Notes on Organizing Arbitral Proceedings' (Arbtiration and Conciliation), UN Doc A/CN.9/WG.II/WP.188.

UNCITRAL Working Group III, 'Draft Summary Possible Reform of Investor-State Dispute Settlement (Addendum)' UN Doc A/CN.9/WG.III/XXXIX/CRP.1/Add.1 [18].

UNCITRAL Working Group III, 'Possible reform of investor-State dispute settlement (ISDS) Dispute prevention and mitigation – Means of alternative dispute resolution' A/CN.9/WG.III/WP.190.

UNCITRAL Working Group III, 'Possible reform of investor-State dispute settlement (ISDS) Dispute prevention and mitigation – Means of alternative dispute resolution A/CN.9/WG.III/WP.190.

UNCITRAL Working Group III, 'Possible Reform of Investor-State Dispute Settlement (ISDS) – Cost and Duration' UN Doc A/CN.9/WG.III/WP.153.

UNCITRAL Working Group III, 'Possible reform of investor-State dispute settlement (ISDS) – Dispute prevention and mitigation – Means of alternative dispute resolution' A/CN.9/WG.III/WP.190.

UNCTAD, 'Denunciation of the ICSID Convention and BITS: Impact on Investor-State Claims' IIA Issues Note, No 2 2010, UN Doc UNCTAD/WEB/DIAE/IA/2010/6).

UNCTAD, 'Dispute Settlement: Investor-State', UNCTAD Series on Issues in International Investment Agreements, UNCTAD/ITE/IIT/30, 26 July 2003.

UNCTAD, 'Investor-State Dispute Settlement: A Sequel' UNCTAD Series on Issues in International Investment Agreements II, UNCTAD/DIAE/IA/2013/2, May 2014, 197.

UNCTAD, 'Investor-State Dispute Settlement: Review of Developments in 2015', 2016 (IIA Issue Note, No. 2, 2016).

UNCTAD, 'Investor–State Disputes: Prevention and Alternatives to Arbitration' UN Doc UNCTAD/DIAE/IA/2009/11, 1 August 2010.

UNCTAD, 'Reform of Investor-State Dispute Settlement: In Search of a Roadmap', IIA Issues Note N2, June 2013.

UNCTAD's Investment Policy Hub, available at <https://investmentpolicy.unctad.org/>.

United Nations Treaty Collection, 'United Nations Convention on International Settlement Agreements Resulting from Mediation', available at <https://treaties.un.org/pages/ViewDetails.aspx?src=TREATY&mtdsg_no=XXII-4&chapter=22&clang=_en>.

United Nations, 'Status: United Nations Convention on International Settlement Agreements Resulting from Mediation, available at <https://uncitral.un.org/en/texts/mediation/conventions/international_settlement_agreements/status>.

United Nations, 'List of Signatory States to the Singapore Convention on Mediation', available at <https://treaties.un.org/Pages/ViewDetails.aspx?src=TREATY&mtdsg_no=XXII-4&chapter=22&clang=_en>.

World Intellectual Property Organization's (WIPO) Arbitration and Mediation Center (WIPO Center), 'Results of the WIPO Arbitration and Mediation Center International Survey on Dispute Resolution in Technology Transactions' (2013), available at <https://www.wipo.int/amc/en/center/survey/results.html>.

World Intellectual Property Organization's Arbitration and Mediation Center, 'Results of the WIPO Arbitration and Mediation Center International Survey on Dispute Resolution in Technology Transactions' (2013).

Wu J, 'Annual Review on Commercial Mediation' in *Beijing Arbitration Commission Commercial Dispute Resolution in China: An Annual Review and Preview* (2014) Beijing Arbitration Commission 44.

Index

www.ingramcontent.com/pod-product-compliance
Lightning Source LLC
LaVergne TN
LVHW010625300926
849162LV00001B/70
* 9 7 8 9 0 0 4 5 3 2 5 3 3 *